Joseph A. Gordon
1984

The White Front Cars of San Francisco

Charles Smallwood

Interurbans Special 44

P.O. Box 6444 Glendale, California 91205

Publisher • Mac Sebree
Editor • Jim Walker

The White Front Cars of San Francisco

© 1978 by Charles Smallwood   First Printing, Fall 1978, Revised Edition

All rights reserved. This book may not be reproduced in part or in whole without written permission from the publisher, except in the case of brief quotations used in reviews.

Library of Congress Catalog Number: 78-71892
ISBN: 0-916374-32-7

This book was manufactured in the United States of America. The text was set in 10 point Garamond with captions set in 10 point Helvetica Condensed and headlines in American Classic of various sizes. Printed on 70-pound Patina dullcoat.

Dust Jacket Photographs

COVER: Here is "California Comfort Car" 979 decked out in its colorful 1930s streamstyling at the end of San Francisco's newest streetcar line, the #31—Balboa Street. It was art deco, Market Street Railway version!

BACK COVER: (TOP) A lineup of White Front Cars at Holy Cross terminal, Colma, on Memorial Day, 1937. (BOTTOM) Down by the gasworks, car 705 pauses at the 23rd and Third terminal of the #30 line, in 1934.
(Three photos taken and hand-colored by Charles Smallwood.)

Endsheet Photographs

FRONT: How's this for a lineup of White Front Cars? All in perfect alignment, all identical at the 28th and Valencia carhouse, 1927. Surely this proves MSR to be the very model of a modern and well-ordered railway! **C.D. Miller**

BACK: In days of yore, when autos were few and traffic was serene, this United Railroads "big sub" had 26th and Mission streets nearly all to itself. It was November 6, 1914, and the White Star Saloon, on the right, was doing a good business in San Francisco Steam Beer. **United Railroads**

Charles D. Miller

Dedication

The author dedicates this history to the memory of the late Charles D. Miller. Mr. Miller was with the Market Street Railway Company throughout its existence; he began his transportation career with the United Railroads in 1907.

Mr. Miller had a great interest in the history of the city's transit lines and much of the historical background, both text and photographs, used in this book came from material he collected over the years. It was he who first suggested to the author in 1950 the idea of putting down on paper the fascinating history of San Francisco's transportation systems.

He was the last Superintendent of Equipment of the Market Street Railway, and continued in that post after the 1944 merger, administering the cars, trolley coaches and buses of Municipal Railway with distinction. In 1951 he was appointed General Manager of Municipal Railway, a post he held until his retirement in 1960.

Foreword

THE ORIGINAL *The White Front Cars of San Francisco,* by Charles Smallwood, was put together by the late Ira L. Swett in 1971. This new edition contains essentially everything that was in the original, plus much additional material furnished by the author. The first edition was typewritten, as was Ira's policy, and this one is typeset. We are very pleased to be able to bring back this fine book, an early sellout in its original form, for the enjoyment of today's readers.

For the balance of this foreword we include the words of Ira L. Swett, founder of *Interurbans,* who wrote in the original edition:

San Francisco is famous in transit history for its cable cars and because it was one of the first big cities of the nation to create a municipal street railway. Today's Municipal Railway enjoys a monopoly of the Bay City's public transit operations, but 'twas not ever so—no, indeed. Prior to 1944 roughly two-thirds of San Francisco's transit patrons rode on the justly famous White Front Cars of the Market Street Railway Company, a private operation. MSR's trolleys climbed Twin Peaks; thundered along busy Market Street on the inside track; sped southward through Daly City and the cemetery district on interurban trackage all the way to San Mateo; often racing steam trains on the way; they conquered steep Fillmore Hill with a novel counterbalance system; squealed around the stately Ferry Building loops where thousands of commuters to The City from Oakland, Berkeley, Alameda and Sausalito were funneled into San Francisco; and wandered through sand dunes in the far western districts, bringing settlers and a bigger and better city.

Market Street Railway Company constructed many of its electric cars in its Elkton Shops, using local labor and products to the betterment of the entire community. Although primarily a rail operation to the very end, Market Street Railway installed the first trolley coach line in the city. Ironically, the company also operated the oldest transit equipment in the city, the venerable cable cars of Powell Street.

Market Street Railway was one of the nation's major street railway companies. Here is its story, of two-man cars, Eclipse fenders, leather seats and hissing trolley wheels—all related by an expert on this subject, Charles A. Smallwood.

Perhaps only Charles Smallwood could write the definitive history of Market Street Railway. Born in San Francisco in 1912 at Hayes and Fillmore streets, within earshot of United Railroads cars on the #6 and #22 lines, Smallwood grew up in a city where the electric streetcar dominated the local transit scene; and the privately owned URR (which became Market Street Railway in 1921) was the major operator.

Charlie grew up on Richland Avenue in "The Mission" and watched the big 1300 Class cars clatter past his home. In 1927 he moved to the Richmond District where he resides today. While yet a youngster he constructed models of streetcars and was one of the first electric railway historians to take photographs, starting that activity in 1933. He entered the employment of Market Street Railway in 1938 and almost immediately was assigned to the Washington and Mason cable car barn. The ensuing years found him working at many Market Street and Municipal Railway divisions, including the Geneva Division, last stronghold today of San Francisco's streetcars; he returned to Washington and Mason as foreman, retiring from that post in 1974.

Interurbans takes great pride in presenting this definitive history of the great Market Street Railway Company.

November 1978   Jim Walker

Table of Contents

Introduction 11

CHAPTER 1 Coming of the White Front Cars 15
Steam Dummies and Horse Cars—Cables—The Electric Era—The United Railroads of San Francisco—Earthquake!—Labor Unrest—The 1907 Strike—Patrick Calhoun—Municipal Pressures—Municipal Railway Opens—Improved Fare, Collection, New Cars—The Exposition—Another Strike—URR Weakened—New Name, Few Changes—Byllesby Management—City Loses Most Scenic Line—The One-Man Car Battle—A Trolley Coach Line—The Long-Lived Nickel Fare—The Bay Bridge Terminal—The MSR Goes To War

    SPECIAL REVENUE SERVICES 26

    TRAGEDY IN VISITACION VALLEY 52

CHAPTER 2 Merger and Obliteration 75
Derision for the MSR—Borrowing for the Muni

CHAPTER 3 The System 85
Listing and Maps of Lines

CHAPTER 4 Electric Passenger Cars 149
Car Series:

1-12	156	746	224
101-180	162	751-756	225
201-265	168	757-771	227
266-305, 778-994	175	772-778	231
401	194	II 725-734	232
402-406	199	II 735-736	238
407-410	202	II 740-759	241
601-662	203	1225-1244	249
681-697	208	1301-1424	257
698-699	210	II 1424	266
701-724	213	1500-1549	269
725-726	218	II 1508	275
727-730	220	1550-1749	279
731-745	222	II 1715, II 1716, II 1722	288

Miscellaneous Cars:

"San Francisco"	294	Funeral Cars	299
Mt. Olivet Car	298	Car 45	300

CHAPTER 5 Service Cars...303
Wreckers, Cranes, Sand Cars, Etc.

CHAPTER 6 Cables..331
Those Hill-Climbers on a Rope

CHAPTER 7 The Bus Gets A Foothold.....................................351

CHAPTER 8 One Very Crooked Trolley Coach Line.........................367

CHAPTER 9 The Transportation Factory..................................371
Transfers—Joint Trackage With Municipal Railway—Communication With Trainmen—Safety—Special Moves—Skip Stops—The Great Ferry Terminal

CHAPTER 10 Laying Track the MSR Way...................................399

CHAPTER 11 The Power Picture...409

CHAPTER 12 The Overhead..419

CHAPTER 13 Elkton Shops..423

CHAPTER 14 Car Houses..435

CHAPTER 15 Putting MSR's Best Foot Forward.............................459

Appendix—History, the Company's Narrative...............................466

Tables:

Operating Results by Routes for Year Ended June 30, 1927 87
Analysis of Car Mileage by Routes......................................88
Analysis of Financial Results of Operation by Routes...................89
Route Mileages, Car Assignments and Car Types Operated 1929-1940.......96
1922-1944: Vital Statistics..97
Maximum Number of Cars Operated by Lines on January 8, 1932............99
All-Time List of Electric Passenger Cars, 1921-1944...............150-151
Schedule of Revenue Rolling Stock as of November 23, 1936.............152
Commercially Built Cars...293
Boneyard Brigade: Car Scrappings by Municipal Railway.................293
Non-Revenue Rolling Stock, August 1921................................329
General Specifications, MSR Motor Coaches.............................354

Maps:

Four-Track System: Market and Church, Church and 16th, Market and Castro 94
System Map at Time of 1944 Merger .... after page 98
Map of System, 1934 .... after page 98
Individual Line Route Maps, 1927 98
San Mateo Interurban Line 134
Elkton Shops 425

Plates:

Market Street Car Movements 91
Car Routes, 1934 92-93
Illustrations of Transfers, Tickets and Forms 393-396
Selected Car Plans 475-482

Acknowledgments

The author is greatly indebted to the following Municipal Railway officials and employees for their many kindnesses in providing old documents, photographs, and much other valued material used in this history:

Bressel Corley
Carl Dietz
Warren DeMerritt
The late Robert English
Frank Farren
Gail Freeman
The late Laurice Holst
Maurice Ittig
Robert King
Joseph Logasa
Leo Logasa

Louis Luini
William Marquardt
Wesley Mason
James Maugham
Frank McQuaid
Marshall Moxom
Clifford Nilan
The late Victor Peterson
The late William Rushing
The late Joseph Slevin
Kenneth Snodgrass

And to the following interested people for their contributions of much valuable material, both photographic and documentary, and especially to Mrs. Charles D. Miller, who kindly made available to the author the large collection of Market Street Railway memorabilia compiled by her late husband while he was Superintendent of Equipment for the company:

Eli Bail
Carl Blaubach
Rudolph Brandt
P. Allen Copeland
Harre Demoro
The late Ralph Demoro
Jack Ferrier
James Gibson
The late Roy Graves
Francis Guido
Addison Laflin
Warren K. Miller
Emanuel Mohr

John McKane
The late Roy Proffer
Vernon Sappers
Richard Schlaich
Lorin Silliman
Fred Stindt
The late Ira L. Swett
Robert Townley
Bert Ward
Paul Ward
Edward B. Watson
Wilbur C. Whittaker
Ted Wurm

The following published material was consulted for much of the factual information:

Inside Track, house organ of Market St. Ry. Co.
Annual Reports, San Francisco Public Utilities Commission
California Public Utilities Commission
United Railroads records, 1904-21
Local newspapers
"Transportation Facilities of San Francisco, 1913" by Bion J. Arnold
"San Francisco's Street Railway Problem," 1927, a report to the Hon. John J. O'Toole, City Attorney, by Delos F. Wilcox
"Chronology of Routes," S.F. Municipal Railway
"Street Railway Journal"
"Electric Railway Journal"
"Transit Journal"
"Electric Traction"

For the most part, the official photographs of the United Railroads and Market Street Railway contained herein were taken by the longtime official company photographer, the late Harry Mentz. Through the eyes of his camera the transportation scene of San Francisco from 1906 to the mid-1940s was professionally recorded.

The United Railroads was a pioneer in the use of photography in conjunction with urban transit, having established a photo department in 1903. The policy of the company was to supplement the written word with pictures in the fields of engineering, construction, accident claims, and for all other purposes where a photographic record would be applicable. The successor company, Market Street Railway, continued the policy and maintained the photo department to the end of its corporate existence. Many thousands of photos were taken of the property's operations during this long period. Most photos taken before 1906, unfortunately, were lost in the great fire when the URR office building at Market and Valencia streets (wherein was located the photo laboratory) was lost. However, most of the photos made after the great disaster exist to this day and thus provide what is said to be one of the most complete photographic records of any transit system in the world.

The Earliest Conveyance

PIONEER STREET RAILWAY for The City was the San Francisco Market Street Railroad, which began service on July 4, 1860, from Third and Market Streets out Market to Woodward's Gardens (14th and Valencia streets). This photograph, the only known view of the steam cars, shows the double-decked car at its Third and Market terminus. This would date the view between 1860 and 1863, for in the latter year the line was extended to the waterfront. The steam cars were ousted from Market Street by horse cars in 1868 because of a city ordinance banning the use of steam operation on that thoroughfare. Access to the top deck seats was via ladder (shown at left), making the roof a strictly masculine domain. The large structure in the center is now the site of the present Examiner Building.

Richard Schlaich

Introduction

THE COOL, GRAY CITY by the Golden Gate sits on its 46-square-mile peninsula tip in regal splendor. To the west, the broad Pacific; to the east, one of the premier harbors of the world. With water on three sides and San Mateo County to the south, San Francisco's confining boundaries have caused the city to grow vertically, not horizontally, and have given the city a unique personality as a dividend.

The topography of the city is uneven; how many hills there are within its boundaries is open to speculation, but there are many. From sea level to 925 feet of elevation climb these hills, carrying on their broad backs the skyscrapers, the factories, the palaces and a broad array of lesser structures. The seven main hills are well known: Nob, Russian, Telegraph, Twin Peaks, Mt. Davidson, Rincon and Lone Mountain. These noble mounts give San Francisco a look all its own.

It also has a climate all its own, invigorating the year round. Steady inshore breezes from the big ocean bring the cooling fog; temperatures seldom exceed 75 degrees maximum, yet 45 degrees is about the minimum. Rain is a familiar visitor, but snow is rare. The city provides a climate that is conducive to exerting oneself to a greater degree than in warmer climes, yet there is a lack of harsh winters, the bane of most cities in the United States.

Living in ever-closer neighborliness around the shores of San Francisco Bay are about five million Californians. The metropolis of this great market is "The City," as San Francisco is known to residents of the state living north of the Tehachapis. The City has not kept up with others in the matter of population; it counts about 750,000 residents and has even lost some in the last census count. Nevertheless, San Francisco claims to be the financial capital of the west, as well as the transportation center, and perhaps the shipping center.

These enterprises mean jobs for the thousands and on workdays some 400,000 commuters pour into town from "bedroom" communities around the Bay. Adding to this impressive total are the visitors who come to The City as tourists—about two million annually.

To carry the working people to and from their jobs and to provide San Franciscans with transportation to recreation points and shopping areas was the task of a remarkable electric railway company. Market Street Railway Company was the last of the great privately owned street railways of The City. Its era, 1921 to 1944, is the purview of this book.

The story of mass transportation in San Francisco is a continuing story which began with the horse-drawn omnibus lines of the 1850s. From that humble beginning the progress and expansion of the organized operators of the city's transit lines kept pace with the rapid growth of the community. From 1861 to the middle 1880s, many new companies entered the field and competition became rife at times. The various companies utilized the most modern technical triumphs of their periods and made use of almost every conceivable method of propulsion devised by man; in the field of rail traction, horse, steam, cable and electric all found their place. In later years the motor bus and the trolley coach were put to use.

During the 1890s a major consolidation of many of the companies providing transit service occurred, and in 1902 the greatest and last important consolidation of the privately owned lines was achieved when the immediate predecessor of Market Street Railway, United Railroads of San Francisco, was formed. Private ownership of most of San Francisco's public transportation came to an end in 1944 when Market Street Railway was, at long last, merged with the city's own Municipal Railway.

The purpose of this volume is to spotlight historically the span of time between 1921 and 1944 when the "landlord" of San Francisco's largest transit system was The Market Street Railway Company. To gain an insight into the background from whence this company sprang, it is necessary to journey briefly into the past and examine the events leading to its formation. Then, too, one may well ponder the fate of this large operation after 1944. Less than a decade later our story ends with the virtual obliteration of the tracks and cars which, for so many years, were familiar sights in almost every part of the city.

Market Street Railway was essentially a "streetcar company," a once-numerous American institution which has almost completely disappeared from the urban scene. During the life of the company, rail transit was its predominate way of doing business; buses and trolley coaches were utilized to a minor degree, mostly during the latter days of the company's existence.

A generation of San Franciscans now walk abroad in The City who have never known the White Front trolley cars of the recent past—their dads' "family car."

THE HORSECAR had its day on Market Street. The passengers of number 14 pose at Post, Montgomery and Market streets, in the 1860s.

Charles Smallwood

(ABOVE) **THERE WERE FOUR TRACKS** on Market Street even in the horse car days. The four horse car tracks from Third Street to the Ferry carried some heavy traffic back in 1882, when this view was made. Note cable slots have been installed in the two center tracks, but cable service was still a few months in the future. **Charles Smallwood** (BELOW) Horse cars lined up at the original Ferry Building in 1875. **Courtesy Mrs. C.D. Miller**

ON A RAINY DAY, 1883, horse car operation is seen at the intersection of 4th, Market and Ellis streets. These horse cars were running to the Southern Pacific depot at Third and Townsend streets, and belonged to the North Beach & Mission Railway, one of the many early predecessor companies of the Market Street Railway.
Charles Smallwood

Coming of the White Front Cars

WHEN THE NEWLY ORGANIZED Market Street Railway Company assumed control of the United Railroads of San Francisco in April 1921, the new company acquired control of 291 miles of street railway system; of this, 276.3 miles was operated by overhead trolley and 14.7 miles by cable. The nearly six hundred cars represented many vintages and styles; all of the cable equipment was able to date its beginnings to the previous century.

As to the remainder of the property (track, car houses, the shops, overhead trolley, etc.), its condition could only be considered fair. Many of these facilities dated back to the cable car era, and one important car barn had its genesis in the horse-car period. San Francisco, as the Pacific Coast's first city, was a pioneer in public transit.

The first settling of the site upon which a city was to emerge was by Franciscan missionaries in 1776. Their settlement was near what is today 16th and Dolores streets, and their church, Mission Dolores, is standing today on its original site. A few years later a village was settled on the shore of the great bay; it was named "Yerba Buena"—"Good Herb."

In 1839 streets were laid out in Yerba Buena and in 1847 the name of the village was changed to San Francisco. The discovery of gold in California in 1849 was the signal for frenzied growth; population of the town mushroomed from 2,000 to 15,000 within the year. Eighteen fifty saw plank-paved toll roads built on several streets—the most important being constructed on Mission and Folsom streets. Horse-drawn vehicles provided the era's only transportation.

By 1852, due to the activity in the gold fields, the population of the city increased to such proportions that organized public transportation facilities became not only economically feasible but a public necessity. The first public transit company in San Francisco thus materialized: a horse-drawn omnibus line operated by the firm of Crimm & Bowman. Known as *The Yellow Line*, it ran between the post office (then located at Kearny and Clay streets) to Mission Dolores via Kearny, Third, and Mission streets. It ran on a thirty-minute headway and functioned Mondays through Saturdays on a 50¢ fare; on Sundays the fare jumped to a dollar.

So successful was this initial transit route in garnering paying passengers that in 1854 Crimm & Bowman inaugurated a second line to Mission Dolores via Folsom and 16th streets. The following year they added still a third line: from 3rd and Townsend to Meiggs Wharf; a 10-minute headway prevailed on this line and (the company must have been prospering) fare on this line was only 15¢—and even this low fare, for that day—was later reduced to 10¢. Competition eventually comes to any business that proves to be a moneymaker and it came to the Yellow Line in 1857 in the form of The Peoples Omnibus Company ("The Red Line"), operating over much the same routes as the Crimm & Bowman company.

By the late 1850s it became apparent that San Francisco, with a population then of 50,000, was rapidly outgrowing its omnibus system. The California Legislature in 1857 granted Thomas Hayes the first franchise for a street railway in the city. Thus was born the first *Market Street Railroad Company*. It opened for service on July 4, 1860, operating from Third and Market Streets out Market to Valencia, terminating at 16th and Valencia. It was the first street railway on the Pacific Coast and was popularly hailed at the time as one of the greatest miracles of western advancement.

The terms of the original charter contemplated it to be operated as a horse railroad but, due to the rugged area traversed (mostly sand dunes), a special act of the Legislature gave the company the option of using steam as motive power until such time as the route was made practical for horse operation.

In 1863 this route was extended down Market St. to the waterfront and out Valencia St. to 25th St. Also about this time a branch was built out Hayes St. to Laguna St., largely to develop a large tract of land owned by Thomas Hayes, the founder of the company.

In those years Market St. was largely a succession of sand dunes. In 1894 Frank McCoppin, first general manager of the line, penned his recollections of those early operations:

> Its roadbed along the center of Market St. from California to Third St., being below grade, was called "McCoppins Canal" in which, during the rainy season many worthy citizens narrowly escaped drowning. The only opening along Market St. west of Third St. was along the line of the railroad, and the daring owners of some vehicles had the temerity to drive over the Company's tracks, but that nonsense was put to a stop by digging several trenches across and under the tracks.
>
> Such was Market St. in those days. Property fronting on the thoroughfare was of such inconsiderable value that its owners put up with The Market Street Railroad and all its concomitants, including wheezy engines, canals and trenches to obstruct travel.

Following the immediate success of the Market St. line, several horse-car companies were incorporated and built

"BALLOON" CAR of the Sutter Street Railroad was the idea of that company's engineer, Henry Casebolt. The circular-shaped car body was mounted on the wheel truck by means of a pivot, which enabled the driver to turn the car around without unhitching the horses. It was fitted with more lavish appointments than ordinary cars on the line, and had upholstered seats and carpeted floors. For this luxury the passenger paid a higher fare (10 cents) instead of the traditional nickel. When the day of these unique cars was over, two bodies were brought to Harbor View Park, where they served as tea rooms. They lasted in this capacity until 1914, when the area was cleared to make room for the Panama-Pacific International Exposition of 1915.
Charles Smallwood

between 1863 and 1875. Among these were the pioneer *Yellow Line* omnibus company (reorganized as *The North Beach & Mission Railroad Company*) and *The Peoples* ("Red Line") which became *The Omnibus Railroad Company*.

In 1868 steam operation on Market St. was banned and Market Street Railroad then changed to horses as its motive power. By 1875 there were eight companies in operation, having 80 miles of single track, 220 cars, with 700 men and 1700 horses employed.

The Cables Come

But the days of the horse car were numbered when a new era of transportation for hilly San Francisco was ushered in on August 1, 1873. On that historic day Andrew S. Hallidie opened the world's first cable-operated car line on Clay St. from Kearny to Leavenworth streets. The financial success of this original line gave great impetus to cable construction throughout the city; many horse-car lines were converted, and new cable lines built between 1876 and 1889.

In 1882 the pioneer Market Street Railroad was taken over by Leland Stanford and associates who formed *The Market Street Cable Railway Company*. They at once set about converting their lines to cable operation. On August 22, 1883, the first line opened for service from the ferries to 28th and Mission streets via Market and Valencia streets. Shortly thereafter other cable lines were opened on Castro, Haight, Hayes and McAllister streets, all terminating at the ferry via Market St. Construction of this system was first class throughout. It was operating intact on the morning of the great earthquake of April 18, 1906, and the roadbed was built so well that it withstood the temblor except in certain instances where its support was entirely carried away.

The Omnibus Railroad Company changed its name to *The Omnibus Cable Company* in 1886; by 1889 it had converted and expanded most of its horse-car lines to cable traction. These lines were: Ellis St. from Market St. to Broderick, via Oak and Stanyan to Haight; on Post St. from Market to Leavenworth and 10th to Howard; the Howard St. horse-car line was converted to cable to 26th St. and a line built on 24th St. to Potrero Ave. To The Omnibus Cable Company went the distinction of building the last cable lines in San Francisco; they were, it is worthy to note, short-lived—for they were constructed on the eve of the birth of electric traction.

THE PARK AND OCEAN RAILROAD was opened to traffic in 1883 to provide service to the Ocean Beach. Prior to construction of this steam line, access to the Cliff House and Ocean Beach area was by horse-drawn Concord stages running along Point Lobos Road from the terminal of the Geary Street cable road at Geary and Central Ave. (now Presidio Ave.) The Park and Ocean road ran from Haight and Stanyan streets, where it connected with cable lines, to the beach via Stanyan, "H" Street (now Lincoln Way) and along the ocean front to a terminal at 49th Avenue (La Playa) and "B" (Balboa) streets. This view is at the roundhouse, near Frederick Street at what is now the site of Kezar Stadium.

Charles Smallwood

Steam Trains

THE FERRIES & CLIFF STEAM LINE, opened on March 1, 1886, ran from California and Central (now Presidio Ave.) to a point above the Cliff House at 48th and Point Lobos. The route was along California Street to 33rd Ave., where the line turned north to follow a very scenic route overlooking the Golden Gate. The line was built by the Powell Street cable system to give them a route from downtown to the Cliff House. This little Ferries & Cliff train was pictured at Fifth Ave. and California Street. Last day of operation for the trains was May 17, 1905, when the city's last steam-operated streetcar line gave way to prepare the route for electrification.

Charles Smallwood

Cable Era

THE DAY OF THE CABLE was at hand in 1885, when this view of the Ferry Building showed a shift to cable traction (compare with view on page 13).

C.D. Miller

CABLE CARS DOMINATE the scene in this 1900 photo from the Ferry Building tower of the terminal below. Mail Car "A" is at lower right. The Sacramento cable car approaches from center right to curve off to its terminal, then back to Clay Street.

Charles Smallwood

FIRST CABLE MACHINERY power plant of the Market Street Cable Railroad was this wooden structure at the junction of Valencia and Market Street. Constructed in 1883, this building gave way to a large brick power plant in the early 1890s as the Market Street Cable system added more lines. The steam dummy train in the foreground ran on the Market Street Extension line and was later replaced by the Castro Street cable line.
Charles Smallwood

(BELOW) **THE OMNIBUS CABLE COMPANY'S** Howard Street line terminated at 24th and Potrero Ave., where this photo was taken about 1888. The horse car at left rear belonged to this same company and ran on Potrero. Note the cable company inspector between carmen; he wears the large, six-pointed star of a city marshal.
Charles Smallwood

THE METROPOLITAN RAILWAY missed out by a few months to the San Francisco & San Mateo Electric Railway for the honor of being San Francisco's first electric street railway when it opened in 1891. Its line started at Eddy and Market and ran via an extremely winding route to wind up eventually at a terminus at 9th Ave. and "H" St. (now Lincoln Way). **Charles Smallwood**

The Electric Era

By 1890 a new form of city transit had been developed that was destined to render obsolete all previous methods of propelling transit cars. The electric trolley car appeared and was so successful from the start that cities throughout the nation rapidly scrapped their horse and cable lines in favor of this mysterious and wondrous new medium.

However, the established San Francisco companies were cautious, reluctant to enter the electric trolley car business until the new-fangled method of propulsion had been thoroughly proved. The city's first opportunity to sample electric trolleys came in 1891 when two brothers, Behrend and Isaac Joost, organized *The San Francisco & San Mateo Railroad Company*. They built their line from Steuart and Market streets to Daly's Hill (now renamed Daly City) via Steuart, Harrison, 14th, Guerrero, Chenery and San Jose Ave. Unfortunately, the Joost line did not pay expenses and was sold at a foreclosure sale on April 11, 1896. It was then reorganized and extended from the county line to Holy Cross Cemetery. At the same time a new line was built on 18th and Waller streets to Golden Gate Park.

San Francisco's second electric railway, *The Metropolitan Railroad*, was opened to traffic a few months after the opening of the Joost brothers road. It built a rambling line from Market St. to Golden Gate Park via Eddy, Hyde, O'Farrell, Scott, Fell, Baker, Page, Clayton and Waller to 9th Ave. and H St. (now Lincoln Way). From the circuitous route followed by this line, it would be forgivable to note that perhaps the promoters of The Metropolitan Railroad desired to obtain franchises on as many streets as was humanly possible for a single route. This company was absorbed by The Market Street Railroad in 1894.

In 1893 was effected San Francisco's first large consolidation of street railway companies. In that year interests identified with The Southern Pacific Railroad organized *The Market Street Railway Company* and the new company at once took over all lines in the city with the exception of the electric railway to Daly City and the Sutter, Geary, California and Union St. cable lines. Market Street Railway, a firm believer in electric cars, thereupon converted many of the old horse and cable railways to electric traction; it also constructed many new electric lines.

THE FIRST DOZEN CARS of the Metropolitan Railway were equipped with an odd six-wheel Robinson Radial truck, shown at left. This arrangement was soon replaced by four-wheel trucks. The company was absorbed by the original Market Street Railway Co. in 1894.
Charles Smallwood

UNTIL ADOLPH SUTRO built his electric line from Presidio Avenue to his Baths and Museum at the Cliff House, a 10-cent fare was required to reach that area from other sections of the city. He opened his line in 1896 and made a transfer agreement with the Sutter Street cable company, thus enabling patrons to reach his popular resort for a single five-cent fare. Here, one of Sutro's attractive cars approaches its outer terminus. The big gabled building in the background is the old Cliff House, which burned in the early 1900s. **Charles Smallwood**

CENTRAL POINT of operations of the San Francisco & San Mateo Electric Railway Company was at San Jose Ave. and 30th Street (ABOVE). The building at left housed company offices and its dispatcher. Crews turned in their receipts here upon completing their runs. Through service from downtown to the county line and Colma was not provided for some time after the company opened its line; passengers were obliged to transfer here.   **Charles Smallwood**

CREW AND PASSENGERS pose at 28th and Guerrero streets, circa 1893. These early electric cars were somewhat cranky and delicate to handle. SF&SM had a novel policy to prevent crews from abusing the equipment. If a car broke down on the road, no matter what the reason, the crew's pay (perhaps 21 cents hourly) ceased abruptly until the car was repaired and back in service. This was the only electric railway company in the city to treat its carmen so, and the practice did little to cement good relations between employees and company.   **Charles Smallwood**

THE ORIGINAL Market Street Railway's initial electrification of the Mission Street lines used this early style of electric car which followed closely the successful California Street cable design—a closed center section between two open sections (still in use today on California Street) (ABOVE) A pioneer electric hauls an old horse car as a trailer, at Ocean Ave. near the Ingleside Race Track in 1898. (BELOW) A closeup of this type of car, at the outer terminal of the line at 29th and Noe Street, 1896.

BOTH: Charles Smallwood

Electrics to the Ocean

THE STEAM-OPERATED Park and Ocean line along Lincoln Way was electrified in 1898. Three large electric motor cars were provided for this service. These cars (601-603) were equipped with motors powerful enough to pull several of the old steam line trailers. They were the first electric cars in San Francisco to be equipped with air brakes. This train was photographed about 1900 at the Beach terminal, and operated from that point to Stanyan and Haight streets. The operation of these large trains was short-lived, however, and by 1902 they were discontinued when regular streetcars of the Ellis, Park and Ocean line took over all service on this route. The cars were subsequently sold to the Pacific Electric Railway, in Los Angeles, where one of them was still in use as late as 1947.

Charles Smallwood

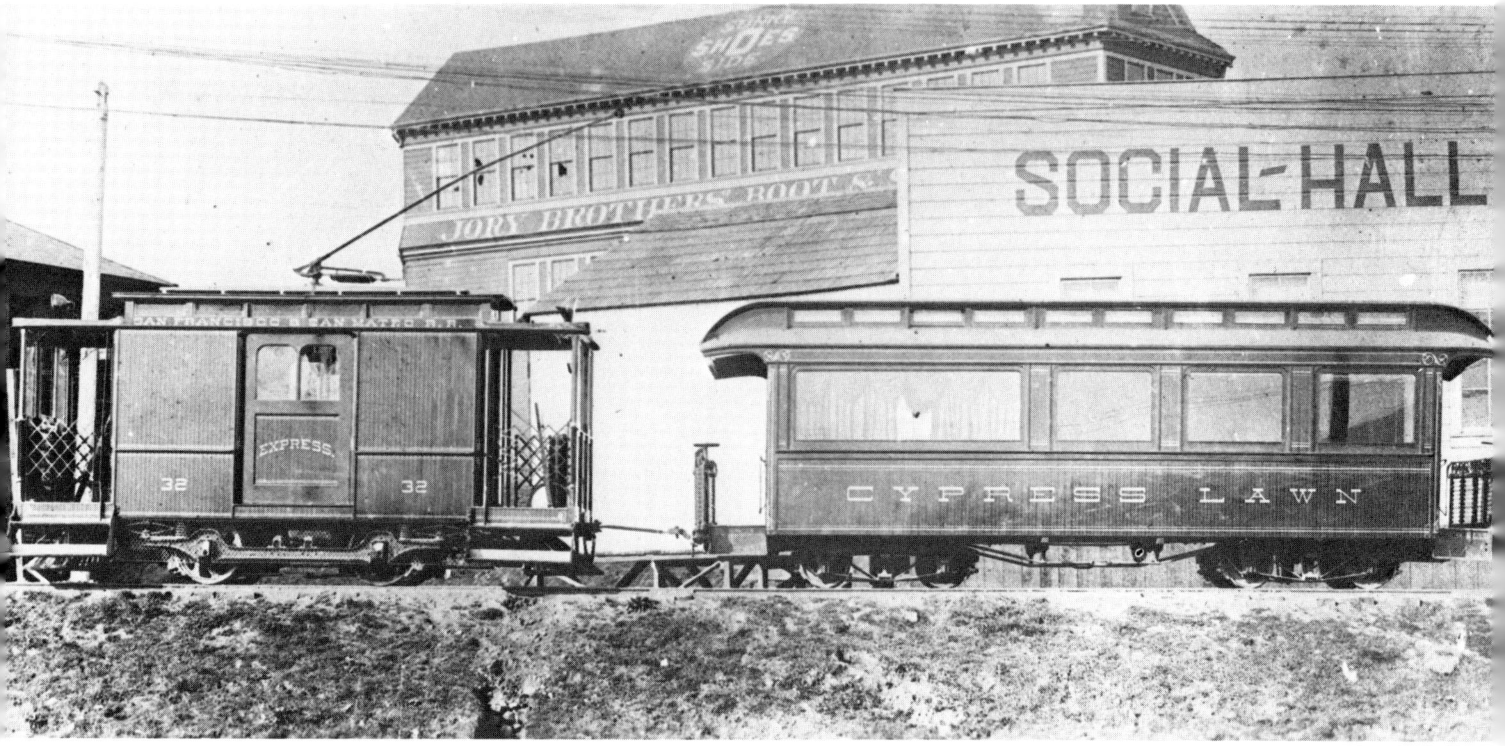

FIRST ELECTRIC FUNERAL TRAIN was this interesting consist that ran on the San Francisco & San Mateo Railroad. Ornate coach ''Cypress Lawn'' was later motorized and became United Railroads Funeral car 1. The tiny express motor briefly gave San Francisco its only trolley package freight service. This picture dates to 1898 and was taken on the old San Mateo line at Glen Park.

Charles Smallwood

Special Revenue Cars

The United Railroads and its predecessors engaged in transportation activities other than their principal chore of hauling the citizenry around the town for a nickel. This extra business was quite diversified and included the movements of U.S. Mail, funerals, sight-seeing tours and catering to private parties, as well as carrying race horses and cleaning up streets. An interesting variety of rolling stock was used for these services. The coming of the motor age doomed this method of transport and by 1917 it was only a memory.

United States Mail

In 1896 the United States Post Office petitioned the original Market Street Railway to provide a Railway Post Office service on the Market Street cable lines. The company agreed, and on September 10, 1896, Railway Post Office service was inaugurated on these lines. This service proved successful from the start and was followed later in the same year with Postal routes on the Sacramento Street cable and Mission Street electric lines.

These Railway Post Office cars were fitted up with the necessary facilities for sorting and canceling mail matter. Cars were equipped with a mail slot on each side to post letters. The public could, at regular car stops, hail the Postal car which would pause while the person posted letters via the slot. Each car carried, besides the operating crew, a mail clerk whose job was to sort the mail picked up at the outlying post offices en route to the Ferry Post Office where each car terminated. Mail posted on the cars while they were under way was canceled on the car, each line having its own cancellation mark.

These mail cars were painted white, the standard United States Post Office color for all street railway cars throughout the country engaged in the Railway Post Office service. They also had the legend UNITED STATES MAIL RAILWAY POST OFFICE painted in gold on both ends and sides.

MARKET STREET cable Mail Car "A" in 1900.   **United Railroads**

CLOSED POUCH United States Mail Car "E" is shown at the southside Ferry Terminal early in 1906. This mail service was short-lived, lasting but eight months. It was not resumed after the earthquake and fire. Car "E" was destroyed in the 1906 disaster.
San Francisco Maritime Museum

(RIGHT) **ODDITY OF THE** single-truck passenger car fleet was "Gate Car" 1180. In 1901 this car was equipped with screened-in open sections and sliding screen gates. As rebuilt it had a varied career as a hospital car (carrying convalescing company employees from the Southern Pacific Hospital for outings around the city), as a one-man car (the city's first so-equipped electric car) on the short Bosworth Street line, and other unusual duties. During the 1904 racing season it was chartered by the Pacific Jockey Club to carry the daily receipts from Ingleside Race Track to the P.J.C. office at Kearny and Washington. On September 2, 1905, this car inaugurated closed pouch mail service from the then-new Main Post Office at Seventh and Mission streets to the Ferry Annex Post Office, and is shown in that service at the south side Ferry Terminal in September 1905 (note mail sacks stacked on front platform). On June 24, 1911, it became 605 and in 1914 it was again rebuilt, into a true one-man car of the 601-605 and 613-616 series. It again ran on the Bosworth line, although a conductor was added after 1918, until the line quit in 1927. It was scrapped at Elkton Yard on July 24, 1927.
Robert H. MacFarland/Charles Smallwood Collection

(RIGHT) **SACRAMENTO STREET** cable Mail Car "B" is seen at the Ferry, 1900.
Charles Smallwood

Both cable mail cars were rebuilt from former Omnibus Cable Company passenger cars.

The standard gauge Market Street cable car was assigned the letter "A" and the narrow gauge Sacramento Street car, which was slightly shorter, was lettered "B". The electric mail car, which was built new for the service, was designated "C". During the period of this street railway mail service, cars in regular passenger service on the same routes as the mail cars would, at times, carry closed pouch mail. When regular cars were engaged in this activity they would carry a small sign in the upper right front window reading "U.S. Mail."

The Railway Post Office service was discontinued on September 2, 1905. However, on the same date a new mail service was established between the new Post Office at Seventh and Mission streets and the Ferry Annex Post Office. Two cars ran in the shuttle service and 34 trips a day were made carrying closed pouch mail and Parcel Post. A spur track had been built from Mission St. into the Seventh St. office. This new service was started using the electric mail car "C" and gate car #1180. Meanwhile, the United Railroads constructed in their shops two cars especially designed for this service. These two cars were rebuilt from 670-class streetcars and, as fitted for the mail service, were designated by the letters "D" and "E", entering service on October 10, 1905, replacing the "C" and #1180. This service was short-lived, however, as both the "D" and "E" were burned on lower Mission St. during the earthquake and fire of April 18, 1906. The U.S. Mail service was never resumed and this phase of the company's business was forever ended.

Funeral Car Service

During the early years of this century, United Railroads developed a considerable side business carrying funerals to the several cemeteries located to the south of the county line on the San Mateo interurban route. This macabre business was established in the 1890s when the pioneer *San Francisco & San Mateo Electric Railway* extended its line from Daly's Hill (now Daly City) to Baden Post Office—just beyond the Holy Cross Cemetery, the most southerly of the group of cemeteries.

When this extension was opened to traffic, several funeral parlors along the San Francisco end of the line, as well as the Cypress Lawn Cemetery Association, petitioned the electric railway company to inaugurate funeral car service, inasmuch as the roads to the cemeteries were very poor and not conducive to safe and comfortable carriage traffic.

The original funeral car for this service was a small, ornate vehicle having a compartment for the casket at one end, with the rest of the car being fitted with wicker chairs for mourners; this car was named CYPRESS LAWN, and, as it had no motors or controls, it had to be towed by a work car. Spurs off the interurban line were built into cemetery grounds in some instances, notably at Cypress Lawn and Mt. Olivet Cemeteries.

When United Railroads succeeded the San Francisco & San Mateo Electric Railway in 1902, it somewhat expanded the funeral car service. In that year CYPRESS LAWN was motorized and a second funeral car was added; this latter car was converted from one of the company's large passenger cars and was given the number 2. In 1903 and 1904 three more cars were added to the funeral fleet; these were constructed by URR at its 28th and Valencia car shops. This new trio was especially ornate, having such niceties as deeply cushioned seats, carpeted floors, window drapes, and lead inserts in wheels and gears to cut down on noise. That the deceased would travel to his final rest in the best that United Railroads had to offer was noted in this 1905 company advertisement: ELEGANTLY EQUIPPED CARS FOR FUNERAL PURPOSES TO ALL CEMETERIES IN SAN MATEO COUNTY, FURNISHED AT REASONABLE RATES. QUICK SERVICE, PRIVACY AND COURTESY ASSURED.

By 1908 the county road south to the cemeteries was greatly improved and this fact, coupled with the advent of the automobile hearse, severely cut into URR's funeral

INTERIOR of Funeral Car 3, 1905.   **United Railroads**

car business. At the close of that year, only the three last-built cars were engaged in this service; at this time car 4 was renumbered 2 when the original funeral car 2 was rebuilt into—of all things—a private party car named SIERRA.

The demand for trolley funeral service steadily declined as more and more automobiles appeared on the streets. The funeral cars were finally discontinued about 1921. The three cars were placed in storage at 24th St. Car House where they remained until taken to Elkton Shops for scrapping in February 1926. Their trucks, the motors and the controls were salvaged and provided many more years of service—being incorporated into new passenger cars built at Elkton and numbered in the 800 class.

FUNERAL CAR 3, immaculate in Brewster green and tile red roof, gold letters and numbers, is seen at Cypress Lawn Cemetery in July 1911.
United Railroads

Observation Cars

On March 31, 1901, the *original* Market Street Railway introduced an Observation Car said to be the first of such vehicles in the west. This car, named CITY OF ATLANTA, was designed (and patented) by General Manager E.P. Vining. The car was 40 feet long, 10 feet wide and had two rows of longitudinal seats on each side with each row facing outward. The inner rows were higher than the outer and entrance to the car was by five doorways on each side. A 17-inch-wide aisle separated the two inner rows and there were seats for 72 passengers. The car made two trips a day, except in inclement weather, and began the tour at Post and Market streets to make a 20-mile, four-hour trip to the principal attractions of the city such as Mission Dolores, Golden Gate Park and the Cliff House. (After 1905 the scenic trip around Land's End was added.) Fare was 25 cents and no transfers were issued or accepted.

The Observation Car was popular from the start and patronage continued to grow to the extent that the United Railroads found it necessary to construct in their shops another car to augment the CITY OF ATLANTA, which was, by now, renamed more appropriately GOLDEN GATE. The new car, named CALIFORNIA, was of more conventional design, having transverse seating

RATES FOR SPECIAL REVENUE services are shown in this page from URR's "Transit Tidings" of May 1, 1904. **Charles Smallwood**

OBSERVATION CARS.

Observation Car "GOLDEN GATE" leaves junction of Market, Post and Montgomery Streets

DAILY AT 10 A. M. AND 2 P. M.

For a Round Trip of 20 Miles, and returns to starting point at 1.30 P. M. and 5.30 P. M.

FARE, 25 CENTS.

Points of interest along the route are pointed out by a competent guide.

Union Square, City Hall,
   The new St. Francis Hotel,
      Lick Monument,
         Mechanics Pavilion and
   St. Ignatius Church and College.

A stop is made at Bryant Avenue Power House of the United Railroads, for inspection, continuing the journey car passes

Mission Dolores,
   Golden Gate Park Pan Handle to
      Affiliated Colleges

where a panoramic view of the City, Golden Gate Park, Mt. Tamalpais and Pt. Bonita is obtained. Thence to the

Ocean Beach, Cliff House,
   Sutro Heights, Sutro Baths,
      Seal Rocks,

returning via Fillmore Street Hill where a magnificent view of the harbor and Marin coast is obtained.

This Trip has been Designed for Tourists Particularly,

but it also offers to the long-time resident a most instructive and invigorating outing.

ALL NIGHT SERVICE

KEARNY AND MISSION, from Washington and and Kearny to Twenty-ninth and Mission. Cars leave Washington and Kearny at 1 A. M. and every 15 minutes until 2 A. M., then every 30 minutes until 5 A. M.
   Leave Twenty-ninth Street at 1:30 A. M., and every 30 minutes until 4:30 A. M.

EIGHTH AND EIGHTEENTH, from Eighth and Market to Sixteenth Avenue. Car leaves Eighth and Market at 1:10 A. M.,2 :20 A. M., 3:30 A. M., 4:40 A. M. Leave Sixteenth Avenue at 1:50 A. M., 2:55 A. M., 4:05 A. M. and 5:15 A. M.

ELLIS AND O'FARRELL, from Depot at Third and Townsend Streets to Park every 15 minutes from 1 A. M. to 2 A. M., then every 30 minutes until 5:30 A. M. From Park every 15 minutes from 12:30 A. M. to 1:30 A. M., and every half-hour from 1:30 A. M. to 5:30 A. M.

EDDY AND FULTON, hourly service from Market Street from 1:45 A. M. From Park hourly service from 1:15 A. M.

RATES OF SPECIAL CARS.

The UNITED RAILROADS OF SAN FRANCISCO is prepared to furnish large and commodious electric cars, seating 48 persons, for special party purposes, at the following rates:

Within the limits of the City and County of San Francisco.
   During the day, $2.00 per hour,
                minimum charge, $ 8.00
   Evenings, from 7:00 P. M. to 1:00 A. M., $10.00
   New suburban cars, evenings, - $12.00

Parlor car "HERMOSA" seating 30 persons:
   During the day, $2.00 per hour,
                minimum charge, $ 8.00
   Evenings, 7:00 P. M. to 1:00 A. M., $10.00

Observation car "GOLDEN GATE"
   Evenings, 7:00 P. M. to 1:00 A. M., $10.00

Rates between San Francisco and Burlingame or San Mateo:
   Cars seating 48 persons, including the new suburban cars, day or evening, six hours only, - $25.00
   Each additional hour, - - $ 2.00
   This rate also applies to the parlor car "HERMOSA."

The number of hours the car is in use is computed from the time the car leaves the car house until its return thereto.

UNITED RAILROADS OF SAN FRANCISCO,
                            G. F. CHAPMAN,
Room 822, Rialto Building,   General Manager.
   New Montgomery and Mission Sts.
   San Francisco, Cal.

FUNERAL CARS.

Elegantly equipped cars for funeral purposes, direct to all cemeteries in San Mateo County, furnished at reasonable rates. Quick service, privacy and courtesy assured. Cars start from the following points: Ferry terminus, 18th and Guerrero Streets, and 30th Street and San Jose Avenue.

Arrangements may be made with undertaker.

San Mateo Suburban Cars leave Fifth and Market Streets every half hour, commencing at 6 A. M. up to 6:30 P. M., and thereafter at 7:30, 8:30, 9:30, 10:30 and 11:30 P. M.

Cars leave San Mateo every half hour after 5:30 A. M. until 7:30 P. M., and thereafter at 8, 9, 10, 11 and 12 P. M. On Sundays cars leave every fifteen minutes between 9 A. M. and 7 P. M.

OBSERVATION CAR "Golden Gate," originally called the "City of Atlanta," is shown (ABOVE) in its original configuration, with outward-facing benches.

AS REBUILT, Golden Gate underwent a complete body style change (RIGHT). One of the points that was a "must see" on the Sight Seeing Car tour was the Affiliated Colleges, at Second Ave. and Parnassus Street. The car passes in 1908. The large University of California Hospital now occupies this site.
BOTH: United Railroads

CAR "CALIFORNIA" poses with sightseers, operating crew and guide, at the Ferry Building, 1912. (BELOW) **AFTER** the electrification, in 1905, of the Cliff steam line, Land's End was a favorite stop on the Observation car route, seen in the 1908 view. **BOTH: United Railroads**

which could accommodate 48 passengers. This design proved more practical for the sight-seeing service than that of the GOLDEN GATE. On the latter car the passengers on the side opposite the attraction the car happened to be passing at the time, especially those seated on the lower row, found trying to see what was going on rather awkward. To correct this fault in design the GOLDEN GATE was rebuilt along the same lines as the CALIFORNIA and rejoined the Observation route on July 20, 1905. With two cars in operation the number of trips per day rose to four. When one of the two Observation Cars was tied up for some reason a 1225-class interurban car took over its duties. After the electrification of the Market Street lines in 1906 the downtown terminal for the Observation Cars was moved from Post and Market streets to the Ferry; a side track was installed in the middle of the loop to hold them.

By 1910 private motor sight-seeing buses appeared on the scene going over much the same route as the cars plus a few other attractions that were not located on the car lines. The growing number of these buses made severe inroads to the Observation Car patronage and the final sight-seeing trip was made in 1917. In 1918 the GOLDEN GATE and CALIFORNIA were altered for regular streetcar service, numbered 698 and 699 and assigned to replace the ill-fated one-man cars on the Visitacion line. They were scrapped in 1927.

PARTY CAR "SIERRA" shines in this 1908 portrait. A bit of yesteryear's elegance for those who could afford it. **United Railroads**

Party Cars

During the first decade of this century it was considered quite chic and fashionable among the affluent to use private trolley cars for any festive occasion. To cater to this charter business the railway company provided special cars that were furnished with the most lavish appointments and conveniences. A popular use of these cars was for evening theatre parties whereby upwards of 40 people could board the car at a prearranged point, ride to a restaurant of the host's choice, dine, and again board their car to be taken to the theatre. After the performance the party would find the car waiting for them and ready to whisk them off to the Cliff House, Beach Chalet or some other fashionable eating place for an after-theatre snack and libations. When the party was

A PRIVATE PARTY basks in the glory of Party Car "Hermosa" at the Cliff House (at left) on the Sutro Baths right-of-way. At the turn of the century, this was the most fashionable way for such groups to travel around the city. **Charles Smallwood**

over the private car would return the participants to the point of origin and a pleasant time was generally had by all. And all this was done for the modest sum of but $10.00 for the private transportation.

Following is a description of the Private Party Cars furnished by the United Railroads during this era:

The St. Louis Car Company constructed in 1898 an ornate special car for the original Market Street Railway. This car, named HERMOSA, had one large center section and a motorman's cab at each end. The exterior was painted Tuscan red with gold striping and lettering, and the interior was finished in cherry with terra cotta colored velour curtains and cushions, rattan chairs, moss green Wilton carpet and a fancy sideboard. An ice chest was provided on one of the platforms. It was a small car, being but 32 feet, six inches in length. It was originally equipped with a Peckham single truck but was given a pair of Brill trucks in 1901. The car was intended for private sight-seeing, theatre parties and other group moves. Flagship of the United Railroads Private Party Car fleet was the SAN FRANCISCO, the most luxurious trolley car ever to roll in the Bay Area. It was built by the St. Louis Car Company in 1901 for the San Francisco & San Mateo Electric Railway as their #61. When that company was taken over in 1902 by the United Railroads the new owners rebuilt the car for the private service. The SAN FRANCISCO was a closed car, 38 feet long, and was divided into three sections. The middle compartment was 19 feet long and was termed the *parlor*. The end compartments contained a buffet, ice chest, clothes closet and motorman's cabs and were also used as smoking rooms. The exterior of the car was painted Brewster green with gold striping and lettering, and the interior was finished in natural oak and furnished with rattan chairs, red plush cushions, red plush curtains lined with cream-colored silk, red portieres, fancy bronze light fixtures, Pullman card tables and had Wilton carpet in the middle section and linoleum in the end compartments.

This car was chartered to private parties, but only on presentation of the *best* of references. It was also used by the officers of the company for state occasions. It was considered quite the proper thing to charter the SAN FRANCISCO for theatre parties, serving a supper in the car after the theatre (with the champagne for the supper chilled in the ice chest). During the early days of the century the

SAN FRANCISCO boasted of such notable passengers as President Teddy Roosevelt and actress Sarah Bernhardt.

These Party Cars were much in demand, and in 1908 the company rebuilt Funeral Car #2 into a party car which it named SIERRA. The SIERRA was fitted out much in the same manner as the SAN FRANCISCO and became very popular with that part of the citizenry affluent enough to charter Party Cars.

The SIERRA almost came to grief once, according to old-time company employees, when one evening in 1910 a party celebrating something or other chartered the car for a trip about the city. Eventually the party ended up at the Beach Chalet for a late supper. Apparently the bubbly was flowing freely and a supply of it was brought back to the car to keep the party going. The car crew was invited to share in the fun, which they did to some considerable degree. The car left the Beach and went rolling down Fulton St. with its hilarious passengers and crew. As the car began to descend the grade past Stanyan St. no one seemed to notice that it was dangerously gathering speed. On reaching the base of the grade at Masonic and Fulton, where the line turned to the left, the SIERRA slammed into the curve with such force that it turned over on its side. Although the passengers were severely shaken up, no one was seriously injured.

By 1915 the chartering of Private Party Cars became passe among the elite and the company phased out this operation. The SIERRA was put in storage at 29th and Mission Car House where it remained until 1927 when it was taken to Elkton Shop and scrapped on July 15. The little HERMOSA was downgraded to ordinary passenger car status and numbered 746. As such it went into service on October 10, 1919, and saw use on the unimportant #28—Ferries-Depot and #34—6th and Sansome lines for a few years until it, too, was finally scrapped at Elkton September 2, 1927. The SAN FRANCISCO fared better than its two partners, having been altered into a special School Car in the mid-1920s. It lasted well into the Municipal Railway era. (See chapter on cars.)

VELVET CURTAINS, wicker seats and carpeting—the many touches of luxury on Party Car ''Hermosa.''
United Railroads

(ABOVE) **THE ELEGANT** "San Francisco," when new, at Geneva Car House, 1904. **United Railroads**

(LEFT) **"SAN FRANCISCO"** heads a lineup of more than 20 cars on School Street, Colma, alongside the Colma Boxing Arena. The car beyond San Francisco is party car "Hermosa." The occasion was the Kelly-Nelson prize fight, 1903. The two private cars were probably used to transport the fighters, officials of the area and other dignitaries. Cars behind are from 1000 and 680 classes. **Charles Smallwood**

The Competition

EARLY-DAY tour buses, like this open-top model of the Pacific Sightseeing Co., were already making inroads when this 1912 view was taken at the Cliff House. They would soon doom the streetcar sightseeing service.
Charles Smallwood

The Tanforan Horse Car

THE TANFORAN HORSE CAR. Among its varied cargoes were racehorses, motorcycles and strike-breakers.
United Railroads

Another unit of unusual revenue rolling stock was the Tanforan Horse Car. This car was merely a motorized box car fitted with stalls to accommodate and transport horses to the Tanforan Race Track on the San Mateo interurban line. The horses were usually picked up at the Ferry Terminal of the transcontinental railroads, or from one of the numerous horse stables in the Western area of the city. At times it was also used to carry motorcycles to Tanforan as the race track also featured motorcycle races during the off-season at the track. For this service a charge of 25 cents for each motorcycle and 10 cents for each rider or attendant was made. This car was officially numbered 0910 but during 1906-07 it was also called MYSTERY. It earned this sobriquet when it was used to secretly move strike-breakers imported from the east, from the railroad stations to the various car houses under the cover of night during a work stoppage.

As the improved motor vans took over the duties of this car and which its use as a revenue unit was over it was taken to the 20th Avenue and Pacheco sand lot and used as a tool car. It was dismantled at this location around 1935 when the sand lot was sold to make way for a real estate development.

Street Sweeping Cars

Least glamorous of all the Special Revenue Car services was that performed by the street sweeping cars. These units were motorized gondola cars and had a motorman's cab at each end. Two large bins, each with an eight cubic yard capacity, were mounted on a steel shaft having a gear and pinion arrangement that permitted the boxes to be tipped and dump their load by means of a crank in each cab. The cars were under contract to the City Street Cleaning Department to carry the street sweepings from the downtown area to the outer portions of Golden Gate Park. The horse-drawn wagons of the City Street Department deposited their loads at a yard on Brannan St. between 7th and 8th streets; here a ramp was provided enabling the wagons to dump their contents directly into one of the street-sweeping cars, which entered the yard via a spur track from the Brannan St. car line. When loaded, the big gondola would then proceed to Golden Gate Park, entering over several spur tracks from Lincoln Way, and there dump its load—used as fill in gullies and other low areas.

For this service the City paid the United Railroads thirty cents a cubic yard. The cars made from eight to ten trips and moved between 100 and 160 yards per day. Earnings to the company averaged $38.00 per day with crew expenses averaging out to $10.00 per day.

Although officially designated as Street Sweeping Cars by the city and United Railroads, the residents along their outbound route had other, less complimentary, names for them due to the liberal sprinkling of horse manure in their loads. Apparently the contract with the city was not renewed after 1906 as there is no record of this operation after that date. When the odorous duty of these cars was ended, they went to work in general track maintenance jobs, only their old numbers reminding the knowledgable of their original service.

(TOP) **STREET SWEEPING** Car 0402 leaves the City Cleaning Department yard, Brannan between Seventh and Eighth streets, for Golden Gate Park, with its aromatic load.

(LEFT) **THE 0402** dumps its manure-laced street dirt in a gully in Golden Gate Park in 1905. Sidings into the park ran from ''H'' Street (later Lincoln Way). A trestle was built over low ground and cars dumped their loads from it. The trestles were eventually abandoned in the fill and many still remain buried in the park. **BOTH: United Railroads**

The United Railroads of San Francisco

The final large consolidation of privately owned street railways in San Francisco came in 1902 when the banking house of Brown Brothers of New York purchased the entire capital stock of the Market Street Railway from Southern Pacific and others, acting in the interest of eastern capitalists. Also purchased at the same time was the *Sutter Street Railroad* and *San Francisco & San Mateo Electric Railroad,* the whole forming the *United Railroads of San Francisco.* This move placed all street railways in the city under one management with the exceptions of the *California Street Cable Railroad, Geary Street, Park & Ocean Railway* and the *Presidio & Ferries Railway.*

The newly formed system comprised 226 miles of single track consisting of 158 miles operated by electric, 52 by cable, 12 by steam motors and 4 by horse. Rolling stock ran the gamut as to methods of propulsion and included:

- 404 Electric passenger cars
- 374 Cable cars
- 77 Horse cars
- 17 Steam car trailers
- 36 Cable and electric trailers
- 6 Steam motors
- 21 Miscellaneous cars

Faced with this heterogeneous network the new company set out to convert to modern electric propulsion except on lines where steep grades made necessary the retention of cable traction. The company, as did its predecessor, urged the replacement of the cable cars by electric traction on the important Market Street corridor. In 1891 the Board of Supervisors, by popular demand, and especially due to pressure from the powerful Merchants Association, passed an ordinance that prohibited the use of overhead trolley wires in the downtown area. The more or less success of an underground conduit employed for electric streetcars in New York and Washington, D.C., as well as public sentiment to eliminate all overhead wires in the downtown area, managed to keep electric cars off Market Street until the great disaster of 1906. The order banning the overhead trolley originally encompassed the entire downtown area. However, it was modified in 1892 to allow the Metropolitan Railway to use the overhead trolley on Eddy, Hyde and O'Farrell streets but continued to be enforced on Market and Sutter streets. The company offered to install and maintain ornamental iron poles which, besides holding the trolley wires, would also be topped by powerful arc lamps that would make Market Street one of the world's most brilliantly lighted streets. But this alluring offer was to no avail, the city authorities remaining adamant that, though electric cars were desired on the city's most important street, the underground conduit must be used.

Meanwhile the United Railroads went forward in modernizing the system, electrifying the horse car lines and the steam line out California Street and around Land's End. The interurban line to San Mateo was built and new, larger cars, modern for their day, were purchased, 145 of them being added between 1903 and 1905.

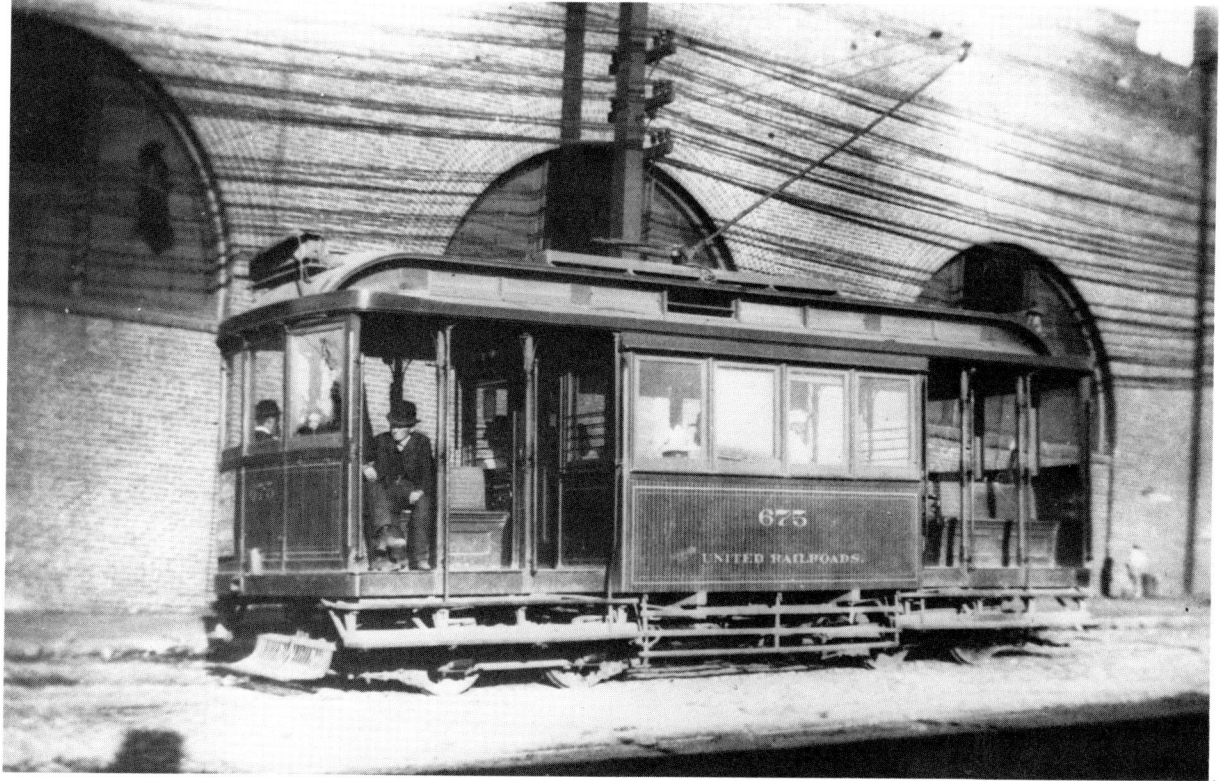

ONE CAR OF THIS SERIES survived into 1978 as Municipal Railway car 0304, the last unit of the private traction company's stock still in service. The disposition of the 10 cars included one car each to the Mt. Olivet Cemetery Association and the Reno Traction Company; two of the cars became Mail Cars "D" and "E". This 10-car order was built by the John Hammond Car Company, of San Francisco, in March 1900, for the San Francisco & San Mateo Railway and bore the numbers 41 to 50 of that road. After acquiring the San Mateo line the United Railroads placed the cars in its 671-680 series. Car 675 is shown (ABOVE) at Bryant and Division streets in 1905.

Robert H. MacFarland

Interurban to San Mateo

AN EARLY United Railroads accomplishment was construction of the interurban line to San Mateo. Here is one of the original large wooden cars, known as "Big Subs," which were original equipment on the Peninsula route, in Colma, 1907. **Charles Smallwood**

AS AN EXPERIMENT, the United Railroads enclosed one of its 1300-1349 class cars. The rebuilt unit, 1313, went into service on the Guerrero and Ocean View Line on April 17, 1906 (the day before the 'quake). It was the first car in San Francisco to be equipped with roller-type destination signs. Car 1313, the only car so rebuilt, wound up as the Fillmore Street crosstown line owl car. In 1911 it was lengthened and changed to Pay-As-You-Enter, as were the other 1300s. **United Railroads**

HERE IS Valencia cable car 3 in front of Sanford Hall, by the 28th and Valencia barn in 1904. These cars were painted light blue, and were sold to the Geary Street cable road after the 1906 earthquake and fire, as the Valencia line was then converted to electric operation. **United Railroads**

WHEN THE EARTHQUAKE HIT the Oak and Broderick Car House, the chimney collapsed, its debris crashing through the roof. Not only was the building damaged, but a number of cars were crushed.

United Railroads

Earthquake!

When disaster struck the city on April 18, 1906, the earthquake and resultant fire completely destroyed the winding machinery of the cable systems on both Market and Sutter streets. Considerable other damage was suffered by the company due to the calamity, much of the overhead electric network was down, the iron trolley poles bent by the heat, rails twisted out of line and carhouses and other buildings either destroyed or heavily damaged. The entire building, machinery and rolling stock of the Powell Street cable system was laid waste as was the cable power plant and car house at Sutter and Polk streets. Almost all of the electric car houses were damaged by the quake to some degree but fortunately all of the electric barns escaped the flames. Oak and Broderick car house sustained much damage as the tall old chimney, a relic of cable days, fell and crashed through the roof severely damaging several cars.

It was urgent to resume streetcar service as soon as possible after the quake and the United Railroads requested and obtained a "temporary" permit allowing the company to install overhead trolley wires on Market and Sutter streets. Meanwhile, all available manpower was put to work cleaning up the lines and preparing them for service. Orders were placed with eastern car builders for new cars which were put in service as soon as they arrived. A total of 262 new cars were in use on the rebuilt lines by 1907.

The company was indeed fortunate that, with the exception of the Powell Street system, most of the damage sustained by it was to the cable lines that the company wanted to get rid of anyway. (Only six electric cars were destroyed by the fire.) The first service to resume following the disaster was nine days later when a few cars were run on the Fillmore-16th Street line. By May 6 the Mission Street line was again running followed by Market Street from Fifth Street to the Ferry. As soon as they could be made ready other lines followed rapidly. However, it was not until January 13, 1907, that the Powell Street lines, the hardest hit of all of the company's divisions, was again back in service and then only to a limited degree. For a few days following the resumption of service after the quake no fares were charged in an effort to alleviate the sufferings of the populace.

THIS RUBBLE is all that was left of Guerrero line car 1310, burned during the April 19, 1906, fire that followed the earthquake. It was sitting at 19th and Guerrero streets when destroyed. **United Railroads**

Electrifying Market Street

IN ITS HASTE to install overhead wires on Market Street after the earthquake and fire (and in an effort to resume service as soon as possible and thwart possible public resistance to this move) United Railroads augmented its own equipment and crews with this tower wagon, rented from nearby Oakland Traction Company. This rig, manned by Oakland linemen and drawn by an Oakland Traction team, is shown stringing trolley wire on Market Street, near Fourth, in front of the ruins of the Humboldt Savings Bank building.

Charles Smallwood

FIRST REGULAR CAR to the Ferry, following the 1906 earthquake-fire, car 1350 posed with celebrants on May 6, when service resumed along Market Street to its traditional terminal. **United Railroads**

A TEMPORARY stub terminal was installed, following the disaster, at the Ferry until the loop tracks could be built. View is from the Ferry tower. **Charles Smallwood**

THIS MOVING MASS of humanity with a trolley pole sticking out of it is a Fillmore line streetcar, seen at Turk and Fillmore streets on April 27, 1906, when the first few cars were run on Fillmore after the disaster. Looks like everybody wanted to go somewhere! **Charles Smallwood**

HOPING TO INCREASE car capacity, the United Railroads experimented with the idea of using obsolete Market Street cable cars as trailers for electric cars. It took only two trips down Mission Street to the Ferry to convince company officials that the plan was not feasible. The experimental train is shown at San Jose and Ocean Aves. on February 15, 1907. **United Railroads**

Labor Unrest

The prevailing wage for carmen at this time was $2.50 for a 10-hour day, a holdover from the old horse and cable car days. On August 26, 1906, the carmen went on strike demanding $3.00 for an eight-hour day, it being charged by the union that the unusual conditions brought about by the quake made it difficult for the employees to adequately provide for themselves and their families at the present rate. Although the United Railroads declared that the carmen were getting higher wages than paid similar employment on other railways both parties agreed to submit the dispute to arbitration. The carmen were satisfied by this action and returned to work on September 6. They were subsequently awarded a 25% increase in wages but the 10-hour day remained. This minor labor dispute was but a prelude to the long and brutal struggle that was to surface the following year.

When the initial shock of the great disaster began to wear off later in the year civic groups began to put the "temporary" permit granted by the municipal authorities for overhead wires on Market Street under closer scrutiny. Their fears were realized when it became known that the United Railroads, with the connivance of the Mayor and Board of Supervisors, intended as permanent this method of operation on that street. The resulting investigation and litigation resulted in a public scandal but in the end the overhead wires remained. True to their promise the company did install the beautiful iron poles surmounted by arc lights. These same poles and lights are still in use on Market Street today.

The 1907 Strike

The company suffered a major setback when on May 5, 1907, the carmen again went on strike for a $3.00 wage and an eight-hour day. The company refused to negotiate with the union and thus began a long, costly and brutal struggle. The company resorted to importing strike-breakers from eastern cities and provided dormitories and dining facilities for these crews at the various car houses. Service using strike-breakers was started on May 13 to a limited degree starting much violence by the striking carmen and their sympathizers by way of retaliation. Just how serious the situation became was clear in these notations from the 29th and Mission Car House daybook:

DURING THE 1907 CARMEN'S STRIKE the company attempted to run cars with strike-breakers. This scene is at Divisadero and California on the first day of the walkout, May 13, 1907. Mounted policemen and police department autos (early versions of today's patrol cars) convoyed the streetcars in an attempt to prevent violence.

Charles Smallwood

ALL MANNER of makeshift vehicles was operated by the General Strike Committee during the 1907 strike in an effort to provide some sort of transit for the public. Here is one of the better ones, a rig that utilized an old horse car body on a wagon bed. Those solid wagon wheels rumbling over cobblestone streets must have made for a very shaky ride!
R.H. McFarland/Charles Smallwood Collection

July 20 8:45 P.M.—Conductor Kawag and Motorman S. Feller were shot at 29th and Noe and then the rioters let car go down the hill to 29th and Mission where it jumped the track and ran into a candy store and toggery store completely smashing the fronts of both stores. The car was a total wreck.

October 19 Riot on car #1575, run 9, Polk-Larkin Line, Conductor Brown and Motorman Purcell both beaten. In protecting themselves they fired several shots hitting three rioters, two of whom were killed.

On May 27 United Railroads Vice President and General Manager George F. Chapman died suddenly. Despite the strike Chapman went to his final rest in a manner befitting an important streetcar company executive. The cortege consisted of one of the company's funeral cars, a floral car and two of the new streetcars to carry the mourners. Company executives operated the cars.

The strike was successfully broken by the company and on September 13 the union finally called it off but violence and ill feeling continued for the remainder of the year. At the time of the Union's surrender the company had over 1,400 men at work, some 250 of whom were former employees who had deserted the union and returned to the company. It was costly to both sides, the final toll being an estimated $1,000,000 in lost revenue to the company and over a half-million dollars in lost wages to the strikers. Three men were killed and 30 wounded, and there was much damage to company property. Car windows were especially vulnerable, a total of 3,539 being shattered by missiles thrown by rioters. The strike also resulted in great inconvenience and hardship to the public and considerable loss to the business community.

Patrick Calhoun

Guiding hand of the company affairs during these early years was its president Patrick Calhoun. To Calhoun fell the task of heading earthquake and fire reconstruction and to weather the brutal labor troubles of 1906-07. He was also one of the principal figures in the municipal litigation over the graft associated with the overhead trolley permit on Market Street.

Calhoun entered the scene in December 1905, when he succeeded Arthur Holland as president of the United Railroads. Son of a wealthy South Carolina plantation owner who was ruined by the Civil War, he was orphaned and penniless at an early age but managed to educate himself and attain a law degree by the time he was 19 years old. At the start of his career he was employed by J.P. Morgan in the capacity of aiding that railroad magnate in his efforts to consolidate several small Southern railroads into a unified system. Still later, on his own, he successfully brought about utilities mergers in several cities before coming to San Francisco to head the United Railroads. In 1909 he was indicted and brought to trial as one of the main figures in the overhead trolley graft scandal, it being alleged that Calhoun, with the notorious political boss Abe Ruef acting as intermediary, bribed the Board of Supervisors for the trolley permit. The trial lasted for 22 months and received much publicity. It resulted in a hung jury and in 1911 the indictments against Calhoun and other company officials were dismissed for lack of evidence.

In the public's view Calhoun *was* the United Railroads during those turbulent years. In 1913 he retired from the presidency of the company and was succeeded by Mason B. Starring. Starring was eventually replaced by Jesse W. Lilienthal as president but returned again to the presidency of the new Market Street Railway in 1925.

Municipal Pressures

During the years 1908 to 1912 the company continued to further improve their property. Several lines were relaid with heavier rail and many new cars were added. These improvements, costing in excess of $12,000,000, were all to upgrade the existing property. The United Railroads had adopted a policy of no further expansion of their system and would not extend their lines into sections of the city, notably the area lying south of Golden Gate Park, that was in dire need of street railway service. Extensions to the system were deemed inadvisable because of the provisions of the new City Charter of 1900 which declared for ultimate Municipal ownership of all street railways. An amendment to this charter in 1902 reduced the term of future franchise grants to 25 years and provided for regulations of service, fares and operation. Another amendment to the Charter in 1910 gave the city the right to purchase, for a fair price, any services provided by these future franchises. The results of the restrictive provisions of this Charter was to discourage private capital from investing in further expansion of the United Railroads.

Since 1902 the company applied for and received only a few franchises covering Gough St. from McAllister to Market, Judah St. from 3rd Ave. to 9th Ave., 9th Ave. from Judah to Pacheco, Sloat Blvd. from Junipero Serra Blvd. to the beach, 20th Ave. from Lincoln Way to Sloat Blvd., a meandering route in the Parkside area, Visitacion Valley and on Mission St. from Onondaga Ave. to Daly City. All of these franchises were of minor importance except those on Mission St. and Sloat Blvd. and the Judah and 9th Ave., Visitacion and the Parkside lines were financed by real estate development interests desiring car service in their largely undeveloped areas. By 1912 the company refrained from establishing any new extensions to their services. The only exception to this policy was a new line built in 1918, on a revocable permit, on Army Street from Potrero Ave. to Third St. This line was financed by the government as a war measure to carry workers to the shipyards along Third St. After 1912 all street railway expansion into undeveloped areas was done by the Municipal Railway.

Municipal Railway Opens

The negative effects of the city's policy, as illustrated by URR's failure to build into new territory, was perhaps one of the factors which caused voters to finally approve a bond issue for the first Municipal Railway lines (after a number of elections).

Muni's Geary St. line was opened to traffic on December 28, 1912, and at once the new line made heavy inroads into paralleling United Railroads routes. Further proof that the city was in earnest in its endeavor to institute a competing street railway system came on August 26, 1913, when the electorate voted by a 37,000 majority to approve a proposition authorizing $3.5 millions in bonds to extend greatly the new Municipal Railway. Another move by the city, viewed with considerable consternation by United Railroads, was the taking over of the privately owned Presidio & Ferries Railway by the Municipal Railway on December 11, 1913.

Improved Fare Collection, New Cars

In 1911 the United Railroads introduced the "Pay-As-You-Enter" method of fare collection by the purchase of 80 new cars (Class 101-180). This new system became highly suc-

Horsecar at the Loop

UNTIL 1913 the Sutter Street horse car shared trackage around the Ferry Loop with the electric cars.　　　**Charles Smallwood**

MAYOR "SUNNY JIM" ROLPH runs the last scheduled horse car up Market Street on June 3, 1913. The ceremonial run is seen at Eighth and Market. Franchise horse cars had run on Market from Sansome to the Ferry until this date.
Charles Smallwood

REAL ESTATE DEVELOPERS built the Burlingame Railway to provide local service from the Easton Station (later Broadway-Burlingame) of the San Mateo interurban line. This battery-powered streetcar ran two miles west from the station until replaced by a bus in late 1917.
Charles Smallwood

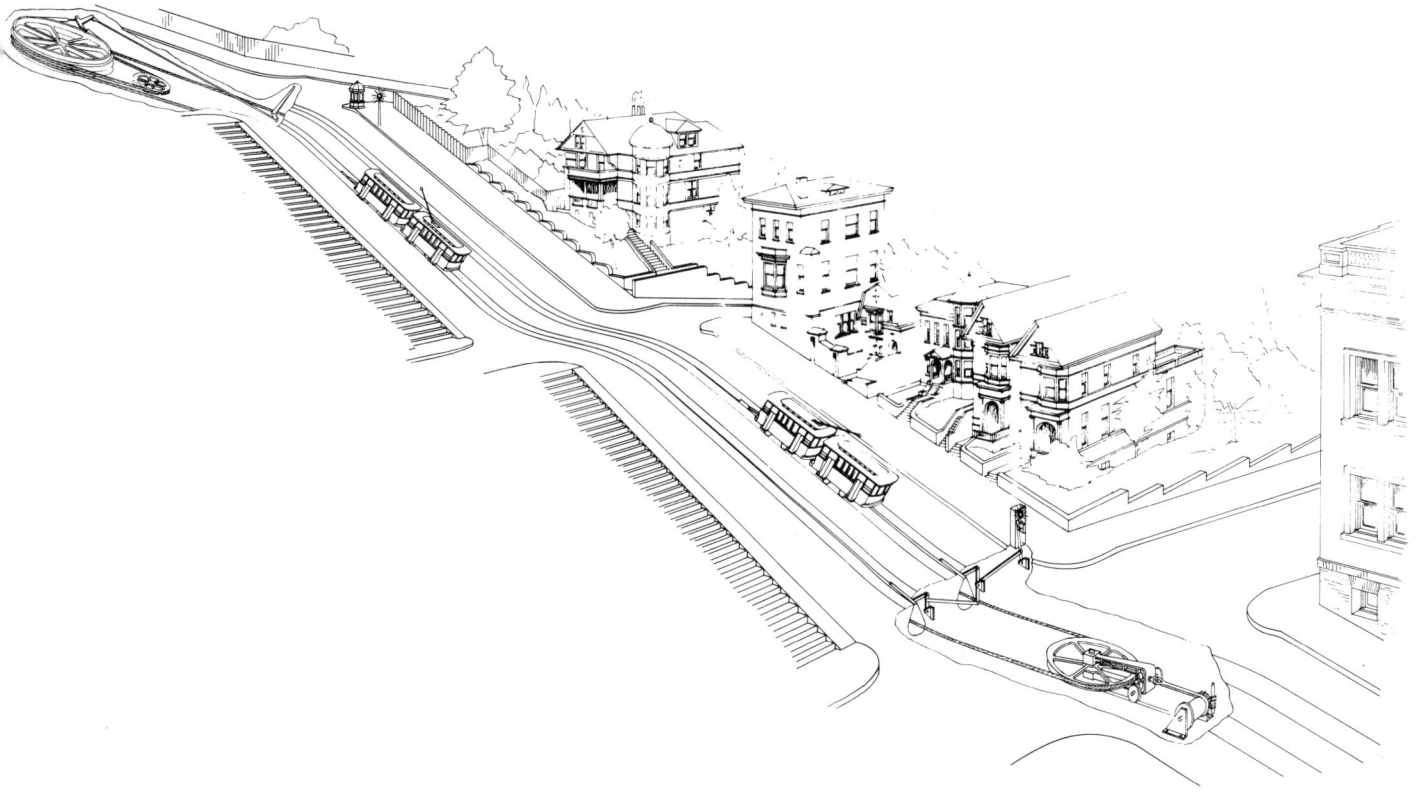

THE FILLMORE COUNTERBALANCE, illustrated in this diagram of its workings, did yeoman service carrying throngs to the 1915 Panama-Pacific Exposition. Photographs of its cars are found in the "Electric Passenger Cars" chapter.   **United Railroads**

cessful after the public and crews became acquainted with it. Prior to the introduction of the Pay-As-You-Enter cars passengers could board the car at either end, take their seats and wait for the conductor to walk through the car to collect their fares. The conductor would ring up the fares collected on a register mounted on the car bulkhead, in the same manner as on today's cable cars. The company and the public were both pleased with this new method of fare collecting as it speeded up service and was safer as both the entrance and exit were at all times under the surveillance of the crew. Also in 1911 the company constructed 24 new cars in their shop (Class 701-724) that were of the Pay-As-You-Enter type and immediately began to change all of the existing double-truck electric cars to PAYE, many of which required a major rebuilding in the process.

The Exposition

The Panama-Pacific International Exposition, held in San Francisco in 1915, was constructed on largely undeveloped and reclaimed land in the Harbor View area, now the present Marina District. The United Railroads had but two lines to this area, the Fillmore Hill counterbalance line and the electric line on Polk St. In an effort to establish adequate transportation service to the area in expectation of the Exposition, the city authorities submitted to the electorate in 1913 a bond issue of $3,500,000 to extend the Municipal Railway service to the Fair. This bond issue passed with a 37,000 majority and during 1914 new lines were constructed from the Mission District (long a United Railroads exclusive stronghold) to the Fair via Potrero Ave., 11th St. and Van Ness Ave. and downtown Market and Stockton via Stockton, Columbus, North Point, Van Ness and Chestnut streets. The section on Chestnut St. provided the Municipal lines with a direct route to the Main Gate of the Exposition.

These new Municipal lines were highly competitive with the United Railroads and what should have been a banner year for the company actually, due to this competition, resulted in a drop of 9,000,000 passengers carried in 1915 over the previous year.

Two further developments did damage to revenues. The city had canceled the franchise on California St., from 6th Ave. to 33rd Ave., on which the #1 line operated, and this was turned over to the Municipal Railway for its C line. Unregulated jitney bus service began that year, soon spreading so these makeshift vehicles paralleled all profitable car lines.

The most important United Railroads line to the Fair was the Fillmore Hill line. This electric line used a counterbalance system to negotiate the very steep grade on Fillmore between Broadway and Green St. Small single-truck cars were used on the route which connected to the Fillmore-16th St. Crosstown line at the Broadway summit of the grade. The small cars would have been totally inadequate to handle the expected traffic that the Fair would generate. To overcome this limitation the company upgraded this line by equipping the small cars for multiple-unit control whereby two of the cars could be permanently coupled together and run as one unit. While this move doubled the capacity of the line passenger movement was somewhat restricted during periods of heavy travel owing to the slow and complicated operation on the two-block counterbalance section. Despite these difficulties the counterbalance line did perform admirably, carrying millions of passengers during the Fair with perfect safety.

The second route serving the Fair area was the #19—9th, Polk and Larkin line. For this line the company constructed a loop, known as Exposition Terminal, on property it purchased on Francisco St. between Van Ness Ave. and Polk St. To augment the #19 line service to this terminal the company established during the run of the Fair three additional routes that also terminated at the loop. These new lines were:

#32—S.P. DEPOT-EXPOSITION From S.P. Depot to Exposition via Townsend, 4th, Ellis, Hyde, O'Farrell and Polk streets.

#33—MISSION-EXPOSITION From 29th and Mission to Exposition via Mission, 9th, Larkin, Post and Polk streets.

#34—SUTTER-EXPOSITION From Ferry to Exposition via Market, Sutter and Polk streets.

The #22—Fillmore-16th streets Crosstown line served the Broadway-Fillmore terminus of the counterbalance line. During the Fair the #23—Fillmore-Valencia line was diverted from its usual terminal at Sacramento and Divisadero streets to Broadway and Fillmore. A new line, designated #35—Haight-Exposition, was established from Carl and Stanyan to Fillmore and Broadway via Carl, Clayton, Frederick, Masonic, Page (return via Oak St.) and Fillmore streets. Travel on the #35 line did not reach expectations and the line was discontinued after a few weeks.

It is interesting to note that, when the Fair closed, the 32, 33, 34 and 35 route numbers were assigned to long-established lines that had no number designation prior to 1916.

"ARMORED CARS" appeared during the 1917 carmen's strike. The wire mesh screen protected the crews, passengers and window glass from missiles hurled by the strikers.   **United Railroads**

Another Strike

During the year 1917 the United Railroads suffered another strike when on August 12 the carmen walked out. As in 1907 the company resorted to the use of strike-breakers. There was considerable violence but not to the extent of the 1907 unrest. So-called "armored cars" were introduced during this strike. These cars had screens of wire mesh nailed over all of the windows and had holes cut in each platform roof for the trolley rope which allowed the trolley to be manipulated from within the car thus thwarting the rioters' favorite mode of harassment, that of smashing car windows and cutting trolley ropes.

Again the company emerged victorious as the strike and boycott was finally called off on November 24.

URR Weakened

The United Railroads had suffered many severe financial setbacks since 1906. Damage and loss of revenue stemming from the 1906 disaster, the costly strikes of 1907 and 1917, unregulated jitney competition, and the most devastating of all, the rapid expansion of Municipal Railway into what had once been exclusive United Railroads territory all took their toll of the financial situation of the system. For several years the company paid no dividends and was financially unable to redeem several series of bonds that were reaching maturity. This state of affairs resulted in the bond holders demanding a reorganization of the company. Just how desperate the situation had become is shown by a memorandum prepared by the statistical department of a prominent brokerage house that had been an active dealer in United Railroads securities. This memorandum was, as a matter of general information, distributed to United Railroads bond and shareholders and points out in part:

Cause of Present Situation

From April 18, 1906, the United Railroads has been subjected to a series of misfortunes or difficulties, all of which together would present almost insurmountable complications for the best and most soundly financed of corporations. We enumerate these without stopping to go into their respective importance financial or otherwise:

1. Earthquake and Fire of 1906,
   resulting in great destruction of physical property not insured, as well as an enormous loss in earnings extending over a period of more than a year.
2. Electrification of Cable Lines,
   with incidental delays and legal expenses thereto, an adverse political conditions.
3. Labor Troubles,
   resulting in a complete tie-up of all business on two distinct occasions and unusual expense extending over a period of months each time.
4. Mismanagement,
   resulting in the misuse of company funds on a large scale.
5. Municipal Street Railway Competition,
   an established policy resulting from a Charter Declaration in favor of Municipal ownership of public utilities in 1900 and resulting in repeated submission of propositions to the voting public and finally in the construction of several lines practically paralleling portions of the United Railroads System.
6. Adverse Public Opinion,
   engendered by antagonism to private street railway enterprises brought out in an extended controversy over the construction of the Municipal lines; as well as by unfavorable labor interests in political control and general dissatisfaction with the financial operations of the Company and the services rendered to the traveling public.
7. Jitney Bus Competition,
   which reached its height in the Exposition period, when the Company would have otherwise have had an opportunity to recoup some of its losses.

The difficulties that the United Railroads of San Francisco have been subjected to have resulted in:

1. Actual property loss of considerable magnitude.
2. Heavy losses in gross earnings.
3. Materially increased operating expenses.
4. Increase in fixed obligations and charges incidental thereto.

These large losses in property and earnings have culminated in a time when certain maturing obligations must be met—obligations for the retirement of which adequate provision had not been made.

In addition to the primary problem of the payment of the actual maturing obligations coming due in 1917 and 1918 it is advisable at this time to meet the problem of an excessive capitalization which has become burdensome with a decrease of net earnings, a capitalization which would sooner or later have to be adjusted in the face of limited franchises.

If all this was not enough to sink the United Railroads, the tragic Visitacion Valley wreck of 1918 was truly "the straw that broke the camel's back." It is discussed in detail in a nearby page, and was a loss from which URR never recovered.

The reorganization came on April 1, 1921 when the control of the United Railroads passed into the hands of the newly formed Market Street Railway Company.

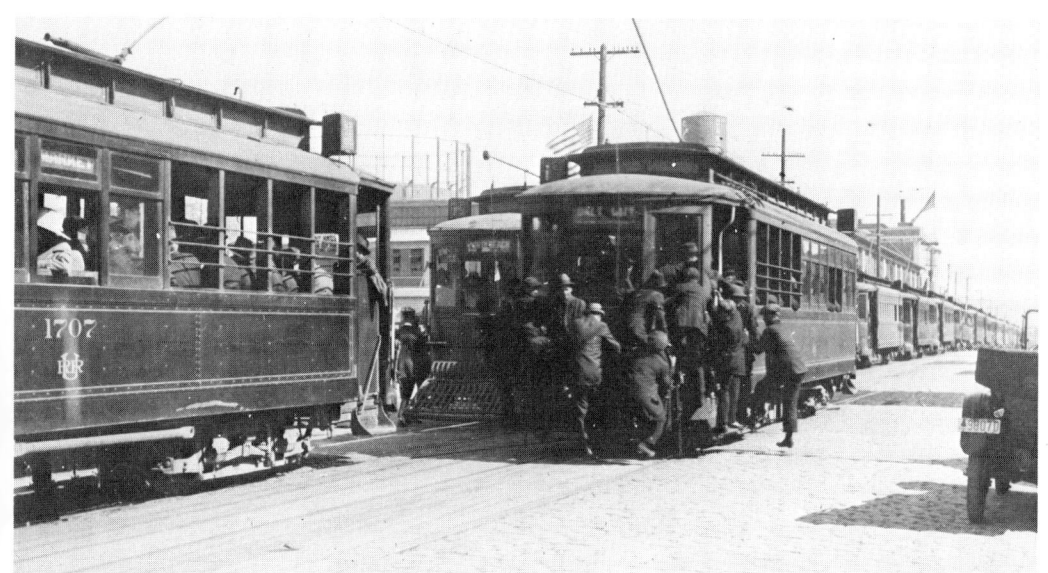

HEIGHTENED ACTIVITY of the City's shipbuilding industry brought about by World War I taxed the facilities of the United Railroads, as shown in this view taken at Third and 20th streets. The cars in this 1918 lineup (looking south) are waiting for homebound shipyard workers from the Union Iron Works.
United Railroads

Tragedy in Visitacion Valley

THE VISITACION VALLEY Line ran right near the County Line. This 1917 view looks west from the spot where #1024's sister car overturned, in July 1918. **United Railroads**

THE COUNTRY was still at war with Germany in July 1918, and shipyards along the Bay in the southeastern section of The City were a beehive of activity turning out the tools of war. An important link in the United Railroads streetcar lines serving the shipyard facilities was the cross-country Visitacion Valley line that ran from Geneva Ave. and Mission St. to the Six-Mile House (now Leland Ave. and Bay Shore Blvd.). This line was very heavily traveled during the war period as it provided a direct route to the shipyard lines for the large working class section of the Outer Mission District.

Normally, travel on the Visitacion line was light except during the morning and evening peak periods and there was little or no auto traffic for cars of this line to contend with as almost all of its route was on private right-of-way. As an economy move, United Railroads instituted one-man car service on this route in July 1914. Three cars of the 1001-1025 class (1022, 1023 and 1024) were extensively rebuilt for this pioneering one-man service.

Saturday morning of July 13 dawned as a sultry, overcast day. Around 7:00 A.M. Visitacion car 1022 was loading passengers at the Mission Street terminal. Almost all of the estimated 100 passengers to board the car were employed at the Schaw-Batcher Shipbuilding Company's plant at South San Francisco. Shortly after 7:00 A.M. car 1022 started a fateful trip that it was destined never to complete. For in a few minutes car 1022 was a total wreck, eight of its passengers dead and more than 70 injured in what was the worst streetcar disaster in California history.

The Visitacion Valley wreck, tragic as it was in terms of human misery, set in motion economic forces which were to destroy United Railroads as a company and plague its successor, Market Street Railway, to its own end as an operating organization. Here is a vivid newspaper account of that most fateful calamity:

8 KILLED, 70 INJURED IN SAN FRANCISCO CAR WRECK

Federal Authorities Investigate Charge Air Brakes Had Been Tampered With by Outsider

Car Loaded With Employees of Ship Building Plant; Motorman Under Arrest

Eight men were killed and 70 others injured—several perhaps fatally—when a United Railroads streetcar of the Visitacion Valley Line, after a mad dash down the steep hill on Wallbridge Street, struck the curve at Schwerin Street and overturned early yesterday, wrecking the streetcar and burying the dead and injured beneath the wreckage.

More than 100 passengers were on the streetcar at the time it started down the grade. Some of them jumped from the car as it hurtled down the grade after the air brakes failed to hold, and thus escaped with minor injuries.

The streetcar was in charge of Motorman-Conductor George W. Sweetman at the time of the accident.

BRAKES MEDDLED WITH

According to Sweetman, the air brakes had been tampered with. The police and government officials are investigating his story, as all of the injured were employed at the Schaw-Batcher Shipbuilding Company's plant at South San Francisco. The plant is working on government contracts exclusively.

According to passengers, the car was operated by a shipyard worker when it started down the hill on Wallbridge Street and the motorman did not take charge of the controller box until the car was more than half-way down the hill. This is denied by Sweetman, who told police that he was at the brakes before the car reached the top of the grade.

Passengers told the police yesterday that the car, which is operated by one man, acting as both motorman and conductor, was usually operated by one of the shipyard workers during the early morning trip while the motorman-conductor went through the car collecting fares.

Captain of Detectives Duncan Matheson, in charge of the investigation, said yesterday: "If the motorman left his post at the control box, as passengers claim, and went through the car collecting fares and transfers while a civilian operated the car, he is guilty of criminal negligence and I propose to run the matter down."

MOTORMAN ARRESTED

After visiting the scene of the wreck Captain Matheson had Sweetman taken into custody by the local authorities.

He was booked at city prison on seven counts of manslaughter. Later in the day Sweetman was released on $1000 bail furnished by United Railroads.

Two companies of local fire department were called to help extricate the injured from the wreckage.

ORDER ENFORCED

To enforce an order of the coroner concerning the disposition of the wrecked car Police Corporal Charles Brown was all but

LOOKING DOWNGRADE along the Wallbridge Street right-of-way in August 1937. The speeding car left the rails at the bottom. **Charles Smallwood**

WHEN THE LINE TURNED SHARPLY at Schwerin St., car 1022 careened off the track and overturned. The toll included eight deaths. This view looks west. **United Railroads**

OVERTURNED CAR 1022 is seen in this view looking south. A Pacific Gas & Electric substation is at left.

United Railroads

forced to use his revolver to compel workmen of the United Railroads to desist from attempts to remove the car.

"I directed Corporal Brown to see that nothing was removed from the wreckage and that no person tampered with it in any manner," said Deputy Coroner Frank Becker, assigned to investigate the accident. "This order was given after I had inspected the wreckage and determined that the closest investigation would be necessary in order to determine the responsibility for the accident.

"To this end I directed a police photographer to make pictures of the wreck and Corporal Brown was instructed to guard it until this was accomplished. The order had scarcely been issued when two wrecking cars of the United Railroads arrived at the scene of the accident. To the foreman of the crew Brown repeated his orders and told the men to let the wreck alone."

CONFLICT WITH FOREMAN

The foreman sought to disregard the order and directed his crew to proceed with the work of clearing away the damaged car.

"I told you about my orders," said Brown, "and I tell you now I am going to enforce them."

The foreman laughed, whereat Brown half drew his revolver, the foreman backed away and the men ran to their wrecking cars which left the scene and the danger of a clash had passed.

Continued Becker: "The car was wrecked when it climbed the rails of the curve at Wallbridge and Schwerin Streets. Three short blocks before it reached that corner it completed the descent of a sharp declivity on which it had gained high momentum. When it approached the curve it must have maintained much of this momentum, for instead of taking the curve the car continued in a straight course, striking a vacant lot some distance away and turning over. The front end of the car was smashed and lay on its top. The rear end of the car was on its side with the wheels facing one as one approached it."

TAMPERING CHARGE

Eugene Byington, chief Inspector for the United Railroads, after the accident said:

"We have had considerable trouble with passengers on the Visitacion Valley line tampering with the light and air compressor switches on the cars and I have had several special police officers of the company riding on the line for the past three weeks endeavoring to apprehend them."

Captain Henry O'Dea of the Bay View Police Station said that he had received complaints from the railroad company to the effect that passengers on the cars had tampered with the lights and brakes, but said that his men had not been able to locate the guilty persons.

UNITED RAILROADS STATEMENT

Jesse W. Lilienthal, president of the United Railroads, made the following statement about the accident:

"After an investigation this morning we have come to the conclusion that either vicious hoodlums or German sympathizers were responsible for the affair. There might be a motive for German influence for the reason that the car carries almost exclusively employees of a shipbuilding plant. The railroad company was not negligent. We had an experienced motorman on the car. He was not absent from his post when the car got away. The air had been exhausted because someone had tampered with it. This might be done while the motorman was at his post.

"For the past three weeks the company has been entering complaints with the police about hoodlums and hoodlumism on some of the cars and on this line particularly. There is no question but that an outsider tampered with the brakes out of maliciousness. The car was not overcrowded and the mechanism and the track were in perfect working order, as our investigation showed. *[With a seating capacity of 30 for this type car and inasmuch as this car was carrying more than 100 passengers at the time of the accident, one wonders what awesome number of passengers a car would have to carry to be considered overcrowded by President Lilienthal. —Author]* The fact that the crew consisted of only one man was not to blame nor is it unusual. All of the passengers, save a very few, get on this car at one terminus and ride through the other one. The motorman collects all of his fares before he starts.

"There are men, as everyone knows, who used to work for the company who have a great deal of malice against it. The company's officials have always to be on the lookout for something they might do."

[The previous year of 1917 the United Railroads suffered a bitter and bloody strike of carmen. The company won the strike and a great many of the strikers were not taken back into the employ of the company, thus generating much bitterness by these men and their sympathizers. This, no doubt, was what Lilienthal was referring to in this statement.]

Lilienthal said he had not heard of a policeman being forced to draw a revolver to keep employees from clearing away the wreckage before the coroner's deputies arrived. He said he did not believe such a thing could have happened.

FORTY POUNDS OF AIR

Examination of the air pressure gauge on the car after the accident showed that only 40 pounds of air were in the tank at the time of the accident. The usual pressure in the tanks is 70 pounds according to officials. One of the peculiar features of the accident was that Sweetman, the motorman, escaped without injury. This is explained by the fact that the rear end of the car, after leaving the tracks, was the first end of the car to tip over. Sweetman, being in the front of the car, climbed out of the window after the car stopped.

Sweetman said after the accident:

"I tested the air brakes just before making the curve at the top of the hill at Wallbridge Street, and at that time the brakes responded. Immediately after starting down the grade I again applied them, but by this time they would not work.

"I remember distinctly while rounding the curve I glanced at the pressure gauge and it registered over 70 pounds, but when I tried the brakes and they failed there was only 40 pounds in the tank. I closed the air and endeavored to set the emergency brakes but did not have time to do this before we were at the bottom of the hill and dashing for the curve. I again tried the air but it was useless. When the crash came I was thrown from my feet, but fortunately escaped injury."

The public sentiment at the time was that the chief cause of the accident was the use of a one-man crew even though it is doubtful if the presence of a conductor would have prevented the runaway. Within days the San Francisco Board of Supervisors unanimously passed an ordinance prohibiting the use of streetcars operated by one man and requiring a two-man crew. Immediately after the accident one-man cars were withdrawn from the few outlying lines that used them. The two remaining cars used on the Visitacion line, 1023 and 1024, were rebuilt into two-man cars and re-numbered 725 and 726.

The aftermath of the accident was devastating to URR. Large damage awards resulting from the wreck were partly responsible for placing the company in receivership in 1921. But the most damaging effect it had on the future of the company was the anti-one-man-car ordinance so quickly enacted after the tragedy.

Repeated attempts by successor Market Street Railway to have this ordinance repealed by voter initiative, especially in the 1930s and 40s, were unsuccessful. The opposition was fanatical. Anti-repeal forces unfailingly raised the spectre of the Visitacion tragedy. Even as late as the 1950s, long after the private company had been absorbed into the Municipal Railway, the city itself attempted to have the voters repeal the ordinance with negative results. Success came finally in 1954, but by that time only five car lines were left.

UNITED RAILROADS rushed crane 0130 to the scene to quickly remove the wreckage, but the coroner ordered otherwise.
United Railroads

VOTE YES *for* 2 MAN STREET CARS

The Eastern owners of the Market Street Railways are trying to fool the people. They are saying that you ought to vote no on the two-man street car ordinance Thursday.

If you want to keep 1000 men working on the two-man street cars you should vote YES!

HERE'S WHAT'S LEFT OF A ONE-MAN STREET CAR

Seven of your fellow citizens were killed in this accident in Visitacion Valley in 1918. A little girl was killed in Parkside by a one-man car. Another of your neighbors lost both legs in a one-man car accident.

Because of this ghastly record one-man cars were prohibited.

Let's make that prohibition permanent and secure by voting YES on the two-man street car ordinance which would for all time ban the one-man car.

YEARS LATER the Visitacion Valley wreck was a cause celebre for retention of two-man cars. This handbill helped defeat a one-man ordinance at the polls. **Charles Smallwood**

FILLMORE STREET: 1921. As the United Railroads was about to retire from ownership of the city's vast transit system, the cars made their daily trips as before, like these 1300-1400 class cars, seen just beyond Fillmore and Sutter. Other timely items worth noting are the iron arches over intersections—unique to Fillmore Street until claimed by World War II scrap drives; note also that Ford Model T jitney at left, one of a myriad which plagued URR in the Teens; and look at that big battery-powered delivery truck in left foreground!
United Railroads

New Name, Few Changes

The Market Street Railway Company on February 16, 1921, filed its amended Articles of Consolidation, Amalgamation and Incorporation with California's Secretary of State and in April of that year (through reorganization and foreclosure proceedings) took over the ownership and the operation of the system of street railways formerly the property of United Railroads of San Francisco.

The takeover was made with little or no fanfare, and the first indication most San Franciscans had that their city's largest transportation system had changed hands was when, overnight, the long familiar "U.R.R." insignia was painted off the sides of the green cars and the new name, MARKET STREET RAILWAY COMPANY, was emblazoned thereon. It took San Francisco quite some time to get used to this new title (after all, to most natives United Railroads had been around practically forever); the writer recalls that as late as 1925 the company was still often referred to as "The United."

The new company carried on the business with no outward changes. Routes and headways were unchanged. United Railroads had always pursued a policy of liberal and frequent service on its lines even into areas which were sparsely settled; the new company wisely continued this policy. Heading the executives of the new company was William Von Phul (former vice president and general manager of United Railroads); Von Phul succeeded Jesse W. Lilienthal, former URR head man. In June of 1922, Von Phul was succeeded by Charles N. Black as president and general manager who continued at the reins until his retirement in May 1925. Mason B. Starring, a veteran street railway executive, then became president of the system.

In Starring, the company seems to have secured its first experienced traction man at its head. His impressive record in the field of urban traction began in 1888, when he entered the employ of *The Chicago City Railway*, soon working his way upward to the post of vice president and general manager of that huge system. He later became president of Chicago's *Northwestern Elevated Railroad*. Starring came to Market Street Railway through The United Railways Investment Company, at that time the holding company of Market Street Railway.

It was under the Starring regime that the company made its

THE BUSY CORNER OF 22nd and Mission streets, 1926, with #24 Line Mission-Richmond car 1330 outbound. The #24 route was one of the city's longest streetcar lines.
Randolph Brandt

first attempt to improve its public relations (a field which seems to have been viewed with considerable suspicion if not outright horror by previous managements). One of the most dramatic evidences of the company's new policy was the introduction on June 9, 1925, of "The California Blue & Gold Car." Actually this car, #2001, was not really painted gold but a brilliant yellow with blue trim and lettering; the colors were inspired by California's Diamond Jubilee which was observed that year in San Francisco. The 2001 was a beautiful car and met with enthusiastic acceptance by the public. It was paraded about town with much fanfare by press and radio. In a vote conducted by the newspapers and the company, public sentiment was 24 to one in favor of the blue and gold livery being applied to all of the cars in MSR's fleet.

The company then publicly stated that in view of the overwhelming popularity of the new paint scheme, all of its cars would be so painted, replacing the somber green color that had been the company's standard livery for two decades. For some reason, perhaps the expense, this did not take place; only a few cars were ever repainted in the brighter raiment. The project was abandoned and the dark green remained the basic color.

ABOUT THE TIME that Market Street Railway was coming into being (1921), the Ocean Shore Railway, a combination electric and steam line from San Francisco along the oceanside to Tunitas Glen, was being phased out. Here is the Ocean Shore depot at 12th and Mission streets.
Market Street Railway

Byllesby Management

In November 1925, one of the most important and far-reaching events in the company's history took place: control of Market Street Railway was acquired by The Standard Power & Light Corporation, a subsidiary of The Standard Gas & Electric Company. Management of MSR was assumed by The Byllesby Engineering & Management Corporation, also in that same month.

The Byllesby organization sent one of its most able executives to San Francisco to head its new acquisition: Samuel Kahn, who was named executive vice president of the company. Kahn had been with Byllesby since 1910 and had successfully managed many of that firm's utilities (Stockton, San Diego, Everett, etc.) before coming to San Francisco.

Mason B. Starring resigned as president of Market Street Railway Company in July 1926. Kahn temporarily filled the post from then until August 1, 1927, when he was elected to the presidency by the directors. Kahn was destined to be the last president of the huge traction company, serving in the office until the private company passed into municipal ownership on September 29, 1944. It was under Kahn's leadership that the company's affairs began to improve and prosper; most important of all, it was through his efforts that, for the first time in the stormy history of the company, public sentiment began turning in its favor.

Many improvement projects were begun after the Byllesby takeover. Most important of these was the construction of 237 new car bodies at Elkton Shops between 1923 and 1933. These new cars were modern for their day, light in weight and comfortable to ride. They replaced old high platform cars, some of which actually dated back to 1895. During this same period many older cars were rebuilt and modernized.

Perhaps the single improvement having the greatest popular appeal was the introduction in February of 1927 of comfortable leather-cushioned seats in the cars. Standard streetcar seats in San Francisco up to that era were either plain wood or rattan upholstered, with many cars having the unpopular longitudinal seating. The new leather-cushioned seats practically eliminated longitudinal seating; this alone met with much popular favor. The new leather seats were installed not only in the new cars but also in many older cars as they were modernized.

The San Mateo interurban line was upgraded during the mid-20s. The large and heavy interurban cars in service on the line since 1906 were replaced in 1923 by refurbished 1200 Class cars, which, incidentally, were the very same cars which originally opened through service to San Mateo back in 1903. In 1927 the company and the County of San Mateo jointly effected a realignment project on the old county road between Colma and the cemeteries; this job straightened some severe kinks in the line which enabled interurban schedules to be speeded up. Much trackage was rebuilt and reballasted, and improved shelters and waiting stations were installed.

The line's power supply was upgraded by the addition of another generator at the Millbrae substation; this generator, of considerable weight and bulk, was moved over the company's lines by a work car from the Turk and Fillmore substation, a moving feat of some magnitude.

The car houses, which had been of no standard color, were repainted green, trimmed with white. The same repainted color scheme was extended to all company buildings with the exception of Geneva Car House and the Bryant & Division

A SIGN OF THE new "air age" was this direction sign painted atop the Elkton Shops paint building. The arrow pointed to Crissy Field. **Charles Smallwood**

Storeroom and Substation. A novel feature of this car house painting project was the emblazoning on the roof of several car houses a huge SAN FRANCISCO in white letters some 12 feet high together with a huge arrow pointing the direction of the city's airport. Thus did Market Street Railway enter the Air Age.

Another minor improvement was the extending of the Fillmore Hill car line several blocks from Bay St. to Marina Blvd. This extension was opened to traffic on August 29, 1925.

On January 13, 1926, car 809 emerged brand new from Elkton Shops with a feature that was to identify the company's cars and buses for the remainder of its corporate life. The 809 was the first White Front car. The gleaming white front, brightly illuminated at night, was a safety feature that, after general adoption, prevented many an accident and was a not inconsiderable factor in saving the company large amounts of money in accident litigation.

So successful did 809's white front prove that all of the company's rolling stock was so treated as rapidly as they could be put through the paint shop. The company applied for and received a patent for its illuminated white front idea in February 1927.

The company's first motor coach line was opened in 1926, running from Mission and Brazil streets over a loop route via Mission, Excelsior, Vienna, Brazil, Prague, Russia, Moscow, Italy, Naples and Brazil to Mission St. The franchise for this route was granted by the Board of Supervisors on April 2, 1926, and the line was placed in operation just four days later. The Excelsior bus line operated in a fairly densely populated area, some portions of which were quite removed from existing car lines. It is doubtful if this pioneer line was remunerative from the revenue standpoint, but it did provide a convenient, needed service in its area and was responsible for generating much public goodwill for the company in the Outer Mission district.

Late in 1926 the company constructed in its Elkton Shops six new cable cars for the standard gauge Castro St. cable line; these new cars were quite a departure from standard cable car construction with their rounded ends and arch roofs.

To accommodate increasing commuter traffic from the downtown area to the Southern Pacific Depot at 3rd and Townsend streets, the company established a new morning and evening peak hour line between 2nd and Market to the depot via 2nd, Brannan and 3rd streets; this new line began operating on February 16, 1927, and was designated Line 41.

The company had long owned an elaborate private trolley car named SAN FRANCISCO. The car was a masterpiece in luxury urban travel and boasted such refinements as a carpeted floor, velvet and satin curtains, and upholstered wicker furnishings. It performed considerable service in the early years of the century transporting visiting notables about the city.

By the mid-20s, however, it was seeing little, if any, use—so Market Street Railway painted the car all white and presented it to the exclusive use of the children of San Francisco. The beautiful car thereupon became known as the "Special Students Car for School Classes," and for many years it was a familiar sight as it transported happy children about the city. One popular trip of the SAN FRANCISCO was to take them from school to the Elkton Shops where a grand tour was given of that facility showing new cars under construction, the brass foundry in operation, and other work in progress. Passengers who rode on the car were given a souvenir of their ride; each student was presented a ruler imprinted with timely safety slogans, while teachers received a brass paper weight in the form of the familiar company shield.

The SAN FRANCISCO was available to public and private schools alike, as well as to children's hospitals and instructions; no charge was made for its use. Many San Franciscans grown old and gray recall with fondness a trip on this fine car. As an ambassador of company goodwill, SAN FRANCISCO had no peer; Market Street Railway received much public praise for its operation of this car in such altruistic service—one of the nicest gestures ever made by a public utility toward the people it served.

On October 7, 1927, the company inaugurated its third motor coach line. Like the pioneer Crocker-Amazon coach route of the year before, the new route also served the Outer Mission district, operating on Silver Ave. between Mission St. and 3rd St.—linking the Mission St. car lines and the heavily traveled industrial district 3rd St. lines; this line is still operating today over essentially the same route as Municipal Railway's #51 line.

Samuel Kahn
President of Market Street Railway

THIS OPEN "BREEZER" ran on the Castro Street cable line until the mid-1920s, on sunny days. MSR was very involved in the cable car business throughout its life. View was taken in earlier years outside the Castro barn. **United Railroads**

THE EARTH SLIDE that put the Number 1 Line out of business, near Point Lobos, February 7, 1925.
Market Street Railway

City Loses Most Scenic Line

On February 7, 1925, the company suffered a major setback when the famed #1-Cliff line was forced to shut down when a portion of the right-of-way along the cliffs near Land's End abruptly slid into the Golden Gate below. Fortunately the slippage occurred during early morning hours when there was no service on the popular line—one of the world's most scenic car lines, providing a breathtaking view of the Golden Gate and the Pacific Ocean from the cliffs around Land's End. After the land subsidence, #1 Line cars terminated at 33rd Ave. and Clement streets; service was never resumed over the scenic route.

Of all of Market Street Railway's varied operations, perhaps the most unique was the archaic cable car line on Pacific Ave. from Polk to Broderick streets. This isolated cable route remained in service until late 1929 with essentially the same type of operation and rolling stock as it did when it first began service in the 1870s. A tiny open grip car pulled a closed single truck trail car. Prior to the disaster of April 18, 1906, the line was part of a busy crosstown route which ran from Pacific and Broderick to 9th and Brannan streets via Pacific, Polk, Post, Larkin and 9th streets. During the post-1906 modernization of cable routes, this line was electrified except for the portion on Pacific Ave. Why was this segment, well suited for electric operation, not electrified? It is one of the classic tales of San Francisco tractioniana.

Unlike those cable lines which remained into the electric car era because their routes were too steep for conversion to trolley operation, the Pacific Ave. line was very suitable for conversion. The residents of Pacific Ave., however, insisted on retaining their elderly cable operation; inasmuch as they included in their number some of the most influential people in the city who brought considerable pressure to bear, the company finally acquiesced to their wishes.

The old cable cars ran for many additional years, quaint little cable trains, completely an anachronism. By 1929 increasing traffic on Pacific Ave. brought even their most ardent admirers face to face with the inescapable fact that their day was over. As the little line was hopeless from the revenue standpoint, Market Street Railway did not need much urging to apply for its abandonment.

The tiny trains, hauled by a cable rope, made their final trip on November 17, 1929. Other than some unimportant outlying shuttle lines that quit, this was the first streetcar abandonment of any size in San Francisco and was a harbinger of things to come.

Many franchises of the company expired in 1929, some of these involving some of MSR's most important car lines. In November 1930 the voters of the city adopted a charter amendment which permitted Market Street Railway to surrender its remaining franchises to the City and County of San Francisco in exchange for a blanket 25-year operating permit. The State Legislature immediately ratified this amendment. The operating permit also provided that the city could purchase the property at a fair price during the life of the permit. Although there was some opposition to the granting of this permit, it would seem that the company's policy of improved public relations paid off; the vote on granting the permit was 80,774 in favor and 64,965 against.

Having assurance of at least a 25-year life, the company set about to carry out some of the promises it had made during the charter amendment campaign. The most ambitious of these promises was to construct a new streetcar line on Turk and Balboa streets. This line was started in the winter of 1931-32 and opened for service on May 15, 1932. The new line was a financial success from the start. Market Street Railway received much praise for this effort, as the construction of the Balboa line provided many jobs during the depth of the Great Depression years. The company estimated the cost of its new line at $400,000.

A COURTEOUS CONDUCTOR helps a lady passenger board Montgomery Street "dinkey" 609. This trackage was a casualty of traffic congestion in the 1920s.
Charles Smallwood

End of the Montgomery Street "Dinkeys"

THE LAST DAY of streetcar service on Montgomery Street called for a civic celebration. Chief participant for this October 6, 1927, event was Mayor James Rolph, seen looking out 635's front window. However, that portion of the line not on Montgomery Street continued in service, terminating at Post and Market for some years.

Charles Smallwood

Opening of Last New Car Line

IT WAS SUNDAY, May 15, 1932, opening day of San Francisco's last new streetcar line, the 31—Balboa Street route. This photo was taken at the new line's western terminal, 30th Ave. and Balboa Street. **Market Street Railway**

WHITE FRONT CARS join the parade in ceremonies commemorating the opening of the new Third Street Bridge on May 12, 1933. The steam train belongs to the State Belt Railroad, which shared the bridge with the Market Street Railway and motor traffic.
Market Street Railway

In 1933 the company sought the repeal of a local ordinance which prohibited operation of streetcars by a one-man crew; this ordinance had been enacted in 1918 as the emotional result of a tragic accident on the Visitacion Valley line in which a one-man car was involved. The company's request for repeal was denied by the Board of Supervisors but the company succeeded in obtaining a temporary injunction against the enforcement of the ordinance in 1934.

The One-Man Car Battle

Armed with this injunction, MSR set about inaugurating one-man car service over some of its lines. The first one-man car appeared on the Folsom St. line March 13, 1935. One-man operation of other lines followed as rapidly as cars could be converted for the new service. Several second-hand one-man cars were purchased from defunct lines in the east and brought to San Francisco to expedite the conversions.

The beginning of one-man car service on Folsom St. was not the first experience that Market Street Railway had had with this type of operation. Since May 27, 1934, the company had been operating one-man cars on its subsidiary *South San Francisco Railway & Power Company* local car line in South San Francisco with success. As the city of South San Francisco was located in San Mateo County (which had no anti-one-man car law) no trouble was experienced in this operation.

Lines converted to one-man operation were mainly those in the South of Market area of the city; among them were some which were heavily traveled. Also converted were the two crosstown routes, #19 and #22, as well as the very heavy Third and Kearny streets group. No attempt was made to convert any of the Market or Mission streets lines, although some one-man lines did use short portions of Mission St. over a part of their routes.

Eventually the company had a total of 174 one-man cars operating over 18 routes. These cars worked out well, and

PASSENGERS BOARD a one-man car on Folsom Street on the first day of service, March 13, 1935.
Charles Smallwood

many were used on some of the heaviest of MSR's lines (such as Third and Kearny and the Fillmore St. crosstown line). Business actually improved on some of the lighter lines under one-man operation, due to closer headways and faster, more modern cars than had been used heretofore.

Meanwhile, the city had appealed the one-man-car case to the United States Circuit Court of Appeals which ultimately rendered a decision upholding the ordinance. The company thereupon appealed this decision in the United States

ONE-MAN CAR 946 loads passengers for Visitacion Valley at Third and Market streets in 1935. It was the tragic wreck on this line which caused one-man service to be dropped until Market Street Railway won a temporary respite from 1935 to 1939. **Charles Smallwood**

RUBBER-TIRED and electrically propelled, Market Street Railway's little fleet of trolley coaches was a pioneer in West Coast city transit. Coach 56 is seen near Waller and Stanyan, the outer terminus of its single electric bus route.
Paul Ward

Supreme Court, but that court refused to review the case. The Circuit Court of Appeals then gave the company six months to reinstate two-man cars on all affected lines; by February 1939 all one-man cars were gone.

Unionization of Market Street Railway's employees came in 1934. This brought about greater operating costs which had been offset to a large degree by the operation of one-man cars. With the loss of the financial advantages of one-man cars in 1939, it became apparent that at least some of the weaker lines could no longer support two-man cars. Understandably, a rapid transition from electric and cable car operation to motor coaches which could legally be operated by one man began in 1939. The number of motor coaches owned by the company rose from 11 in 1938 to 125 by the end of 1942.

Despite the increased use of motor coaches after 1938, several of the lines that were changed were not entirely abandoned to the bus. On routes #36—Folsom, #19—Polk and Larkin, the Kearny and 3rd streets group and the Guerrero and San Jose Ave. lines which were converted to bus operation, several schedules on these lines were actually operated by streetcar; this unusual practice lasted well into the Municipal Railway era on those routes still in existence when the city took over the company.

A Trolley Coach Line

On October 6, 1935, the company began what was at the time claimed to be the first modern trolley coach line on the Pacific Coast. These trolley coaches took the place of two-man cars on the #33—Harrison and 18th St. line which operated over the famous "switchback" on the slopes of Twin Peaks. The new trolley coaches, vanguard of a much larger fleet which would eventually replace almost all of the remaining streetcar lines, were quite successful; they were popular with the public and were able to negotiate the steep grades on the #33 line with ease; powerful electric brakes aided them to make an equally easy descent.

The years following 1939 witnessed the changing of many of the old established routes. Some lines were hopeless even from the bus standpoint (such as #34—6th and Sansome); these were abandoned entirely. Some new service by bus was inaugurated, but it generally was a more efficient routing over that of the streetcar line that the bus supplanted.

(ABOVE) **GRAND AVENUE,** South San Francisco, is the scene of this December 1938 view of one-man car 285. This was two weeks prior to abandonment, and by this time only morning and evening service was provided. **Ted Wurm** (BELOW) **AT THE SWIFT PACKING PLANT,** South San Francisco, 1937. Note the absence of a rear door, unique to this car. **Warren K. Miller**

WHITE FRONT ACTION: Two 1500s circle the Ferry loop on Memorial Day, 1937. Note the Muni B line car, upper left. (BELOW) A 20 Line car pauses in front of the beautiful Southern Pacific depot (now gone), at Third and Townsend streets, 1938.

BOTH: Charles Smallwood

'TWAS THE LAST DAY of the Visitacion Valley streetcar line, July 31, 1937, when this excellent photo was taken at Mission Street and Geneva Ave. Replacing bus is seen at left. (BELOW) A 35 Line car poses at 24th and Rhode Island in June 1939.

TOP: Lorin Silliman BOTTOM: Charles Smallwood

The Long-Lived Nickel Fare

The traditional five-cent streetcar fare lasted longer in San Francisco than in any other major city in the United States. This situation was largely made necessary by the competitive Municipal Railway operations. Rising costs of operation coupled to a rider loss trend made it apparent by 1937 that Market Street Railway no longer could do business on the ruinous five-cent fare. In that year the company applied to the State Railroad Commission (now renamed the State Public Utilities Commission) for an increase in rates.

The Commission, in a decision dated June 21, 1937, denied the company's plea for a seven-cent cash fare, but granted a two-cent transfer charge and an increase from 20¢ to 25¢ for the Sunday and holiday passes. These new rates became effective on July 6, 1937.

In March 1938, under the same application, the company petitioned the Commission to authorize a seven-cent fare with free transfers and a rate of 20 rides for 70¢ for schoolchildren. In a decision dated May 9, 1938, the Commission authorized a seven-cent fare with four tokens for 25¢ on other than interurban cars, 16 rides for 50¢ for schoolchildren, and a seven-cent or token unit fare in place of the five-cent unit fare on the interurban lines. The two-cent charge for transfers was discontinued. These fares became effective on May 29, 1938.

In a second supplemental application, the company sought authority to establish a straight seven-cent fare and to discontinue selling four tokens for 25¢. In a decision dated November 23, 1938, the Commission directed the company to petition the city for authority to abandon operation of certain lines and for relief from jitney competition. The decision authorized the rate hike sought, provided such authority and relief were not received by January 1, 1939. The new fare became effective January 1, 1939. It called for:

—Seven-cent cash fare in San Francisco (except on interurban cars) with free transfer;
—Schoolchildren, 18 rides for 50¢, with free transfers;
—Sunday and holiday pass, for use in San Francisco, 25¢;
—South San Francisco local line, 7¢;
—San Mateo line, seven-cent fare to be in accordance with tariff filed with the Railroad Commission on May 23, 1938.

The California Railroad Commission after several 1943 hearings into MSR's rates, service and facilities, ordered the company's seven-cent fare reduced to six cents effective February 29, 1944. MSR appealed the order immediately, and on March 8, 1944, the California Supreme Court suspended the Commission's order pending court review. In the meantime, however, the Court ordered MSR to issue one-cent refund coupons to all cash and token riders, these to be redeemable if and when the Court found in favor of the Railroad Commission. MSR was required to set aside $100,000 monthly to back up these coupons.

The Bay Bridge Terminal

An old era ended and a new one began on January 15, 1939. On that date, electric trains of three railways began gliding across the San Francisco-Oakland Bay Bridge and into an impressive new terminal building in San Francisco, there to deposit their passengers hard by waiting streetcars and motor coaches of Market Street Railway and Municipal Railway.

The transbay ferry service (except for several boats connecting with steam trains) ended on that day, and San Francisco's historic Ferry Building subsided into minor importance, its day done.

As far back as the early 1930s it was known that a terminal for the bridge railway would be necessary. In 1934, a proposal placed it at Second St., just south of Market St. The expansion loop followed by the bridge trains through San Francisco on elevated trackage made it clear that the most efficient location would be on Mission St. between First and Fremont streets; this location was the one finally selected.

The first structural steel for the imposing new terminal building was erected on January 12, 1938. Costing about $2 million, the new terminal was a model of passenger movement efficiency as well as being clean and functional architecturally.

To deposit their cars on the spacious ramp immediately in front of the new terminal, it was necessary for the two railway companies to construct a new double track loop from Market St. To accommodate the heavy flow of traffic, First St. was made one way southbound while Fremont St. was declared a one-way street northbound.

With Market Street Railway in straitened financial circumstances (as usual), the cost of the loop was borne entirely by Municipal Railway. At one time (June 1938) it even appeared that MSR would turn its cars back on First St. and Mission St., not using the loop at all; President Kahn reported that his company had no money at all to pay its half share of the cost of the new trackage required.

The agreement finally worked out called for Muni to pay the total cost of the loop ($154,046). MSR would then pay Muni an annual rental equivalent to 10% of half the construction costs plus a fair share of maintenance, this to be based on use of the new trackage. This worked out to an annual rental of $7,702—and MSR's share of maintenance was about $5,700 annually.

THE BRIDGE RAILWAY brought Market Street Railway cars face to face with their big brothers from the Eastbay. This #25 car, outbound on Howard Street, shares the San Francisco scene with a two-car Interurban Electric Railway (Southern Pacific) "Big Red Car" train.
Ohio Brass

East Bay Terminal

LINED UP at the streetcar loop in front of East Bay Terminal, at Mission Street between First and Fremont, is a Market Street Railway 900 on the 9 Line, one of Municipal Railway's five "Magic Carpet" streamliners, and Muni 125. The track at left was still active in 1978 while the middle rails were intact for emergency use.
Charles Smallwood

On June 12, 1938, newspapers reported that the Public Utilities Commission had given its approval to begin the emergency construction of the new loop to the Bay Bridge Terminal site. Even at that late date the final route had not been selected. This was to set the tone of the whole loop construction project—delay, followed by feverish activity and culminating on opening day in the worst traffic jam ever experienced in San Francisco.

As constructed, the loop was 0.97 mile in length (equivalent single track). Its twin tracks became three on the ramp, and a control tower jutted out of the upper front windows of the terminal where a switchman routed cars to their proper tracks, much as had been done at the ferries for decades.

As the date for the opening of the bridge railway service neared, construction of the streetcar loop lagged far behind schedule. Night crews were finally placed on the construction project by Muni; owl cars were rerouted (some even replaced by motor coaches) so construction men could install the necessary switches and overhead wires at the junctions on Market St. and on the ramp.

Three days before the new Bay Bridge Terminal was to enter service, the two railway companies made public their proposed service to it. Muni decided that alternate cars, irrespective of route, would operate to the Bridge Terminal; this was to cause monumental confusion and was soon changed—after the damage had been done. MSR was considerably more intelligent; it designated certain lines to terminate at the Bridge Terminal, with the others continuing to operate to the Ferry Building. These lines to terminate at the Bridge Terminal were: 2, 4, 5, 7, 31, 9, 29th and Noe and Cortland Ave. branches; lines continuing to end at the Ferries were 1, 3, 6, 8, 21 and 9—San Jose Ave. and Daly City.

The formal dedication of the East Bay Terminal as it was officially named occurred on January 14, 1939. As Gov. Culbert Olson was ill, he was represented by Lt. Gov. Ellis E. Patterson. Mayor Angelo J. Rossi represented the City of San Francisco. Interurban trains of the three eastbay railways to use the bridge tracks (*Key System, Interurban Electric Railway,* and *Sacramento Northern*) participated in the dedication of the gleaming $2,300,000 structure.

So dawned the fateful day when a city's travel habits were to be drastically altered for all time. As events of that memorable morning were reported in the *San Francisco News:*

Streetcar service on Market Street came to a virtual halt this morning. For more than an hour, inbound cars were backed up Market Street for blocks. E.G. Cahill, in charge of Municipal Railway, said, "We had too little time to educate the public." He reported he found numerous instances where San Franciscans took cars marked for the Ferries when they did not want them, and that transferring of these passengers caused delays.

Other newspapers carried similar stories. All in all, it was far from being an auspicious inauguration of the new terminal. Among the reasons pinpointed for the delays were: a bad trolley wire frog, heavy auto traffic, unfamiliarity of motormen with the route to the East Bay Terminal, improperly operating track switches, a lack of traffic officers, etc.

Line crews worked all day to perfect the overhead and track switches were thrown by hand. That evening the traffic jam was repeated.

But as the shakedown phase passed into history, so did the traffic jams. Little by little, passengers became familiar with the new car routings and East Bay Terminal took its place as the new focus of streetcar operation. Instead of the 20-minute ferry ride to the opposite shore, passengers now walked from the ramp to the upper level, there to board their waiting interurban train to be whisked off over the giant bridge to the eastbay communities. It was indeed a new era.

However, use of the three tracks on the ramp was to be comparatively short-lived. Decrease in number of cars operated plus a big upsurge in motor coaches had its inevitable result. The track closest to the entrance of the terminal building was removed from service on March 16, 1942, and was physically paved over in May 1942. The center track was discontinued on June 10, 1942, and at the same time the operation of the switching tower was abandoned. Of interest is the fact that although most former MSR rail lines were converted to trolley coach operation by Municipal Railway, no trolley coaches have ever used the ramp at East Bay Terminal.

The MSR Goes To War

Our nation's entry into world conflict on December 7, 1941, did not catch Market Street Railway ill-prepared. Fortunately the beginning shift to motor coaches which was well under way by 1941 had not resulted in the physical removal of track on certain converted lines, nor had the company scrapped many cars thus replaced. Thus cars made a comeback on lines converted to bus, and the motor coaches thus replaced were available to serve many wartime emergency lines, such as those serving Hunters Point housing areas and defense industries.

MSR's chronic financial difficulties, however, were pointed up in a 1944 blast at the company by the California State Railroad Commission. MSR, according to the Commission, was unconvincing in claiming that shortage of manpower was responsible for idle rolling stock at a time when every car was needed. The Commission blamed the trouble on obsolete equipment on one hand and "disadvantages accruing from more enlightened and liberal policies of other systems in matters of employee relations, wages and salaries, working conditions, and attitude toward the public in general."

TWO TRACKS ON FIRST STREET, the left one for Municipal Railway and the right for Market Street Railway, were constructed to bring streetcars one block south from Market to East Bay Terminal.
Paul Ward

WARTIME CROWDS are seen in this 1943 view at Third, Kearny and Market. The company did not completely abandon streetcar service on many of the former one-man, two-man lines converted to bus in the late 1930s, thus MSR was able to supplement bus service on the 3rd-Kearny motor coach line with two-man streetcars. Bus 4, at right, is one of the vehicles leased from the War Assets Corporation for the "duration."

Charles Smallwood

The Commission went on to assert that "no satisfactory reason had been supplied by MSR why the large number of idle streetcars owned and classed as operative by the company is not put to much-needed use during this critical war period." As of June 1, 1943, MSR listed 73 electric cars and 12 cable cars as being out of service and a total of 440 electric cars and 39 cable cars classed as operative as of that date. The Commission deplored the fact that more than two-thirds of the electric cars were 20 or more years old and that no streetcars had been bought by MSR since 1936 when it acquired some second-hand cars.

"In that period" [pointed out the Commission] "great progress has been made in modernizing and increasing the operating efficiency of electric streetcars . . . the company has not participated in this progress."

And castigating Market Street Railway even more forcefully, Commissioners went on to state:

There is evidence of longtime neglect, of mismanagement, of indifference to urgent public need, and of other matters inevitably productive of poor service that by no means were caused by the war, and for the consequences of such failure the company must assume responsibility. Not only has there been no betterment in the unsatisfactory service . . . but the condition of the track and equipment, and the character and quality of the service . . . have grown progressively worse until in 1941, 1942 and in 1943 the standard of service has reached the lowest point in the company's history. Consideration of service alone, and of the value of such service to the patron, would justify the fixing of a five-cent fare.

In reply to arguments of President Kahn defending the deferred maintenance as an obligation to stockholders, the Commission held that the first obligation of the company was to its patrons; money allowed in rate proceedings should not be devoted to paying off debts.

The Commission concluded by issuing an order reducing MSR fares from seven to six cents. The company, which had been receiving a seven-cent fare for years, was understandably unhappy and appealed for a rehearing. The California Supreme Court stayed and suspended the order of the Commission pending its review of the case, but ordered MSR to issue one-cent refund coupons to all cash and token riders, these to be redeemable when and if the Court found in favor of the Commission.

In late 1943 MSR made one contribution to the war effort: its Victory Cars. Here all cross seats were taken out and longitudinal seats substituted the entire length of the car. Through this arrangement, MSR claimed to be able to handle four times as many people per car. Victory Cars were assigned to dense lines, such as Third and Kearny where, although not especially popular with tired passengers seeking seats, they did move the crowds.

With competent men off to war, MSR hired anyone it could to operate cars, including members of the gentle sex. A rash of accidents immediately ensued. Among the epidemic of disasters were these: 282 on the #9—Valencia Line ran down the Richland Ave. hill to Andover St. where that line ended; it hurtled into a heavy steel pole, originally placed there for those occasions to protect houses, and was a total wreck. Car 902 on the #12—Ingleside Line was hit by a fast-moving Muni bus while crossing Alemany Blvd. and Onondaga Ave.; 47 passengers on the bus were hurt and its driver killed; no one on the car was injured but the posts and windows were knocked out of line. A Muni B Line car hit a #5 MSR car near the beach. Car 939 on #14—Daly City Line had its front platform completely torn off by a speeding Navy bus at 8th and Mission streets. Car 808 on the Kearny Line hit a steam locomotive and had its whole front end pushed in. Fillmore car 864 also hit a locomotive and was a complete ruin; a motormanette was at the controls.

Market Street Railway continued to limp through the war. President Kahn, valiantly endeavoring to keep his company afloat with the end view of selling it to the city, met innumerable problems with his characteristic calm effectiveness. Kahn was in a highly sensitive and unenviable position throughout the latter part of MSR's life; a lesser man would have thrown up his hands in disgust and fled the scene, but Kahn's dedication in the end brought him out safely: a new election in 1944 saw the Market Street Railway purchase proposal again referred to the electorate. This time the voters were asked to buy the company for but $7.5 million, of which $2 million would be in cash and the remainder paid out of earnings of the combined railways.

Kahn's perseverance paid off; the approval of the purchase proposal was not even close. "Yes" votes totaled 102,640; "No" votes were but 85,000. Probably the single most important influence in the election campaign was San Francisco's new mayor, Roger D. Lapham, who even made a personal appearance at the reins of an old horse car in a colorful parade up Market Street.

Market Street Railway had lasted through the worst part of the war. Its worn-out plant, long denied the succor of adequate financing, was about to receive an infusion of municipal millions. The long journey was ended.

ELECTION EXTRA!

San Francisco Chronicle
The City's Only Home~Owned Newspaper

FOUNDED 1865—VOL. CLVIII, NO. 123 CCCCAA   SAN FRANCISCO, WEDNESDAY, MAY 17, 1944   DAILY 5 CENTS, SUNDAY 15 CENTS   DAILY AND SUNDAY PER MONTH, $1.50

COMPARATIVE TEMPERATURES			
High Low		High Low	
San Francisco	58 50	Chicago	80 63
Oakland	61 45	New Orleans	90 70
Sacramento	69 41	New York	79 62
Los Angeles	67 49	Salt Lake City	77 53
Seattle	66 49	Washington	90 64
Forecast: Rain.			

TROLLEY BUY WINS!

SAN FRANCISCANS AWOKE on May 17, 1944, to learn they had purchased the Market Street Railway, at long last. It was such a major story that World War II was pushed into the background.

Learning of the victory, Major Lapham and other interested parties were on hand bright and early to take out the first Market Street Railway pullout car to its new owners. This historic photograph shows the mayor at the controls, flanked by Commissioner S. McKee, Utilities Manager E.G. Cahill and Commissioner F. Del Carlo. The merger became effective at 5:00 A.M. on September 29, 1944.
**Newspaper Headline: Harre Demoro
Photograph: S.F. Public Utilities Commission**

Merger and Obliteration

ON MAY 16, 1944, citizens of San Francisco went to their polling places to vote on a proposition to buy the operative properties of The Market Street Railway Company by the payment of $2 million in cash and $5.5 million from the earnings of the acquired MSR properties. There was not too much basis for optimism on the part of those favoring acquiring the private company. From November 3, 1925, to April 20, 1943, this same proposal had been turned down by the electorate no less than six times. These were:

NOVEMBER 3, 1925: General Municipal Election. An initiative measure for a bond issue of $36 million for purchasing the MSR properties. Defeated by a vote of 12,435 to 87,315.

SEPTEMBER 27, 1938: Special Election, Proposition No. 8—a bond issue of $24,480,000 to purchase the operating properties of MSR. Defeated by a vote of 52,680 to 93,979.

NOVEMBER 8, 1938: General Election. Declaration of policy, Proposition No. 4—Purchase of MSR operating property for an amount not exceeding $5,000,000. Defeated: 49,932 to 128,320.

NOVEMBER 8, 1938: General Election. Declaration of policy, Proposition No. 5—City to issue $9 million in bonds for passenger buses and facilities therefor to be used with property of MSR if acquired or as adjunct of Municipal Railway. Defeated by a vote of 49,948 to 128,466.

NOVEMBER 3, 1942: General Election. Acquisition of operative properties of MSR financed by issuance of revenue bonds in the amount of $7,950,000. Defeated by a vote of 96,003 to 102,081.

MANY FORMER MSR cars received a complete new Muni paint job. Muni 644 (ex-MSR 244) is seen on Muni's line C in 1946. **Charles Smallwood**

APRIL 20, 1943: Special Election. Purchase of operative properties of MSR for $7,950,000 to be financed by issuance of revenue bonds. Defeated by a vote of 53,619 to 88,418.

With this steady string of defeats a matter of record, Mayor Roger D. Lapham headed an intensive campaign to take over the private company and provide San Francisco for the first time a citywide unified transit network. Much hoopla accompanied the campaign, despite primary preoccupation with the national wartime emergency. Lapham succeeded where his predecessors had repeatedly failed: on the morning of May 17, 1944, the good burghers of San Francisco awoke to the news that they had purchased the Market Street Railway system's operative properties for $7.5 million. The vote was not even close: 108,621 to 84,078.

At 5:00 A.M. on September 29, 1944, the two railway systems were merged and thereafter operated by the city as a consolidated system.

Acquired by Municipal Railway in the merger was the entire MSR fleet of equipment; this included 440 electric streetcars, 38 cable cars, nine trolley coaches and 124 motor coaches. In addition, Muni arranged to rent 35 motor coaches from the United States Navy—these same coaches having been rented by MSR in connection with the war effort.

Total single track acquired in the purchase was 223.854, of which 206.592 was operated; 6.820 miles of this was cable track, and 28.060 miles of electric railway trackage was located in San Mateo County.

Municipal Railway's old five-cent fare was the first casualty of the merger, going to seven cents (as was MSR's) on that memorable merger morning. Offsetting this raise for Muni patrons was a universal transfer, enabling a continuous trip into parts of the city hitherto forbidden to them without paying a second fare.

In normal times, consolidating two major transit systems would have been a formidable task; coming as this one did at the height of the war effort, it was heightened to an almost overwhelming degree. Municipal Railway General Manager William H. Scott put it well:

"The physical condition of the cars and coaches and of the trackage acquired was such that every effort had to be made to maintain these facilities in a condition to render service. It developed that the inventories of materials and supplies, including car and coach parts on hand, for the Market Street Railway facilities were far below requirements and in many cases were depleted entirely. This, coupled with the great lack and scarcity of mechanical help for maintenance repairs, add-

MONEY STARTS ROLLING IN.—Conductor Edward G. Cahill (manager of municipal utilities) is shown here collecting the first 7c fare on the merged streetcar system, from Mrs. Edward G. Cahill.

THE MERGER was big news in this transit-oriented metropolis. This clipping is from the September 18, 1944, San Francisco News. **Harre Demoro**

ed further to the difficulties of operation. The difficulty in securing needed critical materials on account of the war and the ever-present shortage of operating personnel were major factors with which to contend."

It was a big mouthful for Muni. In September 1944, its daily average passenger receipts amounted to $19,812. In October, the very next month, receipts of the merged systems skyrocketed to $48,908.

One of the first big snags to occur was in the field of labor relations. Owing to certain legal actions taken, former MSR employees who were taken over into Muni employ could not be paid wages at Muni rates based on their credits for years of service in MSR. However, Muni made out its payrolls to show the top rates in question, but checks to ex-MSR men were at beginner's rates—with the difference being impounded

New Transportation Era

Birth of the new, unified Municipal Railway yesterday was accomplished with a pleasantly surprising minimum of confusion and poor service. That speaks well for the city's management and indicates the promises of steadily improved service in the future will be realized. It is a credit also to the loyal operating employes of both systems who kept the cars running so well.

The consolidation marks the beginning of a new era in San Francisco's transportation history.

Henceforth, with exception of the California Street Cable Railway, the entire transit system will be city-owned and under a single control. Within a couple of weeks even the California cable line will be included in the uniform fare and universal transfer plan. Thereafter car riders will be able to make a continuous trip from any point in the city to any other point for one seven-cent fare.

No marked changes in service probably will be manifest for a few weeks until the Municipal Railway management can recruit sufficient crews to operate the expanded service, put the idle former MSRy trolley cars into use and secure the new buses as additional equipment on several lines now woefully short of adequate service.

But in the long run unification should prove of tremendous advantage to the city. The old multi-system arrangement was archaic, confusing, wasteful and inefficient. It caused citizens no end of unnecessary time and expense in going about their business. It baffled visitors with its multiplicity of ownership and fares and limited transfer privileges. It fell far short of the kind of transportation system a city of the importance of San Francisco should have.

From now forward we shall expect steady progress to be made toward modernizing and developing the service to the full extent commensurate with San Francisco's requirements. If present predictions regarding San Francisco's future are accurate we will have here within a few years a metropolis vastly greater in every respect than the city of today. The transportation facilities, as indeed all other public utilities, must keep pace with, nay, must anticipate that development.

By reason of its new and expanded responsibilities, the Public Utilities Commission becomes the most important commission of the city government. We must see to it that it is manned continuously by the most capable and far-sighted citizens who can be drafted for the public service.

That is to say, not only the equipment and service must be modernized, but the organization and administration behind it must likewise be maintained at highest level of modern efficiency and understanding of the problems. San Francisco cannot afford to let anything stand in the way of the fulfillment of its destiny.

* * **S.F. News (HD)**

pending the court's decision. Ultimately, of course, the decision was favorable to ex-MSR men; they received their just wages considering years of service.

Another statistic grew impressively as a result of the merger. Muni's total number of employees rose from 1,531 to 4,437.

Three days after the merger, Muni entered into a contract with L.V. Newton, former MSR vice president and general manager, to act as consulting engineer and to make the necessary plans for the consolidation of the acquired MSR properties with those of Muni; he was also charged to prepare plans for improvements in service of Muni as may be possible at the moment; and to make postwar plans for the modernization of the greater system—"including changes in types of service," an ominous portent of a dim future for electric streetcars.

UNDER THE HEADLINE "SUCCESS — 5 A.M. CHAMPAGNE," the September 30, 1944, issue of the San Francisco News reported some of the celebration of the consolidation.   **Harre Demoro**

Derision for the MSR

As city forces grew familiar with the former MSR properties they now operated, the result of deferred maintenance resulted in some rather caustic public utterances by city officials. Probably the most severe was that by Manager of Utilities E.G. Cahill who, in the *Interurban News Letter* of May 1945, was quoted:

"The entire former Market Street Railway of San Francisco will have to be scrapped immediately after the war. In fact, if the war lasts too long it will scrap itself. It is obvious that equipment, every piece of which must be dragged off to the barns for repairs 15 times in five months is in the last stages of decrepitude. It will be a miracle if this rambling wreck of a railway can be held together for the duration, regardless of the amount of money we spend on it."

Trolley Vets Drink Toast To Merged Lines

At 5 o'clock this morning the victorious end of the years-long struggle to consolidate San Francisco's major streetcar systems was celebrated—with a spontaneous champagne party in Muni Supt. William Scott's office in the Geary-st headquarters.

A carload of officials, veteran Muni and Market Street Railway workers, newspapermen and sundry other citizens toasted the new unified lines with champagne thoughtfully provided by Public Utilities Commission members (at their own expense).

None of the bottles was broken over any trolley prows but the contents were used for the purpose intended by the vintners.

"San Francisco," said one predawn celebrant, "still knows how."

One of the old-timers there was also there on Dec. 28, 1912, when Mayor James Rolph Jr. dedicated the new Municipal Railway's first line—from Kearny-st to Golden Gate Park on Geary. He's William Bendel, now general superintendent of equipment. He can't recall any champagne on that occasion.

But older still, in years and service, is Fred Wills, who went to work for the Great United Railways, MSRy predecessor, in 1888. Then, he recalls a horse-car driver had to curry and feed the horse—and sweep out the car—in between runs.

* * *

Muni carmen carried 50,000 pennies in their changemakers and pockets, and tried to remember that when a customer gives you a dime, you give him a nickel and five pennies in return—not two nickels. They were further confused by a habit of many MSRy riders dropping two pennies into the box and giving the dime to the conductor, expecting two nickels in return, one which they put in the box.

WORKING ON THE RAILROAD.—Here is Motorman Roger D. Lapham (the mayor to you) taking the first white front streetcar from the Muny barn on Geary-st.

Cahill revealed that repairs have cost the city $1,255,000 since it took over the system. The total of 528 streetcars broke down 4,198 times, and 497 more were put out of commission for various lengths of time by accidents. Cahill stated that track repairs have reached 'almost fantastic' proportions and that 11,000 miscellaneous track parts had to be built or repaired in the shops.

The only bright spot in Cahill's tale of woe was the financial result of combined operations. "We are paying for the Market Street Railway faster than we anticipated and apparently we will own it outright when the time comes to throw it on the scrapheap," he concluded.

In the last, Cahill proved to be an excellent prophet. Muni paid off its $7.5 million debt in good style, aided by a 1947 refinancing bond fund. The payments were made as follows:

September 28, 1944	$2,000,000.00
January 31, 1945	1,000,000.00
June 30, 1945	1,000,000.00
September 28, 1945	500,000.00
June 28, 1946	813,088.44
September 28, 1946	58,248.68
July 30, 1947	194,315.42
October 3, 1947	52,948.75
Total	$5,618,601.29
May 7, 1948*	1,881,398.71
	$7,500,000.00

*From 1947 Refinancing Bond Fund.

First visible evidence of the implementation of the merger was the rapid disappearance of the Byllesby white front from rolling stock. The patented paint scheme, for which Muni was certainly not willing to pay royalties, was engulfed in a myriad of conjured-up schemes: blue and yellow, cream, blue, and others—some apparently the dream of a bemused car barn foreman. Literally overnight there were no more white fronts in the city.

Despite the war and the critical shortages of certain items, Muni began at once the long process of erasing Market Street Railway from the public consciousness. Selected as the first big track job was reducing Market St. from four tracks to two from Valencia St. to Castro St. This work was performed by a private contractor. The two inner tracks were uprooted and replaced by entirely new construction; when this was completed, the two outer tracks were removed and their former area paved over. Included in this job were all new overhead wire and safety islands. In all, some 11,296 lineal feet of single track was constructed plus 2.1 miles of new overhead trolley.

About 1938 Municipal Railway had adopted a new color scheme for its vehicles: blue and yellow—the same combination of colors with which MSR had briefly experimented prior to Byllesby management. In 1945 this attractive color scheme began to appear on former MSR cars and buses; by June, 10 cars and five coaches of MSR appeared in blue and gold, as did 33 Muni cars and four Muni coaches.

The MSR 24th and Utah barn was selected to be the combined systems' bus garage. It was drastically upgraded and Muni's motor coaches were transferred there from its Arguello garage.

All former Market Street Railway rail and bus line schedules were changed to conform with Muni standards, involving adjustments of service to travel requirements insofar as equipment and manpower permitted. This involved a total of 456 timetable changes and added 46 daily car and coach trips.

End of the Four Tracks

THE OLD CENTER TRACKS of Market Street are uprooted following the 1944 Merger. Brand new center tracks would soon serve the remaining consolidated system, the outer tracks being abandoned.
S.F. Public Utilities Commission

By June 1945, car houses, paint shops, electric shop, fare box department and part of the machine shop divisions of Muni and the former MSR were consolidated.

To avoid confusion due to duplication of numbers, some cars in MSR's 100 and 200 Classes were renumbered, becoming respectively Muni's 400 and 600 Classes. Those not renumbered in these classes had been previously retired from service.

"Owing to the age and condition of the streetcars acquired," declared Muni in its 1944-45 Annual Report, "many were inoperable and practically all were greatly in need of maintenance repairs. A large number of the motor coaches was also in need of rehabilitation. As of June 30, 1945, nine of the streetcars and one of the motor coaches were retired and scrapped."

During that fiscal year, 31 new 44-seat motor coaches were purchased and placed in service. Another 20 buses and 16 trolley coaches were on order. At the close of the fiscal year, June 30, 1945, the consolidated Muni system owned 669 streetcars, 38 cable cars, 195 motor coaches and 18 trolley coaches. In addition to these, the railway rented another 35 motor coaches from the United States Navy. The preponderance still was with the trolley car, but about to gather momentum was a modernization program which would reduce the once mighty streetcar fleet to but a shadow of its former importance.

MUNICIPAL RAILWAY conducted a vigorous campaign in favor of the 1947 Modernization Bonds. One feature of it was the odd pairing of #0601, an old MSR single trucker (as the "old"), and a demonstrator Super Twin motor coach (as the "new") parading up and down Market Street plugging a "Yes" vote for the bonds. They pause at the Ferry Building loop. The motorman of #0601 was railfan Lorin Silliman.
S.F. Public Utilities Commission

Borrowing for the Muni

The 31 new buses mentioned in the preceding paragraph were paid for from the railway operating fund and from the replacement fund. The vehicles on order were also financed from these funds. Clearly, Muni would be a long, long time in getting itself modernized if this dribble of funds was all it could rely on.

The answer came in the form of a bond issue; to be more specific, five bond issues were involved. Taking up each in order:

NUMBER 1—$20,000,000. For modernizing the entire municipal transportation system through purchasing new vehicles, upgrading present equipment, rebuilding tracks, shops, garages and the electrical system.

NUMBER 2—$2,200,000. To pay off the remaining debt to Market Street Railway Company.

NUMBER 3—$22,850,000. For street improvements, including removing approximately 160 miles of street railway track and rebuilding the affected streets from curb to curb, the construction of laterals and tunnels, major thoroughfare extensions, and installing a modern three-light traffic signal system.

NUMBER 4—$5,000,000. To stimulate providing off-street parking facilities to enable maximum use of downtown streets by autos and mass transit vehicles.

NUMBER 5—A Charter Amendment (companion measure to No. 2) legalizing the payment of the balance due on the Market Street Railway properties.

Due to the urgent need for improved and modernized transit facilities, the five bond proposals were submitted to the San Francisco electorate on November 4, 1947. All five general obligation bond issues were approved by large margins.

The die was cast. Money was now available for carrying out the extinction of virtually all car lines of the former Market Street Railway Company.

Muni assumed supervision of the expenditure of funds and of payments for redemption and interest on bond issues No. 1 and No. 2. Nos. 3 and 4 were assumed by other city departments.

No difficulty was experienced in selling the new bonds. Of No. 1, a block of $6,500,000 was sold as of February 1, 1948. A second block of $4,900,000 was sold as of August 1, 1948. No. 2 was likewise well accepted by the financial community; a block of $1,950,000 was quickly sold and from the proceeds of this sale Muni on May 7, 1948, paid the Market Street Railway Company all of the balance on the principal—$1,881,398.71—plus $63,946.99 in interest, thus liquidating all its debt to the private company.

Thus Muni had $11,400,000 to spend as of August 1948. At once orders were placed for 259 motor coaches (44-seat White Model 798) and 190 44-seat trolley coaches. Some 55 streetcars were somewhat modernized; all were Muni's own cars. Other major expenditures from the fund included $886,821 to remodel Geary car house, constructing bus storage and servicing facilities at Ocean Bus Yard ($803,947), erecting trolley coach overhead on the McAllister-Hayes, Haight-Masonic, Haight-Sunset, Fillmore St., and Market St. lines, rebuilding the inner tracks on Market St. from Eddy St. to Valencia St., removing the two outer tracks and repaving the area, and rebuilding the cable turntable at Powell and Market streets.

By August 31, 1948, 209 of the Whites had entered service, replacing streetcars on these lines: 3—Sutter-Jackson; 4—Sutter-Sacramento; 5—McAllister; 6—Haight-Masonic; 7—Haight-Ocean; 21—Hayes; 22—Fillmore; 25—Bryant.

By the same date, the new Ocean bus garage, constructed on the northeastern part of Elkton Shops property, had come along far enough to house 87 buses which ran on 13 routes.

Track removal was well along, this work being performed by the Department of Public Works. Tracks had been removed and repaving was under way on Polk St., Kearny St., Sansome St., Folsom St. and Sacramento St. Track removal was under way on McAllister St. and on that portion of the No. 22 line from 16th and Church streets east.

Muni's own Reconstruction and Replacement Fund and Operating Fund provided additional monies for enlarging the thrust of the bold modernization scheme. Between the merger date, September 29, 1944, and June 30, 1948, Muni had spent more than $5,000,000 of its own—including some $688,751 received from the Market Street Railway Impounded Excess Fare Monies. Some of the big items paid for by this source of funds were:

- 137 44-seat White Model 798 motor coaches.
- 36 new trolley coaches.
- 10 new PCC streetcars.
- Rebuilding Market St. inner tracks from Valencia to Castro Sts., removing outer tracks in same stretch and repaving street.
- Rebuilding of Church St. tracks, including taking out that four-track segment between Market St. and 16th St. (completed in October 1946).
- Reconstruction of inner tracks, Market St., from Fremont St. to Eddy St., completed May 1947; this also entailed removal of outer tracks and repaving street.
- Installing crossing tracks, Market St., Stockton St. and 4th St.
- Modernization and enlarging of 24th and Utah Garage, making it the central bus repair facility.

By August 31, 1948, 170 vehicles acquired from Market Street Railway had been retired. More were to follow in the melancholy parade of old cars to the scrapheap; Muni as of that date had 190 new trolley coaches and 50 motor coaches on order. The rubber tire era had indeed arrived for the city by the Golden Gate.

These basic changes in the city's transportation pattern were carried through after several transit studies had been made by nationally recognized authorities. Included were reports made by the firm of DeLeuw Cather & Company as well as one made by Col. Sydney H. Bingham of New York City. Both these reports concurred in retaining the tunnel rail lines, the Geary and Stockton rail lines and Col. Bingham recommended keeping the cable lines and the trolley coach lines.

TRANSPLANTED to serving a Municipal Railway line, former MSR 160 (now Muni 460) had its front end painted a staid post-merger cream—thus avoiding paying royalties for use of the patented "White Front." Though many other ex-MSR rolling stock simply had ends repainted, other cars emerged in quite bizarre colors.
Charles Smallwood

A POST-MERGER scene at the 5th and Market terminal of the 40 Line. Car 1241 now bears the Municipal Railway's blue and gold livery. **Interurbans**

Muni was in love with the trolley coach, as well it might have been. The city's steepest hills were no challenge at all to these sure-footed, powerful, silent and clean-operating vehicles. Most of the major lines of the old Market Street Railway system eventually were to wind up as trolley coach operations, although first having to endure gas buses while street reconstruction and overhead installations proceeded.

As of August 31, 1948, the total round-trip miles of streets traversed by streetcars and coaches of Muni totaled 524.72 miles, as compared with 492.11 miles on June 30, 1945. Streetcar miles decreased in the period by 101.12 miles; motor and trolley miles increased by 133.73 miles. The true picture of the streetcars' decline in San Francisco was revealed by the fact that a total of 357 round-trip miles were operated by trolley and motor coaches, but only 168 by electric and cable cars.

Motor coaches were stored (as of November 1, 1948) at three locations: 24th and Utah (187 coaches), Ocean Division (132 coaches), and McAllister Division (130 coaches). All major repairs were made at 24th and Utah.

Trolley coaches were centered at Potrero Trolley Coach Base and Geary Car House which had been provided with enlarged outside storage area.

Steadily the street reconstruction program continued, eliminating all traces of what had been Market Street Railway's busiest car lines. By October 1, 1948, the following streets had been detracked, repaved and opened for service:

- Polk St., from Post St. to North Point St.
- Kearny St., from Market St. to Broadway.
- Sansome St., from Bush St. to Chestnut St.
- Folsom St., from Third St. to Steuart St.
- Steuart St., from Folsom St. to Howard St.
- Howard St., from Steuart St. to Embarcadero.
- Folsom St. tracks on the Embarcadero.
- Sacramento St., from Van Ness Ave. to Embarcadero.

The pattern thus established, further abandonments occurred in doleful succession. For some lines, conversion to bus operation came slowly, with buses taking over at night and on weekends. Other lines were converted at one fell swoop.

Some interesting sights were beheld by connoisseurs of trolley equipment in the 1945-1950 years; ex-MSR cars were seen on Muni lines C and H in sizable numbers. Muni cars used Mission St. to the ferries at such times as Market St. was blocked by parades. The big 1200s on the San Mateo line blossomed out in both of Muni's paint schemes: first, blue and gold, then in green and cream; every one of the Twelves was repainted—something no other MSR class could boast. Of the once huge 1550 Class—200 cars—only a few came to Muni in 1944, and but one of these received the Muni paint. At least two MSR lines were merged with Muni lines: the #26—San Bruno Ave. line became part of Muni's H line, while that part of #20—Ellis and O'Farrell south of Market St. became part of Muni's Line F; cars of Muni's K line rolled on up Line 12—Mission and Ocean to a new terminus at Onondaga and Mission. MSR's 8—Market St. line was operated through Twin Peaks Tunnel for only a few days to clear Castro St. for trolley coach overhead construction; as if this were not odd enough, Muni cars were assigned to the #8 line during this period.

The bulk of the conversions occurred on five important days: June 6, 1948 (Lines 5 and 21); July 4, 1948 (Lines 6 and 7); August 1, 1948 (Lines 4, 22 and 25); January 16, 1949 (Lines 9, 11, 14, 40 and 41); and July 3, 1949 (Lines 1, 2, 3, 8 and 31).

So thoroughly did the Department of Public Works perform its street reconstruction job that today there is comparatively little remaining of former MSR trackage. A major electric railway system had been virtually obliterated in a few months.

The cable lines have fared better, owing to the decision to make of them a public monument. The Washington-Jackson cable line was permitted to go, but the three surviving lines, California St., Powell-Hyde and Powell-Bay, seemingly will operate forever.

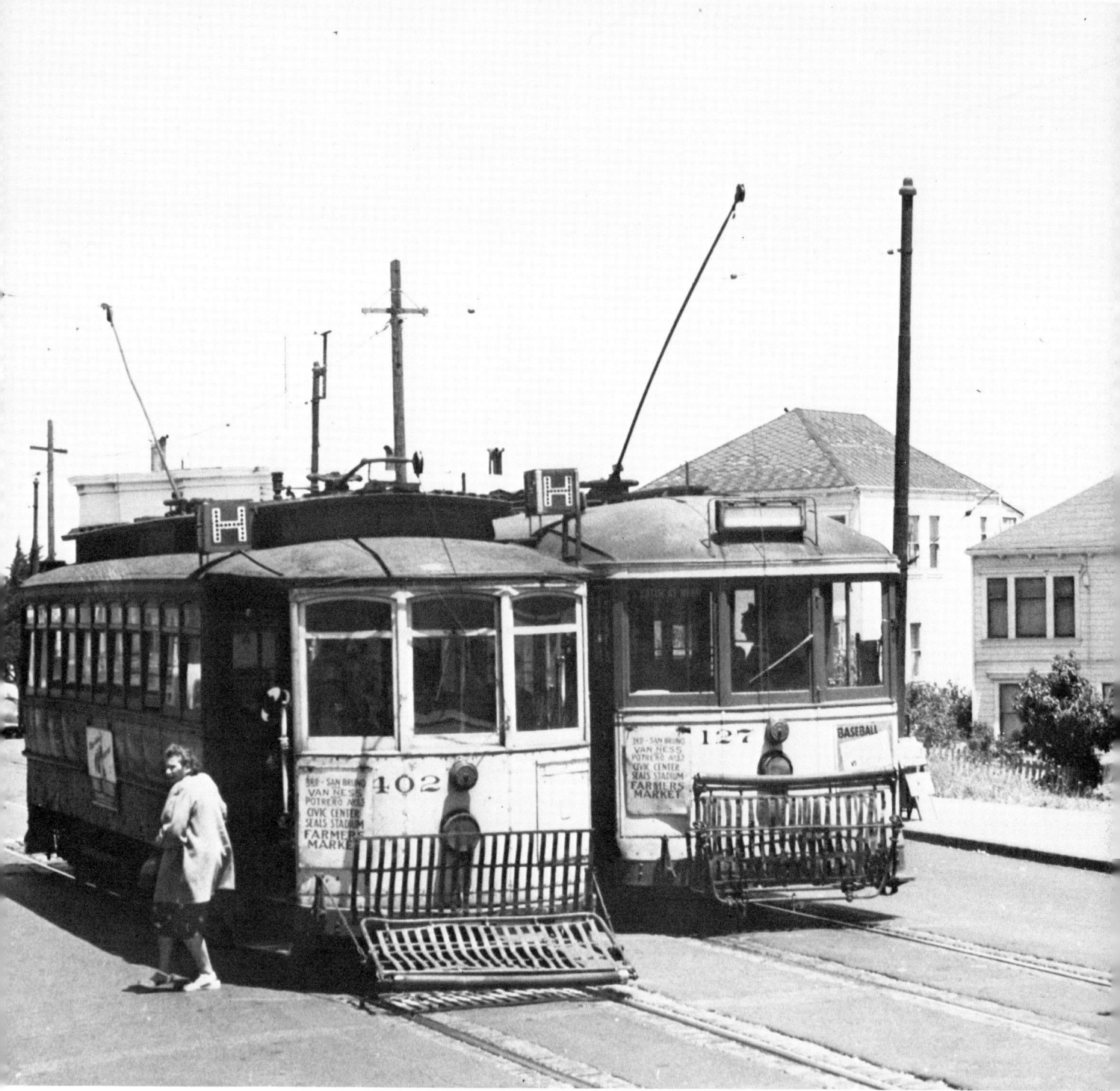

Formerly Neighbors....... Now Partners

THE IMPOSSIBLE HAPPENS in 1948: The scene is at the Five Mile House, San Bruno and Wilde Avenues, which for decades was the traditional terminus of Market Street Railway's #25 line. But now it is the end of the line for Municipal Railway's extended Van Ness-Potrero Line H. Stranger yet is the sight of one of MSR's familiar old Haight Street workhorses signed for a Municipal Railway route. Prior to the 1944 consolidation the two cars above working the same route would have been considered strange bedfellows indeed! **Randolph C. Brandt**

Fillmore Counterbalance

OF ALL THE LINES of the "White Front Car" system, the Fillmore Hill line was perhaps the most unique in its method of operation. Grades on two blocks of Fillmore were so severe that special counterbalance cable machinery was installed so that the weight of descending cars could assist their sister cars coming uphill.

Magna Collection

The System

WHEN THE NEW Market Street Railway took over ownership and operation of the United Railroads of San Francisco's electric railway system in April 1921, it inherited a 288.64-mile (equivalent single track) net of city streetcar lines, plus the interurban line down the peninsula to San Mateo (20 miles). All these lines were operated by overhead trolley except 14.7 miles of cable railways.

The trolley system more or less divided itself into six categories (as of 1927):

1. MARKET STREET-FERRIES LINES
   (Routes 4, 5, 6, 7, 8, 9, 17, 21, 32)

2. SUTTER STREET-FERRIES LINES
   (Routes 1, 2, 3)

3. MISSION STREET LINES
   (Routes 10, 11, 12, 14, 18, 26, 40 and Bosworth, Parkside and Visitacion)

4. SOUTH SIDE LINES
   (Routes 25, 27, 28, 30, 35, 36)

5. THIRD STREET LINES
   (Routes 15, 16, 29)

6. CROSSTOWN LINES
   (Routes 19, 20, 22, including Fillmore Hill, 23, 24, 33, 34, 37, 41, Divisadero Extension, First and Fifth Streets)

What kind of money did these lines earn, without regard to investment involved? One formula for arriving at an enlightening picture is by considering their earning power by charging against each the average cost of operation of the MSR's electric lines for the entire system on a car-hour basis, including taxes and depreciation as a part of the operating cost. The accompanying table shows in the above groupings for the 12-month period ending June 30, 1927. Listed are: (1) gross receipts of the particular route per car hour; (2) system expenses per car hour ($2.917 for electric lines); (3) excess or shortage of actual receipts per car hour for each route as compared with the average expenses; (4) speed in mph on each line; (5) number of car hours operated on each line; and (6) total operating earnings or losses of each route (see table A).

From this table it may be ascertained that the best paying groups of lines, relatively, were those on Sutter Street: Routes 1, 2, and 3—and the Third Street group, Routes 15, 16, and 29. All lines in the Market Street grouping showed profits except Hayes and Oak. Two of the important Mission lines showed losses in addition to the relatively heavy deficits shown by the three minor lines included in this group. Of interest is the fact that 60 percent of the net earnings of the Mission group of lines came from the San Mateo interurban line which was saved from a loss by its high average speed, 15.65 mph. All of the South Side lines and all except three of the crosstown lines were in the red; the Ninth and Polk and the Ellis and O'Farrell lines showed good operating profits, and even the little Second and Market line seemed to be paying its operating expenses. The Fillmore St. line to Broadway only would have shown an operating profit, but this was wiped out and turned into a deficit by the cost of the Fillmore Hill counterbalance operation from Broadway to Marina Blvd.—a separate physical operation but integrally a part of the Fillmore line.

This compilation, however, does not include each line's share of the cost of capital; with the share of return upon investment included the relative profit-and-loss figures undergo some startling changes. Perhaps the most enlightening method to use in arriving at each line's fair share of the cost of capital is by using the cost for reproduction less depreciation, and a rate of return upon the same capital if it were invested elsewhere at seven percent. Rights-of-way could be charged directly against those lines using them. In case of dual use by lines of the same trackage, each line's fair share could be arrived at by ascertaining the relative number of car miles operating by the various lines involved over the affected stretch of track.

Thus we arrive at another table of comparison in which the following items are shown by the same groupings of lines: (1) car mileage operated; (2) approximate route mileage; (3) car miles per route mile during last year of the period; and (4) the proportion of total car miles of all electric lines operated by each route (see Table B).

In arriving at a reproduction cost less depreciation of about $26 million as of 1927 for the Market Street Railway system, such additional items as other land owned, shops and carhouses, machinery and tools, stations and miscellaneous buildings, passenger cars, service equipment, electric equipment of cars, substations, franchises, and the various overheads which were applicable to the above: engineering, legal expenses, interest during construction, injuries and damages, taxes and miscellaneous items must be added. Thus the total figure of $26 million had to be kept in mind in considering the return on capital which, at seven percent, each operating route should earn. When this capital cost was added to the cost of operation, the financial results of operation by groups could be shown on an approximate basis, as in the following table:

(Please refer to Table C)

ONE OF THE EARLY Mission District electric car services was the branch that ran on 29th Street west from Mission to Noe Street; this was the outer end of the important Valencia Street Line. Note the carmen at right waiting to take over their runs; the intersection was an important relief point for the Mission Street Lines.

Lorin Silliman

Table A

MARKET STREET RAILWAY
Operating Results by Routes for Year ended June 30, 1927.

Route No.	Route Designation	Gross Receipts per Car Hour	System Expenses per Car Hour 1926	Excess of Receipts per Car Hour	Deficiency of Receipts per Car Hour	Speed Miles per Hour	Total Car Hours	Total Excess of Receipts	Total Deficiency of Receipts
	Group A:								
4	Turk & Eddy	$3.290	$2.917	$0.37		9.35	93,119	$ 34,454	
5	McAllister Street	3.879	2.917	.96		9.53	188,777	181,226	
6	Haight & Masonic	3.429	2.917	.51		8.63	114,177	58,230	
7	Haight & Ocean	3.355	2.917	.44		9.91	119,449	52,558	
8	Market Street	3.164	2.917	.25		8.37	92,088	23,022	
9	Valencia Street	3.923	2.917	1.01		8.90	141,030	142,440	
17	Haight & Ingleside	3.185	2.917	.27		9.74	74,788	20,193	
21	Hayes Street	3.707	2.917	.79		8.45	91,277	72,109	
32	Hayes & Oak	2.782	2.917		$0.14	8.27	41,748		$ 5,845
	Totals						956,453	$578,387	
	Group B:								
1	Sutter & California	4.221	2.917	1.30		9.50	98,634	$128,224	
2	Sutter & Clement	3.507	2.917	.59		9.89	116,604	68,796	
3	Sutter & Jackson	3.633	2.917	.72		8.23	69,762	50,229	
	Totals						285,000	$247,249	
	Group C:								
10	Sunnyside	2.487	2.917		.43	9.38	50,398		$21,671
11	Mission & 24th Street	3.682	2.917	.77		9.02	87,867	$ 67,658	
12	Ingleside & Ocean	3.081	2.917	.16		11.14	82,481	13,197	
14	Mission Line	4.073	2.917	1.16		10.63	74,319	86,210	
18	Daly City—Cemeteries	3.591	2.917	.67		9.73	30,170	20,214	
26	Guerrero Street	2.498	2.917		.42	10.04	56,439		23,704
39	Visitacion Valley	1.190	2.917		1.73	9.10	12,513		21,647
40	San Mateo	4.657	2.917	1.74		15.65	94,870	165,074	
	Bosworth Street	.458	2.917		2.46	5.66	4,864		11,965
	Parkside	.296	2.917		2.62	9.05	3,343		8,759
	Totals						497,264	$264,607	
	Group D:								
25	San Bruno Ave.	2.701	2.917		.22	9.43	61,119		$13,446
27	Bryant Street	2.366	2.917		.55	8.34	49,204		27,062
28	Harrison Street	2.605	2.917		.31	7.47	22,871		7,090
30	Eighth & Eighteenth	1.831	2.917		1.09	9.23	35,973		39,211
35	Howard Street	2.771	2.917		.15	8.99	49,681		7,452
36	Folsom Street	2.695	2.917		.22	9.37	37,346		8,216
	Totals						256,194		$102,477
	Group E:								
15	Third Street	3.347	2.917	.43		9.36	70,690	$ 30,397	
16&29	Third & Kearny	3.945	2.917	1.03		8.16	122,788	126,472	
	Totals						193,478	$156,869	
	Group F:								
19	Ninth & Polk	3.646	2.917	.73		7.39	88,654	$ 64,717	
20	Ellis & O'Farrell	3.712	2.917	.80		8.71	86,237	68,990	
22	Fillmore Street	2.851	2.917		.07	6.96	178,267		$11,766
23	Fillmore & Valencia	2,531	2.917		.39	8.57	50,064		19,525
24	Mission & Richmond	2.704	2.917		.21	9.00	69,920		14,683
33	Eighteenth & Park	2.105	2.917		.81	8.96	49,840		40,370
34	Sixth & Sansome	2.147	2.917		.77	6.60	36,245		27,909
37	10th & Montgomery	.899	2.917		2.02	6.29	10,725		21,665
41	Second & Market	3.200	2.917	.28		4.82	866	242	
	Divisadero Hill	.029	2.917		2.79	2.83	7,160		19,976
	First & Fifth	1.649	2.917		1.27	6.82	4,322		5,489
	Totals						582,300		$27,434
	Group G:								
	Castro Street Cable	2.073	2.884		.81	5.78	25,276		$20,474
	Jackson Street Cable	3.796	2.884	.91		6.45	54,286	$ 49,400	
	Powell Street Cable	3.956	2.884	1.07		6.12	38,326	41,009	
	Sacramento St. Cable	3.100	2.884	.22		6.69	50,411	11,090	
	Pacific Avenue Cable	.689	2.884		2.20	6.80	11,311		24,884
	Totals						179,610	$ 56,141	
	Total—All electric lines	3.308	2.917	.39		9.14	2,770,689	$1,117,201	
	Total—All cable lines	3.197	2.884	.31		6.37	179,610	$ 56,141	
	Grand Total—All lines					8.97	2,950,299	$1,173,342	

Table B

MARKET STREET RAILWAY
Analysis of Car Mileage by Routes

Route No.	Group Designation	1923	1924	1925	1926	1927	Round Trip Route Mileage	Car Miles Per Route Mile Year Ended June 30, 1927	Per Cent of System Car Miles Electric or Cable
	Group A:								
4	Turk & Eddy	871,225	868,228	876,289	883,682	870,951	12.277	70,942	3.439
5	McAllister	1,592,375	1,721,649	1,757,578	1,765,816	1,798,449	14.706	122,294	7.102
6	Haight & Masonic	987,880	989,897	986,959	986,694	985,102	12.009	82,030	3.890
7	Haight & Ocean	1,157,457	1,167,809	1,184,701	1,188,620	1,183,232	16.312	72,538	4.673
8	Market Street	770,755	771,923	769,503	771,260	770,474	6.900	111,663	3.043
9	Valencia Street	1,228,137	1,232,778	1,235,250	1,255,881	1,255,194	9.845	127,496	4.957
17	Haight & Ingleside	536,888	544,016	562,240	674,453	728,158	15.739	46,265	2.875
21	Hayes Street	529,470	595,639	597,008	652,913	771,202	11.075	69,634	3.045
32	Hayes & Oak	373,312	353,383	349,556	349,077	345,310	8.541	40,430	1.364
	Totals	8,047,499	8,245,322	8,319,084	8,528,396	8,708,072			34.388
	Group B:								
1	Sutter & California	976,499	986,139	967,917	960,970	936,621	12.312	76,044	3.699
2	Sutter & Clement	1,038,133	1,094,018	1,129,342	1,177,118	1,153,231	15.032	76,718	4.554
3	Sutter & Jackson	515,682	510,116	502,686	539,650	573,954	7.435	77,196	2.266
	Totals	2,530,314	2,590,273	2,599,945	2,677,738	2,663,806			10.519
	Group C:								
10	Sunnyside	456,102	457,501	458,304	465,929	472,856	13.630	34,692	1.867
11	Mission & 24th	795,272	798,197	794,618	793,385	792,355	9.880	80,198	3.129
12	Ingleside & Ocean	834,203	843,562	852,663	911,070	918,657	20.790	44,187	3.628
14	Mission Line	542,187	735,201	723,256	774,406	789,988	15.904	49,672	3.120
18	Daly City-C'mteries	176,696*			125,228*	293,550	13.746	21,355	1.159
26	Guerrero Street	500,262	551,092	551,482	497,318	566,390	16.058	35,272	2.237
39	Visitacion Valley	107,860	111,583	114,737	116,287	113,810	4.736	24,031	.449
40	San Mateo	1,607,124	1,628,144	1,626,836	1,566,977	1,485,143	40.569	36,608	5.865
	Bosworth Street	27,539	27,620	27,545	27,549	27,535	1.494	18,430	.109
	Parkside	65,421	61,890	56,646	64,038	30,256*			.119
	Totals	5,162,666	5,214,790	5,206,087	5,342,187	5,490,540			21.682
	Group D:								
25	San Bruno Avenue	565,215	581,540	577,785	574,684	576,243	10.984	52,462	2.276
27	Bryant Street	442,062	418,447	415,567	412,423	410,337	8.262	49,666	1.620
28	Harrison Street	164,847	168,854	169,488	169,995	170,808	3.140	54,397	.675
30	Eighth & Eighteenth	333,322	336,393	335,297	332,128	331,934	11.643	28,509	1.311
35	Howard Street	458,671	460,390	453,067	447,257	446,707	8.895	50,220	1.764
36	Folsom Street	328,861	346,324	351,371	350,230	349,857	8.437	41,467	1.381
	Totals	2,292,978	2,311,948	2,302,575	2,286,717	2,285,886			9.027
	Group E:								
15	Third Street	699,247	685,684	672,134	661,700	661,602	5.278	125,351	2.613
16&29	Third & Kearny	960,681	990,388	992,323	986,650	1,001,325	15.027	66,635	3.954
	Totals	1,659,928	1,676,072	1,664,457	1,648,350	1,662,927			6.567
	Group F:								
19	Ninth & Polk	529,544	547,084	579,563	638,227	655,344	5.701	114,952	2.588
20	Ellis & O'Farrell	754,605	756,105	750,208	750,271	750,909	9.441	79,537	2.965
22	Fillmore Street	1,175,997	1,195,507	1,196,917	1,228,654	1,240,446	12.072	102,754	4.899
23	Fillmore & Valencia	428,907	429,935	428,666	428,693	429,016	10.429	41,137	1.694
24	Mission & Richmond	632,514	631,199	627,559	628,363	629,094	14.960	42,052	2.484
33	Eighteenth & Park	473,432	451,177	445,471	445,790	446,597	9.772	45,702	1.764
34	Sixth & Sansome	244,722	244,966	243,524	242,899	239,151	5.752	41,577	.944
37	10th & Montgomery	120,025	119,527	119,077	117,357	67,428	5.474	12,318	.266
41	Second & Market					4,178*	2.129	1,962	.017
	Divisadero Hill	20,215	20,277	20,220	20,230	20,229	.403	50,196	.080
	First & Fifth	25,131	25,048	26,395	29,083	29,460	5.183	5,684	.116
	Totals	4,405,092	4,420,825	4,437,600	4,529,567	4,511,852			17.817
	Totals, Electric Lines	24,098,477	24,459,230	24,529,748	25,012,955	25,323,083			100.
	Group G:								
	Castro Street Cable	146,529	146,959	146,804	146,649	146,034	1.801	81,085	12.757
	Jackson St. Cable	349,602	349,467	350,854	351,409	350,309	4.551	76,974	30.601
	Powell Street Cable	233,282	234,455	234,809	235,084	234,386	3.357	69,820	20.475
	Sacramento S. C'ble	334,555	336,979	335,672	337,108	337,099	4.523	74,530	29.447
	Pacific Avenue Cable	97,344	97,681	97,259	95,935	76,925	2.282	33,709	6.720
	Total, Cable Lines	1,161,312	1,165,541	1,165,398	1,166,185	1,144,753			100.

*Not full year.

Market Street Railway

Table C — Analysis of Financial Results of Operation By Routes, Including 7 Per Cent Return on O'Shaughnessy's Cost New Less Depreciation.

Route No.	Route Designation	Total Excess of Receipts	Total Deficiency of Receipts	Interest at 7% on Cost New Less Depreciation	Excess Over Cost of Service	Deficiency Below Cost of Service
	Group A:					
4	Turk & Eddy	$ 34,454		$ 55,636		$ 21,182
5	McAllister Street	181,226		96,632	$ 84,594	
6	Haight & Masonic	58,230		51,548	6,682	
7	Haight & Ocean	52,558		66,283		13,725
8	Market Street	23,022		35,046		12,024
9	Valencia Street	142,440		59,575	82,865	
17	Haight & Ingleside	20,193		40,359		20,166
21	Hayes Street	72,109		42,012	30,097	
32	Hayes & Oak		$ 5,845	17,103		22,948
	Totals	$578,387		$ 464,194	$114,193	
	Group B:					
1	Sutter & California	$128,224		$ 45,901	$ 82,323	
2	Sutter & Clement	68,796		64,738	4,058	
3	Sutter & Jackson	50,229		29,942	20,287	
	Totals	$247,249		$ 140,581	$106,668	
	Group C:					
10	Sunnyside		$ 21,671	$ 29,603		$ 51,274
11	Mission & 24th Streets	$ 67,658		43,097	$ 24,561	
12	Ingleside & Ocean	13,197		65,249		52,052
14	Mission Line	86,210		42,893	43,317	
18	Daly City—Cemeteries	20,214		16,501	3,713	
26	Guerrero Street		23,704	45,295		68,999
39	Visitacion Valley		21,647	9,293		30,940
40	San Mateo	165,074		147,659	17,415	
	Bosworth Street		11,965	3,117		15,082
	Parkside		8,759	8,116		16,875
	Totals	$264,607		$410,823		$146,216
	Group D:					
25	San Bruno Avenue		$ 13,446	$ 52,193		$ 65,639
27	Bryant Street		27,062	37,564		64,626
28	Harrison Street		7,090	13,521		20,611
30	Eighth & Eighteenth		39,211	37,757		76,968
35	Howard Street		7,452	48,550		56,002
36	Folsom Street		8,216	38,317		46,533
			$102,477	$ 227,902		$330,379
	Group E:					
15	Third Street	$ 30,397		$ 34,420		$ 4,023
16 & 29	Third & Kearny	126,472		79,355	$ 47,117	
	Totals	$156,869		$ 113,775	$ 43,094	
	Group F:					
19	Ninth & Polk	$ 64,717		$ 40,402	$ 24,315	
20	Ellis & O'Farrell	68,990		56,265	12,725	
22	Fillmore Street		$ 11,766	74,152		$ 85,918
23	Fillmore & Valencia		19,525	30,073		49,598
24	Mission & Richmond		14,683	36,750		51,433
33	Eighteenth & Park		40,370	41,954		82,324
34	Sixth & Sansome		27,909	27,114		55,023
37	10th & Montgomery		21,665	18,574		40,239
41	Second & Market	242		358		116
	Divisadero Hill		19,976	1,399		21,375
	First & Fifth		5,489	7,501		12,990
	Totals		$ 27,434	$ 334,542		$361,976
	Total—All Electric Lines	$1,117,201		$1,691,817		$574,616
	Group G:					
	Castro Street Cable		$ 20,474	$ 18,045		$ 38,519
	Jackson Street Cable	$ 49,400		34,006	$ 15,394	
	Powell Street Cable	41,009		23,661	17,348	
	Sacramento Street Cable	11,090		35,814		24,724
	Pacific Avenue Cable		24,884	20,722		45,606
	Total—Cable Lines	$ 56,141		$ 132,248		$ 76,107
	Grand Total—All Lines	$1,173,342		$1,824,065		$650,723

Thus, as of 1927, the only lines earning seven percent or more on their share of the $26 million were McAllister, Haight and Masonic, Valencia St. and Hayes St. in the Market Street group; the three Sutter St. lines; Mission and 24th, Mission, Daly City-Cemeteries and San Mateo interurban in the Mission St. group; Third and Kearny, Ninth and Polk, and Ellis and O'Farrell. As a group, the Mission group fell behind $46,000; the lines on the South Side ran $330,000 behind; the crosstown lines lost $574,000.

On October 10, 1927, the Board of Supervisors of San Francisco hired expert Delos F. Wilcox to prepare a report on the feasibility of bringing all privately owned transit operations into the Municipal Railway. Wilcox came to San Francisco and, with his staff, made a quite remarkable study of Market Street Railway, line by line. It is quite revealing, even at this remove in time, and this report is the basis of the following analysis of lines of Market Street Railway as they existed at that time:

The Market Street Lines

Lines of the Market Street Railway Company which use Market Street are as follows:

Route #4—Turk and Eddy
Route #5—McAllister Street
Route #6—Haight and Masonic
Route #7—Haight and Ocean
Route #8—Market Street
Route #9—Valencia Street
Route #17—Haight and Ingleside
Route #21—Hayes Street
Route #32—Hayes and Oak

Taking these lines individually, it was found that:

Line #4—Turk and Eddy used lower Market St. except during the evening rush hours when cars turned back on Eddy St. at Market. This line made money, turning in $34,500 over operating expenses. This, however, turned into a $21,000 deficit when the line was charged up with a seven percent return on its appraised evaluation.

Route #5—McAllister was MSR's most profitable; it returned $181,000 more than its share of operating expenses and about $84,500 over a seven percent return.

Route #6—Haight and Masonic was also profitable, showing an operating surplus of $58,000 and a net profit over a seven percent return of $6,600.

Line #7—Haight and Ocean returned $52,500 over operating expenses but fell $14,000 short of a seven percent return.

Route #8—Market Street made only $23,000 over its costs of operation which became a deficit of $12,000 when a seven percent return on its investment was considered.

Route #9—Valencia Street was a good money maker; it had an operating surplus of $142,000 and a clear profit of about $83,000 above a seven percent return.

Line #17—Haight and Ingleside was identical with Line #7 as far as Lincoln Way and 20th Ave., at which point it struck off easterly across the Sunset and Parkside districts to Sloat Blvd. It was not a money maker.

Route #21—Hayes Street returned a profit, showing $72,000 above operating expenses and $30,000 more than a seven percent return on its investment.

Line #32—Hayes and Oak was weak in this group. It had an operating deficit of almost $6,000 and was $23,000 in the red when a seven percent return was counted in.

Taken all together, these Market Street lines had a profit of $114,000 over a seven percent return and accounted for no less than 50 percent of the total operating surplus off the Market Street Railway system.

Market Street, the main thoroughfare of the city, thrusts through the community on the bias to all streets north of it—a broad river of traffic into which lesser streets to the north flow, and to which streets from the south lead, often to dead-end. From the Ferry Building at its foot to Castro St. at its head, Market Street's three-mile stretch was traversed by no less that four electric railway tracks.

Of these, the two inner tracks, the original, were the property of Market Street Railway. The two outer were owned by Municipal Railway from Castro St. down to Sutter St., and jointly from there to the Ferry Loop by Muni and MSR. The three-track loop itself was jointly owned by the two competing street railways.

Cutting through San Francisco's main shopping and financial district, Market Street served the important function of carrying the lion's share of traffic to and from the community's heart twice daily.

In addition, Market Street was traveled two times every day by the army of commuters who resided in the East Bay but worked in San Francisco. As the center of the business district was about 1.5 miles north of the Ferry, streetcars looping in front of that terminal carried tremendous loads during the morning and evening peaks; it was claimed that a streetcar loaded and departed from the Ferry every nine seconds during the peak hours, making that terminal the busiest in the world.

Thus those lines traversing Market St. were a dream operation in the electric railway world. Not only did the cars carry maximum loads downtown from outlying neighborhoods—they immediately carried swinging loads up Market Street on their return trips. Small wonder it required four tracks to meet the stern challenge of this state of affairs.

In addition to the many lines which used the inner tracks, the following MSR lines used the two outer tracks from the ferry to Sutter St.:

Route #1—Sutter and California
Route #2—Sutter and Clement
Route #3—Sutter and Jackson

These same two outer tracks also carried Muni's lines from Geary St., Church St., Duboce St. and the Twin Peaks tunnel lines.

An attempt was made in 1921 to distribute the load more equally by diverting some 22 inbound MSR cars over 12th St. to Mission St., looping back to Market St. at 4th St. and thence outbound. Another attempt to diminish streetcar traffic on Market St. at that time was the deadening of some 18 Eddy St. cars at Market St., making a transfer mandatory for their passengers who desired to continue further down Market.

These diversions resulted in some 18 MSR cars looping at the ferry, plus 101 Muni cars. These cars transported 36,000 passengers from the business section to outlying residential districts from 5 to 6 PM on the average weekday evening—of which MSR carried 26,000.

Moving this armada of cars safely and with a minimum of delay was accomplished in several ways. First of all, the cars themselves were designed for two-man operation, had drop platforms for quick loading, and many had longitudinal seats to permit more passengers on board. Second, inspectors and flagmen were stationed along the busiest part of the four tracks, so cars were spaced to best advantage both in and out of the ferry loops. And third, street loaders were used; 13 loaders as of 1921 collected fares at the cars' front doors and were credited with increasing the average load of the cars by about 40 passengers per trip.

The four-track system certainly greatly increased the capacity of Market Street itself, but added an element of danger which undoubtedly generated a certain amount of delay. The clearance between cars on inner and outer tracks was but 16 inches between grab handles, windowsills, etc., of the largest cars when passing. Passengers desiring to board MSR cars on the inner tracks thus had to center themselves in this narrow space or risk being hit. This same peril was the lot of the unfortunate pedestrian who, in seeking to cross Market St., found himself caught in this devilstrip while MSR and Muni cars bore down on him at speed. Another opportunity for tragedy to occur was present in rush hours, when large numbers of passengers clung to steps of cars; this clump of humanity, bulging outwardly from car ends, bore down on prospective boarders like a juggernaut of doom.

Time was of the essence always on Market St., and cars raced from stop to stop seemingly always at the uppermost limit of speed. A would-be patron of an inner-track car had to act lively or he risked being blocked by a car on the outer track cutting him off—in which case he was forced to wait for the next car. Chances were taken which today would be looked upon with horror; yet, somehow, the four-track system worked and its victims—innocent or no—were the exception rather than the rule.

An excellent illustration of the extreme usage to which the streetcar rails on Market St. were subjected is revealed in the fact that in 1909 the inner tracks were rebuilt with 9-inch, 141-lb. girder rail on redwood ties on 2-foot centers with 9 inches of crushed rock ballast, this being the heaviest type of contruction used in such work; 14 years later all this had to be redone, for 11/16 of an inch of the rail head had been worn off by the thousands of car passings in the interim.

A unique factor in rebuilding of track on lower Market St. was the constant settling of that street which was caused by the settling of the fill—for all of the bay front below Montgomery St. was originally at the bottom of the bay. Every few years it was necessary for the railway companies to raise tracks as much as 18 inches to counteract this settling. Such raising made mandatory the complete rebuilding of all trackage. The presence of four tracks, however, made track rebuilding much simpler, for two tracks could be reserved for work equipment during off-peak periods—greatly facilitating the heavy work and resulting in much saving of time.

To distribute cars equitably on the three loops at the ferry, certain MSR lines were switched inbound to the outer track at Market and Spear streets, two blocks away from the Ferry Building. A switching tower mounted on a pole located on the sidewalk at the southeast corner of the intersection controlled the switch. Lines 4, 8, 21 and 32 were thus switched to the outer track.

The nine MSR lines using Market Street diminished to eight at Eddy St., where Line #4 cut off. At McAllister St., Line #5 was claimed. Lines 21 and 32 left Market at Hayes St., while Haight St. claimed Lines 6, 7, and 17. At Valencia St., Line #9 went on its own way, leaving only Line #8 to continue up Market St. as far as Castro St., where it, too, turned off. At this point the 120-foot-wide thoroughfare ended; remaining Municipal Railway cars entered Twin Peaks Tunnel and automotive traffic began the narrow, winding climb up the steep rise of the twin mounts.

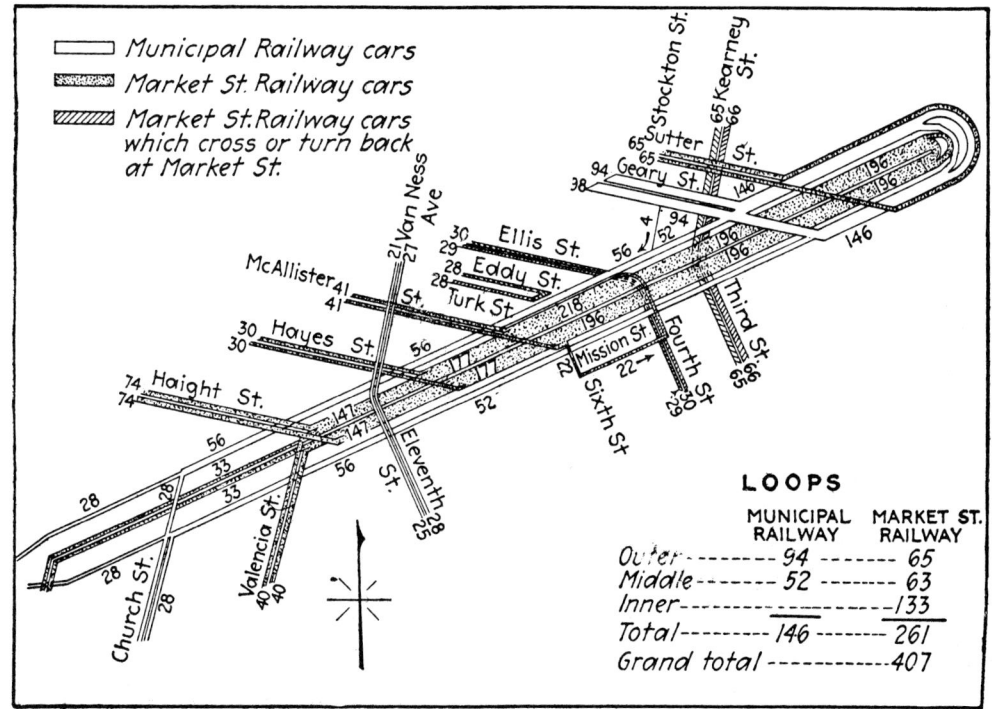

TO SAY THAT MARKET STREET was a busy transit thoroughfare is an understatement! This schematic diagram, circa 1927, shows the volume of cars on both Market Street Railway and Municipal Railway lines during a typical 4:30 to 6 P.M. rush hour.

Directions for the Riders

THE PUBLIC TIMETABLE for the White Front Cars contained a foldout map (the 1934 edition has been reproduced at the beginning of this chapter) and information about points of interest, fares and schedules. At the bottom of this page, and on the next page, is a listing of the system as it was in 1934.

CAR ROUTES

The word "OWLS" designates all night service. Unless Owls are mentioned the first set of figures at the end of each paragraph indicates the leaving time of the first and last cars from the Ferry Building—and the last set of figures, the first and last cars from the outer terminal unless other terminals are mentioned.

1—**SUTTER AND CALIFORNIA STS.**, from the Ferry Bldg. via Market, Sutter, Presidio Ave., California, 6th Ave., Clement, 33rd Ave. Owls.

2—**SUTTER AND CLEMENT STS.**, from the Ferry Bldg. via Market, Sutter, Presidio Ave., California, Parker Ave., Euclid, Arguello Blvd., Clement, 33rd Ave. and Geary to Sutro Baths and the Cliff House. Owls.

3—**SUTTER AND JACKSON STS.**, from the Ferry Bldg. via Market, Sutter, Fillmore, Jackson, Presidio Ave. to California St., 6:53 a. m.— 1:05 a. m.; 6:31 a. m.—12:46 a. m.

5—**McALLISTER ST.**, from Ferry Bldg. via Market, McAllister, and Fulton Sts. to Golden Gate Park, Chutes at the Beach and Amusement Concessions. Owls.

Car routes are indicated by numbers

Ride the City-Wide Green Cars

6—HAIGHT AND MASONIC AVE. from Ferry Bldg. via Market, Haight, Masonic Ave., Frederick, Clayton, Carl, Stanyan, Parnassus, Judah, 9th Ave. to Pacheco. Owls.

7—HAIGHT AND OCEAN, from the Ferry Bldg. via Market, Haight, Stanyan, Frederick and Lincoln Way to Golden Gate Park, Chutes at the Beach, Amusement Concessions and Ocean Beach. Owls.

8—MARKET ST., from Ferry Bldg. via Market and Castro to 18th St. Owls. Cable from 18th (5:25 a. m.-1:30 a. m.) to 26th (5:33 a. m. to 1:22 a. m.)

9—VALENCIA ST., from the Ferry Bldg. via Market, Valencia and 29th to Noe St. Owl service to Daly City via Mission. No Owls on 29th. 5:50 a. m.-1:15 a. m.; 5:23 a. m.; 1:40 a. m.

10—SUNNYSIDE, from the Ferry Bldg. via Mission, 14th St., Guerrero, San Jose Ave., 30th St., Chenery, Diamond, Monterey Blvd. to Westwood Park. Terminates at 8th and Market Sts. and Sundays after 6:26 p. m. Owl service from 5th and Market—1:08 a. m. to 5:08 a. m.

11—MISSION AND 24TH STS., from the Ferry Bldg. via Mission, 22nd St., Chattanooga, 24th St. to Hoffman Ave. Return via 24th St., Dolores, 22nd, Mission to Ferry Bldg. 5:37 a. m.-12:30 a. m. Cross town Owl service from 24th and Utah Sts. to 24th and Hoffman, 1:01 a. m. to 4:31 a. m.

12—INGLESIDE AND OCEAN, from Ferry Bldg. via Mission, Onondaga, Ocean Ave. and Sloat Blvd. to Ocean and Fleishhacker Pool—6:30 a. m.-12:32 a. m.; 5:11 a. m.-1:09 a. m. After 6:20 p. m. downtown terminal at 5th and Market.

14—MISSION LINE, from the Ferry Bldg. via Mission St. and Mission Road to Daly City. To Colma and Cemeteries on certain holidays. Transfers to Visitacion Valley line. 5:50 a. m.-12:40 a. m.; 5:30 a. m.-11:57 p. m.

15—KEARNY AND NORTH BEACH, from the Southern Pacific station (Third and Townsend Sts.) via Third, Kearny, Broadway and Powell Sts. to North Beach. Owls.

16—3RD AND KEARNY STS., from the Ferry Bldg. via Embarcadero, Broadway, Kearny and 3rd Sts. to Sunnydale Ave.—5:52 a. m.-1:00 a. m.; 5:00 a. m.-12:15 a. m.

17—HAIGHT AND INGLESIDE, from the Ferry Bldg. via Market, Haight, Stanyan, Frederick, Lincoln Way, 20th Ave., Wawona and 19th Ave. to Sloat Blvd. On Sundays via Sloat Blvd. to Fleishhacker Pool. Owls.

18—DALY CITY, from 5th and Market via Mission to Daly City, 5th and Market—6:45 a. m.-12:16 a. m.; D. C.—6:11 a. m.-11:44 p. m. To Cemeteries on Sundays and certain holidays.

19—9TH AND POLK STS., from Brannan St. via 9th St., Larkin, Post, Polk to Fort Mason and North Point. Owls.

20—ELLIS AND O'FARRELL STS., from Southern Pacific Station (3rd and Townsend Sts.) via 4th St., Ellis, Hyde, O'Farrell, Divisadero and Oak Sts. to Golden Gate Park. Return via Page, Divisadero, Ellis and 4th Sts. to S. P. Station. S. P. Station—5:55 a. m.-1:00 a. m.; 5:24 a. m.-12:36 a. m.

21—HAYES ST., from the Ferry Bldg. via Market, Hayes, Stanyan, Fulton, 8th Ave. to Clement. 5:50 a. m.-1:15 a. m.; 6:25 a. m.-12:50 a. m.

22—FILLMORE ST., from 23rd and Third Sts. via 18th St., Connecticut, 17th St., Kansas, 16th St., Church, Duboce and Fillmore Sts., to Marina Blvd. Owls. Broadway to Marina—5:15 a. m.,-1:45 a. m.

23—FILLMORE AND VALENCIA STS., from Holly Park via Richland, Mission, Valencia, Gough, McAllister, Fillmore and Sacramento to Divisadero. Holly Park—5:39 a. m.-12:11 a. m.; Sacramento and Divisadero—6:12 a. m.-12:42 a. m.

24—MISSION AND RICHMOND, from Golden Gate Park via 8th Ave., Clement, 6th Ave., Lake, Sacramento, Divisadero, Page, Fillmore, Duboce, Church, 16th St., Mission, Cortland Ave. to Banks St. Park—5:24 a. m.-1:15 a. m.; Banks—5:21 a. m.-12:30 a. m.

25—SAN BRUNO AVE., from Market St. via 5th St., Bryant, Army and San Bruno Ave., to 3rd and Wilde Sts. Owls.

26—GUERRERO ST., from the Ferry Bldg. via Mission, 14th St., Guerrero, San Jose Ave., 30th St., Chenery, Diamond, San Jose Ave. to Daly City. Downtown terminal, 8th and Market and Sundays after 6:16 p. m. 6:10 a. m.-6:16 p. m.; 5:31 a. m.-12:15 a. m.

27—BRYANT ST., from Market St. via 2nd St., Bryant and 26th to Mission. Return via 26th St., Bryant, 8th, Brannan and 2nd Sts. Market—5:59 a. m.-5:50 p. m.; 5:36 a. m.-5:25 p. m. (Night service 26th St. from Bryant to Mission only. 6:19 p. m.-12:30 a. m.)

28—HARRISON ST., from the Ferry Bldg. via Embarcadero, Howard, Steuart, Harrison, Stanley Place, Bryant, 2nd, Brannan and 3rd Sts. to Southern Pacific Station (3rd and Townsend Sts.) 6:00 a. m.-12:12 a. m.; 5:48 a. m.-12:00 midnight.

29—KEARNY AND BROADWAY, from Broadway and Davis via Kearny and 3rd Sts. to Sunnydale Ave. Davis—6:53 a. m.-6:20 p. m.; 6 Mile House—6:27 a. m.-5:38 p. m.

Car routes are indicated by numbers

Ride the City-Wide Green Cars

30—ARMY ST., from Mission via 22nd, Howard, 26th, Folsom and Army Sts. to 3rd St. Mission—5:28 a.m.-12:15 a.m.; 5:43 a.m.-11:55 p.m.

31—BALBOA STREET LINE. Ferry via Market, Eddy, Divisadero, Turk, Balboa to 30th Ave. Return via Balboa, Turk, Mason, Eddy, Market. Owls.

33—18TH AND PARK, from 3rd St. via Harrison, 14th St., Guerrero, 18th St., Falcon, Caselli, Clayton, Ashbury, Frederick, Clayton, Waller to Golden Gate Park. (Terminates at 8th and Harrison Sts. after 6:20 p. m.) 5:32 a. m.-6:20 p. m.; Park—5:05 a. m.-12:23 a. m.

34—6TH AND SANSOME STS., from the Embarcadero via Sansome, Bush, Kearny, Post, Taylor and 6th to Brannan. Embarcadero—6:02 a. m.-6:22 p. m. Brannan—5:40 a. m.-6:00 p. m.

35—HOWARD ST., from the Ferry Bldg. via Embarcadero, Howard and 24th Sts. to Rhode Island St.—5:34 a. m.-12:36 a. m.; 5:10 a. m.-12:13 a. m.

36—FOLSOM ST., from the Ferry Bldg. via Embarcadero, Howard, Steuart, Folsom and Precita Sts.—5:30 a. m.-7:00 p. m.; 5:08 a. m.-6:36 p. m.

40—SAN MATEO INTERURBAN, from 5th and Market Sts. via 5th St., Mission and Peninsula Highway to Daly City, Colma, Cemeteries, Stanley (Tanforan), San Bruno, Millbrae, Lomita Park, Broadway, Burlingame, Hillsborough and San Mateo. Transfers to South San Francisco line. S. F.—6:10 a. m.-12:00 a. m.; Sat.—1:20 a. m.; S. M.—5:20 a. m.-1:05 a. m.

41—2ND AND MARKET STS., from 2nd and Market to S. P. Station, daily except Saturday afternoon, Sundays and holidays. Leave S. P. Station morning: 7:48, 8:03, 8:13, 8:23, 8:33, 8:43, 9:03, 9:23. Leave Market St. evening: 4:11, 4:51, 5:03, 5:15, 5:25, 5:37.

EIGHTH STREET LINE, from Market via 8th and Bryant Sts. to 16th St. Market—6:30 a. m.-5:50 p. m.; 6:20 a. m.-5:40 p. m.

VISITACION VALLEY, from Mission and Geneva to Visitacion Valley and San Bruno Ave. (6 Mile House). Mission—5:30 a. m.-12:35 a. m.; 6 Mile House—5:45 a. m.-12:55 a. m.

POWELL-JACKSON CABLE, from Powell and Market via Powell and Jackson to Steiner. Return via Washington and Powell to Market Market—6:10 a. m.-1:00 a. m.; Steiner—6:14 a. m.-12:40 a. m.

POWELL-BAY CABLE, from Powell and Market via Powell, Mason, Jackson, Columbus and Taylor to Bay St. Market—6:22 a. m.-12:55 a. m.; Bay—6:07 a. m.-12:40 a. m.

SACRAMENTO CABLE, from the Ferry Bldg. via Sacramento to Fillmore St. Return via Sacramento, Larkin and Clay Sts. 5:56 a. m.-1:00 a. m.; 6:16 a. m.-12:40 a. m.

MOTOR COACH LINES

MISSION ST. AND SAN BRUNO AVE., from Mission and Maynard, Craut, Silver Ave., San Bruno Ave., Felton, Bowdoin and Silver Ave. to Mission St. Lv. Mission—6:00 a. m.-12:20 a. m.

EXCELSIOR, from Mission and Silver Ave. via Silver, Edinburgh, Excelsior, Naples, Persia, Mission, Brazil, Moscow, Persia, Naples, Excelsior and Mission to Silver. Lv. Mission—5:45 a. m.-12:50 a. m.

CROCKER-AMAZON, from Mission and Persia Sts. via Persia, Naples, Cordova, Baltimore Way, South Hill Blvd., Naples, Russia to Mission. Mission—5:45 a. m.-12:55 a. m.

SOUTHERN HEIGHTS, from 16th and Bryant, San Bruno Ave., 19th St., Vermont St., 20th St., Rhode Island St., Southern Heights Blvd., 22nd St., Wisconsin St. to 23rd St. Return same route to 17th St. and San Bruno Ave., 17th St., Bryant to 16th St. Lv. Bryant 5:50 a. m., 11:40 p. m.

SUNSET, from 25th Ave., Lincoln Way, 24th Ave., Irving St., 25th Ave., Noriega St., 27th Ave., Moraga St., 25th Ave. and Lincoln Way. Lv. Lincoln Way 6:00 a. m., 12:00 a. m.

CAR STOPS

As a rule, all cars stop on the near side of the crossings. "Enter car here signs" are painted on the pavement at most loading points to indicate where the car entrance stops. Patrons can save themselves much time and trouble if they will stand at the spot so marked. In a few cases cable cars stop on the far side of the crossing, which is indicated by the previously described marker. An overhead "cars stop here" sign designates a few places where electric cars stop on the far side of the crossing. On Market Street the car stop marks on the inside tracks are located several feet back of those on the outside track, thus leaving the platform of the inside track cars clear for intending passengers. When both cars are approaching at once a hand signal to the inside track motorman will indicate you wish to board his car, but this signal is ordinarily unnecessary.

Car routes are indicated by numbers

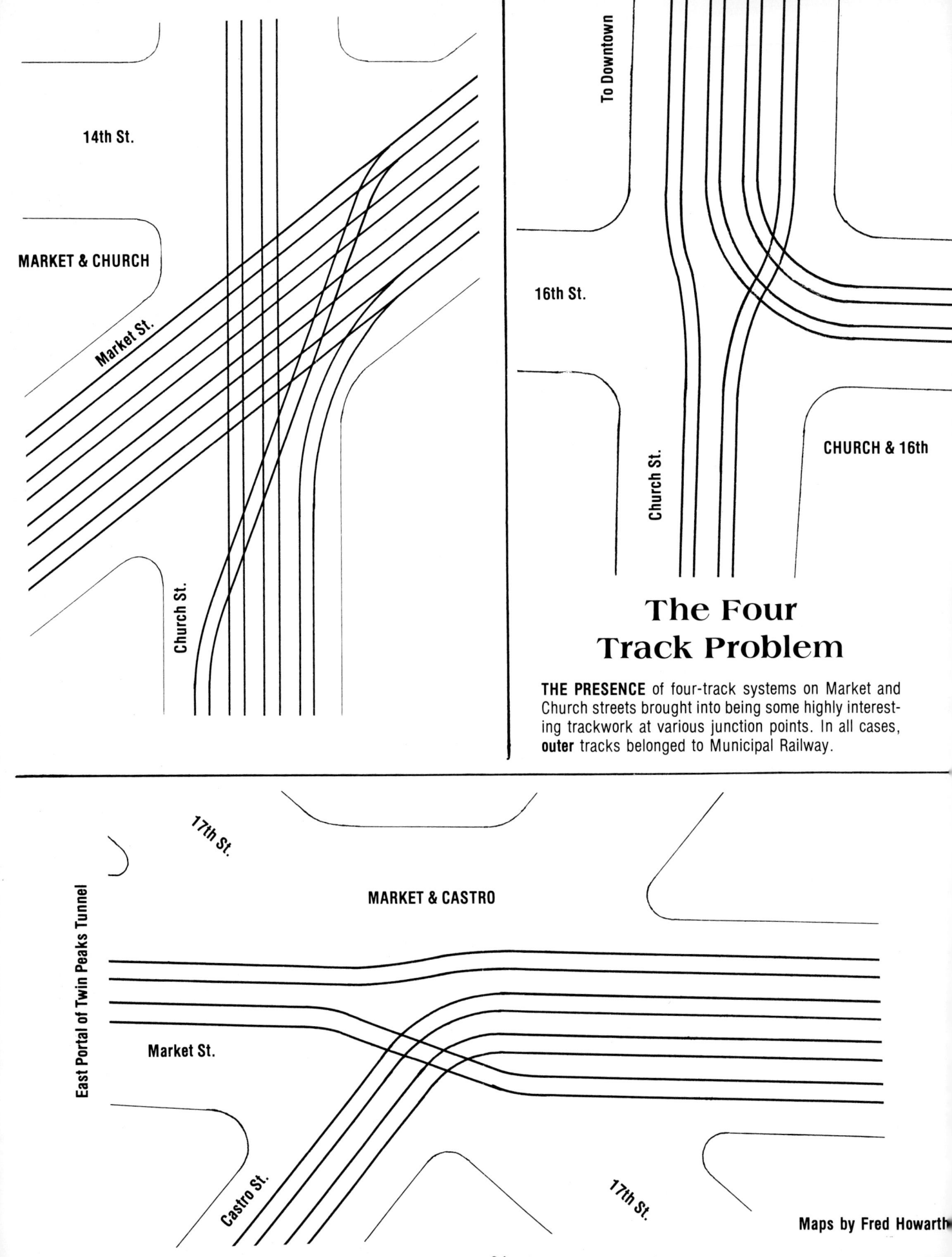

The Four Track Problem

THE PRESENCE of four-track systems on Market and Church streets brought into being some highly interesting trackwork at various junction points. In all cases, **outer** tracks belonged to Municipal Railway.

Maps by Fred Howarth

The Sutter Street Lines

The Sutter Street Lines—Routes #1, #2 and #3, used the outer tracks on lower Market St., switched onto Sutter St. and proceeded out that thoroughfare to Fillmore St. At that intersection, Route #3 branched off on Fillmore to Jackson, to Presidio Ave. and thence south to Calfornia St.

Route #2 continued out Sutter St. to Presidio Ave. and then followed Presidio, California, Parker Ave., Euclid Ave., Arguello Blvd., Clement, 33rd Ave., Geary, 48th Ave., and private right-of-way to a terminal at the Sutro Baths near the Cliff House. This was the only one of the Sutter St. lines which regularly operated all the way to the ocean.

Route #1 followed the same trackage as Route #2 as far as Parker Ave., then continued along California St. to 6th Ave. to Clement (where it joined #2 again), and then out to 33rd Ave., its usual terminal; at certain times its cars continued on out to Sutro Baths.

These three lines were all profitable ones. As of 1927, Route #1 showed a profit of $128,000; Route #2 had a black ink figure of $69,000; Route #3 showed a surplus of $50,000 (all figures given are before a seven percent return).

Groups I and II comprised all the MSR routes that operated on Market St. to the ferries. Together they comprised about 45 percent of the total car miles (electric) on the system and they earned about 70 percent of the operating surplus. They showed a net profit of $220,000 above a seven percent return; the balance of the MSR system showed a loss of $870,000 below a seven percent return.

The Mission Street Lines

The third group of MSR electric car lines consisted of the heavy trunk lines out Mission St. from the Embarcadero (ferries) to Daly City, plus their satellites. Lines found in Group III were:

#10—Sunnyside
#11—Mission and 24th streets
#12—Ingleside and Ocean
#14—Mission Street
#18—Daly City-Cemeteries
#26—Guerrero Street
—Visitacion Valley
#40—San Mateo Interurban
—Bosworth Street
—Parkside
—South San Francisco

Routes #10 and #26 left Mission at 14th St. thence via Guerrero St. and others to Diamond St. and San Jose Ave., where #10 switched off to follow Monterey Blvd. to Genesee Ave. in the Sunnyside district; #26 continued out San Jose Ave. to its junction with Mission St. in the heart of Daly City. Both lines were heavy losers. These lines did not run to the ferries after the evening rush hour but shared Route #30's terminal at 8th and Market streets.

Route #11—Mission and 24th streets, went out Mission from the Embarcadero to 22nd St., then followed 22nd St., Chattanooga, Dolores and 24th to Hoffman Ave. in Noe Valley. This line made a modest profit of $25,000 above seven percent on its appraised value.

Line #12—Ingleside and Ocean went out Mission St. to Onandaga Ave., thence over Onandaga and Ocean Ave. to Junipero Serra Blvd., then via private right-of-way in Junipero Serra and Sloat Blvds. to Ocean Beach near Fleishacker Pool. A curiosity of this line was the fact that Municipal Railway's "K" Line shared its trackage on Ocean Ave. to Brighton Ave. Faced with heavy competition from Muni, this line was a loser.

Route #14—Mission St. traversed the entire length of Mission St. within the city limits, starting at the ferries and terminating in Daly City. This was a profitable line, returning $43,000 above a seven percent return.

Route #18—Daly City-Cemeteries started at Market and 5th streets and used Mission St. from 5th St. all the way to Daly City; part of the time its cars continued on to serve the several cemeteries immediately south of Daly City. The #18 Line was not operated continuously, its operation being suspended during off-peak hours, but nevertheless (perhaps due to its curtailed service) it returned a small profit.

Route #40—San Mateo Interurban was unique in that it was San Francisco's one and only classic interurban operation, running from the Fifth and Market terminus to the city of San Mateo down the peninsula, achieving an average speed of 15.65 miles per hour because of the large percentage of its journey made on private right-of-way. Of course, from Daly City in, interurbans shared the Mission St. trackage with several local lines and their speed was but little greater, if any, than that of the slower cars. This was a profitable line, enjoying an operating surplus of $165,000 which translated into a net of about $17,500 above a seven percent return on the appraised valuation of this long line.

The Visitacion Valley route was unique in that it was a single-track, cross-country line, partly within and partly without the San Francisco city limits. Its chief function was to connect the Third and Kearny Line #16 with the Mission St. routes at Geneva Ave. It was owned by *The Gough Street Railroad Company* and was operated under lease by MSR. Originally built to stimulate real estate sales in Visitacion Valley, this line, despite its small size, was a champion money loser—showing an operating deficit of almost $22,000.

The Bosworth St. line was a little single-track affair, connecting with the Mission St. lines and losing just about as much money as its limited operations would permit. Probably this line should have been made a through route, going into downtown San Francisco over Mission St., but since Mission St. already had more than enough of such anaemic parasites it certainly did not need yet another.

Altogether the Mission Street group of lines posted a profit of $264,607 which became a deficit of $146,216 after being charged with a seven percent return on their appraised value. Without the San Mateo interurban line, the operating profit would have been much less and the final deficit below cost of service would have reached about $164,000. This would have been an even more dismal showing had it not been for the generally high operating speeds achieved by the lines in this group.

Route Mileages, Car Assignments and Car Types Operated

Compiled by James K. Gibson

Route	Name	ONE-WAY MILES 1929	ONE-WAY MILES 1943	PEAK CARS 1929	PEAK CARS 1943	1921-1925	1926-1930	1931-1935	1936-1940
1	Sutter and California	6.01	6.85	24	9	C	C	C	C
2	Sutter and Clement	7.39	7.39	28	10	C	C	C	C
3	Sutter and Jackson	3.78	3.52	16	10	BC	BC	CM	C
4	Turk and Eddy[1]	5.82	5.00	15	6	Q	QM	M	—
5	McAllister and Fulton	7.08	6.82	47	21	PQ	PM	M	M
6	Haight and Masonic	5.81	5.81	24	10	B	B	B	B
7	Haight and Ocean	7.96	7.71	26	13	BQ	B	B	B
8	Market St.	3.33	3.76	23	3	M	MQ	Q	Q
9	Valencia St.	4.78	5.28	31	19	Q	Q	Q	QM
10	Guerrero and Sunnyside	6.50	--	13	--	O	O	OM	M
11	Mission and 24th	4.79	4.79	20	9	O	OM	M	M
12	Mission and Ingleside	10.25	--	17	--	Q	QM	QMN	QN
14	Mission and Daly City	7.83	7.83	19	40	NQ	Q	Q	QM
15	Kearny and North Beach	2.64	--	15	--	Q	QM	QM	M
16	Third and Kearny	7.47	--	12	--	Q	Q	QM	M
17	Haight and Ingleside	7.70	7.25	20	12	B	B	B	B
18	Mission and Daly City	6.77	--	23	--	OQN	OQN	Q	—
19	9th and Polk	2.79	2.10	17	1	G	M	M	M
20	4th-Ellis-O'Farrell[2]	4.52	8.02	22	19	Q	Q	M	M
21	Hayes	5.24	5.24	25	17	P	PQ	QP	B
22	Fillmore and 16th	5.11	4.55	30	25	O	OM	M	M
23	Fillmore and Valencia	5.08	--	9	--	O	OM	M	—
24	Mission and Richmond	7.32	--	13	--	O	OM	MP	M
25	San Bruno Ave.	5.35	5.35	15	8	OLI	OLPI	P	MZ
26	Guerrero and Daly City	8.03	8.05	14	2	O	OM	M	—
27	Bryant St.	3.89	--	13	--	FOLI	FOLGPI	PXZ	Z
28	Harrison and Depots	1.47	--	6	--	HJ	HJGM	MX	Z
29	Kearny and Broadway	6.36	--	14	--	Q	Q	M	M
30	8th and Army	5.76	--	7	--	FJ	FG	M	G
31	Balboa	--	5.69	--	18	—	—	M	M
32	Hayes and Oak	4.10	--	7	--	BQ	Q	—	—
33	18th and Park	4.90	--	9	--	K	K	K	TC
34	6th and Sansome	2.83	--	9	--	JGH	G	G	—
35	Howard St.	4.62	--	11	--	OFGIL	OFGPIL	PVWX	—
36	Folsom St.	4.44	4.44	7	6	OFGIL	OFGIP	PWX	—
40	San Mateo Interurban	19.98	19.98	16	11	AN	N	N	N
41	2nd and Market—SP Depot	1.01	--	3	--	—	GQI	QGMX	MZ
42	1st and 5th	2.60	--	2	--	—	—	M	M
--	Fillmore Hill	0.87	--	4	--	E	E	E	E
--	10th and Post	2.27	--	1	--	E	—	—	—
--	Visitacion Valley	2.32	--	2	--	★	O	OGY	Y
--	Divisadero Extension	0.18	--	1	--	E	E	E	—
--	Bosworth St.	0.73	--	1	--	E	E	—	—
--	South San Francisco	2.88	--	3	--	OM	OM	OMX	MX
	Total Streetcars:			**634**	**269**				
--	Washington and Jackson	2.23	2.23	14	11	T	T	T	T
--	Powell and Mason	1.61	1.61	8	7	T	T	T	T
--	Sacramento and Clay	2.28	--	10	--	S	S	S	S
--	Castro St.	0.90	--	5	--	R	R	R	R
--	Pacific Ave.	1.14	--	2	--	U	U	—	—
	Total Cable Cars:			**39**	**18**				
	Total Cars, Electric and Cable:			**673**	**287**				

(1) Sutter-Sacramento in 1943
(2) Ellis-O'Farrell and Kearny in 1943

Data from: 1929: Street Railway Requirements of San Francisco, O'Shaughnessy, page 129.
1943: California Railroad Commission Staff Ex #10 in Case 4680, July 15, 1943, Table 2-1.

Note: 1943 listing of peak cars does not reflect certain important factors such as partial bus substitution, inability to obtain full crews due to wartime manpower shortages, as well as certain line consolidations such as #14 and #18 lines.

Car Type Code:

A 1-12, Suburban, Flush Platform
B 101-180, PAYE, Drop Platform
C 201-265, PAYE, Drop
E 601-662, Single Truck California
F 681-697, PAYE, Flush
G 701-724, PAYE, Flush
H 727-730, PAYE, Flush
I 731-745, PAYE, Flush
J 751-755, PAYE, Flush
K 756-771, PAYE, Flush
L 772-778, PAYE, Flush
M 266-305, 778-994, PAYE, Drop
N 1225-1244, PAYE, Interurban, Drop
O 1301-1423, PAYE, Flush
P 1500-1549, PAYE, Drop
Q 1500-1749, PAYE, Drop
V 402-406, PAYE, One-Man, Flush
W 407-410, PAYE, One-Man, Flush
X 725-734, PAYE, One-Man, Drop
Y 735-736, PAYE, One-Man, Drop
Z 740-759, PAYE, One-man, Drop
★ 698-699, Non-PAYE, Drop and Flush
TC Trolley Coach

Cable Cars

R 1-7, Double end, California, Standard gauge
S 15-26, Double end, California, 3' 6" gauge
T 501-527, Single end, Powell type
U Pacific Ave. train

Market Street Railway Company, 1922-1944: Vital Statistics

Year	Revenue Passengers (000) Rail	Bus	Total	Passenger Revenue Rail and Bus	Miles of Track	Car Miles (000)
1922			191,925	$9,517,316	289	25,092
1923			196,515	9,745,825	289	25,391
1924			197,376	9,788,393	289	25,768
1925			198,278	9,829,219	289	25,807
1926			198,031	9,815,087	289	26,572
1927			196,556	9,739,558	285	26,666
1928			193,767	9,668,384	284	26,764
1929	193,523	906	194,429	9,504,931	281	26,060
1930	185,554	906	186,460	9,112,106	280	25,400
1931	173,511	879	174,390	8,488,343	280	24,300
1932	157,656	1,125	158,781	7,739,168	285	23,600
1933	149,825	1,118	150,943	7,347,445	285	22,800
1934	147,514	1,100	148,614	7,225,951	285	22,000
1935	148,733	1,042	149,775	7,260,560	273	22,000
1936	152,925	986	153,911	7,437,039	269	20,400
1937	141,073	899	141,972	7,115,448	266	19,500
1938	110,874	913	111,787	6,415,758	265	17,900
1939	93,288	2,275	95,563	6,366,996	255	16,100
1940	79,629	10,295	89,924	6,011,855	252	13,800
1941	71,477	18,378	89,855	6,010,757	234	12,000
1942	84,849	26,554	111,403	7,515,637	220	11,800
1943			124,700	8,499,787		
1944			126,629	8,725,932		

Sources

Ex 10, California Railroad Commission Staff Exhibit dated July 15, 1943, in Case #4680; also, "Street Railway Transportation Requirements of San Francisco," 1929, by M.M. O'Shaughnessy. Data for "Revenue Passengers" from Ex 10, Table 3-2, and page 16. Data for "Passenger Revenue" from Ex 10, Table 3-1. Data for "Miles of Track Operated (Equivalent Single Track)" from Ex 10, Chart 2-1. Data for "Car Miles" from O'Shaughnessy (1922-1928) from Ex 10, Tables 4-19 and 4-15 (1929-1942). Data for "Revenue Passengers" and "Passenger Revenue" for 1943 and 1944 from California Railroad Commission-203 Reports. 1944 figures are for 12 months, including two months under City of San Francisco operation. (Courtesy James K. Gibson, California PUC)

South Side Lines

Group IV consisted of those lines operating in that part of the city south of Market Street—the revered "South of the Slot," so much a part of the lore of San Francisco back in the pre-1906 cable car era.

In this group were the following lines:

Route #25—San Bruno Avenue
Route #27—Bryant Street
Route #28—Harrison Street
Route #30—Army Street
Route #35—Howard Street
Route #36—Folsom Street

These lines were all money losers and taken together toted up an operating loss of $102,477—which translated into a deficit of more than $330,000 below a seven percent return.

Route #25—San Bruno Avenue operated from 5th and Market via 5th, Bryant, Army and San Bruno Ave. to Wilde St. and 3rd. Mere operation of this line cost MSR $13,500 annually and this increased to a deficit of more than $65,000 after taking into account the seven percent return on appraised valuation.

Route #27—Bryant ran from a 2nd and Market terminal via 2nd, Bryant and Brannan and 26th to Mission. Line #27 lost about $27,000 a year in operating expenses alone.

Route #28—Harrison St. was a short line which ran from the ferries at the foot of Market St. to the Southern Pacific Depot at 3rd and Townsend. It ran on the east pair of the four tracks on the Embarcadero at the ferries. It lost about $7,000 in operating costs which increased to a loss of more than $20,000 after taking into account a seven percent return on its valuation.

Route #30—Army St. started on 8th St. at Market, then meandered all over the south side before achieving a terminal at 22nd and Mission streets. Its operting loss was a whopping $39,000 which became a deficit of $77,000 if a seven percent return were figured in.

Route #35—Howard Street ran from the ferries via the Embarcadero, Howard and 24th streets to Rhode Island St. Its operating loss was about $7,500 and its deficiency below a seven percent return on its appraised value was about $56,000.

Route #36—Folsom Street operated from the ferries via the Embarcadero, Howard, Steuart, Folsom and Precita streets. Its operating loss was about $8,000 annually and its deficit below a seven percent return was about $46,500.

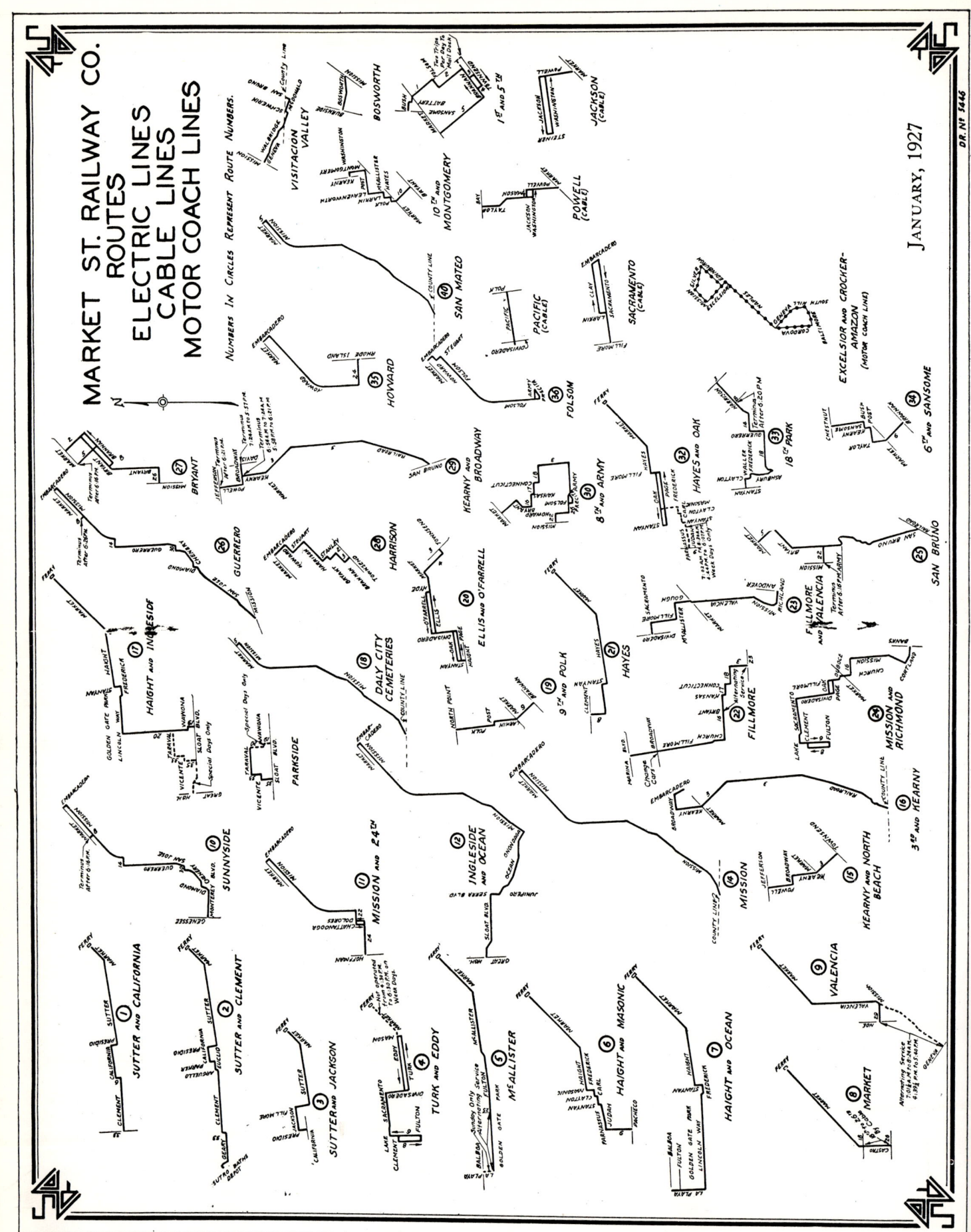

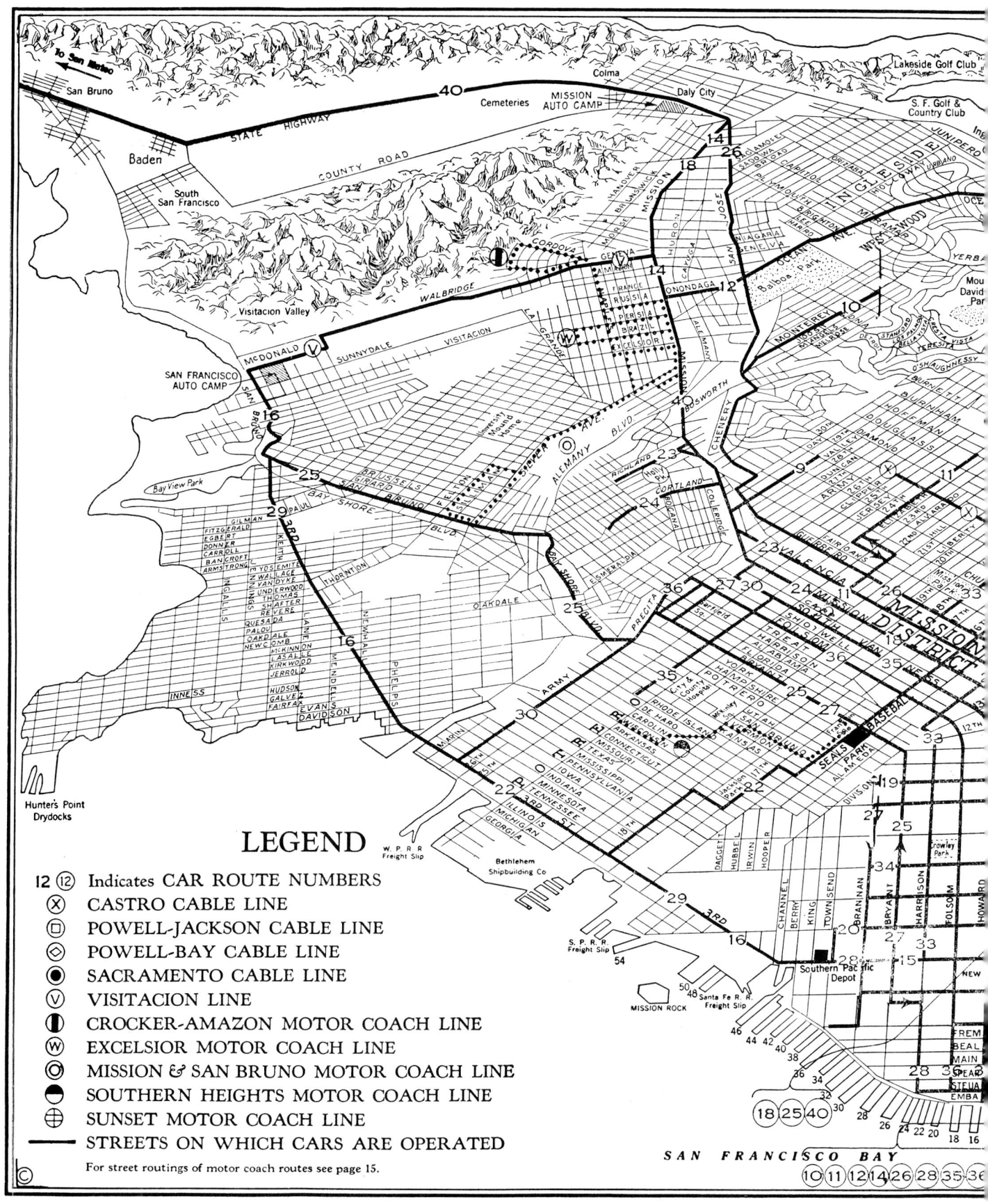

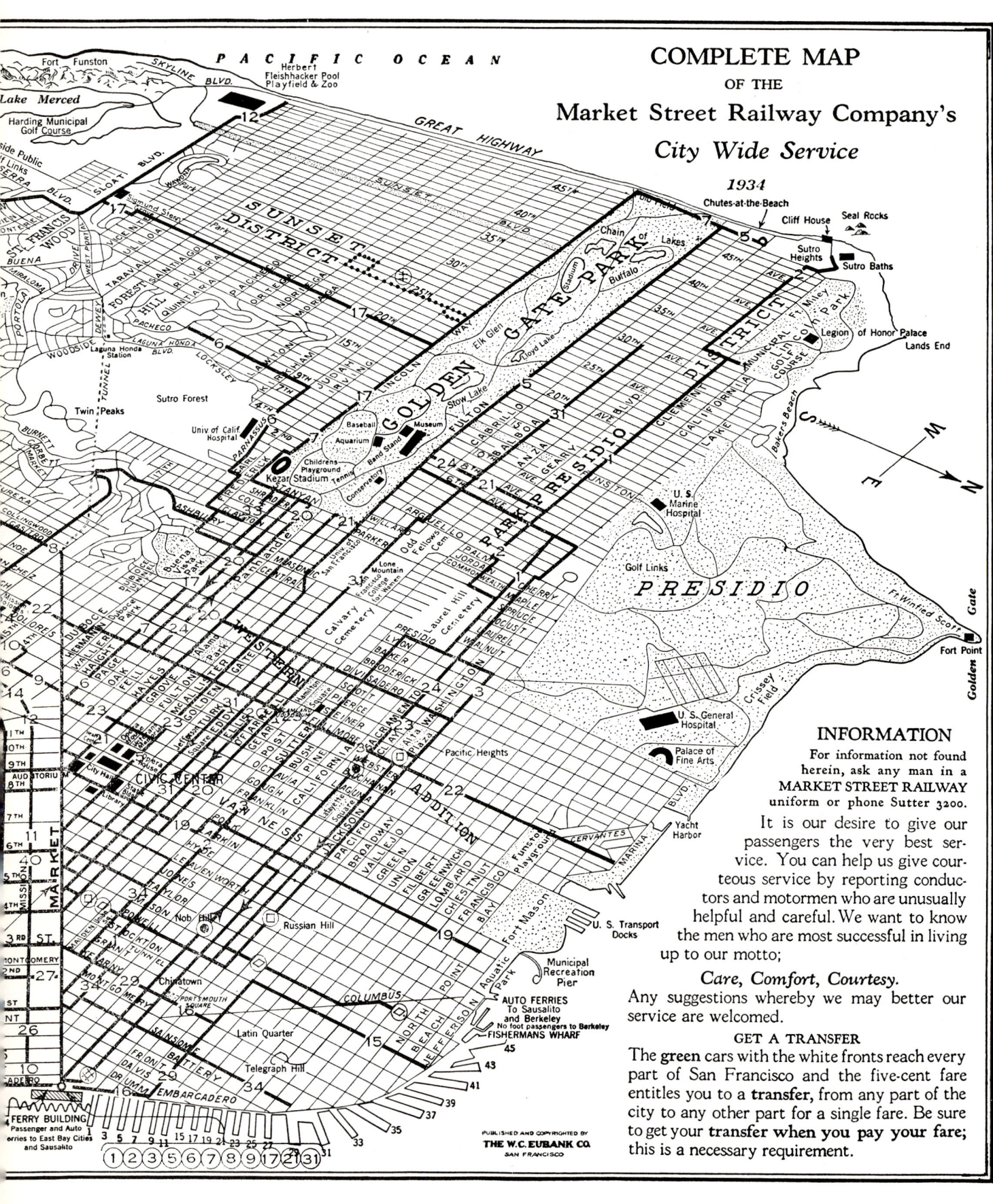

The Third Street Lines

Considered as a whole, the Third Street group of lines was profitable. Three lines were in this category according to MSR's published route descriptions, but the company's monthly statistics put all Third St. operations under but two routes. The three routes described were:

Route #15—Kearny and North Beach
Route #16—Third and Kearny streets
Route #29—Kearny and Broadway

Apparently in its accounting procedure, MSR put #29 in with #16. This group, taken as a whole, showed an operating profit of nearly $157,000 and a net of $43,000 above a seven percent return. Line #15, by itself, showed a small deficiency of $4,000 below seven percent, but Route #16 and #29 showed a net of $47,000.

Route #15 had its northern terminus at North Beach but Route #16 traveled around by way of Broadway and the Embarcadero to the ferries, where it terminated at the north side of the ferry loop.

On the south end, Route #15 terminated at the 3rd and Townsend depot of the Southern Pacific, but Line #16 continued on out Third St. and San Bruno Ave. to the county line at Six Mile House where it connected with Visitacion Valley Line.

The Crosstown Lines

Of the eleven lines comprising this grouping, only three showed an operating profit and but two could post a surplus of income above a seven percent return on their appraised value. Taken together, these lines showed an operating loss of $27,434 and a deficiency of $361,976 below a seven percent return.

Lines which we include in the crosstown group are:

Route #19—Ninth and Polk
Route #20—Ellis and O'Farrell
Route #22—Fillmore Street
Route #23—Fillmore and Valencia
Route #24—Mission and Richmond
Route #33—18th and Park
Route #34—6th and Sansome
Route #37—10th and Montgomery
Route #41—2nd and Market
　　　—Divisadero Hill
　　　—First and Fifth streets

Route #19—Ninth and Polk streets was profitable, its operating surplus being nearly $65,000 and its net over a seven percent return about $24,000. It ran from Brannan St. via 9th, Larkin, Post and Polk to Fort Mason and North Point.

Route #20—Ellis and O'Farrell was also profitable; it posted an operating profit of about $69,000 and had a net above a seven percent return of about $13,000. It operated from the Southern Pacific Depot at Third and Townsend streets via Townsend, 4th, crossed Market into Ellis St., and followed Ellis and O'Farrell streets to Divisadero; from there cars on this line reached Golden Gate Park at Stanyan St. by way of Divisadero, Oak and Page streets. Muni long had had its eyes on the 4th St. tracks of this line, for by connecting them with its Line F—Stockton St. across Market St. a very fine through route to the S.P. Depot would be created; as a

Maximum Number of Cars Operated by Lines on January 8, 1932

Line	Route	Maximum Cars Operated
1	Sutter-California	21
2	Sutter-Clement	24
3	Sutter-Jackson	16
4	Turk-Eddy	16
5	McAllister	45
6	Haight-Masonic	19
7	Haight-Ocean	21
8	Market	20
9	Valencia	26
10	Sunnyside	12
11	Mission-24th	18
12	Ingleside	17
14	Mission	14
15-29	Third & Kearny	26
16	Third St.	13
17	Haight-Ingleside	23
18	Daly City & Cemeteries	15
19	Ninth, Polk & Larkin	17
20	Ellis & O'Farrell	18
21	Hayes	27
22	Fillmore-16th	24
23	Fillmore & Valencia	9
24	Mission & Richmond	11
25	San Bruno Ave.	13
26	Guerrero	13
27	Bryant	10
28	Harrison	6
30	Eighth & Eighteenth	6
32	Hayes & Oak	3
33	Eighteenth & Park	8
34	Sixth & Sansome	9
35	Howard	10
36	Folsom	7
40	San Mateo Interurban	16
41	Second & Market-Depot	3
	Visitacion	2
	Divisadero	1
	Tenth & Post	1
	First & Fifth	3
	South San Francisco	2
	Sacramento & Clay Cable	10
	Powell & Mason Cable	9
	Washington & Jackson Cable	14
	Castro Cable	5
	Crocker-Amazon Motor Coach	2
	Silver Ave. Motor Coach	2
	Excelsior Motor Coach	2

Maximum Totals:
　Electric Cars　　565
　Cable Cars　　　38
　Motor Coaches　　6
　　Grand Total　609

matter of fact, this was actually carried out after the acquisition of MSR by Muni in 1944.

Route #22—Fillmore St. ran from 23rd and 3rd streets via 18th St., Connecticut, 17th, Kansas, 16th, Church, Duboce and Fillmore streets to Broadway. Here those passengers who desired to continue down the steep grade to the Marina had to transfer to the Fillmore counterbalance cars—single truckers whose mode of operation was to hook onto a cable so that a car coming uphill would balance a car going down the severe grade. With the financial drag of the counterbalance operation included, this line lost about $12,000 directly, which increased to a seven percent loss of nearly $86,000. This was a long crosstown operation and a large percentage of its patrons boarded via transfers.

Route #23—Fillmore and Valencia was a money loser. From Sacramento and Divisadero this line operated via Sacramento, Fillmore, McAllister, Gough, Valencia, Mission and Richland. Line 23 lost nearly $20,000 annually and this mounted to nearly $50,000 below a seven percent return on value.

Route #24—Mission and Richmond ran from Cortland Ave. and Banks St. to 8th Ave. and Fulton St. via Cortland, Mission, 16th, Church, Duboce, Fillmore, Page, Divisadero, Sacramento, Lake, 6th Ave. and Fulton St. Cars returned via 8th Ave., Clement to 6th Ave. and Oak St. between Divisadero and Fillmore. This line had an operating loss of $15,000 and a deficit of $51,000 below a seven percent return.

Route #33—18th and Park started on Harrison St. at 3rd and then ran via Harrison, 14th, Guerrero, 18th, Market, Clayton, Ashbury, Frederick, Clayton and Waller streets to a terminus at Waller and Stanyan at Golden Gate Park. This line lost $40,000 per year out of pocket, and its deficit below a seven percent return was more than $82,000. This dismal showing doubtless went far in causing this line to be changed over to one-man trolley coach operation in 1935.

Route #34—Sixth and Sansome operated at the slow speed of 6.29 mph, even slower than the cable lines. It was a comparatively light line but even so was able to run up an operating loss of about $28,000—a deficiency of $55,000 when the line was charged with seven percent return on its appraised value.

Route #37—Tenth and Montgomery was another heavy loser. Before its Montgomery St. franchise was surrendered it lost nearly $22,000 a year on operation—and ran about $40,000 behind a return of seven percent on its appraised value. So undesired was this line along Montgomery St. that financiers reportedly paid MSR $18,000 as an inducement to withdraw the little single-truck cars.

Route #41—Second and Market, operating between the Southern Pacific Depot and Market St. on a "meet the trains" basis, rolled up the magnificent operating surplus of $250, which speedily translated into a deficiency of about $115 when charged with a seven percent return.

The Divisadero Hill line, which could have been considered an extension of Route #23, was one of the most decrepit lines on the system. It gave but little service yet managed to set an operating deficit of nearly $20,000 annually—to which had to be added about $1,400 for return on the appraised value of the property used.

The First and Fifth streets line was another route of so little importance that no route number was assigned to it. Its cars traveled sporadically from a dead end on Battery St. at California St. to the S.P. Depot; sometimes the cars even found their way along Townsend, 4th, Brannan and 5th to Market. Rendering but little service, this line was able to amass an operating loss of about $5,500, which grew to a $13,000 deficit when charged with a seven percent return.

These, then, were MSR's trolley lines as evaluated by expert Wilcox and his staff in 1928. Now, the individual histories of these lines as compiled from official records by the author:

On The Rocks

THE OCCASIONAL SHIPWRECK in the Land's End area of the Golden Gate was a mammoth generator of traffic for the #1—Cliff Line. The car line was usually the only method of transportation in this rugged area, and such a calamity was sure to strain MSR's resources in coping with the throngs who came to gawk. Seen here is the tanker LYMAN STEWART on the rocks on October 8, 1922 (a total loss). More than 100 trippers operated on the #1 Line on this date.
Lorin Silliman

1—Sutter and California

ROUTE: From ferry to 48th-Point Lobos Station, via Market, Sutter, Presidio, California, 6th Ave., Clement and private right-of-way, 7.75 miles. Dash sign colors: orange and red to 1925, then blue.

HISTORY: Began operating as an electric line on May 26, 1905, from Presidio Ave. and Sutter St. to Point Lobos Ave. via Presidio and Sutter and the Land's End right-of-way. On July 4, 1906, operation was extended down Sutter to Market, thence over the outer Market St. tracks to the ferry. On June 1, 1908, inner terminus was cut back to Sansome and Sutter due to a dispute with the city over its franchise; horse cars shuttled passengers from there to the ferry. Service to the ferry was restored on June 3, 1913. On September 5, 1915, the franchise on California St. from 6th Ave. to 33rd Ave. was taken over by the city; this line was thereupon diverted to 6th Ave. and Clement St. On February 7, 1925, operation on the private right-of-way around Land's End ceased due to a washout; outer terminus became 33rd Ave. and Clement St.

On September 29, 1944, Line #1 became the property of Municipal Railway. On November 5, 1945, its outer terminal became 45th Ave. after 6:30 A.M.; the outer terminal became Sutro Depot after 5:12 P.M. on that same day. On February 24, 1947, streetcars were operated only from 45th to Sansome, weekdays only, 9:00 A.M. to 4:00 P.M., a distance of 6.22 miles. October 5, 1947, saw streetcar service operated only until 6:46 P.M. weekdays, 6:16 P.M. Saturdays, with cars running from 45th to Sansome; buses took over from 48th and Pt. Lobos to Sansome St. on weekday nights, Saturday nights and all day Sundays. Three days later cars began operating through to the ferries from 9:00 A.M. to 4:00 P.M.. On July 3, 1949, all streetcar service on this line gave way to motor coach operation. All tracks were removed from Sutter St. during the first half of 1950. On January 20, 1951, motor coaches ran for the last time on this line; next day trolley coach line #1 began operating.

CONVERTING THE OLD STEAM LINE to electric operation at Land's End, United Railroads' work cars toil on both track and overhead, in 1905. This became the #1 Line. **United Railroads**

At Land's End

THIS EARTH SLIDE, on February 7, 1925, put the scenic Land's End line out of business, and thereafter the #1 Line was cut back to 33rd Ave. and Clement St.
Courtesy Mrs. C.D. Miller

THE LAND'S END LINE . . . lonely and breathtakingly beautiful . . . was a part of the #1 Line until the 1925 washout. Car 240, with URR insignia painted over but without MSR lettering, is signed for the #2 Line in this company-posed shot on the Cliff Line in 1921. Occasionally a regular #2 car might be routed this way, especially when crowds traveled to see the entry of noteworthy ships through the Golden Gate. **United Railroads**

2—Sutter and Clement

ROUTE: From ferry to Sutro Baths terminal via Market, Sutter, Presidio, California, Parker, Euclid, Arguello, Clement, 33rd Ave., Geary, 48th Ave. and on private right-of-way, 7.50 miles. Color of sign: red.

HISTORY: Started operation as *Sutro Railroad* on February 1, 1896, running from Presidio and Sutter to Sutro Baths Terminal via Central (Presidio Ave.), California, Williamson Ave. (Parker), Euclid, First Ave. (Arguello), Clement, Point Lobos, 48th Ave. and private right-of-way. On March 18, 1902, Sutro Railroad was taken over by United Railroads. On July 4, 1906, this line opened on Sutter St., Presidio to Market St. History to ferry same as #1 line.

With Municipal Railway taking over this line on September 29 1944, Line #2 entered its last era as a streetcar operation. O February 24, 1947, this line ran from Sutro Depot to an inner te minal at Sansome St. between the hours of 9:00 A.M. and 4: P.M. on weekdays. On October 6, 1947, partial bus operatic commenced, with cars running until 6:46 P.M. on weekdays ar until 6:16 P.M. Saturdays with buses taking over after those hou and all day Sundays, running from Pt. Lobos to Sansome. B three days later cars resumed running through to the ferries fro 9:00 A.M. to 4:00 P.M. with buses continuing to aid. This line w cut back to 45th and Geary on February 12, 1949, due to t burning of its Sutro Terminal. It was converted to bus operatic on July 3, 1949.

THE SUTRO BATHS-CLIFF HOUSE terminal of the #2—Sutter and Clement Line contained hot dogs, coffee, protection from the elements; and lots of streetcars! This shot was taken in 1928.
S.F. Public Utilities Commission

THE NUMBER 2 LINE had a dramatic terminus hard by Sutro Baths, above the Pacific. (RIGHT) Two #2 cars pass at the double-tracked terminal at the ocean resort, in 1938. Dash signs call attention to a dead whale washed up at Point Lobos; such events ranked with shipwrecks for "rubberneckers" and produced big crowds on the cars.

(BELOW) A car winds down the twisting way from 48th Avenue and Point Lobos, the #2 Line terminus, in this 1938 view.

BOTH: W.C. Whittaker

A UNIQUE STRUCTURE was this, the Sutro Baths-Cliff House terminal, seen in this 1928 view with its freshly installed Byllesby emblem and paint. It was destroyed by fire on February 12, 1949.

S.F. Public Utilities Commission

3—Sutter and Jackson

ROUTE: From ferries to Presidio and California via Market, Sutter, Fillmore, Jackson and Presidio, a distance of 3.75 miles. Color of dash sign: green.

HISTORY: Began operation as an electric line on July 4, 1906. On March 19, 1911, this line enjoyed the first operation of Pay As You Enter cars in San Francisco. History to ferry same as #1 line.

Muni took over operation of this line on September 29, 1944. On October 7, 1945, Line #3 was transferred to Muni's Geary Street Division. A service change occurred exactly one year later: streetcar service until 7:00 P.M. weekdays and Saturdays, bus service after 7:00 P.M. weekdays and Saturdays and all day Sundays from Presidio Ave. to an inner terminal at Van Ness and Sutter. On February 24, 1947, the cars' inner terminal became Sansome St., but on October 8, 1947, the turnback at Market St. was eliminated with cars continuing through to the ferries. On August 1, 1948, cars of this line were moved to Sutro Division, operating shuttle service between Sutter and Fillmore and the East Bay Terminal. Last day of streetcar operation on Line #3 was July 2, 1949, with buses taking over. The buses were themselves succeeded by trolley coaches on January 21, 1951.

THE SPLENDOR of Golden Gate Park unfolds behind #4 car 812, when its smoking sections were not glassed in and it still had wooden seating. **Market Street Railway**

4—Turk and Eddy

ROUTE: From ferries to 6th Ave. and Fulton via Market, Eddy, (Turk St. inbound) Divisadero, Sacramento, Arguello, Lake, 6th Ave., Clement, 8th Ave., Fulton to 6th Ave. Inbound via 6th Ave. Distance, 5.75 miles.

HISTORY: Began as electric line on February 1, 1897. On May 15, 1932, its route on Turk and Eddy was taken over by the new #31—Eddy and Balboa line. Single car owl service continued over the old route until June 16, 1935. On that date this line began operating as a new line, running from ferries via Market, Sutter, Fillmore, Sacramento and via old route to 6th and Fulton; its name was then changed to Sutter and Sacramento Line. Dash signs were blue for Turk and Eddy, blue and yellow for Sutter and Sacramento. Buses partially replaced cars on April 14, 1940, running after 6:30 P.M. weekdays, all day Sundays and holidays from the Park to Fillmore and Sutter; no cars ran from Fillmore to the ferry while buses operated.

On September 29, 1944, Municipal Railway took over operation of this line, and made its terminals 6th and Fulton and the East Bay Terminal, five miles. On October 8, 1945, Line #4's cars were transferred to the McAllister Division where they remained until December 9, 1946, when they were taken to Geary Division. Starting February 24, 1947, cars were turned back at a new inner terminal: Sansome St. on weekdays between 9:00 A.M. and 4:00 P.M., but on October 8, 1947, cars were again routed through to East Bay Terminal. July 31, 1948, was the last day of streetcar operation.

But the replacement motor coach service was not to last long. Bus line #4 on July 5, 1949, was discontinued from 6th and Fulton, then began running from Sansome and Sutter via Sutter to Divisadero. On September 24, 1949, even this service was discontinued, it being felt that the area was served sufficiently well by Lines 1 and 2.

PLAYLAND AT THE BEACH was the big weekend attraction for #5 Line riders. Its premier ride was "The Big Dipper," shown above as an atmospheric backdrop for car 111 as it departs for the downtown section in 1941, at Fulton and La Playa.

Charles Smallwood

5—McAllister

ROUTE: From ferries to the beach at La Playa and Balboa loop via Market, McAllister, private right-of-way and Fulton St., a distance of 6.75 miles.

HISTORY: This was originally a cable line and was rebuilt into an electric railway after the disaster of 1906. As of 1906, a shuttle car was operated along Fulton from 12th Ave. to 24th Ave. On March 13, 1911, this line was extended to the beach with all cars operating through. Color of dash sign: yellow.

Municipal Railway operation started September 29, 1944, with this line operating between Balboa and La Playa and the East Bay Terminal, 6.91 miles. On November 18, 1946, buses were substituted for cars after 7:00 P.M. weekdays and Saturdays and all day on Sunday, operating from Balboa and La Playa to an inner terminal at McAllister and Jones. On March 10, 1947, cars were turned back also at McAllister and Jones, due to track reconstruction, between 9:00 A.M. and 4:00 P.M.. Track rebuilding was completed to Eddy St. and through operation to the East Bay Terminal was resumed on October 2, 1947. Another track rebuilding project on Market St. caused all cars to terminate at Jones and Market after March 15, 1948—which condition prevailed until streetcar operation on Line #5 was abandoned, with bus operation taking over on June 6, 1948. This line was converted to trolley coach operation on July 3, 1949.

6—Haight and Masonic

ROUTE: From ferries to 9th Ave. and Pacheco via Market, Haight, Masonic, Frederick, Clayton, Carl, Stanyan, Parnassus, Judah and 9th Ave., 5.75 miles.

HISTORY: On February 7, 1916, this line started as a new line. On July 12, 1943, the inner terminal was changed to Haight and Fillmore after 6:30 P.M. weekdays and all day Sundays and holidays. On October 19, 1945, this line was changed to bus operation after 6:30 P.M. weekdays and all day Sundays and holidays, operating only to an inner terminal at Haight and Masonic with no service to or from the ferries at night or Sundays; streetcars ran through at other hours. Color of dash signs: blue.

On December 9, 1946, this line was moved to the McAllister Division. On March 15, 1948, all cars were rerouted to the Ferry Building via Mission St. due to track work on Market from Eddy to Gough. April 26, 1948, saw cars of this line turned back at Market and Gough, because of track work on Market St. This track work was duly completed, and on June 7, 1948, cars resumed running down Market to the ferries. July 3, 1948, was the final day of streetcar operation on this line; buses took over the following day, and were in turn succeeded by trolley coaches on July 3, 1949.

This route was known as the "Hayes and Masonic" line from June 10, 1906, to February 7, 1917. The Hayes-Masonic line was entended from 3rd Ave. and Parnassus to 9th Ave. and Pacheco on June 15, 1912.

CLIMBING HAIGHT STREET, #7 Car 121 heads to Playland and the beach in 1933. **Charles Smallwood**

7—Haight Street

ROUTE: From ferry to Haight and Stanyan by way of Market and Haight streets, 7.75 miles.

HISTORY: Originally a cable line. Started as an electric line on December 26, 1906. On February 7, 1916, this line was extended over the former #20 Line to the beach at La Playa and Balboa via Stanyan, Frederick, Lincoln Way and private way through Golden Gate Park and was renamed the Haight and Ocean Line. On December 23, 1945, alternate cars ran to 20th Ave. and Lincoln Way, due to abandonment of #17 Line. Owl service was provided. Dash signs were red.

Cars of this line were headquartered at McAllister Division after December 9, 1946, due to abandonment of Haight Division. Buses took over the outer end of #7 Line on February 23, 1947; cars terminated at Lincoln Way and 47th and buses ran from there to Balboa and La Playa. Buses provided owl service after May 11, 1947, running only to Van Ness and Market. Another service change became effective on February 8, 1948: the outer terminal was established at Waller and Stanyan evenings, Sundays and holidays, with bus line #20 providing service from Stanyan to Playland (La Playa and Balboa). Streetcar service was suspended entirely on evenings, Sundays and holidays starting March 14, 1948, due to extension of Line #20.

The next day all cars were rerouted to the Ferry via Mission St. due to track work on Market St. from Eddy to Gough. On April 26, 1948, #7 Line's cars were turned back at Gough and Market, due to track reconstruction on Market St. On June 7, 1948, this work had been completed and cars resumed running to the ferry. Final day of streetcar operation was July 3, 1948, with buses taking over the following day. Buses gave way to trolley coaches one year later to the day.

FERRY-BOUND Haight Street car 122 speeds over the picturesque right-of-way in Golden Gate Park along Ocean Beach. This #7 Line track was the only trolley operation permitted in the famous park, dating back to the old steam railroad line of the pre-park era. **Charles Smallwood**

(ABOVE) **WADING THROUGH** high water at Market and Church streets on a wintry day in 1931, #8 car 1569 seems to be winning its race with that Willys Knight at left. (RIGHT) **AT THE 18th AND CASTRO** terminus of the #8—Market Line. Car 1553 was one of a half-dozen cars of its class to survive into Municipal Railway days and was the only one in its entire class (originally 200 cars) to receive a Muni paint job.
BOTH: Charles Smallwood

8—Market and Castro

ROUTE: From ferry to Castro and 18th streets via Market and Castro streets, 3.25 miles. A white dash sign was displayed.

HISTORY: Line #8 was originally a cable line; after the 1906 quake, it was electrified only as far as Castro and 18th; the balance of the old line was kept as a cable operation, running from 18th to 26th streets on Castro, as grades were considered too steep for electric car operation.

On September 29, 1944, Municipal Railway took over ownership and operation. On December 17, 1944, as a wartime conservation measure, Line #8 was discontinued; it resumed on a morning-and-evening rush hour service on November 5, 1945.

Rush hour service ran to 18th and Danvers from the late 1920s; owl service was also provided to 18th and Danvers.

This line's cars, in Muni days, had a most difficult time in keeping a home. As of May 6, 1946, they operated out of Haight Division. As of December 9, 1946, they were based at McAllister Division. On June 7, 1948, they moved to Geary Division.

Starting on June 27, 1949, Line #8 was extended through Twin Peaks Tunnel to a new outer terminal at West Portal and Ulloa streets, the only instance of a former Market Street Railway line's using this facility in regular service. Reason: track work at Market and Castro streets. This operation through the tunnel lasted but a few days, for on July 1, 1949, streetcar service on the #8 Line ended.

9—Valencia Street

ROUTE: Converted from cable over same route: Ferry to 28th and Valencia via Market, Valencia, Mission and 29th St. Electric operation was extended to 29th and Noe streets, 4.75 miles.

HISTORY: Began operation as an electric line on November 1, 1906, to 29th and Noe. On June 16, 1935, this line began two outer terminals: 29th and Noe, and Cortland and Banks (5.00 miles). Certain rush hour trips at that time ran to Geneva and Mission. The Courtland and Banks line replaced outer terminus of #24 Line. On April 16, 1938, one additional outer terminal was added: Richland and Andover, replacing the #23 line. On June 13, 1939, cars of this line ran to Daly City via 29th, San Jose Ave., 30th and Chenery, replacing the #26 line—thus giving this line no fewer than *four* outer terminals. On November 5, 1939, these were cut to three when service was discontinued to Daly City via 29th St. and San Jose Ave. On September 29, 1944, San Francisco Municipal Railway took over operation, sending alternate cars to ferries and East Bay Terminal; mileage was 10.64 from Cortland and Banks and 10.10 from Richland and Andover.

February 4, 1945, saw this line rerouted over 14th to Mission, then down Mission to the ferries. On November 25, 1945, owl service formerly provided by this line was taken over by the #14 line. The Cortland Ave. service was discontinued on December 16, 1946, and the line's outer terminus was changed to Richland and Leese streets. It was extended to Murray and Richland on May 21, 1947. The last day of streetcar operation was January 15, 1949. Buses started running on this line at that time, but were succeeded by trolley coaches on March 18, 1950.

Owl service was provided for many years on a 15-minute headway to Daly City via Market, Valencia, Mission, Onandaga, San Jose and Mission Loop; alternate trips went the opposite way around this loop.

Dash signs' colors were as varied as this line's multitudinous terminals. A blue dash sign signified a car bound for 29th and Noe; if the dash sign were white, that car was headed for Cortland and Banks; an orange sign was for the Geneva Ave. run; a red and green dash sign meant a Daly City car; and a blue dash sign was on cars bound to Murray and Richland.

MULTIPLE TERMINALS gave the #9—Valencia Street a varied personality. Longest of the many branches was to Daly City via San Jose Avenue, inherited from the #26 line. Service was generally given with 900-type cars and 1586, shown on the viaduct over the Southern Pacific Ocean View spur, was a rare sight on this line. Geneva Car House is in left background. In 1978 work has started to build new streetcar track on this spot to connect the outer terminals of Muni lines K and M.   **Charles Smallwood**

ALONG THE #9 LINE:
(ABOVE) **OUTBOUND TO DALY CITY** at Chenery and Mateo.
(BELOW) **LOOKING EAST** on 30th Street, from the old Southern Pacific overpass.
                              BOTH: Charles Smallwood

A NEW BRANCH of the #9—Valencia Line, established on June 16, 1935, ran out Cortland Avenue from Mission Street to Banks Street. Cortland Avenue was single-track with turnouts, a unique practice on San Francisco streetcar lines. Prior to the above date the line was part of #24—Mission and Richmond Crosstown. We look east from Mission Street. **Lorin Silliman**

(BELOW)   Car 1597, on a Cortland run, discharges passengers at 25th and Valencia. **Charles Smallwood**

LINE 9 AND 10 CARS meet at their junction at Diamond and Monterey Blvd. in June 1940. **Charles Smallwood**

9, 10 and 11 Cars

(BELOW) **A FEW MONTHS** before the end of the Market Street Railway's existence, a conductor poses at the terminus of the 11 Line at 24th and Hoffman streets. **Randolph Brandt**

10—Sunnyside

ROUTE: From Ferry Building to Monterey Blvd. (formerly Sunnyside Ave.) and Genessee via Mission, 14th, Guerrero, San Jose Ave., 30th, Chenery, Diamond, and Monterey Blvd., 6.50 miles.

HISTORY: Line #10 was converted to partial bus service in the midthirties. It was completely converted to motor coach operation on January 28, 1940, with the bus route being designated line #10—Glen Park.

While streetcars operated, night and Sunday service terminated at 8th and Market.

Color of dash signs: white and green.

11—Mission and 24th Street

ROUTE: From ferries via Mission, 22nd, Chattanooga, 24th St. to Hoffman Ave., returning via 24th St., Dolores, 22nd, Mission to Ferry Building, 4.75 miles.

HISTORY: On May 5, 1906, this line resumed operation after the earthquake and fire. Owl service from 24th and Hoffman to 24th and Utah was discontinued on August 13, 1934; this service had operated via 24th, Dolores, 22nd, Howard and 24th. Muni took over operation on September 29, 1944, and immediately cut back night and Sunday service to 22nd and Mission, 2.96 miles. Motor coaches replaced cars nights and Sundays to 22nd and Mission on August 18, 1946. Buses took over completely on January 15, 1949.

Color of dash signs: blue.

12—Mission and Ingleside

ROUTE: From the ferries to Sloat Blvd. and Great Highway (Ocean Beach) via Mission, Onondaga, Ocean Ave., Junipero Serra Blvd. and Sloat Blvd. The 10-mile length of this line made it the longest local streetcar line in San Francisco. Much additional flavor was added by the fact that tracks on Junipero Serra and Sloat Blvd. were on private right-of-way.

HISTORY: Service resumed on May 6, 1906 after the quake and operated with no change until June 23, 1940, when cars were replaced by buses after 6:00 P.M., the coaches operating from the ocean to Onondaga and Mission where downtown passengers had to transfer. Municipal Railway succeeded to ownership on September 29, 1944. On April 8, 1945, the outer terminus was changed to Mission and Geneva, 6.43 miles, with cars making all trips. On January 18, 1948, pull-out cars to St. Luke's Hospital were discontinued with pull-outs then operating to 26th and Mission, thus eliminating the final streetcars from Valencia St. The last day of streetcar operation on this line was October 31, 1948. Service was provided by bus line #18 to Onondaga and Mission only. May 18, 1952, saw a new trolley coach line #12 established; it ran from the ferry via Mission, Ocean Ave. to Phelan Loop at City College.

Dash signs were white and yellow originally; they later were changed to a very striking picture design.

When Fleishacker Zoo and Pool were opened in the early 1920s, weekend patronage on this line increased to the point where several tripper runs were operated from Third St. Division.

THE INGLESIDE LINE had the longest private right-of-way of any San Francisco line. Car 1553 sits at the Beach Terminal on Sloat Blvd. in 1937. The Fleishacker Zoo and Pool are to the right of the street.   **Charles Smallwood**

Along Sloat Boulevard

(ABOVE) **LINE 12—INGLESIDE AND OCEAN** enjoyed some wide-open spaces in the early twenties. The scene is Sloat Blvd. near 37th Ave., in 1926, and car 1674 is inbound from its ocean terminal. Today this area is one of the finest residential neighborhoods in The City. (BELOW) **ON TRACKAGE SHARED WITH** Municipal Railway's K Line, this #12 Line car passes Commodore Sloat School, on Junipero Serra Blvd. and Ocean Ave., in 1939.
BOTH: Charles Smallwood

14—Mission Street

ROUTE: From ferries to Daly City via Mission St., 7.75 miles. On certain holidays (such as Memorial Day and Christmas) service was extended to Holy Cross on the San Mateo interurban line to serve the numerous cemeteries.

HISTORY: Service was resumed on May 6, 1906, and operated continuously until conversion to buses and trolley coaches on January 16, 1949.

Owl service to Daly City was changed from the #9 line to this line on November 25, 1945, by Muni. On May 11, 1947, all owl service on this route was provided by motor coach. April 4, 1948, saw all cars operating through to Holy Cross Cemetery on Sundays from 11:00 A.M. to 4:30 P.M.

January 15, 1949, was the last day of streetcars on this line with buses taking over the following day. On January 6, 1952, all regular service on this line was taken over by trolley coaches with buses making express runs.

Color of dash signs: red.

During the 1930s, one morning rush and one evening rush trip operated from the Ferry Building over this line to South San Francisco. Such service used one of the San Mateo interurban line's cars 1715, 1716, or 1722 which were fitted with swing bolster trucks.

AN OUTBOUND #14 Car runs along lower Mission Street en route to Daly City in 1937.

Charles Smallwood

(ABOVE) **A #14 CAR** awaits departure time for Daly City at the Ferry in 1940. (BELOW) **OCCASIONAL RUSH HOUR TRIPS** on the #14 Line continued through Daly City on the San Mateo interurban line as far as Leipsic Junction, where connection was made with the South San Francisco local line. This car leaves the Junction on its return trip in 1934. **BOTH: Charles Smallwood**

Meeting the Commuter Trains

SOUTHERN PACIFIC'S Peninsula commute service, operating from the beautiful Third and Townsend Depot, generated much business for Market Street Railway's Third Street lines. Cars of the #15 line share the spotlight with #28 and #42 line vehicles in this late 1930s view. The site of the structure is now occupied by a recreation vehicle parking area and commuters use a small, plain depot at 4th and Townsend.

Charles Smallwood

15—Kearny and North Beach

ROUTE: From Third and Townsend streets, where the Southern Pacific Depot was located, to North Beach, via Third, Kearny, Broadway and Powell to Jefferson St., 2.50 miles. Cars displayed a red dash sign.

HISTORY: This route was a part of the old *North Beach & Mission Railway Company's* horse car line; it was electrified around the turn of the century. All Sunday service was provided by buses starting June 23, 1940; cars were withdrawn completely on September 12, 1941. World War II brought cars back on May 15, 1945; they ran from Jefferson and Powell via Broadway, Kearny, Third, Mariposa and Illinois to 19th in rush hours only. Cars left this line for good on October 7, 1946.

(ABOVE) **TWO #15 CARS PASS** at Powell and North Point streets in 1941. (BELOW) **DURING WORLD WAR II YEARS** the Third Street line was extended from the Southern Pacific Depot to Union Iron Works, partly (as this view shows) on S.P. freight trackage on Illinois Street.
BOTH: Charles Smallwood

16—Third and Kearny

ROUTE: From Ferry Building to Six Mile House (County Road and Sunnyvale Ave.) via Embarcadero, Broadway, Kearny and Third streets, 7.5 miles. Dash signs: red and white. (County Road today is Bayshore Blvd.) Cars gave way to buses on this route on September 12, 1941.

(ABOVE) **ON OUTER THIRD STREET,** a #16 car operates below Five-Mile House in 1938. **Charles Smallwood**

THE #17—HAIGHT AND INGLESIDE LINE shared Haight Street with the #6 and #7 Lines. Car 116 is seen on Haight at Buena Vista West in 1938 . . . long before the invasion of the "flower children" to the Haight-Ashbury. **W.C. Whittaker**

17—Haight and Ingleside

ROUTE: From Ferry Building to 19th Ave. and Sloat Blvd. via Market, Haight, Stanyan, Frederick, Lincoln Way, 20th Ave., Wawona and 19th Ave., 7.75 miles. Red dash sign. This route was opened as a new line on February 17, 1916, using tracks of the #7—Haight and Ocean Line from 20th Ave. and Lincoln Way to downtown, and over the former Parkside Transit Company's line on 20th and 19th Avenues.

HISTORY: On Sundays and holidays cars of this line continued down Sloat Blvd. to Fleishacker Pool at the beach via the #12 Line.

On December 29, 1937, tracks were forced off 19th Ave. due to a State Highway widening project; cars then terminated at 19th Ave. and Wawona, 7.25 miles.

A route change occurred on February 4, 1945; cars turned off Market St. at 12th St. to Mission St., thence down Mission St. to the ferries—7.83 miles. This line was discontinued on December 22, 1945.

(ABOVE) **THE TALL TREES** along 19th Ave. were a pleasant sight for #17 Line patrons. Car #120 operates along that thoroughfare on December 29, 1937, the last day before the route was cut back to Wawona and 19th Ave. The cutback was caused by the widening of 19th Ave. to make it a state highway. **W.C. Whittaker** (BELOW) **TERMINUS OF** the #17 line: 19th Ave. and Sloat Blvd. On Sundays and holidays some cars would continue onto Sloat Blvd. and use the #12 line tracks to the beach. **Lorin Silliman**

18—Fifth-Market-Mission

ROUTE: From Fifth and Market to Daly City via 5th, Mission, 6.77 miles. No dash signs were displayed.

HISTORY: This line was primarily a rush hour line by the 1920s. It fell victim to the Depression and was discontinued entirely by 1935. However, cars displaying #18 signs did appear on the Memorial Days of 1936 and 1937 in service on Mission St. to the cemeteries.

THIS 1941 EXCURSION view shows how the #18 Line cars served the cemeteries on Memorial Day. In later years the line gave only rush-hour service on Mission Street from 5th to Daly City. **Charles Smallwood**

19—Ninth-Polk-Larkin

ROUTE: From Ninth and Brannan streets to Polk and North Point streets via Ninth, Larkin, Post and Polk streets, 2.75 miles. Yellow dash sign.

HISTORY: Until the 1906 disaster, this was a 5'0" gauge cable line, running from Ninth and Brannan via Ninth, Larkin, Post, Polk, Pacific to Divisadero; after 1906 this line was reconstructed as a standard gauge electric line and ran out Polk St. to Lombard until the opening of the Panama Pacific International Exposition in 1915 caused it to be extended to North Point. The line from Polk to Divisadero on Pacific was continued as a cable line until it was abandoned November 17, 1929.

Streetcars were replaced by buses on June 25, 1939, but on July 15, 1940, cars were added and the line was operated with both cars and buses. After Municipal Railway took over operation on September 29, 1944, cars were operated from Hayes and Larkin to North Point, and buses from North Point to Brannan. Buses were extended to Fisherman's Wharf on February 4, 1945, and on September 29, 1945, the final car ran on this line.

20—Ellis and O'Farrell

ROUTE: From Southern Pacific Depot at Third and Townsend to Golden Gate Park (Stanyan and Haight) via Townsend, Fourth, Ellis, Hyde (outbound), O'Farrell, Divisadero, Oak (outbound, Page St. inbound), and Stanyan. Originally this line ran out Lincoln Way and La Playa to the beach, but on February 6, 1916, when the #7 Line was extended to the beach, #20 Line was cut back to an outer terminal at Haight and Stanyan—4.50 miles. Green sign.

HISTORY: Service was resumed after the fire on April 29, 1906. Municipal Railway took over operation on September 29, 1944. On January 27, 1946, cars were replaced by buses Sundays and holidays. The following day this line was cut in two: buses ran from the Park to Divisadero on weekdays and Saturdays—and from the Park all the way through to the depot on Sundays and holidays; cars operated from Divisadero to the depot on weekdays and Saturdays.

On December 9, 1946, bus service was extended to the depot at night, followed by bus service from the Park to the depot on Saturday afternoons, effected April 26, 1947. This nibbling away of car service continued. On July 7, 1947, the remaining car operation was cut in two while new special work was installed at Fourth and Market to permit Muni's F Line cars to reach the depot from their Stockton St. trackage. Cars of the #20 Line then ran from Divisadero and Ellis to Market, and from Market to the Depot on 4th St. Line #20 cars were discontinued on Fourth St. on September 8, 1947, when Muni's F Line cars began operating on that thoroughfare from Market St. to Townsend St. The last day of streetcar operation on the remaining segment of this line was September 27, 1947.

(ABOVE) **THE MOTORMAN MANHANDLES** the Eclipse fender as this #19—Polk-Larkin-9th Street car switches back at Hayes and Larkin streets, in 1943. Although the #19 Line was converted to bus operation in 1939, this route (like the Third and Kearny Lines) was not completely motorized. For a time a few schedules continued to operate by streetcar.
Charles Smallwood

(RIGHT) **A SCENE** at the Haight and Stanyan terminus of the #20 line. Car #265, operating one-man, lays over back in 1938.
Warren K. Miller

21—Hayes Street

ROUTE: Until the fire of 1906 this line was one of the five cable lines on Market St. and ran from the ferry out Market, Hayes to Hayes and Stanyan. Cars were painted green. When rebuilt as an electric line, it entered service on June 10, 1906, but, as grades were too steep between Fillmore and Divisadero, electric cars were detoured from Fillmore via Oak, Masonic, Frederick, Clayton, Carl, Stanyan, and Parnassus to 33rd Ave.

As the grades between Fillmore and Divisadero had been regraded, the Hayes Street line ran direct to Stanyan and over that street to Fulton as of February 7, 1916. Later this line was extended over Fulton and 8th Ave. to Clement. During the early 1920s this line was extended to a terminus at La Playa and Balboa streets on Sundays and holidays only, running to the beach via Fulton St. In the early 1930s this line was extended full time to 8th Ave and Clement St., a total run of 5.25 miles. Green dash signs.

HISTORY: Municipal operation started on September 29, 1944. On August 18, 1946, buses started operating on this line nights and Sundays, with the inner terminal Larkin St., a distance of 3.46 miles. March 10, 1947, saw the inner terminal for cars and buses at Larkin St. from 9:00 A.M. to 4:00 P.M. weekdays only, 3.46 miles. On October 2, 1947, through service at all times was re-established from 8th and Clement to the ferry, 5.24 miles. Due to track rebuilding, all cars turned back at Larkin St., effective March 15, 1948. June 5, 1948, was the final day of streetcar operation on this line, with replacement bus line operating through to the ferries. Buses were succeeded by trolley coaches on July 3, 1949.

22—Fillmore Street

ROUTE: At the time United Railroads took control in 1902, this was a single-truck car line running from Bay and Fillmore, Duboce, Church, 16th to Bryant St.; at Green St. cars were hooked onto the Fillmore Hill Cable and ascended the hill to Broadway, where they were unhooked and proceeded to Bryant St. URR cut this line into two parts, using double-truck cars south from Broadway and Fillmore, and establishing the Fillmore Hill Line from Broadway to Bay St. using single-truck cars. Later this line was extended from 16th and Bryant to the Kentucky (Third St.) Car House at 23rd and Third, looping through the car barn. Total distance: 5.11 miles. A green dash sign was displayed by cars terminating at 16th and Bryant; cars going through to 23rd and Third showed a white and green dash sign. About 75 percent of the service terminated at 16th and Bryant.

HISTORY: This line was the first line in the city to resume service after the 1906 earthquake and fire. One-man cars were used on this On September 12, 1941, service was cut back to 18th and Third, due to widening of Third St. Mileage thereafter was 5.53. The Fillmore Hill counterbalance was discontinued the same day.

The Muni era began on September 29, 1944, and a minor service change was effective that day: alternate cars terminated at 16th and Bryant. On March 27, 1946, a sewer construction project at Church and Market cut this line into two parts, with shuttle buses connecting the two parts; buses operated via Dolores St. Through car service was resumed on October 23, 1946.

Owl service was provided by buses after May 11, 1947. July 31, 1948, was the last day of streetcars. Trolley coaches took over this line on January 16, 1949.

ONLOOKERS WATCH as a #22 Line car "fords the stream" crossing Market Street at Church Street, bound for Third Street.
Charles Smallwood

TOO STEEP for regular electric cars, this portion of Fillmore Street was served by these counterbalance cars, which took on passengers at Broadway from the #22 Line car. Then, as this car went downhill, another began its uphill journey from Green Street, two blocks below.

Fillmore Hill Counterbalance

ROUTE: From Fillmore and Broadway to Marina Blvd. via Fillmore St., about 1.00 mile; blue and yellow dash signs.

HISTORY: This line was constructed in 1895 as the north end of the Fillmore and 16th St. line. The two blocks between Broadway and Green streets were too steep for electric car operation without some kind of mechanical aid, so a counterbalance was installed on this grade. Single-truck cars equipped with a gripping device were used on this line; they were San Francisco's only cars equipped with multiple unit controls and actually operated in two-car trains during the 1915 Panama-Pacific Exposition.

On August 29, 1925, this line was extended from Fillmore and Bay streets to Fillmore and Marina Blvd.

Buses replaced the counterbalance cars on this line on April 6, 1941.

AT THE BOTTOM of the grade, a hook tender applies a coupling device (known locally as "the wish-bone") to an upbound car. (NOTE: Both views were taken on April 5, 1941, last day of service.)

BOTH PHOTOS THIS PAGE: Charles Smallwood

(ABOVE) **THE HILL LINE** provided its passengers with a spectacular view of San Francisco Bay. Here cars 623 and 625 pass at midpoint (Vallejo Street) of the counterbalance on the last day of operation, April 5, 1941. **Charles Smallwood** (BELOW) **LETTING THE THIRD CAR** down in the morning; Fillmore and Green Streets in 1940. **Warren K. Miller**

Towing the Dummy

HOW TO SHUT DOWN the counterbalance line? Something had to go downhill each time a car came uphill, so when closing time came a regular #22—Fillmore car brought out this "dummy" car which was stored at the carhouse during the day, to the top of the counterbalance grade. This evening view is at Fillmore and Jackson (note Washington-Jackson cable track in foreground).

HAVING SPENT THE NIGHT in the middle of Fillmore and Vallejo Streets (too often the target of nocturnal motorists although marked with a lantern), the dummy car, weighted to match the passenger cars, is brought up the hill to be towed to the barn for the day. It is seen at Fillmore and Green, midpoint of the counterbalance.

BOTH: Warren K. Miller

AN OVERFLOW load packs counterbalance car 627 on the opening day of the Golden Gate Bridge, as it climbs the steep grade. Below Vallejo, these cars operated in regular streetcar fashion. **Charles Smallwood**

23—Fillmore and Valencia

ROUTE: From Sacramento and Divisadero to Richland Ave. and Andover St. via Sacramento, Fillmore, McAllister, Gough, Market, Valencia, Mission and Richland Ave., 5.00 miles. Blue dash sign.

HISTORY: This line began service on September 6, 1914. On June 16, 1935, this line was discontinued and shuttle service was established on Richland Ave. between Mission St. and Andover, using a one-man car which ran weekdays and Saturdays; later the #27 Line, also one-man, was extended to Richland and Andover from 26th and Mission. On October 28, 1937, the #23 Line was reestablished from Richland and Andover to 5th and Market via Richland, Leese (inbound) and Mission streets, using two-man cars.

On April 16, 1938, the Richland-Andover service became a branch of the #9 Line.

DURING ONE-MAN CAR DAYS, the #24 Line was a shuttle. Car 180 is seen as a one-man car at Divisadero and Sacramento Streets in 1938.
Ted Wurm

24—Mission and Richmond
(16th and Divisadero)

ROUTE: From 8th Ave. and Fulton St. to Cortland and Banks streets via 8th Ave., Clement, 6th Ave., Lake, Arguello, Sacramento, Divisadero, Page (Oak St. outbound), Fillmore, Duboce, Church, 16th, Mission and Cortland Ave. Outbound cars reached their 6th Ave. terminus via 6th Ave. and Fulton St. 7.25 miles, white dash sign.

HISTORY: The #24 was established as a new line on May 20, 1906, running from 29th and Mission to 8th Ave. and Fulton. On June 16, 1935, the route was changed to 16th and Bryant, from Divisadero and Sacramento via Divisadero, Page (Oak St. north bound), Fillmore, Duboce, Church and 16th. Some #9 cars were diverted to Cortland and Banks that date.

In 1936 this line operated as a one-man shuttle from Divisadero and Sacramento to Page and Fillmore, returning west on Oak St.

One-man cars were outlawed on February 25, 1939, so two-man cars took over the shuttle service. On April 6, 1941, street cars gave way to buses.

Along Bay Shore Boulevard

(ABOVE) **THE WIDE OPEN SPACES** of Bay Shore Blvd. frames #25 Line car 275, outbound to Five-Mile House, 1940.   **Charles Smallwood**

(RIGHT) **INBOUND #25 LINE** car 273 passes Market Street Railway's General Stores Building at Bryant and Division Streets, in 1939.   **Randolph Brandt**

25—San Bruno Avenue

ROUTE: From Fifth and Market to San Bruno Ave. and Wilde Ave. (Five Mile House) via Fifth, Bryant, Army, private right-of-way (later Bayshore Blvd.) and San Bruno Ave., 5.35 miles, red dash sign.

HISTORY: After the stop caused by the 1906 disaster, this line resumed operation on May 1, 1906, with an outer terminal at Dwight St. and San Bruno Ave. and an inner terminal at 26th and Folsom. Sometime later the line was brought downtown to 5th and Market. The outer end was extended to Wilde Ave. on February 9, 1914.

In 1935, due to construction work on the Oakland Bay Bridge which required removal of tracks on Fifth St. between Mission and Bryant streets, this line was diverted to Sixth St., terminating at 6th and Market; however, it returned to its Fifth and Market terminus via 6th, Mission and 5th on April 5, 1936.

Coaches replaced streetcars on February 16, 1937, but effective September 8, 1942, cars were used again while buses continued nights, Sundays and holidays.

Municipal Railway operation began September 29, 1944, with this line operating from Arleta to 5th and Market, a distance of 5.60 miles. The inner terminal became the Ferry Building (via Mission) on April 9, 1945.

On July 1, 1946, this line was cut in two by sewer construction on Bryant St. One part ran south from 16th St., the other from 9th St., with shuttle buses running between. Through service was resumed on August 6, 1946.

On December 5, 1946, the outer terminus became Army and Potrero, cutting this line to 4.18 miles. Municipal Railway's car line "H" was extended over San Bruno Ave. to Five Mile House, effective this same date.

July 31, 1948, was the last day of streetcar operation.

26—Guerrero Street

ROUTE: From Ferry Building to Daly City via Mission, 14th, Guerrero, San Jose Ave., 30th, Chenery, Diamond and San Jose Ave., 8.00 miles. Brown and white dash sign.

HISTORY: This line followed a portion of the route of the first electric car line in San Francisco (the *San Francisco & San Mateo Electric Railway Company,* 1891). At nights and on Sundays this line terminated at 8th and Market streets.

On April 16, 1938, line #26 was discontinued and a branch of the #9 Line took over that portion of its route from 29th St. south to Daly City. This #9 Line branch was discontinued on January 14, 1939.

During World War II line #26 was reestablished from Mission and Onondaga to Daly City via Onondaga, Ocean and San Jose Ave.; this was effective September 23, 1944, six days before start of Municipal operation. Cars were discontinued on February 4, 1945.

SECOND AND MARKET, downtown terminal of the #27—Bryant Street route is the scene of this rare view of a "Chicago" car working a South of Market line. This photo of car 1509 was taken on the last day of two-man operation. **Charles Smallwood**

27—Bryant Street

ROUTE: From Market and Second via Second, Bryant and 26th to Mission St., 4.00 miles, green and yellow dash sign. Inbound route was via 8th and Brannan originally; in June 1937 it was changed to inbound via Bryant St., the same as outbound. Shuttle service was provided from 6:30 P.M. to midnight (all day Sundays and holidays) on 26th St. from Mission to Bryant.

HISTORY: During the 1920s and early 1930s this line was extended from 26th and Mission to Cortland and Banks during the morning and evening peaks on weekdays. During the one-man car era (mid-1930s) this line was extended to Richland and Andover with one-man cars.

On January 28, 1940, motor coach service was inaugurated but streetcars ran during morning and evening rush hours along with the buses. The Municipal era began September 29, 1944.

July 11, 1948, saw this line undergo a rerouting: inbound from 26th and Folsom streets via Folsom, Precita and Bryant and regular route; outbound, from 26th and Bryant via Bryant, Precita, Folsom to 26th and Folsom and then the regular route. August 13, 1948, was the last day of streetcar operation on this line.

28—Ferries & Southern Pacific Depot

ROUTE: From Ferry Building to S.P. Depot at Third and Townsend via Embarcadero, Howard, Steuart, Folson, Second, Brannan and 3rd, 1.50 miles, blue dash sign. This line operated over Rincon Hill prior to the construction of the San Francisco-Oakland Bay Bridge, then was diverted to the above route.

HISTORY: This line was used mainly by S.P. main line passengers transferring between the Third and Townsend Depot and the Ferry Depot.

In March 1928, obsolete types of cars used on this line were replaced, with some fanfare, by brand-new Comfort Cars with leather-upholstered seats. Although this line was hopeless from a revenue standpoint, it was thought that the traveler passing through San Francisco between the two train depots would have a better impression of the city if he had a comfortable streetcar ride.

One-man cars were used on this line in the 1930s; streetcars were replaced by buses on April 1, 1940.

On January 15, 1939, this line was diverted to East Bay Terminal by way of Third, Brannan, Second, Folsom and First to just north of Howard.

29—Third and Sansome
(Kearny-Broadway)

ROUTE: From Broadway and Davis to Third and Wilde (Five Mile House) via Broadway, Kearny and Third, 6.36 miles. Red and white dash sign. Originally Line #17 but changed to #29 in 1911 due to confusion with #15 and #16.

HISTORY: This line did not operate evenings, Sundays and holidays after 1930. When one-man cars began operating on this line in 1935, it was extended to Six Mile House all day.

On September 15, 1936, the northern terminus was changed from Broadway and Davis to Seawall and Embarcadero via Bush and Sansome streets. A replacement rush hour line, #43, was established between Kearny and Broadway and the S.P. Depot. The last day of streetcar service was September 12, 1941.

LOOKING DOWN on Third Street in 1936 from the roof of the Southern Pacific depot, #29 Line car 952 is seen southbound, approaching the Third Street bridge. The S.S. PRESIDENT HOOVER is in the background. **Charles Smallwood**

OUTER THIRD STREET gave this #29 car a bit of wide open running. Car 944 is en route to Visitacion Valley during the last days of this trackage in 1941. During its last years the commuter-station zone of the route was augmented by cars bearing a #43 designation. — **Charles Smallwood**

30—Army Street

ROUTE: From 8th and Market to 22nd and Mission streets via 8th, Bryant, 16th, Kansas, 17th, Connecticut, 18th, 3rd, Army, Bryant, 26th, Howard and 22nd streets, 5.75 miles with white dash sign.

HISTORY: In the early 1930s this line was cut back from 22nd and Mission to 23rd and Third streets. One-man cars were installed during the mid-1930s. On about July 1, 1940, a rerouting took place: from 23rd via Third, Army, Bryant, and 26th to Mission. Last day of service was May 11, 1941. However, wartime service was restored on December 7, 1942, from Third and Army to 26th and Mission.

31—Balboa Street

ROUTE: From Ferry Building to Balboa and 30th Ave. via Market, Eddy, Divisadero, Turk and Balboa streets, returning via Turk St. to Mason to Eddy, 5.75 miles, white dash sign.

HISTORY: This was the last new streetcar line built in San Francisco, opening for service on Sunday, May 15, 1932. It replaced Route #4—Turk and Eddy.

Municipal Railway took over ownership and operation of this line on September 29, 1944.

On February 12, 1947, the inner terminus became Eddy and Powell from 9:00 A.M. to 4:00 P.M.. On October 2, 1947, cars resumed operating through to the Ferry Building all day. Four days later cars were replaced by buses nights and Sundays, with the bus inner terminal being set at Market and Mason. On March 21, 1949, all cars terminated at Market and Eddy streets, because of track rebuilding on Market St.

The last day of car operation was July 2, 1949.

32—Hayes and Oak Street

ROUTE: From Ferry Building to the Stanyan-Haight entrance of Golden Gate Park via Market, Hayes, Fillmore, Oak and Stanyan—four miles, with green dash sign. The return route was via Page St. instead of Oak St. During morning and evening peaks, Line #32 operated to 9th Ave. and Judah St. via Masonic, Frederick, Clayton, Carl, Stanyan, Parnassus and Judah streets. This line was the weakest of all lines operating on Market St. and fell an early victim to the depression. It was gone by 1932.

33—18th and Park

ROUTE: From 3rd and Harrison to Stanyan and Waller (Golden Gate Park) via Harrison, 14th, Guerrero, 18th, Market, Clayton, Ashbury, Frederick, Clayton and Waller streets, 5.00 miles; white dash sign to Third St., red dash sign to Eighth St.

HISTORY: This was one of the pioneer electric lines in San Francisco, having been built in the early 1890s by the *San Francisco & San Mateo Electric Railway Company*. After the 1906 quake and fire, it started up again on May 6, 1906, running from Market and Steuart streets via Steuart, Harrison, 18th, Clayton and Waller streets to the park. It had the famed "switchback" on the side of Twin Peaks at Market and Clayton streets.

This line was converted to trolley coach operation October 6, 1935—the first line in the west to have modern electric buses.

The Switchback

(ABOVE) **LOOKING DOWNHILL** on Upper Market Street, the famous #33 Line "switchback" is seen. Uphill cars proceed from Market (on the right), went past the switch in the foreground, then changed directions to proceed up Clayton, at the left.   **Paul Ward**

(RIGHT) **ENTERING THE SWITCHBACK** from Clayton (looking the other direction from above view) this #33 Line car has claimed the right-of-way from the Studebaker sedan at right, circa 1928.   **Charles Smallwood**

#34 LINE car 716 is seen passing the classic facade of the San Francisco Curb Exchange in 1929.

Charles Smallwood

34—Sixth and Sansome

ROUTE: From Chestnut and Sansome (Seawall) to Sixth and Brannan streets via Sansome, Bush, Kearny, Post, Taylor and Sixth St., 2.83 miles; blue and red dash sign. The company's franchise on Post St. was due to expire on September 15, 1936, and this line was discontinued shortly after this date. Line #29 was diverted t­ Chestnut and Sansome on this date via Kearny, Bush and San­ some.

35—Howard Street

ROUTE: From Ferry Building to 24th and Rhode Island via Embarcadero, Howard, Van Ness Ave. South and 24th St., 4.50 miles; white, red and green dash sign.
HISTORY: The last cars operated on this line on November 5, 1939. Service on this line was discontinued because the franchise covering Howard St. and Van Ness Ave. South had expired and th city desired to install its first Municipal Railway trolley coach li on this route (Line "R"). Line "R" began operating o September 7, 1941, from Army St. to Beale St., a distance of 6.8 miles.

(ABOVE) BUSY JUNCTION: Howard Street and the Embarcadero is the meeting place for #35, #36 and #28 cars in this June 1939 view. Behind are portions of the Pier structures on the waterfront. **Charles Smallwood**

(LEFT) CAR 1581 IS AT the Precita Ave. terminus of the #36—Folsom Street Line, 1937.
Charles Smallwood

36—Folsom Street

ROUTE: From the Ferry Building to Precita Ave and York St. via Embarcadero, Howard, Steuart, Folsom and Precita Ave., 4.50 miles; green and yellow dash sign.

HISTORY: On March 14, 1935, the city's first one-man cars entered operation on this line. Two-man cars returned on February 25, 1939.

This line was converted to 100 percent bus operation on January 28, 1940, but World War II brought about the return of cars to all schedules on October 26, 1942.

Municipal Railway operations began on September 29, 1944. The line was converted to bus operation on January 28, 1945.

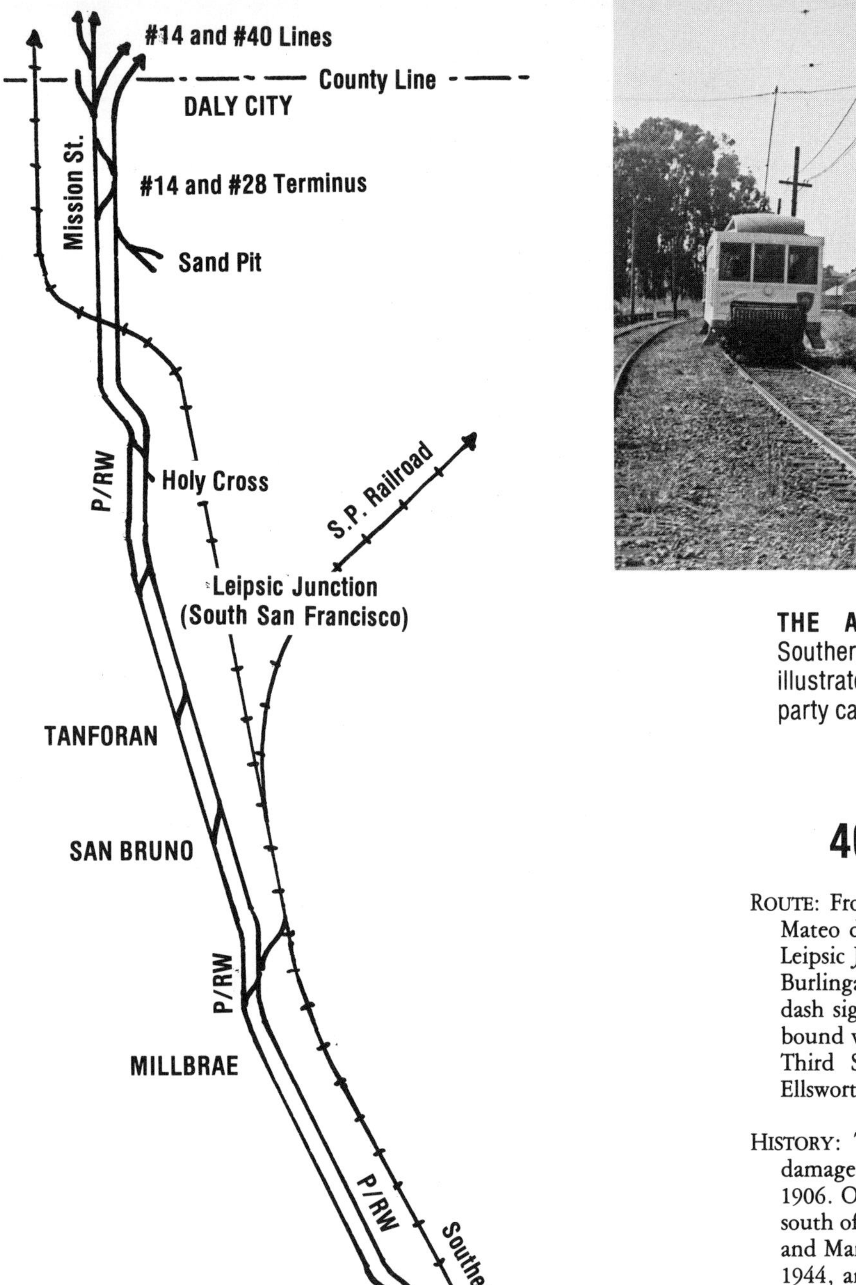

THE ADJACENT OPERATION of steam-powered Southern Pacific trains along the #40 Line is well-illustrated in this 1940 view of an excursion on MSR's party car SAN FRANCISCO. **Jack Ferrier**

40—San Mateo Interurban

ROUTE: From Fifth and Market streets to the Southern Pacific San Mateo depot via Mission Street, Daly City, Colma, Holy Cross, Leipsic Junction, San Bruno, Millbrae, Lomita Park, Broadway, Burlingame, Hillsborough, and San Mateo, 20.00 miles; yellow dash sign. A loop was made within the city of San Mateo: outbound via San Mateo Drive, Griffith Ave., Baldwin Ave., B St., Third St., Railroad Ave.; inbound via Second St., B St., Ellsworth St., Poplar to Griffith Ave. and return to main line.

HISTORY: This line began operation on August 1, 1903. It was damaged by the 1906 disaster but service resumed on May 6, 1906. On August 16, 1943, cars were operated by one-man crews south of Daly City and by two-man crews from Daly City to Fifth and Market. Municipal operation commenced on September 29, 1944, and service operated by one-man crews from Daly City to San Mateo.

On October 1, 1944, two-man operation resumed and all cars operated through to Fifth and Market from San Mateo.

In an effort to avoid heavy traffic on Mission St., cars of this route were rerouted on March 4, 1945; cars left Mission at 14th St. and operated over Valencia St. to 28th, thence regular route.

Effective August 17, 1947, Sunday service was operated only from Daly City to San Mateo. On the following day, through service from Fifth and Market was changed to only morning and evening peak periods. At all other times, this line's inner terminal was Daly City.

January 15, 1949, was the last day of streetcar operation of Line #40.

(ABOVE) **TRADITIONAL SAN FRANCISCO TERMINUS** of the San Mateo interurban line was at Fifth and Market streets, where the big cars stub-ended. Our view looks south from across Market as a 1200 Class car awaits its next 20-mile journey to San Mateo.
Ted Wurm

A TWO-MAN OPERATED #40 Car leaves Fifth and Market during a short period in 1943-44 when service connected with one-man operated at Daly City. Car 1228 is on one of a few rush-hour trips run to San Bruno with a two-man crew. **Charles Smallwood**

(ABOVE) **A LONG STRETCH** of street running along Mission Street adversely affected the schedule of the San Mateo Line (its private right-of-way did not begin until the County Line). Sharing this trackage with numerous local car lines made matters worse. This scene is at Mission and Richland. **Lorin Silliman**

(BELOW) **A SWITCHMAN** "bends the iron" for tripper 1241 at Holy Cross siding on Memorial Day, 1934. **Charles Smallwood**

(ABOVE) **A NORTHBOUND #40 CAR** approaches Leipsic Junction, 1937. The city of South San Francisco lies in the distance and the water tower belongs to adjacent Southern Pacific. (BELOW) **NEARING ORANGE AVE.**, San Bruno, another northbound interurban rolls along a tangent section of the San Mateo line, 1938. **BOTH: Charles Smallwood**

Burlingame's Trees

A LONG ROW OF eucalyptus trees characterized the Burlingame portion of the San Mateo interurban line. An inbound #40 car enters the Oak Grove crossing in 1939.

RAILFANS MEET a regular 1200 Class San Mateo car at Millbrae substation (behind excursion car 1731), in September 1942.

BOTH: Charles Smallwood

(ABOVE) **BROADWAY BURLINGAME** station was shared by patrons of MSR and SP. The White Front interurban crosses Broadway on a warm day in July 1937 on its way to The City. **Ernest M. Leo**

(RIGHT) **THE MOST ORNATE** company-owned waiting room on the #40 line was at central Burlingame. **S.F. Public Utilities Commission**

(ABOVE) **ON THE STREETS OF SAN MATEO:** Interurban 1237 runs along California Ave., approaching Mt. Diablo Ave., 1939.

(BELOW) **ROUNDING THE CURVE AT "B" STREET,** this #40 car is near the San Mateo terminal, 1939.

BOTH: Charles Smallwood

In San Mateo

41—Second and Market-S.P. Depot

ROUTE: From Second and Market to S.P. Depot at Third and Townsend via Second, Brannan and Third streets; white dash sign, 1.01 miles.

HISTORY: This was established as a new line on February 16, 1927. It operated on weekdays only on a 10-minute headway from 8:03 A.M. to 9:03 A.M. and from 4:51 P.M. to 5:37 P.M. It was essentially a convenience for the benefit of railroad commuters. Line #41 was discontinued on January 15, 1949, as Municipal Railway's Line F took over the service.

SANSOME AND SEAWALL (Chestnut Street) was the terminal of the #42 Line, a commuter route which used a portion of the former First and Fifth streets trackage. Pier 29, at left, is on the Embarcadero, while the tender of a State Belt Railroad steam locomotive is seen in its storage yard, at right. **Charles Smallwood**

42 & 43 Lines

NOTE: Both were established over portions of other lines. For #42 Line data see (unnumbered) First and Fifth streets line. #43 information is found in the #29—Third and Sansome (Kearny-Broadway) line description.

Visitacion Valley

ROUTE: From Mission and Geneva Ave. to Sunnydale Ave. (Six Mile House) via Geneva, Walbridge, Schwerin, McDonald and private right-of-way (later Bayshore Blvd.), 2.50 miles in length. This line opened on October 25, 1909, as a new car line. It was changed to one-man cars in April 1935. It became a bus operation on August 1, 1937, when it was consolidated with the Crocker Amazon bus line.

(ABOVE) **THE VISITACION VALLEY LINE** had some wide open spaces. Car 736 passes the quarry, 1937.

(LEFT) **THE TWO** Visitacion Valley cars meet, also in 1937.

BOTH: Charles Smallwood

THE MOST REMOTE of all MSR Lines, the Visitacion Valley Line was the stamping ground of the twin Williamsport deck roofers. (ABOVE) The line, looking east on Wallbridge Street, 1936. (BELOW) The passing track, also in 1936. The disastrous 1918 wreck involving car 1022 (see United Railroads chapter) occurred at the foot of the grade in the top photograph.

BOTH: Charles Smallwood

South San Francisco

ROUTE: From Leipsic Junction on the San Mateo interurban line to the W.P. Fuller Paint Company plant in South San Francisco via East Grand Ave. and private right-of-way, 3.00 miles. Opened December 31, 1903.

HISTORY: On June 18, 1916, this line's inner terminal was changed from Holy Cross to Leipsic Junction. One-man cars began operating on this line on May 27, 1934, and it ceased operation on December 31, 1938.

ALONG THE PRIVATE right-of-way of the South San Francisco line, one-man car 285 operates in 1935. Note the absence of a rear door.
Charles Smallwood

Tenth and Montgomery Streets

ROUTE: From 10th and Bryant to Kearny and Washington streets via 10th, Polk, Hayes, Larkin, McAllister, Leavenworth, Post, Montgomery, Washington to Kearny, a distance of 2.75 miles; brown and white dash sign.

HISTORY: Before 1906 this line was important; after that year of reconstruction it became mostly an operation to protect its franchise. It operated on an irregular schedule and was assigned o single-truck, hand brake car.

On October 6, 1927, after a spirited campaign to oust it fro Montgomery St., this line was abandoned on Montgomery a Washington streets, terminating at Post and Market. Final aba donment occurred in 1932.

THIS 1927 PHOTOGRAPH of Montgomery, "Wall Street of the West," shows well the narrowness of the thoroughfare. Congestion was quite heavy in this area, with the diminutive streetcar adding another traffic hazard.
Charles Smallwood

Parkside

ROUTE: From 20th Ave. and Taraval St. to 35th Ave. and Sloat Blvd. via Taraval, 33rd Ave., Vicente and 35th Ave., about 1.50 miles. On April 12, 1919, Municipal Railway began operating its Taraval St. line jointly with United Railroads over a portion of this route—Taraval from 20th Ave. to 33rd Ave. The Parkside Line was abandoned in late 1927.

Bosworth Street

ROUTE: From Mission and Bosworth streets to Glen Park via Bosworth St., about 0.75 miles. This was an unimportant branch line operated by a single car. It was gone by 1928.

First and Fifth Streets

ROUTE: From Fifth and Market to Battery and California streets via Fifth, Brannan, Second, Folsom, First and Battery streets, 2.50 miles; red and white dash sign. On its return trip, it looped via Third, Townsend, and Fourth St. to serve the Southern Pacific Depot.

HISTORY: In early years this was known as the "Mail Dock" line and ran down a short spur on Brannan St. to the Embarcadero to the Pacific Mail Steamship Company's dock. An unimportant line operated with but one car, this line was gone by 1930.

In the early 1930s a new commuter line (#42) was established over a portion of the old route from Battery and California via Battery, First, Folsom, Second, Brannan and Third streets. It was rerouted in 1938 via Third, Kearny, Bush and Sansome to Chestnut, and abandoned on May 12, 1941.

Former Trackage Operating

Although much of the following trackage has been completely reconstructed by Municipal Railway since the 1944 merger, historically these pieces of trackage must be classified as Market Street Railway remnants. Thus San Franciscans and visitors who ride over the following segments of track can claim remote kinship to the White Front cars:

- Junipero Serra Blvd., Sloat to Ocean
- Ocean Ave., Junipero Serra to San Jose Ave.
- San Jose Ave., Ocean to Geneva
- Market Street, Fremont to Castro
- Duboce Ave., Church St. to Fillmore St.
- Carl Street, Cole to Stanyan
- Church Street, 16th to Market
- Taraval Street, 20th Ave. to 33rd Ave.
- First Street, Market to Mission

In 1973, trackage was re-extended on Church from Market to Duboce (once part of the #22 line) in connection with BART subway detours. This trackage will become permanent.

Still Life on Mission Street

SO SPOKE THE CAPTION of this photograph when it appeared in an October 1937 San Francisco newspaper. Let us quote the balance of the newswriter's text, which so eloquently describes the scene: "Trucks, automobiles and streetcars make movement an impossibility. Subways on Market Street, additional lanes for automobiles as a result, would relieve the pressure of through traffic on Mission and other downtown streets. During the rush hours the above picture would become more crowded, if possible. Deliveries to downtown stores inch along! Shoppers waste time in getting to their stores! Commuters rise extra early and eat dinner extra late! Transit has become stagnation."

Paul Ward

Elkton-Built

MARKET STREET RAILWAY'S own Elkton Shops turned out over 250 of these "California Comfort Cars" between 1920 and 1933. In this view, 914 growls uphill on Chenery Street, passing Fairmount Grammar School, in 1940. **Charles Smallwood**

Electric Passenger Cars

AT THE TIME Market Street Railway came into possession of United Railroads, there were on the property a grand total of 772 electric and cable passenger cars and more than 60 pieces of rail service equipment. This conglomeration of rolling stock was of great variation as to types and ages but all cars were in fairly good physical condition.

Of the double truck passenger cars, 210 were of the flush (straight) platform type; due to the necessity of climbing three steps to board these cars, loading and unloading was slow and inconvenient; United Railroads had begun a policy in 1921 of replacing these obsolete cars with a more modern type of drop platform car built in its own shops. The new company continued this car replacement program, and the last flush platform car was withdrawn from service in 1936.

Market Street Railway gradually incorporated many new innovations in its cars, both new and older types, to better riding qualities and to made the cars more comfortable—the chief improvements being the lavish use of deep cushioned cross seats in almost all cars. There can be no doubt that these improvements (especially the luxurious seats) did much to attract riders from the competing Municipal Railway lines, whose cars retained their original wooden benches.

Contrary to the general practice throughout the electric railway industry that seemed to indicate that a change in the exterior color of cars was advisable when a new owner took control, the new Market Street Railway retained the green and red color scheme of United Railroads. After a few years the old tile red roof color gave way to a hue called by the company "French Gray." Then in 1925 came a brief experiment with the attractive "Blue and Gold" livery, but MSR soon reverted to the old green body, red trim and gray roof scheme with the advent of the famous White Front policy.

In the mid-1930s the red trim on window sash and doors gave way to all-green sash on the sides and white sash on ends. In 1937 some cars of the 200 and 800-900 Classes were treated to a somewhat streamlined paint job consisting of a medium yellow roof (which included everything on the roof:

Market Street Railway Company
All-Time List of Electric Passenger Cars
1921 – 1944

CAR SERIES	TYPE	BUILDER	SEATS	WEIGHT	LENGTH	WIDTH	TRUCKS	CONTROL	MOTORS
1-12	Closed Interurban Straight bottom	St. Louis Car Co. 1906	56	75640	52' 1"	9' 4"	St. Louis MCB 61A	C6K	4-GE73
101-180	Deck roof D.T. Closed Drop platform	Jewett Car Co. 1911	46	48616	47' 0"	8' 9"	Standard 0-50	K28J	4-GE216
201-265	Arch roof D.T. Calif. Drop platform	American Car Co. 1913	50	50202	47' 0"	9' 0"	Brill 27GE1	K28J	4-GE216
266-285	Arch roof C.T. Calif. Drop platform	United Railroads 1920-21	50	43020	47' 0"	8' 9"	Standard 0-40	K28E	4-GE216
286-305	Arch roof D.T. Calif. Drop platform	Market St. Ry. 1924-25	50	38948	47' 0"	8' 9"	Standard 0-40	K12	4-GE247
401	Arch roof D.T. Calif. Ramp platform	United Railroads 1915	50	34215	47' 0"	9' 0"	Pittsburgh	K12	4-GE247
402-406	Arch roof D.T. Closed Ramp platform 1-man	St. Louis Car Co. 1927	48	36136	47' 3"	8' 8"	St. Louis E1B64	K75	4-GE264A
407-410	Arch roof D.T. Closed Ramp platform 1-man	St. Louis Car Co. 1924	44	34860	45' 0"	8' 8"	St. Louis AM64	K35	4-GE264A
601-605 613-616	Deck roof S.T. Calif. Straight Bot., 1-man	Hammond Car Co. 1895 Rebuilt U.R.R. 1914-15	26	20300	26' 10"	8' 8"	Peckham single	K10	2-GE1000
606-612 617-620 628-662	Deck roof S.T. Calif. Straight bottom	Hammond Car. Co. 1895 Holman Car Co. 1896	26	20700	26' 10"	8' 4"	Peckham single Brill 21	K10	2-GE1000
621-627	Deck roof S.T. Closed Fillmore Hill cars	Hammond Car Co. 1895 Rebuilt MSR 1925	26	23846	26' 10"	8' 4"	Peckham single	K10	2-GE216
681-697	Deck roof D.T. Calif. Straight bottom	St. Louis Car Co. 1901	50	38240	44' 8"	8' 10"	Brill 27G	K12	4-GE1000
698	Deck roof D.T. Closed Straight bottom	Original MSR 1901 Ex "Golden Gate"	48	40280	42' 0"	8' 4"	Brill 27G	K12	4-GE1000
699	Deck roof D.T. Closed Drop platform	United Railroads 1904 Ex "California"	48	43140	42' 0"	8' 10"	Peckham 14-B-3	K12	4-GE1000
701-724	Arch roof D.T. Calif. Straight bottom	United Railroads 1911-12	44	38710	41' 4"	9' 8"	Brill 27G	K12	4-GE1000
725-726(I)	Deck roof D.T. Calif. Straight bottom	Hammond Car Co. 1895 Rebuilt U.R.R. 1918	30	35840	33' 8"	9' 3"	Peckham 14-B-3	K12	4-GE1000
725-734(II)	Arch roof D.T. Closed Drop platform 1-man	J.G. Brill Car Co. 1914	40	38100	42' 6"	9' 6"	Brill 39E	K36J	2-WH306
727-730(I)	Railroad roof D.T. Closed Straight bottom	St. Louis Car Co. 1901 Rebuilt U.R.R. 1918	33	32720	29' 6"	9' 3"	Brill 27G	K12	4-GE1000
731-745(I)	Deck roof D.T. Calif. Straight bottom	Holman Car Co. 1897 Rebuilt U.R.R. 1915	44	37600	42' 2"	9' 8"	Peckham 14-B-3	K12	4-GE1000
735-736(II)	Deck roof D.T. Closed Drop platform 1-man	J.G. Brill Car Co. 1906	40	41430	43' 9"	8' 11"	Brill 27G	K35	4-GE264A
740-749(II)	Arch roof D.T. Closed Drop platform 1-man	St. Louis Car Co. 1918	40	42050	41' 0"	8' 8"	Brill 27 GE1	K28	4-GE200E
750-754(II)	Arch roof D.T. Closed Drop platform 1-man	St. Louis Car Co. 1918	40	37400	41' 0"	8' 8"	Brill 27 GE	K75	4-GE264B
746(I)	Deck roof D.T. Closed Straight bottom	St. Louis Car Co. 1896 Ex "Hermosa"	28	36300	32' 6"	9' 3"	Brill 27G	K12	4-GE58
751-756(I)	Deck roof D.T. Calif. Straight bottom	Hammond Car Co. 1895 Rebuilt U.R.R. 1916	46	36560	42' 8"	9' 8"	Peckham 14-B-3	K12	4-GE1000
755-759(II)	Arch roof D.T. Closed Drop platform 1-man	St. Louis Car Co. 1918	48	44380	46' 4"	8' 8"	Brill 27 GE1	K28	4-GE203P
757-771(I)	Arch roof D.T. Calif. Straight bottom	United Railroads 1918	44	37060	42' 9"	9' 4"	Peckham 14-B-3	K12	4-GE1000
772-778(I)	Arch roof D.T. Closed Straight bottom	United Railroads 1919	44	37160	42' 6"	9' 3"	Brill 27G	K12	4-GE1000

Electric Passenger Cars—Continued

CAR SERIES	TYPE	BUILDER	SEATS	WEIGHT	LENGTH	WIDTH	TRUCKS	CONTROL	MOTORS
778-922	Arch roof D.T. Calif. Drop platform	Market St. Ry. 1923-30	50	38895 40116	47' 0"	8' 9"	Peckham 14-B-3 Brill 27G	K12	4-GE1000 4-GE203
923-941 944-988 990-994	Arch roof D.T. Calif. Drop platform	Market St. Ry. 1930-33	50	45840	47' 0"	8' 9"	Brill 27 GE2	K28	4-GE90B
942-943	Arch roof D.T. Calif. Drop platform	Market St. Ry. 1930	50	43100	47' 0"	8' 9"	Standard 0-40	K12	4-GE247
989	Arch roof D.T. Calif. Drop platform 1-man	Market St. Ry. 1933	44	45400	47' 0"	8' 9"	Standard 0-40	K28	4-GE216
1225-1244	Deck roof D.T. Inter. Drop platform	Laclede Car Co. 1903	40	56138	48' 1"	9' 6"	Brill 27 E	K28	4-GE57
1301-1349	Deck roof D.T. Calif. Straight bottom	St. Louis Car Co. 1903	52	42290	45' 5"	9' 6"	Peckham 14-B-3	K12	4-GE1000
1350-1374	Deck roof D.T. Calif. Straight bottom	St. Louis Car Co. 1904	52	44780	45' 11"	9' 6"	Peckham 14-B-3	K12	4-GE1000
1375-1423	Deck roof D.T. Calif. Straight bottom	St. Louis Car Co. 1905	48	43510	44' 11"	9' 6"	Peckham 14-B-3	K12	4-GE1000
1500-1549	Deck roof D.T. Closed Drop platform	American Car Co. 1906	44	50990	45' 9"	9' 0"	McGuire 10 A	K28	4-GE80 4-GE90
1550-1749	Deck roof D.T. Closed Drop platform	St. Louis Car Co. 1907	44	54420	45' 4"	8' 9"	Brill 27 GE 2	K28J	4-GE90
45	Railroad roof D.T. Calif. Straight bottom	St. Louis Car Co. 1901	30	32720	29' 6"	9' 8"	Brill 27 G	K12	4-GE1000
1, 2, 3	Deck roof D.T. Funeral Straight bottom	United Railroads 1903-04	32	45260	45' 0"	9' 6"	Peckham 14-B-3	K12	4-GE58
San Francisco	Railroad roof D.T. Private Straight bottom	St. Louis Car Co. 1901 Rebuilt U.R.R. 1904	26	38300	37' 0"	9' 8"	Brill 27 G	K12	4-GE1000
Sierra	Railroad roof D.T. Private Straight bottom	St. Louis Car Co. 1901 Rebuilt U.R.R. 1908	28	39160	37' 6"	9' 8"	Peckham 14-B-3	K12	4-GE1000
2001-2014	See cars 837-843 and 299-305								
1424	Renumbered 778 (see above)								

Notes on Passenger Cars

180 rebuilt to one-man car.

265 rebuilt to one-man car.

266-305 rebuilt to one-man, two-man cars.

401 was formerly numbered 301.

402-410 from East St. Louis Railways.

698 and 699 were formerly observation cars. They were used exclusively on Visitacion line while in regular passenger service.

725 and 726(I) were formerly one-man cars 1023 and 1024 and were used on Visitacion line until wreck of 1918.

725-734 and 735 and 736 were from Williamsport Railways.

740-759 were from East St. Louis Railways.

778, 800-825, 837-838, 850-884, 941-962, 989, and 991-994 were one-man, two-man cars.

1227 rebuilt to one-man car in 1935 but never used as such. Rebuilt back to two-man car.

1391 was an all-steel car built by Pressed Steel Car Co. in 1905. When built it was numbered 1350.

1527 had number changed to 1499 in 1919. Was renumbered back to 1527 about 1924.

1508 had new body of arch roof California type built in 1915 following destruction of original car in accident.

1715, 1716 and 1722 had new arch roof California type bodies built following destruction of original cars.

2001-2014 were the short-lived "Blue and Gold" cars of 1925.

1424 built for South San Francisco service.

MARKET STREET RAILWAY CO. — SCHEDULE OF REVENUE ROLLING STOCK

TYPE OF ELECTRIC CAR	No. of Cars	Serial Number of Car	Weight of Car Equipped	Seating Capacity	Length Over Bumpers	Length Over Closed Section	Length Over Open Section or Platform	Width Over Steps	Width Over Drips	Truck Centers	Name of Builder and Date	Type of Controller	Number of Motors	H.P.	Type	Gear Ratio	Brakes / Type of Compressor	Type of Trucks	Motor Outside or Inside Hung	Wheel Base	Dia. of Wheel Steel or Cast
P.A.Y.E. Drop platform, closed & open bodies	80	101-180 ••	48616	46	47'-0"	32'-4"	7'-4"	8'-9"	9'-2"	20'-10"	Jewett Car Co. 1911	K-28-J	4	50	G.E. 216E	15-71	C.P.27 A-4	Standard 0-50	Outside	4'-6"	33" C.I.
P.A.Y.E. Drop platform, open ends	65	201-265 ••	50202	50	47'-0"	15'-4 3/8"	15'-9 5/8"	9'-0"	9'-2"	20'-10 1/2"	American Car Co. 1913	K-28-J	4	50	G.E. 216E	15-71	A-5	Brill 27 G.E.I.	Outside	4'-6"	33" C.I.
ONE-M & TWO-M Drop plat., closed plat. & body	18	266-283	43020	44	47'-0"	15'-6 1/2"	14'-11"		9'-3"	20'-10"	Market St. Ry. Co. 1920	K-28-E	4	50	G.E. 216	19-67	D-H-10	Standard 0-40	Outside	4'-6"	30" C.I.
ONE-M & TWO-M Drop plat., closed plat. & body	20	286-305	38948	44	47'-0"	15'-6 1/2"	14'-11"		9'-3"	20'-10"	Market St. Ry. Co. 1924 1925	K-12	4	40	G.E. 247D	15-76	A.A.I.	Standard 0-40	Outside	4'-6"	30" C.I.
P.A.Y.E. Ramp platform, open ends	1	401 •	34215	50	47'-0"	15'-6 1/2"	15'-8 7/8"	9'-0"	9'-1 1/2"	21'-3"	Market St. Ry. Co. 1915	K-12	4	40	G.E. 247A	14-57	M.W.I	Pittsburgh	Inside	5'-6"	24" C.I.
One Man Drop platform, closed plat. & bodies	2	S.S.F.R.R.&P. Co. 284-285	44650	52	47'-0"	15'-6 1/2"	14'-11"	8'-9"	9'-3"	20'-10"	Market St. Ry. Co. 1920; Rebuilt Market St. Ry. Co. 1932	L.B.4 Handle K-28-E	4	50	G.E. 216	19-67	C.P.27	Standard 0-40	Outside	4'-6"	30" C.I.
One Man Ramp platform, closed plat. & bodies	5	402-406	36136	48	47'-9"	31'-4"	8'-0"		8'-7 1/2"	22'-8"	St. Louis Car Co. 1927; Received by Mkt. St. Ry. Co. 1936	K-75	4	25	G.E. 264A	15-72	C.P.27	St. Louis E-1 B-64	Outside	5'-4"	26" Steel
P.A.Y.E. Drop platform, open ends	166	778-943 •• ◊	38895 40116 43100	50	47'-0"	15'-6 1/2"	14'-11"	8'-9"	9'-3"	20'-10"	Market St. Ry. Co. 1923 1930	K-12	4 / 4 / 4	40 / 35 / 50	G.E. 247 C.D. / G.E. 1000 / G.E. 203 APQ	15-58 / 15-76 / 17-67 / 15-69 / 17-67	C.P.27 / M.W.I / A.A.I	Peckham 14-3-B.S.; Brill 27G & G1	Outside; Outside	4'-1"; 4'-0"	30" C.I.
P.A.Y.E. Drop platform, open ends	50	944 - 988 ••; 990 - 994	45840	50	47'-0"	15'-6 1/2"	14'-11"	8'-9"	9'-3"	20'-10"	Market St. Ry. Co. 1931 1932 1933	L.B.2 Handle; L.B.4 Handle; T.A.6 Handle; K-28	4	50	G.E. 90B	19-67	C.P.27	Brill 27 G.E.2	Outside	4'-4"	33" C.I.
P.A.Y.E. Drop platform, closed plat. & body	20	1225-1244 +	56138	40	48'-1"	17'-0"	6'-1 1/2"	9'-6"	9'-6"	23'-0"	St. Louis Car Co. 1908; Rebuilt Market St. Ry. Co. 1932	Field Cont. K-28-B	4	50	G.E. 57	22-63	A-4	Brill 27E.	Inside	6'-0"	33" Steel
ONE-M. Drop plat., closed plat. & body	10	725 - 734	38,100	40	42'-6"	28'-1"	5'-6"	9'-1"	8'-5"	19'-4"	J.G. Brill 1918; Received by Mkt. St. Ry. 1936	K-36-J	2	60	W.H. 306	15-69	C.P.27	Brill 39 E	Outside	4'-8"	21" Steel; 33" "
ONE-M. Drop plat., closed plat. & body	2	735 - 736	41,430	40	43'-9"	28'-0"	5'-11"	8'-11"	8'-3"	16'-0"	J.G. Brill 1918; Received by Mkt. St. Ry 1939	K-36-J	2	40	G.E. 80	15-71	C.P.27	Brill 27G	Outside	4'-1"	21" Steel; 33" "
One Man Ramp plat., closed plat. & body	4	407 - 410	34,860	44	45'-0"	29'-6"	7'-9"		8'-7 5/8"	20'-9"	St. Louis Car Co. 1924; Received by Mkt. St. Ry 1936	K-35	4	25	G.E. 264A	15-72	C.P.27	St. Louis A.M.-64	Outside	5'-4"	26" Steel
One Man Drop plat., closed plat. & body	10	740-749	42,050	40	41'-0"	26'-4"	7'-4"		8'-8"	15'-2"	St. Louis Car Co. 1918 Rebuilt 1927; Received by Mkt. St. Ry. 1936	K-28	4	40	G.E. 200E	14-67	C.P.27	Brill 27 G.E.I	Outside	4'-6"	33" Steel
One & Two Man. Drop plat., closed plat. & body.	1	989	45400	44	47'-0"	15'-6 1/2"	14'-11"	8'-9"	9'-3"	20'-10"	Market St. Ry. Co. 1933	L.B.2 Handle K 28	4	50	G.E. 216	19-67	C.P.27	Standard 0-40	Outside	4'-6"	30" C.I.
One Man Drop plat., closed plat. & body	5	750 - 754	37,400	40	41'-0"	26'-4"	7'-4"		8'-8"	15'-2"	St. Louis Car Co. 1918 Rebuilt 1927; Received by Mkt. St. Ry. 1936	K-75	4	25	G.E. 264B	16-97	C.P.27	Brill 27 G.E	Outside	4'-6"	33" Steel
One Man Drop plat., closed plat. & body	5	755 - 759	44380	48	46'-4	31'-8"	7'-4		8'-8"	21'-9 1/2"	St. Louis Car Co. 1918 Rebuilt 1927; Received by Mkt. St. Ry. 1936	K-28	4	50	G.E. 203P.	17-67	C.P.27	Brill G.E.I	Outside	4'-6"	33" Steel
P.A.Y.E. Drop plat. closed & open body	47	1501-1503, 1505-1533, 1535-1547, 1549	52096	44	45'-9"	32'-4"	6'-8 1/2"	9'-8"	9'-0"	20'-6"	American Car Co. 1906; Rebuilt Mkt. St. Ry. 1923	K-28-E; K-28-J	4	50	G.E. 80; G.E. 90	15-71	A-4; A.A.4	McGuire 10-A	Inside	6'-0"	33" C.I.
P.A.Y.E. Drop platform, closed & open body. See storage list.	144	1550-1615(?), 1617-1619, 1621-1626, 1628-1632, 1634-1638, 1640-1641, 1644-1647, 1649, 1651-1652, 1655-1659(?), 1664, 1666, 1672, 1675-1679, 1681, 1683-1684, 1686-1690(?), 1696, 1700, 1702, 1714-1716, 1718-1722, 1725-1756(?), 1758-1769(?) ✧	56714	44	45'-4"	32'-4"	6'-6"	8'-9"	9'-2"	21'-6"	St. Louis Car Co. 1907	K-28-J	4	50	G.E. 90	15-71; 19-67	A-4	Brill 27 G.E.2	Outside	4'-4"	33" C.I.
Private Car	1	San Francisco	38300	26	37'-0"	29'-6"	4'-0"	9'-8"	8'-10"	22'-0"	Rebuilt Mkt. St. Ry. Co. 1904	K-12	4	35	G.E. 58	22-66	A.A.I	Brill 27G	Outside	4'-0"	30" C.I.
P.A.Y.E. Single truck, Fillmore Hill cars	7	621-627	23846	26	26'-10"	10'-7 1/2"	8'-1 1/2"	8'-4"	8'-4"		Rebuilt Mkt. St. Ry. Co. 1915	K-10	2 / 2	35 / 50	G.E. 1000 / G.E. 216	15-69 / 15-71	C.P.25	Peckham Single	Inside	7'-0"	30" C.I.
TYPE OF TROLLEY COACH									OVER SIDES									REAR TIRES	FRONT TIRES		
TROLLEY COACH closed body	9	51-59	19425	37	32'-11 1/2"				8'-0"		J.G. Brill 1935 1936	G.E. / W.H.	2 / 2	65 / 65	G.E. 1184A / W.H. 1429 C.T.9	9.25-1 / 9.29-1	C.P. 25	22-9.75	22-10.50	16'-3 1/4"	
TYPE OF MOTOR COACH													ENGINE					SIZE OF TIRES			
Fageol Bus Closed body	6	1-6	11960	29	28'-3 1/2"				7'-9"		Fageol 1926 1927		6-Cyl.		Hall Scott Waukesha		Westing.	38 x 7.00		19'-5 1/2"	
Fageol Bus Closed body	2	7-8	16380	30	30'-3 5/8"				8'-9"		Fageol Chassis, Calif. Motor Coach Body 1932		6-Cyl.		Hall Scott		Westing.	20 x 9.75		19'-6 5/8"	
G.M.C. Bus Closed body	1	21	7120	17	20'-9"				7'-5 1/2"		G.M.C T26C 711 1932		6-Cyl.		Buick		Mech.	20 x 7.00		13'-11"	
TYPE OF CABLE CAR												TRACK GAGE	FRONT TRUCK		REAR TRUCK	DIA. OF WHEELS	NOTE See supplement on One Man Cars				
Castro St. combination	1	1	13640	30	31'-8"	8'-6"	9'-11"	8'-2"	7'-0"	18'-8"	Market St. Ry. Co. 1924	4'-8 1/2"	5'-3 1/2"		4'-11"	22" C.I.					
Castro St. combination	1	2	13040	34	34'-0"	11'-0"	11'-6"	8'-0"	7'-8"	22'-6"	Market St. Ry. Co. 1907	4'-8 1/2"	5'-3 1/2"		4'-11"	22" C.I.					
Castro St. combination	4	3-6	13190	30	31'-8"	8'-6"	9'-11"	8'-2"	7'-0"	18'-8"	Market St. Ry. Co. 1926 1927	4'-8 1/2"	5'-3 1/2"		4'-11"	22" C.I.					
Castro St. combination	1	7	13020	30	31'-8"	8'-6"	9'-11"	8'-2"	7'-0"	18'-8"	Rebuilt Mkt. St. Ry. Co. 1933	4'-8 1/2"	5'-3 1/2"		4'-11"	22" C.I.					
Sacramento St. combination	12	15-26	15240	34	34'-0"	11'-0"	11'-6"	8'-0"	7'-8"	22'-6"	Market St. Ry. Co. 1907	3'-6"	5'-3 1/2"		4'-11"	22" C.I.					
Powell St. one end open, one end closed	27	501-527	12180	29	27'-0"	12'-0"	15'-0"	7'-10 1/2"	7'-8"	11'-8"	Mahoney Bros. 1893; 509 Rebuilt Mkt. St. Ry. Co. 1928	3'-6"	5'-3"		4'-0"	22" C.I.					

• FORMERLY 301 CHANGED 3-10-25 ✧ CARS 1715-1716-1722 McGUIRE 10-A TRUCKS G.E. 90 MOTORS USED ON SAN MATEO LINE CLOSED BODIES ◊ CARS 942-943 G.E. 247 MOTORS + 1229 G.E. 90 MOTORS

•• 180 265 ONE-M CARS
778, 942 943 ONE-M & TWO-M CARS
944-948 ONE-M & TWO-M CARS

REVISIONS | Correct to Date C.M.L. 12-22-33. | Correct to date C.M.L. 12-16-36 | Correct to date C.M.L. 1-7-36 | Correct to date C.M.L. 11-23-36

MARKET STREET RAILWAY COMPANY
EQUIPMENT DEPARTMENT
SCHEDULE OF REVENUE ROLLING STOCK

DRAWING No. M.M. 2011
SCALE None INCH ONE FOOT
DRAWN BY C.M. Lang Compilled by C.D. Miller
CHECKED BY DATE 12-31-32
APPROVED BY SUPT. of EQUIP.

MM 2011

trolley poles, ventilators, sign boxes, etc.) and a large variated white stripe trimmed with yellow on the sides. The style of numbering was also modified to give a somewhat streamlined appearance. This wild color scheme on the few cars which received it and the green-gray-white scheme remained the standard colors during the remaining life of the company. Strangely, after the takeover of Market Street Railway in 1944, Municipal Railway adopted green as its official body color.

Cars used on the cable lines of the system were all of early origin. Those on Powell St., whose pair of lines was the heaviest traveled cable lines on the system, dated back to 1887 and 1891-93. The large cars on Sacramento-Clay and the isolated standard gauge Castro cable lines were 1907 rebuilds of former open cable cars used on Market St. prior to the April 18, 1906, disaster and dated back to the 1880s. The archaic Pacific Ave. cable trains of grip car and trailer dated back to the late 1870s. In 1927 the company constructed six new cable cars for the relatively unimportant Castro cable; these new cars, which incidentally were the last new design of cable cars ever built, were pleasing in appearance with their arch roof and rounded ends. Why Market Street Railway chose to build new cars for the Castro cable while the important Sacramento-Clay line (which used the same type of car) had to carry on the original rolling stock for another 15 years is open to speculation.

One interesting feature of San Francisco's street railways, both on Market Street Railway and Municipal Railway, was the use of colored destination signs which hung on the right front dash. Each line, whether cable or electric, with few exceptions, had its own color or combination of colors, some of

(FACING PAGE) **HERE IS THE 1936** version of Market Street Railway's passenger car roster, when streetcars were still preeminent.

EVEN THE WHITE FRONT paint scheme had variations, as these photos prove. (ABOVE) **CAR 945** when new had the white front, but note roof, sash and buffer treatment. **Paul Ward** (BELOW) **THE GARISH SCHEME** of the 1940 era reflected the trend of the times . . . remember those railroad streamliners? **W.C. Whittaker**

which were quite attractive. The signs gave, in most cases, the most important streets traversed by the route, the terminals, and, in some cases, the important points of interest. This practice had its origin about 1900, at which time it was customary for each route to have its own distinctive colored cars; when it became necessary, say, to run a yellow car on a red line for some reason, a red colored dash sign (or "board," as they were known in those days) stating the route of the red line was hung on the front dash of the yellow car.

After 1902, when the use of differently colored cars for each line was discontinued in favor of a single system-wide color scheme, the use of the dash signs continued, the signs retaining the original color of the early routes. As new lines were opened, the use of dash signs was retained as they provided a convenient means of passenger route identification. This method of route identification was still in use on the two Powell St. cable lines until 1970, when large-scale thefts by souvenir hunters of these removable signs required the installation of a type of sign that is permanently attached to the dash.

Included in the rolling stock acquired by Market Street Railway were almost 70 pieces of rail service equipment. Even for a property the size of the former URR system this was an ample supply of work cars. These cars could do just about any job that might be faced in maintaining and improving its property. There were cars for every conceivable need: the usual heavy duty gondolas and flat cars for road work, line cars to maintain the overhead power system, wreckers, sand cars, and cars for a host of other duties. Among these highly specialized cars were some beauties: one for washing windows in car houses and other buildings; another for spraying paint on car houses and other structures; still another was fixed up to spray weeds along open track on private way.

Many of these service cars had been rebuilt from obsolete passenger cars, while others were built new for the purpose for which they were intended—some at major expense.

In the mid-1920s motor trucks took over a substantial number of service car duties, especially in construction and wrecker work, as well as in the Line Department. As long as the company enjoyed ample space in which to store the old service cars, they were kept on the property; but when in the late 1930s several car houses were closed as an economy measure and space became at a premium, the supplanted work equipment had to be taken to Elkton Yard and scrapped.

In this chapter we concern ourselves only with MSR's electric passenger cars.

RIDING THE FENDER was one way to catch a ride on an already-overloaded White Front Car, like in this typical rush hour scene; Market and Church, 1933.
Paul Ward

A CHARACTERISTIC FEATURE of San Francisco streetcars was the "fender", a metal basket-like affair decreed by law to be affixed to the operating end of every car. When lowered in position in the direction the car was going, this contraption was intended to scoop up any luckless person chancing to stumble into the fast-moving trolley's path. The rear fender was chained in an upright position. Fenders were first installed on San Francisco cars in 1908.

(ABOVE) **SMALL BOYS** were quick to discover that the raised rear fender provided some jim-dandy toe and hand holds, and thus for generations of San Francisco youths the sport of "nipping the fender" was an adventuresome and economical, albeit hazardous, mode of transportation. This scene is at 26th and Army streets in 1943. **Charles Smallwood**

(RIGHT) **CAR 1722 MODELS MSR'S** colorful Ingleside line dash signs . . . the only ones made of baked enamel. The small plate below reads "White Front patented February 15, 1927." **Lorin Silliman**

The Big Subs

THE ORIGINAL CONDITION of the Big Subs is seen in this October 1907 photograph taken at Geneva Barn. Note the interurban-style wooden pilot, as ordered by the Philadelphia & Western Railway. P&W's inability to pay for the order coincided with United Railway's nationwide search for equipment following the earthquake and fire.
United Railroads

Cars 1—12

The 12 "Big Subs" of San Mateo line interurban fame were the largest and most impressive electric cars ever to roll in San Francisco.

Numbered 1-12, these giants were part of an order constructed by St. Louis Car Company in early 1906 for The Philadelphia & Western Railway for use on its then-building line from Philadelphia west to Norristown. P&W ordered 20 cars, but when St. Louis Car completed the order, P&W had fallen on difficult times and was unable to pay for them.

At that precise moment President Pat Calhoun of United Railroads of San Francisco was scouring the nation for any available electric cars for use on his several lines then being converted to electricity from cable as a consequence of the earthquake and fire. An inspection at St. Louis Car's factory of the P&W orphans so impressed Calhoun that he purchased 12 of them on the spot for his San Mateo line.

Calhoun's giants entered service on the San Mateo line immediately, replacing the 1225 class suburban cars in that service. Thus, for the first time, San Francisco enjoyed interurban cars; it wasn't long before the impressive cars won their soubriquet: "The Big Subs."

Little changes were made in the Big Subs during the years of their epic assignment down the peninsula. Their original spoked wheels were replaced by rolled steel wheels of smaller

General Specifications, Cars 1-12

Body type	Interurban, closed, flush platforms, railroad roof
Builder	St. Louis Car Company
Date built	1906
Weight	75,640 lbs.
Seats	56
Length over buffers	52'1"
Length over closed section	40'0"
Length over platforms	6'6"
Width over steps	9'4"
Width over drips	9'0"
Truck centers	29'4"
Controller	C-6-K
Motors	Four GE 73, 75 hp.
Gear ratio	21:54
Compressor	West. D2EG
Trucks	St. Louis 61A
Motors hung	Inside
Truck wheelbase	6'8"
Wheels	34" steel

(FACING PAGE) **MASSIVE HIGH-BACKED** leather seats featured the Big Sub's interiors. **Charles Smallwood**

THE CARS LOOKED less impressive by this 1913 view, also at Geneva Barn. Their massive wooden pilots had given way to fenders, while their 36-inch spoked wheels had been replaced by 33-inch steel wheels, lowering the entire car slightly. They were still big, however, compared to the rest of the URR fleet. **United Railroads**

(RIGHT) A NORTHBOUND P&W CAR at speed near Oak Grove on the San Mateo interurban line, 1922.
Charles Smallwood

(ABOVE) THIS END VIEW of a P&W car clearly shows construction indicating a train door. Originally built for train service, these doors were closed off at the factory for San Francisco service. The big cars never operated in trains.
United Railroads

AT THE SAN MATEO DEPOT in 1923; capturing the conductor on film. Even at this time the rebuilt 1200-class cars were filling most schedules on the interurban line.
Charles Smallwood

diameter in 1909; at the same time their wooden pilots gave way to fenders, in compliance with a city ordinance. Never did the Subs operate in multiple unit; all had slotted drawbars for emergency use.

Entering San Francisco via Mission St. with its numerous heavy grades and curves, the Big Subs had no appreciable difficulties in the early years. But with the rapid growth of that section and the attendant increase in street traffic, both streetcar and vehicular, the less-than-agile Subs began to pose problems. Quite apart from their sheer bulk, they consumed prodigious amounts of power, especially on the long grades— power badly needed by the burgeoning fleet of local cars. By 1923 it was reluctantly decided to withdraw the Subs. Their replacement? The very same cars which they had themselves ousted from the San Mateo line in 1906: the 1225 class. The 1225s were put through Elkton Shops, extensively refurbished, and replaced the Big Subs in the autumn of 1923.

Into dead storage at 24th Street Car House went the 12 behemoths.

For 10 long years they slumbered, becoming more of a legend with each passing month. The end came for half of the big cars in 1933 when 24th Street Car House was partially rebuilt to accommodate buses, reducing storage trackage. Orders came to remove six of the cars to Elkton Yard for scrapping—the other six even then apparently being considered too valuable to discard. In July 1933, cars 2, 3, 6, 7, 9 and 11 were hauled to Elkton and burned.

In 1935 came further bus expansion at 24th Street Car House, dooming the six remaining cars. Making the melancholy trip to Elkton that spring were cars 1, 4, 5, 8, 10 and 12. Last to suffer the torch was car 10; as its stately body went up in smoke on March 25, so did San Francisco's brief personal encounter with interurbans.

BIG SUBS 10 and 1 effectively dwarf other cars in Geneva Barn, including 1230 at left. This photo dates from August 1920.

PLOWING THROUGH HIGH WATER, Big Sub 5 almost becomes a submariner on County Road between Cypress Lawn and Holy Cross cemeteries, Colma, in January 1914.
United Railroads

Cars 1—12

Cars 1—12

A RARE SHOT of a Big Sub with headlight. Geneva Barn, 1922. **Randolph Brandt**

Big Sub To San Mateo

THE CLASSIC LINES of this southbound Big Sub are seen on the San Mateo interurban line, near Millbrae, circa 1919. **Silliman Brothers**

Cars 101—180

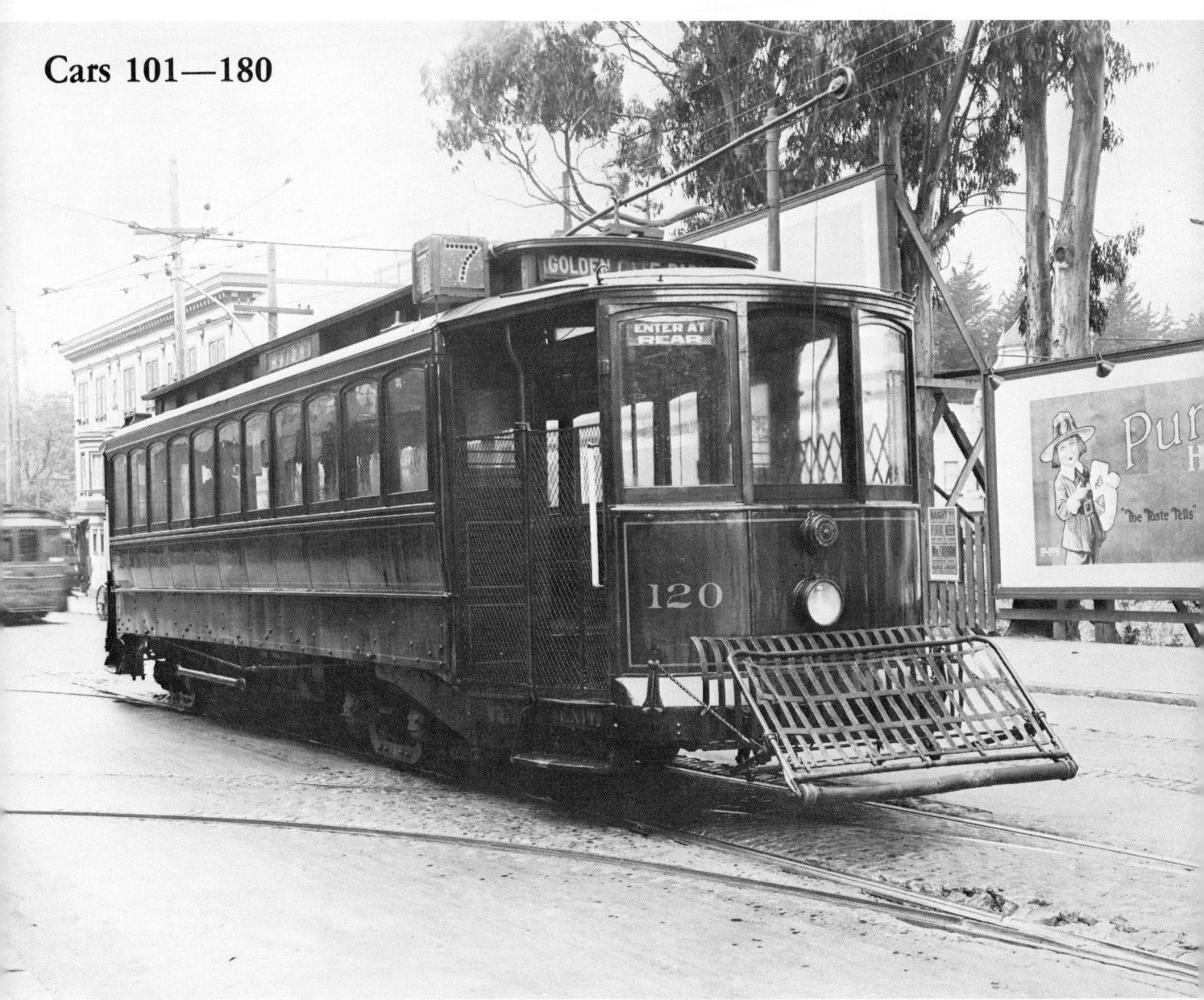

SAN FRANCISCO'S FIRST Pay As You Enter cars, the 100s, were purchased in 1911. Here is 120, in its United Railroads livery, at Haight Street Car House, circa 1920.
United Railroads

Cars 101—180

These 80 cars were the first Pay As You Enter cars purchased new for San Francisco service. They were built by Jewett Car Company of Niles, Ohio, in 1911 under designs prepared by Ford, Bacon & Davis, a large New York public utilities engineering firm. The cars were of the all-enclosed, single-compartment type known to the electric railway trade as "box cars." Lack of a smoking section and uncomfortable longitudinal seats throughout did not do much toward giving the riding public a very favorable opinion of them.

When the 101 class arrived, it was used on the Sutter St. lines but was shifted to the Haight St. line in 1914. These cars were replaced on the Sutter lines by the 201-265 class which arrived in that year.

In January 1927, Market Street Railway began a program of upgrading this class. Movable side windows replaced the stationary sash for better ventilation; best of all, the hard longitudinal seats were replaced by comfortable deep-cushion cross seats upholstered in Spanish grain leather, making the 100s among the city's most pleasant cars in which to ride. Smoking compartments were also provided in this modernization.

The 101-180 class ran out almost its entire life on Haight St. Division lines. A few were transferred to McAllister Division in the late 1930s for use on the #21—Hayes St. line. These cars were not used south of Market (except one-man 180) until World War II years when the Bryant-San Bruno and Fillmore-16th St. lines received a few of them. Some also went on the #9—Valencia line.

Passing into Municipal Railway ownership on September 29, 1944, there was an immediate numbering conflict with

AS DELIVERED, interiors were very plain, like 109 above. **United Railroads** (BELOW) **DEEP CUSHIONED** cross seating was part of a 1927 upgrading program, making these cars far more pleasant for riders. S.F. Public Utilities Commission

Cars 101—180

BRAND NEW! Car 142 models the appearance of the 100 class soon after its delivery. Photo was taken in June 1911.

United Railroads

Muni's own 100 class. This was solved by renumbering the former MSR 100s into a new Muni class, the 400. Never carried through insofar as all ex-MSR 100s were concerned, nevertheless about half did run as Muni 400s. All were retired by the end of 1949.

Note: Car 123 had been retired prior to 1944 and did not come to Muni in the 1944 merger.

Municipal Railway Renumbering Data:

The following 101-180 class cars were renumbered by Municipal Railway into its 400 class:

101: 401	130: 430	151: 451	165: 465
102: 402	131: 431	152: 452	166: 466
104: 404	132: 432	154: 454	167: 467
105: 405	133: 433	157: 457	168: 468
110: 410	135: 435	158: 458	171: 471
111: 411	137: 437	160: 460	172: 472
112: 412	139: 439	161: 461	173: 473
124: 424	144: 444	162: 462	180: 480
126: 426	150: 450	164: 464	

General Specifications, Cars 101—180

Body type	Closed, PAYE, drop platforms, deck roof
Builder	Jewett Car Company
Date built	1911
Weight	48,616 lbs.
Seats	46
Length over buffers	47' 0"
Length closed section	32' 4"
Length over platform	7' 4"
Width over steps	8' 9"
Width over drips	9' 2"
Truck centers	20' 10"
Controller	K-28-J
Motors	Four GE 216-E, 50 hp
Motors hung	Outside
Gear ratio	15:71
Compressor	CP 27 A4
Trucks	Standard O-50
Truck wheelbase	4' 6"
Wheels	33" Cast Iron

THERE WAS NO MISTAKING A 100 for any other type of MSR car. Their long platforms, long deck roof, single closed section, rub rail and uniform window arrangement set them apart. (ABOVE) **CAR 126,** in service on the 22 line, crosses the Cal Cable at Fillmore and California streets, 1932. (BELOW) **CAR 121** at 20th Avenue and Wawona Street in December 1937.

BOTH: W.C. Whittaker

(ABOVE) **100s WERE FIXTURES** on the very scenic private right-of-way through Golden Gate Park. Car 131 heads for the Ferry.
Charles Smallwood

(BELOW) **INBOUND ON TURK STREET**, near Stanyan, in January 1944, 127 climbs up the grade. 100-class equipment was used only as trippers on the 31 line.
W.C. Whittaker

One-Man Car

Cars 101—180

AFTER COURT ACTION, MSR inaugurated one-man car service on some lines. Car 180 was the only 100 so modified. Note in this 1937 photo, taken on the 24 line at Divisadero and Post, the "Enter Front" sign in the front window.
W.C. Whittaker

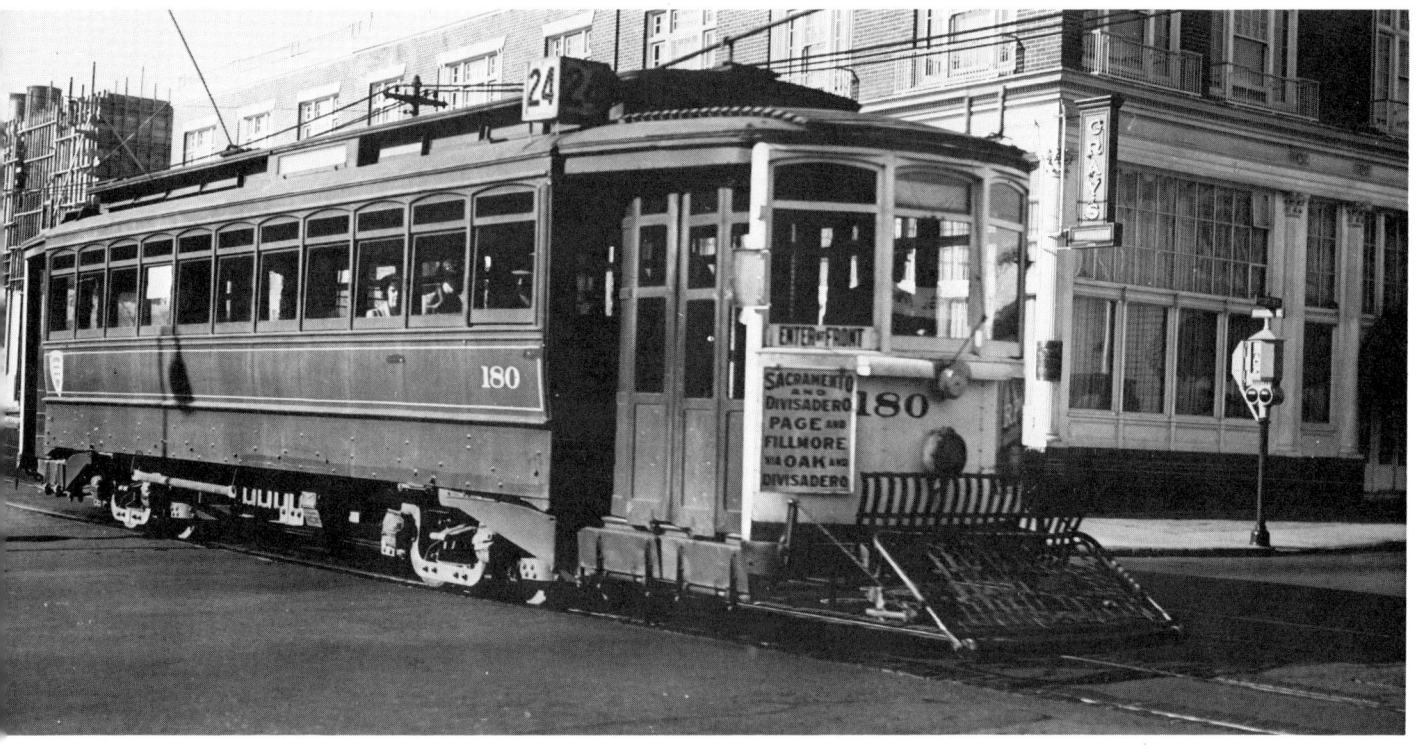

IN 1916 about 15 of the 101-180 class cars were rebuilt to include a four-window open section on one end. The closed section retained the longitudinal seats but wooden cross seats were installed in the open section. These cars retained this open end feature until the 1927 modernization when all cars of this class were equipped with leather seats; at that time the open ends were again enclosed. Car 174 is on Oak Street c.1920.
United Railroads

THIS FINE CAR DESIGN became the pattern for all subsequent units ordered by MSR and the Municipal Railway. Car 206 is seen at Sutro Barn in October 1914.
United Railroads

Cars 201—265

The most successful car design to be developed in San Francisco during the electric streetcar era had its nucleus in 65 cars ordered by and delivered to United Railroads in 1913. This type of car was designed by W.B. Farlow, chief draftsman for URR and was constructed by American Car Company of St. Louis.

These cars, numbered 201-265, were of a modified California type; a closed center section had an open section at either side. If any one type of car ever used in San Francisco deserved to be known as "The San Francisco Type," it was this one. The basic design became the pattern for all subsequent cars ordered for the city both by the private company and also Municipal Railway up until the advent of the PCC car.

The 201-265 represented the ultimate development of the very successful California Type, which had its origin in San Francisco. Easy access and rapid loading were made possible by the use of a large drop platform. Two different seating arrangements were used, varying only in the closed section; the closed section of cars 201-235 was equipped with longitudinal seats, but cars 136-265 had reversible cross seats on one side. Open sections had reversible cross seats of wood slat construction with natural finish to match the interior of the car. Folding seats for six passengers were also provided on the platforms but were used only on the front end. Wire plate glass was standard on the side windows of the ends to minimize the danger from flying glass in the event of collision.

The interior of this class presented an attractive appearance. Woodwork was white ash, stained and varnished in natural finish. Ceiling headlining was painted white, and all hardware was polished brass.

Upon arrival from St. Louis, all cars of this class were assigned to the Sutro Division and placed in service on the Sutter St. group of lines: Clement, California and Jackson. Over the years a few found their way to other lines, but most spent their entire service life of more than 35 years on the original Sutter St. runs.

The personnel of Sutro Division, both operating and shop forces, took unusual pride in these cars and for many years the records of "turn ins" (cars unable to complete their scheduled run due to defects) was the lowest on the entire MSR system.

In 1935 car 265 was rebuilt for one-man operation. It was then assigned to certain lines using that type of operation where it performed quite well. No doubt the rest of the class would have been rebuilt similarly if MSR's one-man policy had been permitted to continue and expand. After one-man cars were abandoned the 265 entered storage; later it was converted back to two-man operation after Municipal Railway succeeded to ownership.

When these cars became the property of Municipal Railway in 1944, many saw considerable service on Muni lines, especially on Geary St. Many were renumbered by Muni to avoid conflict with its own 200 class; these cars entered Muni's 601-665 class.

Cars 201—265

General Specifications, Cars 201—265

Body Type	PAYE, 3 section, arch roof, drop platform
Builder	American Car Company, St. Louis
Date built	1913
Weight	50,202 lbs.
Seats	50
Length over buffers	47′0″
Length closed section	15′5″
Length open section	15′9⅝″
Width over steps	9′0″
Width over drips	9′2″
Truck centers	20′10¼″
Controller	K-28-J
Motors	4 GE 216-E, 50 hp.
Gear ratio	15:71
Compressor	A-5
Trucks	Brill 27-G, E1
Motors hung	Outside
Truck wheelbase	4′6″
Wheels	33″ Cast Iron

SLIDING GATE, bayonet stool, unlined hood, roof sign crank and bare Mazda bulbs—all were typical of MSR standards, as shown in this view of 241's number one end. **Market Street Railway**

Municipal Railway Renumbering Data

On September 29, 1944, cars 201-265 became the property of Municipal Railway; a numbering conflict then existed automatically, as Muni's own 200 class was very much in existence. It was decided to renumber the MSR cars into Muni's new 600 class; this process was never carried through, but the following ex-201 class cars did receive 600 class Muni numbers:

601-613, 622, 635, 638, 644, 647, 651, 654, 657, 659, 660, 662, 663, 665.

Scrapping Data

226, 252 (1947); 218, 239, 243, 250 (1948); 214-217, 219-221, 223-225, 227-234, 236, 237, 240-242, 245, 246, 248, 249, 253, 255, 256, 258, 261, 264, 601-605, 608, 611, 612, 613, 622, 651, 654, 657, and 663 (1949); 606, 607, 609, 610, 635, 638, 644, 647, 659, 660, 662, and 665 in 1950, winding up this class.

It is worthy of note that this class, older by many years than MSR's home-built copies, outlasted all of the latter cars except eight 900s with which it was even—the last survivors being sold for scrap on April 4, 1950.

CAST BRASS numbers and company shield were tried out briefly on cars 236 and 260, as well as on several work cars. This idea, thought up in 1933, was abandoned as being too costly. **Market Street Railway**

THE SPARTAN SIMPLICITY of the interiors of the first group of Sutro 200-class cars (ABOVE) contrasts with this 1928 view (BELOW), showing the rattan and upholstered seating applied to all 65 cars. **United Railroads; S.F. Public Utilities Commission**

Cars 201—265

(ABOVE) **CAR 239 POSED** for a broadside at 33rd and California streets in 1914, in its original state. **United Railroads** (BELOW) **IN THE LATE 1920s,** Sutter car 226 was equipped with Timken Roller Bearings as an experiment. These bearings worked out well; the car was very free-wheeling and was said to use less power. Apparently the company felt that, despite the advantage, the bearings did not justify the high initial cost and no further cars were so equipped. This Elkton view illustrates that when these cars were first enclosed, only one side of each side section was glazed. **Market Street Railway**

171

(ABOVE) **BELLWETHER OF ITS CLASS,** Car 201 poses at the 18th and Castro terminus of the 8 Line in July 1940. (BELOW) **ABOUT TO CROSS** the Jones cable tracks, 3 Line car 210 is seen at Sutter and Jones in April 1942.
BOTH: W.C. Whittaker

(ABOVE) **THE VERY IMPRESSIVE** Temple Emanu-El co-stars with car 264 in this January 1939 study at Sacramento Street and Arguello Blvd.
W.C. Whittaker

SNOW IN SAN FRANCISCO! During one of the city's extremely rare snowfalls, back in February 1932, #1-Sutter St. car 206 lays over at 33rd Avenue and Clement Street.
Charles Smallwood

(ABOVE) **ONLY ONE-MAN CAR** of the 201 class was its top unit, 265, shown here as such at Divisadero and Post streets in January 1938. Municipal Railway rebuilt this car back to a two-man type and renumbered it 665. (BELOW) **CAR 261 MAKES** one of its innumerable passes through the financial district. It is seen at Sutter and Montgomery in May, 1944.

BOTH: W.C. Whittaker

MORE THAN 250 of these handsome "California Comfort Cars" were turned out by Elkton Shops from 1920 to 1933. First of the fleet, 266, posed on August 11, 1920, two months after its unveiling.

United Railroads

Cars 266—305 • 778—994

Cars 266-285 started Market Street Railway on an ambitious car building program which saw more than 250 fine, attractive cars constructed by its Elkton Shops between 1920 and 1933. United Railroads turned out 266 on June 10, 1920, and that first order was completed on December 7, 1921, when the 20th car, 285, was ready for service.

These company-built cars, in the main, followed the design of the very successful 201-265 class, introduced by United Railroads back in 1913. However, these new cars were of much lighter construction than the 201 class. Actually, only bodies were new, as electrical equipment, trucks, controls, brake system, etc., were salvaged from a large number of obsolete cars scrapped during the period of their construction—predominantly from the 1301 class and later (from 944 on) from the 1550-1749 class.

During the 1920s and early 1930s, a completed car left the sprawling Elkton Shops every 15 days. The company took considerable pride in its car building program and lost no opportunity to boast of it on every possible occasion. Every home-built car, on the inside of each bulkhead, carried a neat decal sign stating: THIS CAR A SAN FRANCISCO PRODUCT BUILT IN THE SHOPS OF THE MARKET STREET RAILWAY COMPANY. During the course of the construction period many innovations for the comfort and convenience of passengers were incorporated into the new cars, such as leather-cushioned seats which started with car 844 in January 1927.

Upon the completion of car 808 on September 2, 1924, the use of second-hand trucks from obsolete cars was discontinued for a time; new Standard 0-40 trucks were purchased for the new cars. Thus, the next car turned out (and the first with the new trucks) on September 30, 1924, was numbered 286. This numbering series was a continuation of the 266-285 series which also was equipped with the Standard 0-40 trucks.

The next significant change came on June 12, 1925, when what was scheduled to be car 299 emerged from the shops as car 2001. This was the first of the very attractive but short-lived "Blue and Gold" cars, which continued for the next 14 cars built—inspired by the Golden Jubilee of the State of California (held in San Francisco that year) and the state colors of blue and gold. The cars, however, were not painted gold, but a bright yellow with blue trim. After a half-dozen or so of these Blue and Gold cars appeared on the streets, the company began a poll among passengers and in the newspapers as to the public's preference of the new paint scheme versus the old standard green color of cars; the new paint scheme of blue and gold was roundly preferred by a seven-to-one margin. Market Street Railway thereupon announced that it would officially adopt the blue and gold as its standard

Cars 266—305 • 778—994

scheme and all cars would wear the new, bright livery. In the meantime, car 2008 appeared with Peckham trucks from a scrapped 1300 class car and the use of new trucks was stopped.

The last day of 1925 also ushered out the last of the "Blue and Gold" cars, 2014. The first weeks of 1926 brought out the first White Front car (on January 13) which was the same old green paint scheme plus the addition of white painted ends which were illuminated at night by shielded light bulbs. This car was numbered 809 which carried on the original numbering series. Favorable public opinion or no, this ended the short era of the attractive yellow cars.

The Market Street Railway's public relations department acclaimed this new White Front car over both press and radio as being the ultimate in safety. There can be no doubt it was a great safety improvement over the dark green color, especially on lines operating in districts near the ocean and subject to San Francisco's famed fogs. The writer has often wondered why, especially in light of such favorable public opinion as the yellow cars engendered, MSR did not incorporate the illuminated dashers on the yellow paint scheme. Certainly a bright yellow car would have been a great safety factor, both day and night; in the final analysis one must conclude that MSR officials did not deem economical the expense of repainting the hundreds of cars in a whole new paint scheme.

Between April and October of 1927 the Blue and Gold cars disappeared from the streets; they were taken to the shops, fitted with dash lights and repainted the dark green with white fronts. Those fitted with the the Standard 0-40 trucks were renumbered 299-305; cars with old trucks were renumbered in the 800 series.

Car 935 emerged from the car building shop on September 10, 1930, bearing a minor change in basic body design which was continued in the remaining cars built. The change constituted removing the side and front roller destination signs from their locations on the roof to the top of the right front window on ends and to the top of the first side window next to the entrance. This change, minor as it may seem, did much to change the exterior appearance of the cars.

A FEW CARS EMERGED from the shops in blue and gold livery. Though popular with the public, it was quickly superseded by the Byllesby "White Front" scheme.   **Market Street Railway**

A TYPICAL ELKTON SHOPS product, car 899, with its new body on old trucks, is seen above in 1943 when it served the chopped #26 line. This line during World War II operated from Mission and Onandaga to Daly City via San Jose Avenue, a shadow of its one-time greatness when it ran from the Ferry Building via Mission, 14th, Guerrero, 30th, Chenery, Diamond and San Jose Avenue to Daly City.

Charles Smallwood

On June 26, 1933, car 989 was placed in service on the 23—Fillmore-Valencia line as a one-man, two-man car. Initially it was used as a two-man car, but was intended to acquaint city officials with one-man operation. In March 1935, the Board of Supervisors gave MSR permission to operate its cars one-man; 989 was the first one-man car to operate under this order, inaugurating one-man service on March 13, 1935 on the #36—Folsom line. The 989 had the distinction of being the only car prior to the introduction of Municipal Railway's PCC cars to have been built as a one-man electric car for San Francisco.

In May 1932, cars 284 and 285 were rebuilt into one-man cars for the South San Francisco line, entering service on that line on May 27. Both cars had their old rear entrance doors paneled over.

The two years 1934 and 1935 saw a total of 131 of these home-built cars remodeled for one-man service. Full one-man safety devices were installed as well as air-operated folding doors on all four corners. Automatic treadle-operated folding doors were used at the rear for exit. During the short period of one-man car operation, these cars operated very well and were able to handle adequately the passenger flow on the heaviest lines.

When one-man cars were ruled out in 1938 the cars of this class which had been rebuilt into one-man cars retained their air-operated doors; as two-man cars the rear doors remained open and the front exit doors were operated by the motorman the same as in one-man service.

In constructing these home-built cars, the company did the best it could with the limited funds and equipment available. The end product was a car of pleasing design, comfortable to ride in and economical to operate and maintain. These cars were regarded by the public with much good will and for the 20 years that they ran the gave both the public and the company good service.

In 1944 these cars passed into the ownership of the Municipal Railway which immediately repainted ends in varying colors and designs other than the simple white, which was protected by patent. As cars 266-299 conflicted with Muni's own 200 class cars, it was decided to renumber them into Muni's new 600 class; this was never carried through to completion. Eleven cars did receive corresponding numbers in the 600 class: 271, 274, 277, 281, 283, 284, 286, 291, 294, 296 and 298.

THE BALBOA HIGH-SPEEDS are typified by 977, seen here when new on September 1, 1932. **Market Street Railway**

CAR 822, snapped at Third Street Car House in 1932, was experimentally equipped with an exit gate top panel in 1930. The modified gate was tested for possible application to the new 900 class.
Market Street Railway

Cars 266—305 • 778—994

TWO PERIODS in the career of the California Comfort Cars. (ABOVE) **CAR 271,** seen at Sutro Barn in 1929, models the partly closed end sections. (BELOW) **CAR 298,** sitting at Third and 23rd in 1935, shows the totally enclosed body plus air doors, installed when one-manned.
TOP: Market Street Railway   BOTTOM: Charles Smallwood

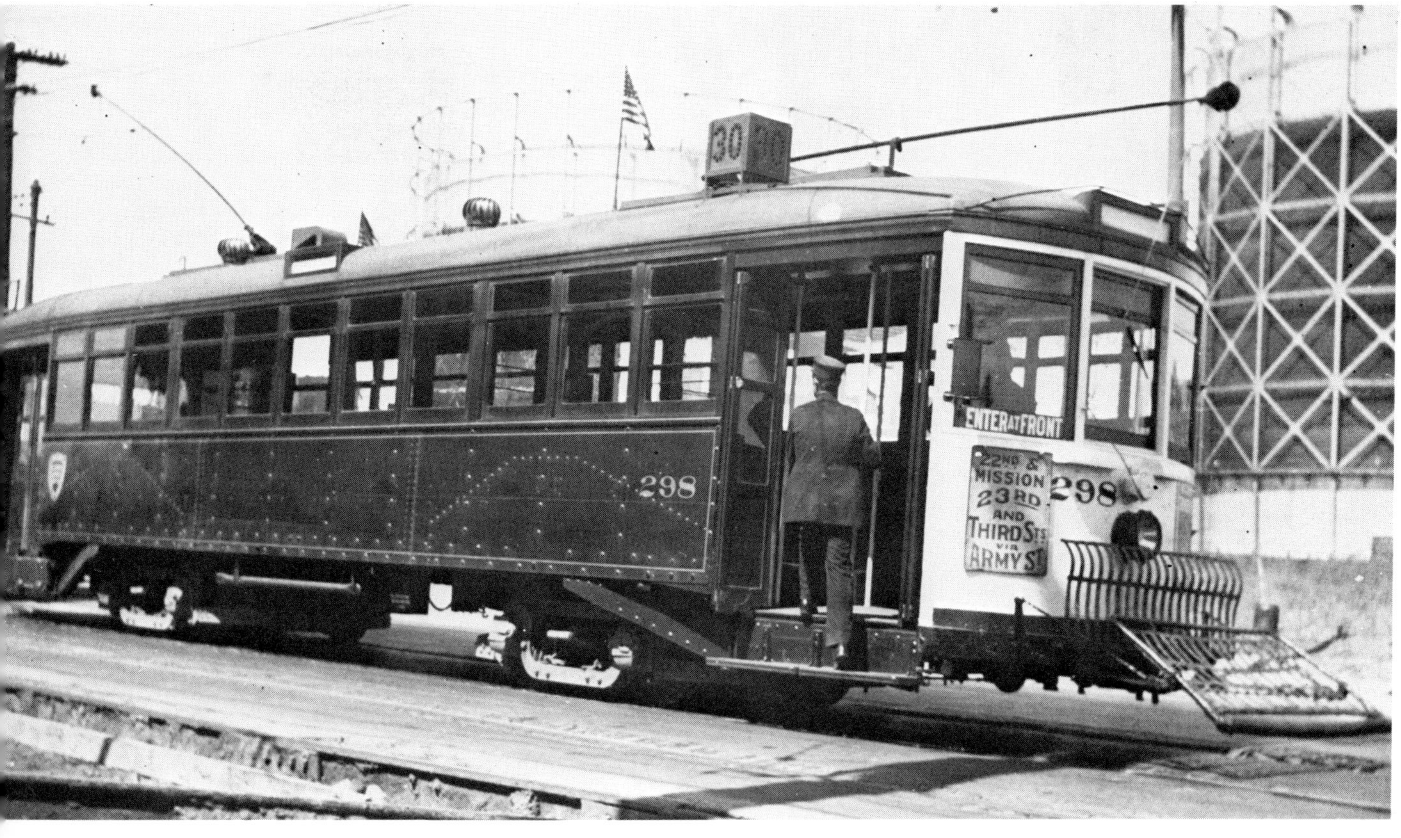

ONE-MAN CARS: Not all cars of this class were rebuilt for one-man operation. Only the following cars were so altered:

266-305	40 Cars
778	1
800-825	26
837-838	2
850-884	35
941-962	22
989	1
991-994	4
	131 Cars

Scrapping Data

These home-built copies of MSR's 201-265 class were scrapped before those hardy old standbys of Sutter St. fame (except for eight of the newest). Municipal Railway retired and sold for scrap these cars as follows:

1945: 282, 290, 808, 815, 847, 854, 895, 900, 902.

1946: 276, 280, 301, 779-799, 835, 836, 839, 841-844, 846, 848, 865, 872, 875, 886, 888, 889, 892-894, 896, 897, 901, 905, 909, 910, 917, 919, 920.

1947: 809, 810, 822, 852, 862, 874.

1948: 266, 267, 273, 275, 278, 287-289, 292, 293, 295, 297, 299, 300, 302-305, 691, 694, 696, 698, 778, 800-807, 811-814, 816-821, 823-834, 837, 838, 840, 845, 850, 851, 853, 855-861, 863, 864, 866-871, 873, 876-885, 887, 890, 898, 899, 903, 904, 906-908, 911-913, 915, 918, 921, 922, 932, 942-949, 951, 956, 957, 963, 982.

1949: 268-270, 272, 279, 285, 601-605, 608, 611-613, 622, 651, 654, 657, 663, 671, 674, 677, 681, 683, 684, 686, 849, 914, 923-929, 933-938, 940, 941, 950, 952-955, 958-962, 964-973, 977-981, 983-994.

1950: 891, 916, 930, 931, 939, 974*, 975, 976. (*974 was sold for preservation to Bay Area Electric Railroad Association on January 20, 1950.)

Individual Car Histories

No.	Date Out	Job No.	Date Retired
266	6-30-20	72A	10-5-48
267	4-17-20		10-5-48
268	8-4-20		1-31-49
269	8-18-20		1-31-49
270	12-8-20		1-31-49
271	12-7-20	72B	1-31-49
272	12-8-20		1-31-49
273	12-8-20		10-5-48
274	12-15-20		1-31-49
275	1-4-21		6-16-48
276	1-17-21	72C	6-22-46
277	2-14-21		1-31-49
278	4-4-21		10-5-48
279	4-28-21		1-31-49
280	5-25-21		2-11-46
281	6-6-21	72D	1-31-49
282	7-6-21		6-13-45
283	9-14-21		1-31-49
284	11-7-21		1-31-49[1]
285	12-7-21		1-31-49[2]
286	9-30-24	228	1-31-49
287	10-8-24		10-5-48
288	10-17-24		10-5-48
289	1-3-25		10-5-48
290	1-6-25		5-19-45
291	1-8-25	232	10-5-48
292	1-10-25		10-5-48
293	2-2-25		10-5-48
294	2-16-25		10-5-48
295	3-4-25		10-5-48
296	3-31-25	237	10-5-48
297	4-18-25		10-5-48
298	5-14-25		10-5-48
299	6-12-25		10-5-48[3]
300	6-18-25		10-5-48[4]
301	6-24-25	250	11-19-46[5]
302	7-10-25		10-5-48[6]
303	7-28-25		10-5-48[7]
304	8-21-25		10-5-48[8]
305	9-21-25		10-5-48[9]

Notes

[1] Converted to one-man for South City line, 5-13-32. [2] Converted to one-man for South City line, 5-11-32. [3] Was Blue and Gold car 2001, changed 4-16-27. [4] Was Blue and Gold car 2002, changed 4-28-27. [5] Was Blue and Gold car 2003, changed 5-5-27. [6] Was Blue and Gold car 2004, changed 5-21-27. [7] Was Blue and Gold car 2005, changed 5-29-27. [8] Was Blue and Gold car 2006, changed 6-18-27. [9] Was Blue and Gold car 2007, changed 6-24-27.

Muni Renumbering

MSR	Muni	Date
271	671	2-23-48
274	674	3-9-48
277	677	12-16-47
281	681	5-7-47
284	684	6-27-47
286	686	8-29-47
291	691	2-12-48
294	694	1-12-48
296	696	12-18-47
298	698	8-12-47

Only 10 of the 40 cars of this class were renumbered by Muni. Their career on Muni was short, encompassing the period from September 29, 1944, to January 31, 1949, when the last were retired.

The first group of 20 cars (266-285) were officially described by Muni as follows (in its June 30, 1949, roster of rolling stock):

"Closed body, three compartment, drop platform, wood frame with steel sides and end panels. Length over bumpers, 47'0"; length over center section, 15'6½"; length over end section, 14'11"; width over steps, 8'9"; width over drips, 9'3"; truck centers 20'10". Seating capacity, 44 passengers. Equipped with two Standard O-40 trucks, 30" cast iron wheels, air and hand brakes. Westinghouse D-H-10 air compressor, Eclipse C Fenders, Golden Glow headlights, roller side and end destination signs, route number signs, and Johnson fare box. Weight, 43,020 lbs. Electric equipment: G.E. Type 216, 50 hp., four motor equipment with double type K-28-E control. Cost per PUC Bureau of Engineering Valuation Report, $16,904 each. Note: Cars 266-684 equipped for one-man operation; add $2,181 to cost."

The second group of 20 cars (286-305) received much the same official description in the same roster:

"Closed body, three compartment, drop platform, oval roof, wood body, wood frame with steel sides and end panels. Length over bumpers, 47'0"; length over closed section, 15'6½"; length over open section, 14'11", width over drips, 9'3"; width over steps, 8'9"; truck centers, 20'10". Seating capacity, 44 passengers. Equipped with two Standard O-40 trucks, 30" cast iron wheels, air and hand brakes, National AA-1 air compressor, Eclipse C fenders, roller side and end destination signs, route number signs, interrupter type signals, Johnson fare boxes. Weight, 38,948 lbs. Electric equipment, G.E. Type 247-D, 40 hp., four motor equipment with double Type K-12 control. Cost, per PUC Bureau of Engineering Valuation Report, $16,416 each. Note: Above cars equipped for one-man operation; add $2,181 to cost."

ONE-MAN MODIFICATIONS: (ABOVE) With fixed steps, tucked well inside the body, the California Comfort Cars looked like this prior to one-manning. Here, car 911 pauses at 16th and Guerrero in 1936. (BELOW) **WITH THE REBUILDING** of these cars for one-man/two-man operation, folding doors and air operating folding steps became standard equipment. Car 884 models this condition on Bryant Street in 1939.
BOTH: Charles Smallwood

Cars 266—305 • 778—994

One-Man Operation

LOOKING CLOSELY, we see the entrance and controls of one-man car 285 in May 1934. Note the seat where the opposite door had been. **Market Street Railway**

(BELOW) RECENTLY REBUILT into a one-man car, 266 posed at the 24th Street Car House in 1935. **Market Street Railway**

Cars 266—305 • 778—994

SAME CAR, SAME LOCATION, but five years apart. (ABOVE) Car 949 as built, in 1934. (BELOW) After rebuilding for one-man operation, in 1939. Both photos show the car standing at Six Mile House on Bay Shore Blvd. **BOTH: Charles Smallwood**

Cars 778—994

Individual Car Histories

The following listing is keyed to Job Numbers under which Market Street Railway constructed cars; usually five cars comprised such an authorization, but as shown below, 10 cars were on some orders and as few as three on others. For several months in 1928 and again in 1930 this Job Number procedure was abandoned; we continue the car building program in groups of five throughout the affected time periods for the convenience of the reader.

For renumberings of certain of these cars by Municipal Railway, see separate list.

All these cars became the property of San Francisco Municipal Railway on September 29, 1944, and all were subsequently disposed of by that owner.

No.	Date Out	Job No.	Date Retired
778	1-22-23	160	10-5-48[1]
779	5-21-23	182	7-5-46
780	6-11-23		7-5-46
781	6-26-23		7-5-46
782	7-17-23		7-5-46
783	8-3-23		7-5-46
784	3-25-23	160	7-5-46[2]
785	5-2-23		7-5-46[3]
786	9-28-23	183	7-5-46
787	10-10-23		7-5-46
788	10-27-23		7-5-46
789	11-9-23	184	7-5-46
790	11-24-23		7-5-46
791	12-14-23		7-5-46
792	8-23-23	183	7-5-46[4]
793	9-12-23		7-5-46[5]
794	1-19-24	202	7-5-46
795	2-14-24		7-5-46
796	3-11-24		7-5-46
797	3-22-24		7-5-46
798	4-7-24		7-5-46
799	4-22-24		7-5-46
800	5-6-24		10-5-48
801	5-21-24		10-5-48
802	5-31-24		10-5-48
803	6-16-24		10-5-48
804	7-9-24	226	10-5-48
805	7-22-24		10-5-48
806	8-7-24		10-5-48
807	8-18-24		6-16-48
808	9-2-24		6-4-45
809	1-13-26	272	12-15-47[6]
810	2-2-26		3-3-47[7]
811	2-18-26		10-5-48[8]
812	3-15-26	280	10-5-48[9]
813	3-31-26		10-5-48[10]
814	4-9-26		10-5-48[11]
815	4-23-26		6-18-45[12]
816	5-1-26		10-5-48[13]
817	5-22-26	293	10-5-48[14]
818	5-29-26		10-5-48[15]
819	6-8-26		10-5-48
820	6-15-26		10-5-48
821	6-28-26		6-16-48
822	7-20-26	301	1-22-47
823	7-30-26		10-5-48
824	8-7-26		10-5-48
825	8-14-26		10-5-48
826	9-1-26		6-16-48
827	9-8-26	309	10-5-48
828	9-18-26		2-12-48
829	9-27-26		10-5-48
830	10-13-26		10-5-48
831	10-23-26		10-5-48
832	11-2-26	312	10-5-48
833	11-10-26		10-5-48
834	11-19-26		6-16-48
835	12-3-26		5-1-46
836	12-28-26		7-5-46
837	10-9-25	263	10-5-48[16]
838	10-22-25		10-5-48[17]
839	11-2-25		7-5-46[18]
840	11-13-25		10-5-48[19]
841	11-30-25		7-5-46[20]
842	10-28-25	272	7-5-46[21]
843	12-31-25		12-26-46[22]
844	1-17-27	316	7-5-46[23]
845	2-4-27		10-5-48[24]
846	3-1-27		7-5-46[25]
847	3-9-27		9-10-45[26]
848	3-20-27		7-5-46[27]
849	3-26-27	331	1-31-49
850	4-16-27		10-5-48
851	4-26-27		10-5-48
852	5-16-27		9-17-47
853	5-26-27		10-5-48
854	6-6-27	339	6-25-45
855	6-17-27		10-5-48
856	7-7-27		10-5-48
857	7-22-27		10-5-48
858	7-30-27		10-5-48
859	8-17-27	348	10-5-48
860	8-26-27		10-5-48
861	9-24-27		10-5-48
862	9-28-27		7-21-47
863	10-17-27		10-5-48
864	10-27-27	360	10-5-48
865	11-15-27		3-15-46
866	11-23-27		10-5-48
867	12-6-27		10-5-48
868	12-22-27		10-5-48
869	12-31-27		10-5-48
870	1-21-28		10-5-48
871	1-31-28		10-5-48
872	2-17-28		2-11-46
873	3-1-28		10-5-48
874	3-17-28		2-7-47
875	3-27-28		2-26-46
876	4-21-28		10-5-48
877	5-4-28		10-5-48
878	5-21-28		10-5-48
879	5-31-28		6-16-48
880	6-16-28		10-5-48
881	6-30-28		10-5-48
882	7-18-28		10-5-48
883	7-27-28		10-5-48
884	8-13-28		10-5-48
885	8-18-28		10-5-48
886	8-29-28		7-5-46
887	9-15-28		10-5-48
888	9-29-28		7-5-46
889	10-20-28		7-5-46

No.	Date Out	Job No.	Date Retired
890	10-30-28		6-16-48
891	11-19-28		4-4-50
892	12-1-28		7-5-46
893	12-18-28		7-5-46
894	12-22-28		7-5-46
895	1-31-29		1949[28]
896	1-23-29	409	7-5-46
897	1-31-29		7-5-46
898	2-12-29		10-5-48
899	2-27-29		10-5-48
900	3-7-29		9-10-45
901	3-25-29	418	12-18-46
902	3-29-29		5-19-45
903	4-9-29		6-16-48
904	4-16-29		6-16-48
905	4-30-29		7-5-46
906	5-7-29	426	10-5-48
907	5-23-29		10-5-48
908	5-29-29		6-16-48
909	6-19-29		7-5-46
910	6-20-29		7-5-46
911	6-29-29	433	6-16-48
912	7-20-29		10-5-48
913	7-25-29		10-5-48
914	8-10-29		1949
915	8-23-29	435	10-5-48
916	8-31-29		4-4-50
917	9-25-29		7-5-46
918	9-28-29		6-16-48
919	10-19-29	437	7-5-46
920	10-31-29		7-5-46
921	11-14-29		6-16-48
922	2-5-30		10-5-48
923	2-19-30		1949
924	3-8-30		1949
925	3-31-30		1949
926	4-14-30		1949
927	4-28-30		1949
928	5-10-30		1949
929	5-26-30		1949
930	6-6-30		4-4-50
931	6-16-30		4-4-50
932	7-8-30		10-5-48
933	7-29-30		1949
934	8-20-30		1949
935	9-10-30		1949
936	9-19-30		1949
937	10-3-30		1949
938	10-8-30		1949
939	11-5-30		4-4-50
940	11-19-30		1949
941	12-5-30		1949
942	12-17-30		10-5-48[29]
943	12-31-30		10-5-48[29]
944	1-20-31		10-5-48[30]
945	2-4-31		10-5-48
946	2-30-31	473	10-5-48
947	3-12-31		10-5-48
948	4-2-31		10-5-48
949	4-21-31		10-5-48
950	5-6-31	486	1-31-49
951	5-22-31		10-5-48
952	6-10-31		1-31-49
953	6-30-31		1-31-49
954	7-17-31	498	1-31-49
955	8-1-31		1-31-49
956	8-18-31		10-5-48
957	9-2-31		10-5-48
958	9-23-31	612	1-31-49
959	10-9-31		1-31-49
960	10-29-31		1-31-49
961	11-25-31		1-31-49
962	12-16-31	621	1-31-49
963	12-31-31		10-5-48
964	1-22-32		1949
965	2-11-32		1949
966	2-29-32	629	1949
967	3-16-32		1949
968	3-29-32		1949
969	4-13-32		1949
970	4-29-32	636	1949
971	5-20-32		1949
972	6-20-32		1949
973	6-27-32		1949
974	7-18-32	643	4-4-50[33]
975	7-29-32		4-4-50
976	8-16-32		4-4-50
977	8-31-32		1949
978	9-16-32	648	1949
979	9-30-32		1949
980	11-2-32		3-29-45[31]
981	11-2-32		1949
982	12-1-32	652	10-5-48
983	12-5-32		1949
984	12-21-32		1949
985	1-6-33		1949
986	1-31-33	662	1949
987	3-8-33		1949
988	4-4-33		1949
989	6-26-33		1-31-49[32]
990	8-1-33	680	1949
991	8-30-33		1-31-49
992	10-3-33		10-31-49
993	11-1-33		1-31-49
994	12-28-33	670	1-31-49

(995-1009, on same order, cancelled)

Notes

[1]Built as car 1424. [2]Was 725, renumbered 784, 12-15-23. [3]Was 726, renumbered 785, 12-18-23. [4]Was 784, renumbered 792, 12-11-23. [5]Was 785, renumbered 793, 12-13-23. [6]First White Front car, was to have been Blue and Gold car 2015. [7]Was to have been Blue and Gold car 2016. [8]Was to have been Blue and Gold car 2017. [9]Was to have been Blue and Gold car 2018. [10]Was to have been Blue and Gold car 2019. [11]Was to have been Blue and Gold car 2020. [12]Was to have been Blue and Gold car 2021. [13]Was to have been Blue and Gold car 2022. [14]Was to have been Blue and Gold car 2023. [15]Was to have been Blue and Gold car 2024. [16]Was Blue and Gold car 2008, changed 7-9-27. [17]Was Blue and Gold car 2009, changed 7-30-27. [18]Was Blue and Gold car 2010, changed 8-4-27. [19]Was Blue and Gold car 2011, changed 9-15-27. [20]Was Blue and Gold car 2012, changed 9-20-27. [21]Was Blue and Gold car 2013, changed 8-20-27. [22]Was Blue and Gold car 2014, changed 10-10-27. [23]Trucks from funeral car 1. [24]Trucks from funeral car 2. [25]Trucks from funeral car 3. [26]Trucks from car 693. [27]Trucks from car 729. [28]Renumbered 980, 3-29-45. [29]Standard O-40 trucks. [30]Trucks from car 1711. [31]Destroyed by fire, 3-29-45—see 895. [32]Built as one-man, two-man car with Standard O-40 trucks and G.E. 216 motors. [33]Sold to Bay Area Electric Railroad Association.

THE ONLY DEVIATION from MSR's white front paint scheme was this one: Car 990 appeared on August 1, 1933, with a startling paint job of aluminum ends, roof and poles, maroon window sash, blue car numbers on ends, green end letterboards and buffer bands. Sides were the usual MSR standard scheme. Car 990 was soon repainted to conform with its sisters.

Market Street Railway

General Specifications, Cars 266-305, 778-994

Sub-Class	Built	Weight	Motors	Gear Ratio	Trucks	Compressor
266-285	1920	43,020	4 GE 216 (50 hp)	19:67	O-40	DH-10
286-305	1924	38,948	4 GE 247D (40 hp)	15:76	O-40	AA1
778-799	1923	38,895	4 GE 1000 (35 hp)	17:67	27-G	MW-1 & AA1
800-922	1924-30	40,116	4 GE 247CD (40 hp)	15:63	14-B3-S	AA1
		43,100	4 GE 203 (50 hp)	17:67		CP-27
923-941	1930	45,840	4 GE 90 (50 hp)	19:67	27-GE-2	CP-27
942-943	1930	38,948	4 GE 247CD (40 hp)	15:63	O-40	CP-27
944-994	1931-33	45,840	4 GE 90 (50 hp)	19:67	27-GE-2	CP-27
		47,860				

Controllers: K-12 except K-28 for GE 216 and GE 90 motors.

General Information

These cars, of the California Comfort car type, used the same body design but mechanically and electrically there were sufficient variations to produce some interesting sub-classes.

The body was of the following dimensions:

Length over buffers	47'0"
Length closed section	15'6½"
Length open section	14'11"
Width over drips	9'3"
Truck centers	20'10"

The body design was of the Pay As You Enter, three-compartment, arch roof, drop platform type originally— later modified for one-man, two-man operation by adding air doors, folding steps and rear treadles.

Unfortunately, a minimum of steel was used in constructing these cars. Underframes were of Oregon pine as were all posts and plates. What steel there was consisted of No. 12 gauge steel siding. Ends were designed to give readily upo impact; accidents which would have resulted in minor dam age to the considerably heavier bodies of 201-265 resulted i much more severe damage in the case of these home-bui cars.

As the years passed, the wooden frames suffered somewh: from wear and tear and it was not uncommon for these cars assume more or less permanently postures which the designers certainly did not contemplate.

All cars had these in common: 30-inch cast iron wheel Golden Glow headlights, outside hung motors, and Johnso fare boxes.

Trucks had these variances: Standard O-40 had a 4'(wheelbase; Brill 27-G had a 4'0" wheelbase; Peckham 14-E had a 4'1" wheelbase.

Cars 923-941 and 944-994 were fastest, due to a 19:67 ge ratio. Roofs of these over ends were given a reinforcing wi slats to prevent damage if trolley wheel came down forcefull one conductor was actually killed in an accident of this typ

While trucks, motors, controllers, and various other equi ment came from retired cars, these components were tho oughly overhauled and modernized where possible.

(ABOVE) **THE INTERIORS** of the 800-900 class cars appeared thusly in the 1930s. Heavy leather seats invited the weary traveler to rest if he remained in the center section, while cane seats were used in the former open ends, now equipped with window sash. Note the fare register and natural wood finish.

(LEFT) **CAR 792 POSED** for this attractive photograph at the 24th Street Car House back in 1930. **BOTH: Market Street Railway**

(ABOVE) **TWO-MAN CAR 942** is inbound at La Playa and Cabrillo streets in 1934. The motorman probably got rebuked by the first inspector he met for not changing the front destination sign to read ''Ferry.'' MSR had a very strict policy regarding its cars being correctly signed. (BELOW) **THE SAME CAR,** rebuilt with doors and steps, inaugurated one-man service on the Visitacion Valley Line. About a week later it was replaced by ex-Williamsport cars 735 and 736. The car is seen here at Six Mile House on the Visitacion Line. Note the Standard O-40 trucks. **BOTH: Charles Smallwood**

Cars 266—305 • 778—994

Minor Variations

CALIFORNIA COMFORT cars 284 (above, at 9th and Brannan in February 1939) and 951 (below, at Five Mile House, 1936) model minor differences in the San Francisco type car. Note the position of destination signs and trucks... Standard 0-40s above, Brill 27-Gs below.
BOTH: Charles Smallwood

BUILT AS A one-man/two-man car, brand new 989 is seen on its first day, June 26, 1933. It is signed up for the South San Francisco Line. This was the only car originally built for one-man service. In the photo below, its complicated control panel (above the motorman's position) is shown. **BOTH: Market Street Railway**

Cars 266—305 • 778—994

Pre-1938: White Front

THE OLD AND NEW paint schemes of Market Street Railway: (ABOVE) Car 958 models the pre-1938 colors (medium green body with yellow striping and numbers, white ends with black numbers, light gray roof with yellow route signs). (BELOW) The post-1938 scheme added a white letterboard, a white streamstyled flourish on the sides, modernized numbering, topped with a yellow roof. **BOTH: Charles Smallwood**

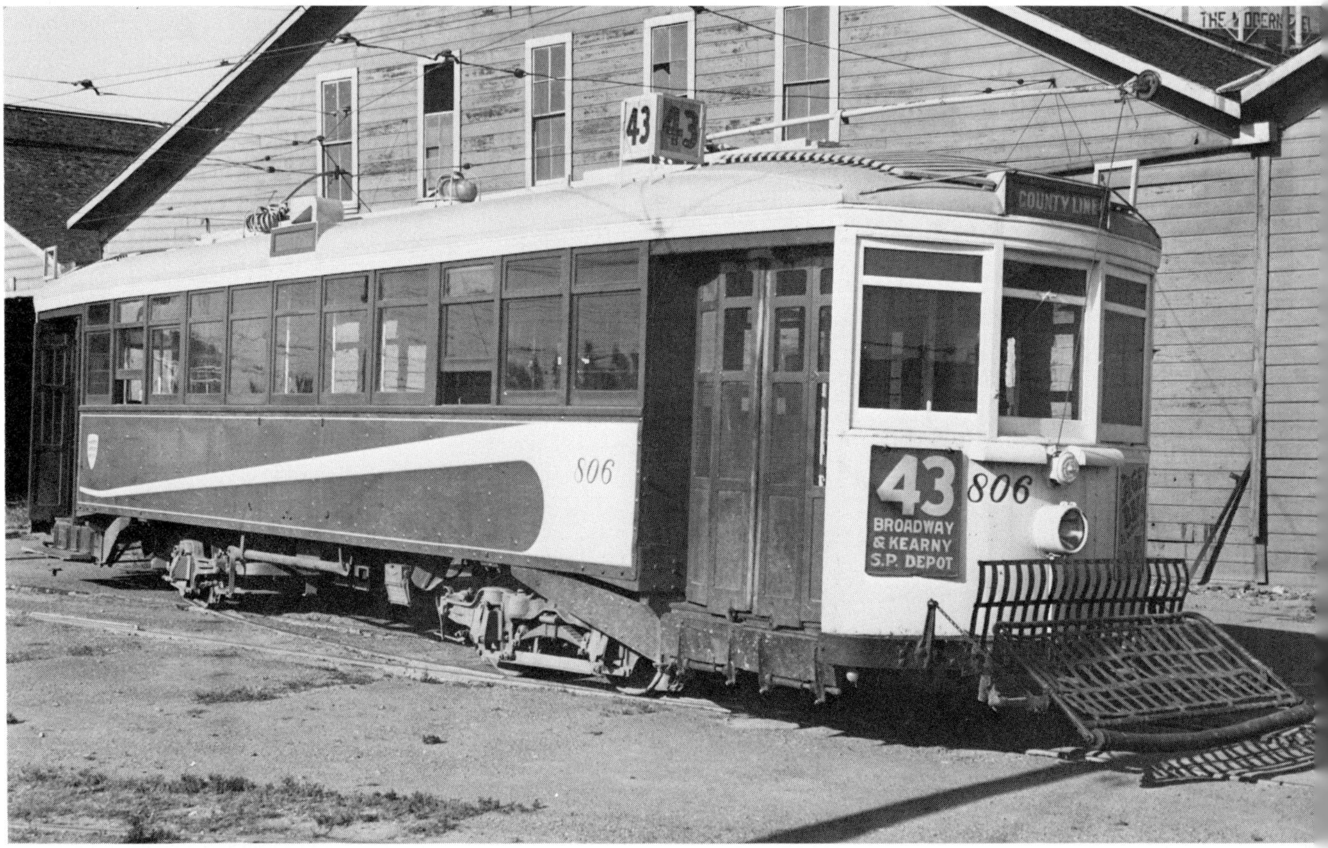

Post-1938: An Added Flourish

(ABOVE) **STREAMSTYLED 806** is seen at Third Street Car House in May 1941. **Charles Smallwood** (BELOW) **CARS 923-941,** originally similar to the other 900s, were revised in the 1930s. Brill 27G trucks and GE 90 motors replaced Peckham 14-B3 and GE 1000 motors. Car 926 models their appearance after these changes had been effected. **W.C. Whittaker**

THE POST-1938 paint scheme brought a completely white front to the California Comfort Cars. A visor over the center end window was also applied to many cars.

Market Street Railway

THE LOW FLOOR CAR: Brand new car 301 is shown at Sutro Barn (33rd Avenue and Clement) early in January 1915, preparatory to a test run.
United Railroads

Car 401

During 1914 United Railroads constructed at Elkton Shops a car following a highly successful design developed in Pittsburgh two years before. This car featured but a single step from the ground to the car floor, a feat made possible by a car truck of Pittsburgh design; small wheels (24-inch diameter) and a special type of baby motor especially designed by General Electric Company for this style of car made the low floor innovation possible.

The pair of experimental Pittsburgh trucks with two 30-hp. motors in each arrived in San Francisco in April 1914. A new car body was planned for the trucks but in the meantime the company was anxious to see what this set of motors and trucks could do. To find out, a flush platform car of the 1300 class (1367) was revamped to take the low floor trucks, thus bringing the floor of the former high platform car some 12 inches closer to the ground. The 1367 was tried out on the very hilly Fillmore St. line. Although, as was pointed out, this kind of truck and motor arrangement was operated with considerable success in Pittsburgh (which also had many car lines with heavy grades) it soon became apparent to United Railroads engineers supervising the Fillmore St. experiment that the car body to be mounted on these low floor trucks would have to be much lighter than the 22-ton 1300 class car they were testing. What operated well on Pittsburgh's hills did not do nearly as well on San Francisco's grades. Thus the 1367 experiment was somewhat of a disappointment to the company,

and trials with 1367 were terminated by the end of the month.

However, the company was reluctant to adandon the low floor experiment entirely, so later in 1914 it was decided to construct an entirely new car body; work got under way at Elkton Shops early in October. On December 28th there emerged a car which was possibly the finest and best-constructed electric car in the long car building history of Elkton craftsmen. The new car 301 greatly resembled the then-new 201-265 class cars of 1913. Construction was first class throughout (something which could not be said about some later types that were built there), and when fully equipped and ready for service, car 301 weighed a mere 17 tons—almost eight tons lighter than the 201 class. In 1914 this weight was considered extremely light for a 47-foot car with 50 seats.

How was this weight saved? Headlining was eliminated; size of carlines was reduced; the center of the arch roof was lowered eight inches; drop platforms gave way to ramp platforms which rose 4.5 inches within the eight feet from the platform edge to bolster line.

Amid national fanfare, new car 301 entered service on January 4, 1915, on the company's showpiece line, the #8—Market Street route; this line traversed the most important thoroughfare in the city from the ferries to Castro St.

After a short time it became obvious that the car with its four small motors was considerably underpowered when carrying a capacity load (about 150 passengers) even for the somewhat gentle grades of the #8 line. The company's worst fears, following the ill-starred 1367 experiment, were fully realized and 301 was placed in storage after about a year in service.

In the early 1920s the car was put back in service, this time condemned to the ignominious task of carrying two large billboards as the "Baseball Car." As such, 301 ran only during the baseball season and informed citizens of the identity of teams playing at Old Recreation Park.

On March 10, 1925, the car's number was changed from 301 to 401, anticipating the "Blue and Gold" 2000 class renumbering into the 299-305 series in April-May of 1927. That 301 was removed from the 300 series two years prior to the 2000 class renumbering leads to speculation that Market Street Railway never intended to leave Blue and Gold cars, even if they had remained in those colors, in the rather unrealistic 2000 series.

In July 1927, 401 was relieved of the baseball sign-toting duty, being replaced by obsolete car 1303. The 401 then went to work in passenger service again on the #35— Howard St. line. Even this return to the service for which it had been intended was of dubious honor, as it was the practice of MSR to run out the mileage of obsolete cars on the Howard St. run before sending them to Elkton Shops for scrapping—a custom which prevailed until the introduction of one-man cars on Howard St. in 1935.

When 401 was finally forced out of passenger service for the last time by one-man cars, it was again put in dead storage at 29th and Mission Car House. There it remained for six years, being scrapped at Elkton on July 30, 1941.

Car 301 (401) really was years ahead of its time. The Pittsburgh cars and 301 were the forerunners of the many hundreds of lightweight, low floor cars which became standard throughout America in later years. This type remained in favor until the advent of the PCC car.

Ironically this little-known car, perhaps the finest electric car ever to be constructed in San Francisco, proved to be its least successful.

General Specifications, Car 401

Body type	PAYE, ramp platform, 3 section, arch roof
Builder	United Railroads of San Francisco
Date built	1915
Weight	34,215 lbs.
Seats	50
Length over buffers	47'0"
Length closed section	15'6¼"
Length open section	15'8⅞"
Width over steps	9'0"
Width over drips	9'1¾"
Truck centers	21'3"
Controller	K-12
Motors	4 GE 247-A, 40 hp.
Gear ratio	14:57
Compressor	M-W 1
Trucks	Pittsburgh
Motors hung	Inside
Truck wheelbase	5'6"
Wheels	24" Cast Iron

WHEN BRAND NEW, in 1915, 301's wooden seating was hardly a rider-pleaser. New leather seats were installed in the closed section in the Twenties.
United Railroads

(BELOW) **SPECIALLY POSED,** this comparison photograph showed the extremely low floor advantage enjoyed by car 301 in contrast to the standard type car used in 1914. Units 301 and 1724 are seen on Sloat Blvd. on December 28, 1914, during one of 301's numerous test trips.

United Railroads

401's Last Journey

(LEFT) **EVEN THE ELEMENTS** conspired on 401's last day on the streets of San Francisco. The grey, gloomy weather was a suitable backdrop for the melancholy occasion pictured in these views. The conductor rides the fender while tending the trolley rope as car 401 leaves 29th and Mission Car House storage for its last trip—to Elkton Shops to be destroyed. This experimental unit could not cope with the local terrain, and was taken out of service after about a year of use.

Charles Smallwood

(BELOW) **ARRIVING AT ELKTON,** car 401 switches into the yard from Ocean Avenue for its rendezvous with the torch.

Bert Ward

Rail Sedans

A NEW LOOK came to Market Street Railway's fleet when Rail Sedans 402-406 entered service. This photograph was taken on the first day of service, in 1936, at 22nd and Howard streets. **Charles Smallwood**

ALONG THE EMBARCADERO: The five Rail Sedans were familiar sights on the Embarcadero between the Ferry Building and Howard Street. Car 402 passes Santa Fe's new "Golden Gate" streamliner, on exhibit, in 1938. **Charles Smallwood**

Cars 402—406

The five cars in this class, purchased in 1936 from *East St. Louis & Suburban Railway,* were the most modern cars ever owned by Market Street Railway. They were constructed by St. Louis Car Company in 1927, and were of that car builder's type known as "Rail Sedans." This class had a speedy, streamlined look, although not especially fast. Their appearance on San Francisco's streets aroused much favorable public comment.

During the short period of their use in San Francisco, however, they were confined entirely to the obscure #35—Howard St. line. The writer once inquired of an MSR official why such fine cars were not used on a more important route; the answer of explanation, logically enough, was that inasmuch as there were but five of the cars, it was not considered practical for them to be run on a busy line with cars of lesser status. He did express regret that so few of them were available, and said that the company would have bought all which they could have gotten.

After the close of one-man service in 1939 the five cars of the 402 class were placed in storage and were finally sent to Elkton for scrapping in September and October of 1941.

THE FLASHY PAINT scheme of the East St. Louis & Suburban Railway car was widely publicized. Car 351 is pictured when brand new, in 1927.
W.J. Clouser

IN THEIR ORIGINAL HABITAT: Rail Sedan 353 is on the East St. Louis side of the Eads Bridge on July 1, 1932. (BELOW) Unit 352 at Eads Bridge trolley station, St. Louis, circa 1930. **BOTH: R.V. Mehlenbeck**

(BELOW) **NOW NINE YEARS OLD**, car 351 has come west and reposes in Elkton Yard awaiting MSR colors. Not only was the automotive aspect emphasized in the spring bumpers (removed by MSR and replaced by fenders), but also in side windows which were lowered from the top. **Charles Smallwood**

AT THE FERRY, car 403 awaits passengers for its Howard Street assignment in 1937. **Charles Smallwood**

A GOOD VIEW of the St. Louis AM-64 trucks on cars 407-410 is afforded in this 1937 shot of #407 at the Ferry.
Charles Smallwood

Cars 407—410

These four cars were included in the 1936 used car purchase from the *East St. Louis & Suburban Railway*. Built by St. Louis Car Company in 1924, they were said to have been constructed from plans made for a large order of cars for Milwaukee, Wisconsin. There was much steel used in their construction and they had metal window sash, an innovation in San Francisco cars at that time. Of all the cars purchased from East St. Louis & Suburban, these four were the least attractive and were rather hard riding and quite noisy.

The 407 class cars were used mainly on the #35— Howard St. line, along with the five fine Rail Sedans, which provided quite a contrast in riding comfort.

These cars were provided with a novel feature that caused considerable consternation to the Elkton Shop forces making them ready for San Francisco service. It seems that no one could find how to get the light bulbs in the front end Hunter destination signs to light; all of the cars' other lights would burn, but not those of the signs. When, in frustration, it was decided to rewire the sign boxes, someone luckily discovered that the signs would only illuminate when the air brakes were applied. The shop force thought this feature quite amusing and never did change it. A prospective passenger, waiting at a dark car stop at night, thus had to wait until the operator applied his brakes to find out where the car was going.

The 407-410 class went into storage when one-man service was abolished in 1939 and was scrapped at Elkton during September and October of 1941.

General Specifications, Cars 407—410

Body type	Closed, arch roof, one-man, ramp platform
Builder	St. Louis Car Company
Date built	1924
Weight	34,860 lbs.
Seats	44
Length over buffers	45′0″
Length closed section	29′6″
Length of platform	7′9″
Width over steps	—
Width over drips	8′7⅜″
Truck centers	20′9″
Controller	K-35
Motors	4 GE 264-A 25 hp.
Gear ratio	15:72
Compressor	C.P. 27
Trucks	St. Louis AM-64
Motors hung	Outside
Truck wheelbase	5′4″
Wheels	26″ Steel

ONE OF THE single-truck California cars displays its URR livery before renumbering into a 600, at 24th Street Car House in July 1911.
United Railroads

Cars 601—662

When United Railroads took control of the street railways of San Francisco in 1902, it became the owner of hundreds of small single truck California type cars, most of which had served to inaugurate trolley service back in the '90s. As newer and larger electric cars were placed in service from 1903 on, many of these single truckers became surplus. After the 1906 disaster with the very large number of new cars then purchased taking control of the car fleet, storage space for the old single truckers became somewhat of a problem. In an effort to rid itself of so many of these obsolete cars, URR began an elimination campaign. Some of the little cars were sold to other companies for further use (the largest block going to the *Presidio & Ferries Railway* of San Francisco, that company taking 29); some were made over into work equipment; bodies of still others were even sold for use as houses and sheds. But after all of this, about a hundred of the single truckers remained in use on lighter lines.

In 1912, URR selected 62 of the better ones and renumbered them 601-662; the remainder were scrapped at that time.

In 1914, a few were rebuilt for one-man service, for use on the Parkside, Bosworth St. and other light lines. However, the 1918 Visitacion Valley accident involving a one-man car ended their use in that year; all those little cars remaining, although unchanged, were operated with two-man crews.

In 1915, several were rebuilt for multiple unit operation on the Fillmore Hill line. This was necessary because of the Panama-Pacific International Exposition which was located at the lower end of the Hill line. These cars were also modified further to accommodate the Pay As You Enter method of fare collection. In 1925 an upgrading of the Fillmore Hill service saw four of these care rebuilt; the result was a quite boxy appearance.

Almost from the day of the 1912 renumbering the total number of cars in this class began to diminish. Hardly a year went by but that some of them were scrapped. By the mid-30s only the Fillmore Hill line continued to use them. That line was converted to bus operation on April 5, 1941, and the era of single-truck passenger cars on Market Street Railway was finally ended.

In 1923 MSR bought back from Municipal Railway 19 of these dinkies which URR had sold to the *Presidio & Ferries Railway* in 1907. After salvaging the motors and controllers, MSR then scrapped all 19 veterans.

Cars 601—662

The Dinkeys Of Montgomery Street

(FACING PAGE, ABOVE) **THE CORNER NEWSBOY** hitches a ride as car 609 swings into Montgomery Street from Washington Street in 1927.

(FACING PAGE, BELOW) **NORTHBOUND 635** traverses Montgomery Street between Sutter and Bush streets, circa 1926.

BOTH: Charles Smallwood

General Specifications, Cars 601—605, 613—616

Body type	Single truck, California, deck roof, PAYE, one-man
Builders	Hammond, Holman, etc.
Date built	1895-1898
Rebuilt	United Railroads of San Francisco, 1914-1915
Weight	20,300 lbs.
Seats	26
Length over buffers	26'10"
Length closed section	11'3"
Length open section	7'9¼"
Width over steps	8'8½"
Width over drips	8'3"
Controller	K-10
Motors	2 GE 1000, 35 hp.
Gear ratio	17:67
Compressor	—
Brakes	Lever Hand
Trucks	Peckham and Brill
Motors hung	Outside
Truck wheelbase	7'0"
Wheels	30" Cast Iron

ONE-MAN SINGLE TRUCKERS: United Railroads in 1914 made an attempt to cut losses on several of its lightly patronized lines by introducing one-man cars. Lines affected were Parkside, Bosworth Street, Divisadero Extension and Visitacion Valley. For service on these lines (except Visitacion) URR rebuilt some of its standard single-truck cars for one-man operation, this resulting in the enclosed of this type as shown in the photo below of car 602, taken in 1914 on Oak Street.

The tragic 1918 Visitacion accident involving a one-man car brought an end to one-man operation. Nevertheless, some of the rebuilt Dinkeys ran for several additional years unchanged; the conductor stood alongside the motorman. The last of these one-man Dinkeys, car 604, was scrapped at Elkton Yard in July 1935.

United Railroads

Multiple Unit

AN IMPRESSIVE ARRAY of cables, couplers, jumpers and chains was used by United Railroads in its only attempt at multiple unit operation— and all on its smallest electric cars! These photos were taken in April 1915. Note that but one trolley pole was used in this train operation.
BOTH: United Railroads

General Specifications, Cars 606—612, 617—622, 627—631, 633—644, 643—647, 655—657 659—662, 650

Body type	Single truck, California, deck roof
Builders	Hammond, Holman, etc.
Date built	1895-1898
Weight	—
Seats	26
Length over buffers	26′10″
Length closed section	11′8″
Length open section	7′7″
Width over steps	9′2″
Width over drips	8′4″
Controller	K-10
Motors	2 GE 58 or GE 1000, 35 hp.
Gear ratio	17:67
Brakes	Lever Hand
Trucks	Peckham or Brill
Motors hung	Outside
Truck wheelbase	7′0″
Wheels	30″ Cast Iron

Cars 601—662

General Specifications, Cars 623—626, 641—642, 648—649, 651—654, 632, 658

Body type	Single truck, California, deck roof, PAYE (Fillmore Hill cars)
Builders	Hammond, Holman, etc.
Date built	1895-1898
Rebuilt	United Railroads of San Francisco, 1915
Weight	23,300 lbs.
Seats	26
Length over buffers	26'10"
Length closed section	10'7½"
Length open section	8'1¼"
Width over steps	8'4"
Width over drips	8'4"
Truck centers	—
Controller	K-10, K-12
Motors	2 GE 1000, 35 hp.
Gear ratio	15:69
Compressor	GE 25-C
Truck	Peckham
Motors hung	Inside
Truck wheelbase	7'0"
Wheels	30" Cast Iron

BEFORE AND AFTER the 1921 rebuilding: (LEFT) extra car 626 (which saw little service) never was rebuilt, retaining its curved sides, wire gates and multiple unit receptacles until the end. The others received a major rebuilding, as modeled by 626, in 1938 (BELOW). It is readily apparent that even the counterbalance cars were susceptible to MSR's standardization policies, as witness car 625, in 1941, pulling into summit at Broadway.
BOTH: Charles Smallwood

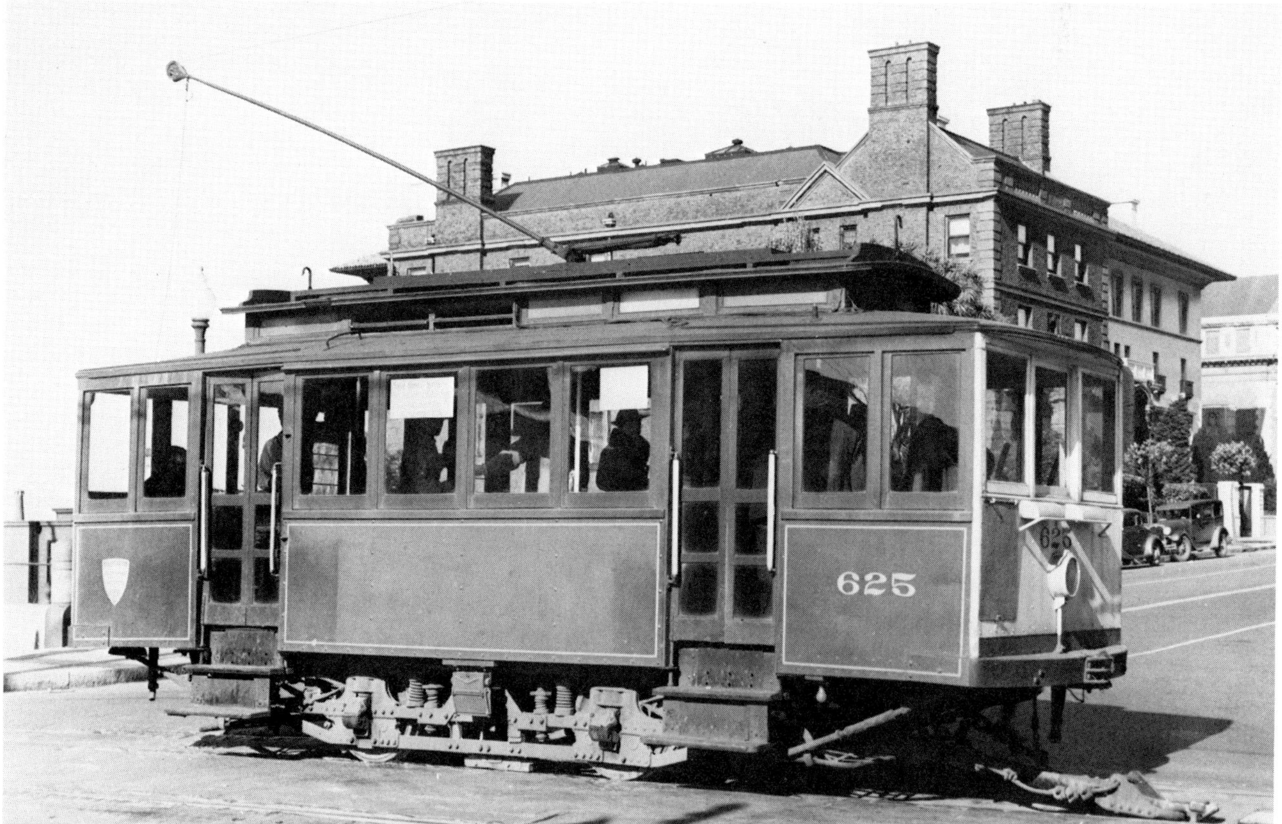

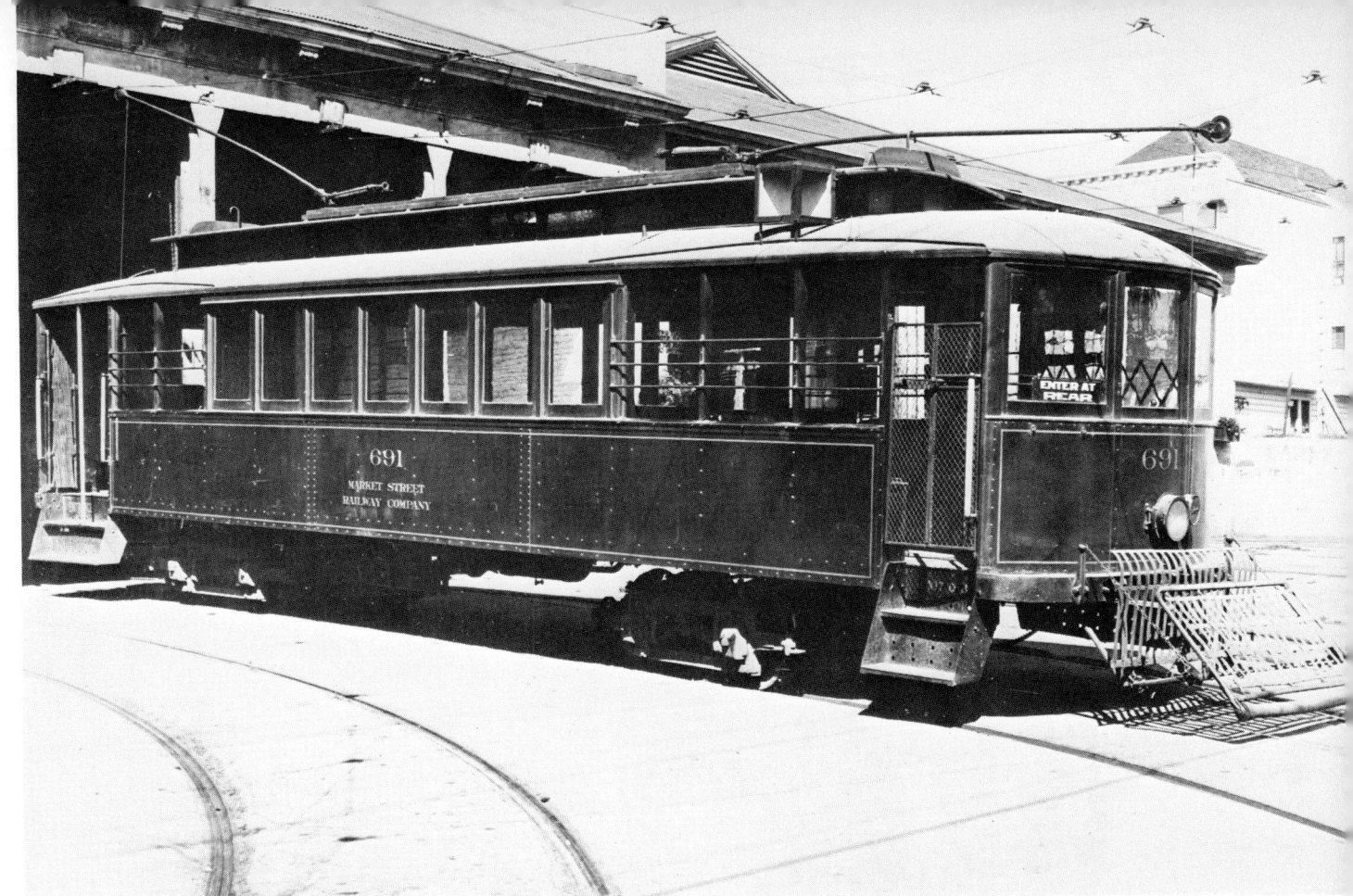

IT WAS 1925, and car 691 was approaching its final terminal when this photo was taken at 24th and Utah Car House.

Market Street Railway

Cars 681—697

In 1900-01 the San Francisco & San Mateo Electric Railway purchased from the St. Louis Car Company 20 large California-type suburban cars; they were numbered 51 through 70.

United Railroads, upon taking over that company in 1902, rebuilt car 61 into an ornate private car which was named SAN FRANCISCO. At the same time car 67 was made over into a funeral car and numbered 2. The rest of this class was numbered 681-698. Around 1907, car 696 was rebuilt into a wrecker (0507) and in 1915 car 698 was renumbered 696.

In 1908 funeral car 2 was rebuilt into a private party car and named SIERRA.

The year 1915 saw the 17 cars still in passenger service taken to Elkton Shops and rebuilt into three-compartment Pay As You Enter cars; in this process the cars lost their distinctive railroad roofs when the platforms were extended for the prepayment feature.

These cars under Market Street Railway management were assigned to lines south of Market St. They fell early victims to the company's policy of phasing out flush platform equipment and all were scrapped at Elkton in 1926-7. None ever received the White Front treatment.

General Specifications, Cars 681—697

Body type	California, deck roof, PAYE
Builder	St. Louis Car Company, 1900
Weight	38,240 lbs.
Seats	50
Length over buffers	44'8"
Length closed section	19'0"
Length open section	12'10"
Width over steps	9'6"
Width over drips	8'10"
Truck centers	22'0"
Controllers	K-12
Motors	4 GE 1000, 35 hp.
Gear ratio	17:67
Compressor	AA-1
Trucks	Brill 27-G
Motors hung	Outside
Truck wheelbase	4'0"
Wheels	30" Cast Iron

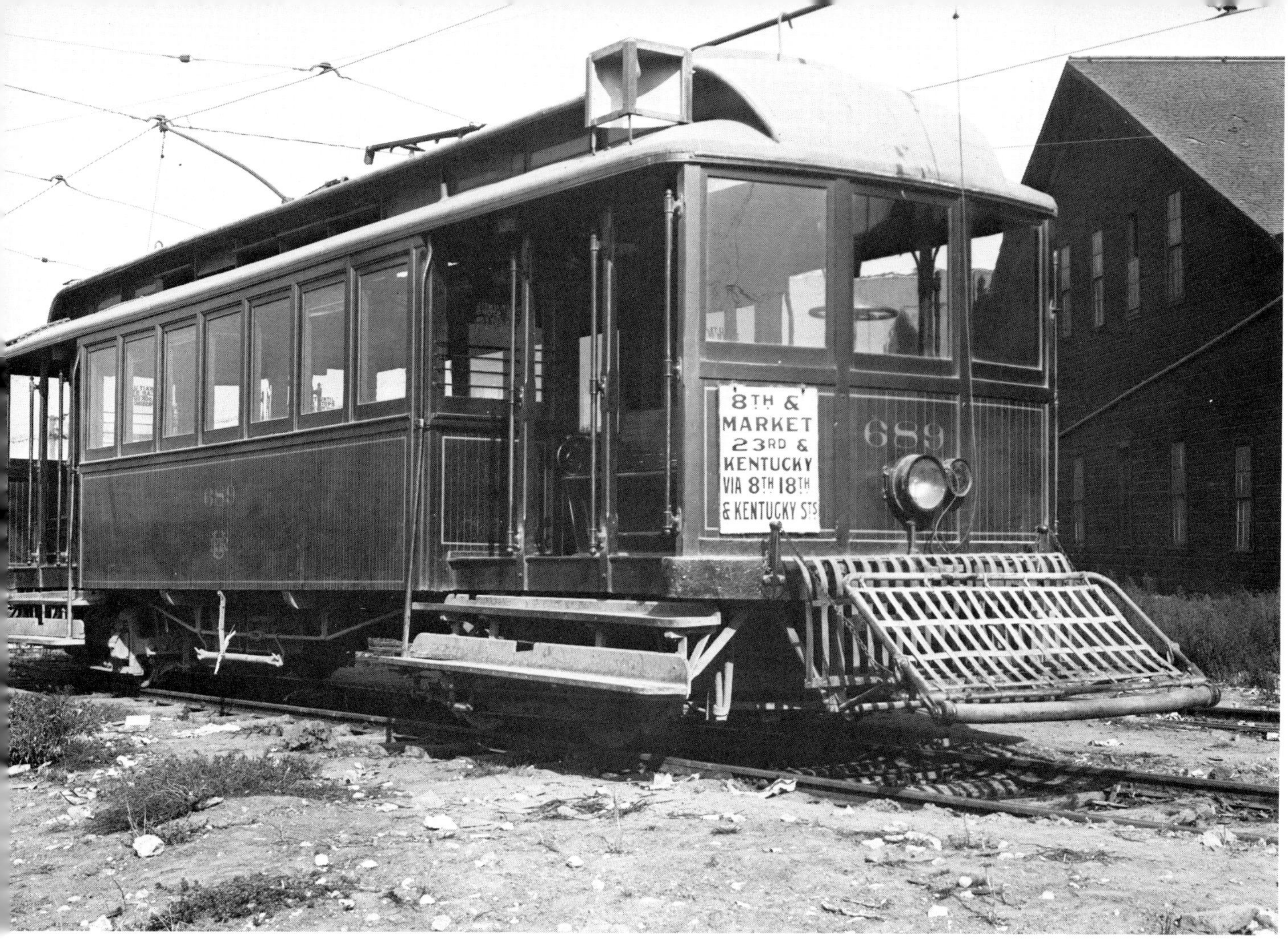

EXTENSIVELY MODIFIED: (ABOVE) Car 689, shown at the rear of Kentucky Barn on November 24, 1914, models the original appearance of this class. (BELOW) The same car after its visit to Elkton Shops; 689 posed for this photo on Third Street near Army Street on June 3, 1915.

BOTH: United Railroads

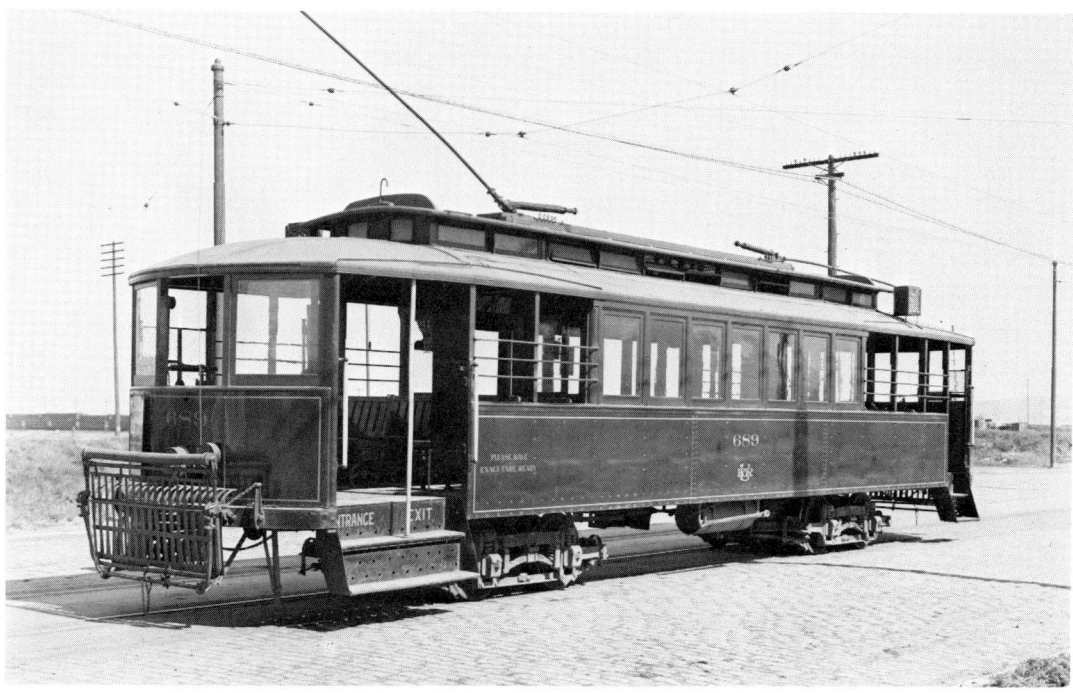

SIGHTSEEING CAR "Golden Gate" poses at Land's End Station in 1908. When motor buses captured the market, this car became regular passenger car 698, in 1918. **United Railroads**

Cars 698—699

In March 1901, the original *Market Street Railway* inaugurated a "Seeing San Francisco" sightseeing car service. There was constructed at the then shops of the company (28th and Valencia streets) an ornate open double-truck observation car, designed (and patented) by MSR's general manager, E.P. Vining. The new car was named CITY OF ATLANTA and was said to have received this seemingly inappropriate name in honor of Mrs. Vining's hometown—this action probably condoned by Mr. Vining in the interest of family peace.

The observation car service was popular and very profitable from the start. In 1904 URR built another observation car along somewhat different lines; this new car was named CALIFORNIA and shared sightseeing duties with the form[er] CITY OF ATLANTA which under URR management was r[e]named GOLDEN GATE.

After 1915 motor bus sightseeing tours began to make i[n]roads into the once-profitable trolley observation car busine[ss] and by the late 'teens this service was discontinued. GOLD[EN] GATE and CALIFORNIA were rebuilt into regular passenger ca[rs] and bore numbers 698 and 699 respectively. The cars spe[nt] the remainder of their years on the unimportant Visitaci[on] Valley line, replacing the ill-fated one-man cars in 191[?]. Literally beaten to pieces running on the extremely rou[gh] track of this route, the two cars were retired and scrapped [in] 1925.

Details of Party Car SIERRA are found in the "Spec[ial] Revenue Cars" section of Chapter One. Its specifications [are] shown below.

General Specifications, Party Car SIERRA

Body type . . . . Closed, railroad roof, flush platforms	Width over drips . . . . 8'10"
Builder . . . . St. Louis Car Company	Truck centers . . . . 22'0"
Year built 1901	Controller K-12
Rebuilt . . . . United Railroads of San Francisco, 1908	Motors . . . . 4 GE 1000, 35 hp.
Weight . . . . 39,160 lbs.	Gear ratio 17:67
Seats 28	Compressor AA-1
Length over buffers . . . . 37'6"	Trucks . . . . Peckham 14-B-3-S
Length closed section . . . . 29'6"	Truck wheelbase . . . . 4'1"
Length of platform . . . . 4'0"	Wheels . . . . 30" Cast Iron
Width over steps . . . . 9'8"	

Cars 698—699

A FORMER SIGHTSEEING CAR, 699 sits in wrecked condition at Elkton Shops in January 1919. This is the only known view of 699 as a regular passenger car.
United Railroads

General Specifications, Car 698

Body type	Closed, deck roof, flush platforms
Builder	Market Street Railway (original company)
Date built	1900
Weight	40,820 lbs.
Seats	48
Length over buffers	42′0″
Length closed section	32′0″
Length of platform	5′0″
Width over steps	9′0″
Width over drips	8′8″
Truck centers	22′0″
Controller	K-12
Motors	4 GE 1000, 35 hp.
Gear ratio	17:67
Compressor	AA-1
Trucks	Brill 27-G
Motors hung	Outside
Truck wheelbase	4′0″
Wheels	30″ Cast Iron

General Specifications, Car 699

Body type	Closed, deck roof, flush platforms
Builder	United Railroads of San Francisco
Date built	1904
Weight	43,140 lbs.
Seats	48
Length over buffers	42′0″
Length closed section	32′0″
Length of platform	5′0
Width over steps	9′3″
Width over drips	8′10″
Truck centers	21′0″
Controller	K-12
Motors	4 GE 1000, 35 hp.
Gear ratio	17:67
Compressor	AA-1
Trucks	Peckham 14-B3-S
Motors hung	Outside
Truck wheelbase	4′1″
Wheels	30″ Cast Iron

Cars 701—724

UNITED RAILROADS took this builder's view of car 700 (later 712) on the photogenic Cypress Lawn Cemetery spur in 1911. There is a startling resemblance to Los Angeles Railway's type H cars, built about 10 years later than URR's 700s. **United Railroads**

Cars 701—724

Built by United Railroads in 1911 and 1912, these 24 cars were the first to have been built in the city for prepayment operation. The steel underframes, trucks, motors and controls of California electric cars of the 900, 1000, 1100 and 1200 classes were utilized in their construction. It is interesting to note that the old cars thus cannibalized were themselves rebuilt from cable cars!

Cars 701-724 were considered by many to have been the best of all types ever turned out by Elkton Shops; notable was the interior finish of their closed section; quarter sawed oak, stained dark. Headlining was used on the ceiling, the only time this luxury was included by Elkton.

When new, 701-724 saw service on some of the most important lines in the city, along with standard main line equipment such as the 1550 class. Using flush platform cars in regular service on lines such as Third and Kearny, Ingleside, etc., was an unusual practice; of the many flush platform types in service, 701-724 were the only such cars thus utilized.

These were the last flush platform type cars of the old California type to have been used in San Francisco, operating until the mid 1930s—then being replaced by one-man cars. The last of the 701s went in 1935.

OUT ON THIRD STREET: Car 707 switches back at the 23rd and 3rd streets terminus of Route 30 in 1931. In the distance, 285 is operating on the #22 Line.   **Charles Smallwood**

Cars 701—724

General Specifications, Cars 701—724

Body type	California, PAYE, arch roof, flush platforms
Builder	United Railroads of San Francisco
Date built	1911-1912
Weight	38,710 lbs.
Seats	44
Length over buffers	41'4"
Length closed section	14'6"
Length open section	13'5"
Width over steps	9'8"
Width over drips	8'4"
Truck centers	23'0"
Controller	K-12
Motors	4 GE 1000, 35 hp.
Gear ratio	17:67
Compressor	AA-1
Trucks	Brill 27-G
Motors hung	Outside
Truck wheelbase	4'0"
Wheels	30" Cast Iron

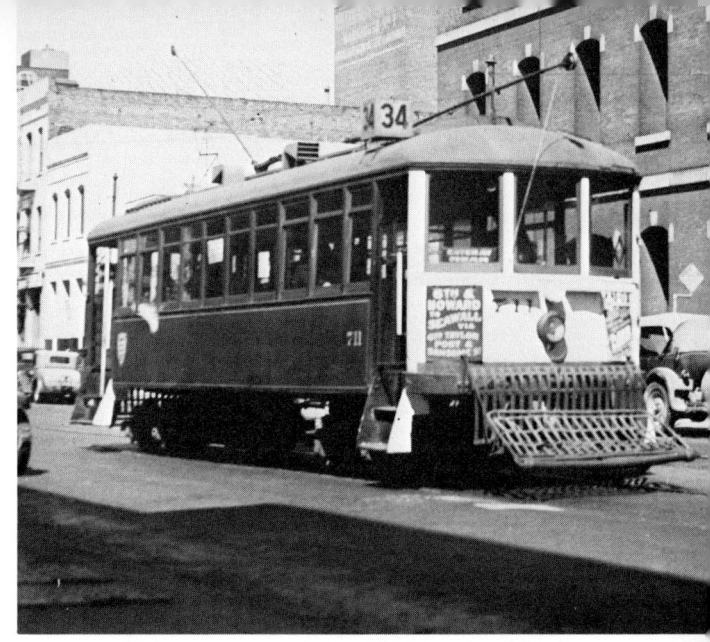

CAR 711 speeds along Sansome Street, near Clay, in 1933.   **Charles Smallwood**

AT 24th AND UTAH, car 723 is viewed in 1920. United Railroads color scheme: body, brewster green; window sash, dark red; roof, tile red; lettering, gold; trucks, light gray.   **United Railroads**

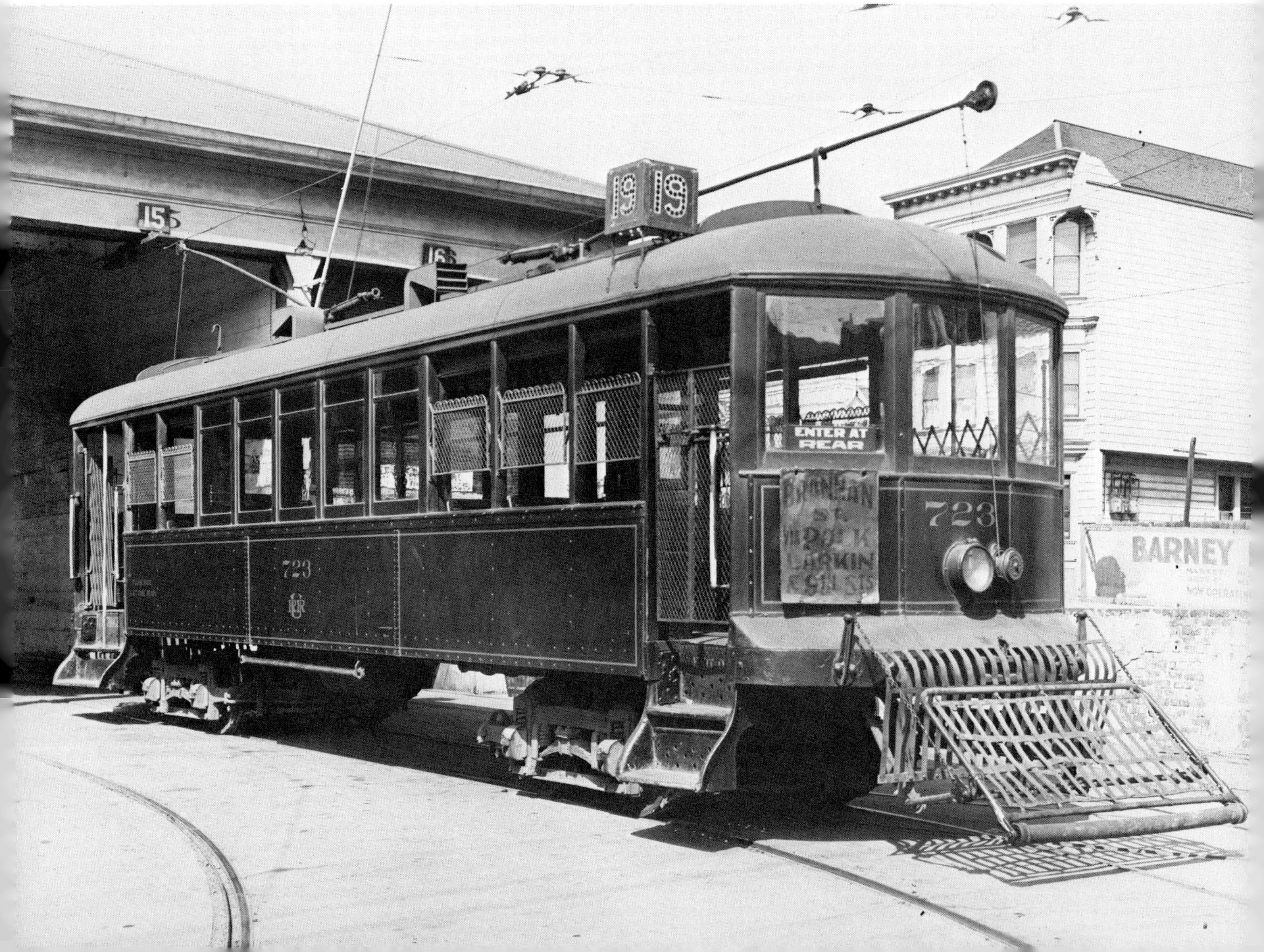

(ABOVE) **PAUSING AT** the 23rd and 3rd streets terminus of Line 30, car 705 was snapped in 1934. **Charles Smallwood** (BELOW) **AN EARLY INTERIOR** view of 710 shows the wood slat seats in end sections and cane-covered longitudinal seats in the center compartment.   **S.F. Public Utilities Commission**

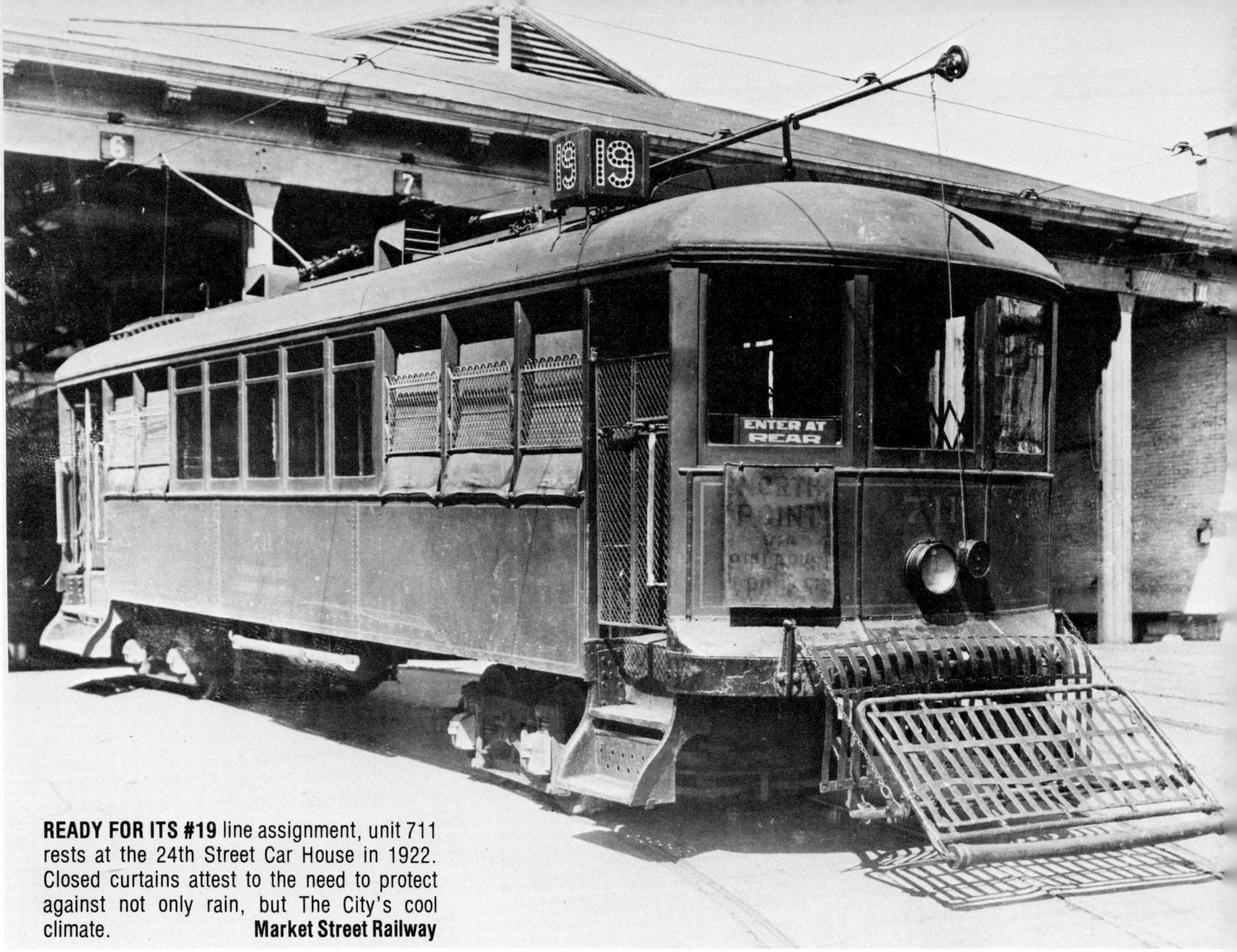

READY FOR ITS #19 line assignment, unit 711 rests at the 24th Street Car House in 1922. Closed curtains attest to the need to protect against not only rain, but The City's cool climate. **Market Street Railway**

THE APPEARANCE of 701-724 was drastically altered in 1923 when the cars' open ends were enclosed. No longer a California car, 711 appeared as below in 1934, at Seawall and Sansome, opposite the State Belt enginehouse, terminal #34. Line 34 was the last to use these flush platform cars.
Charles Smallwood

THE INTERSECTION of Sansome and Pacific streets was enlivened by this speeding trolley car on a warm summer day back in 1933.
Charles Smallwood

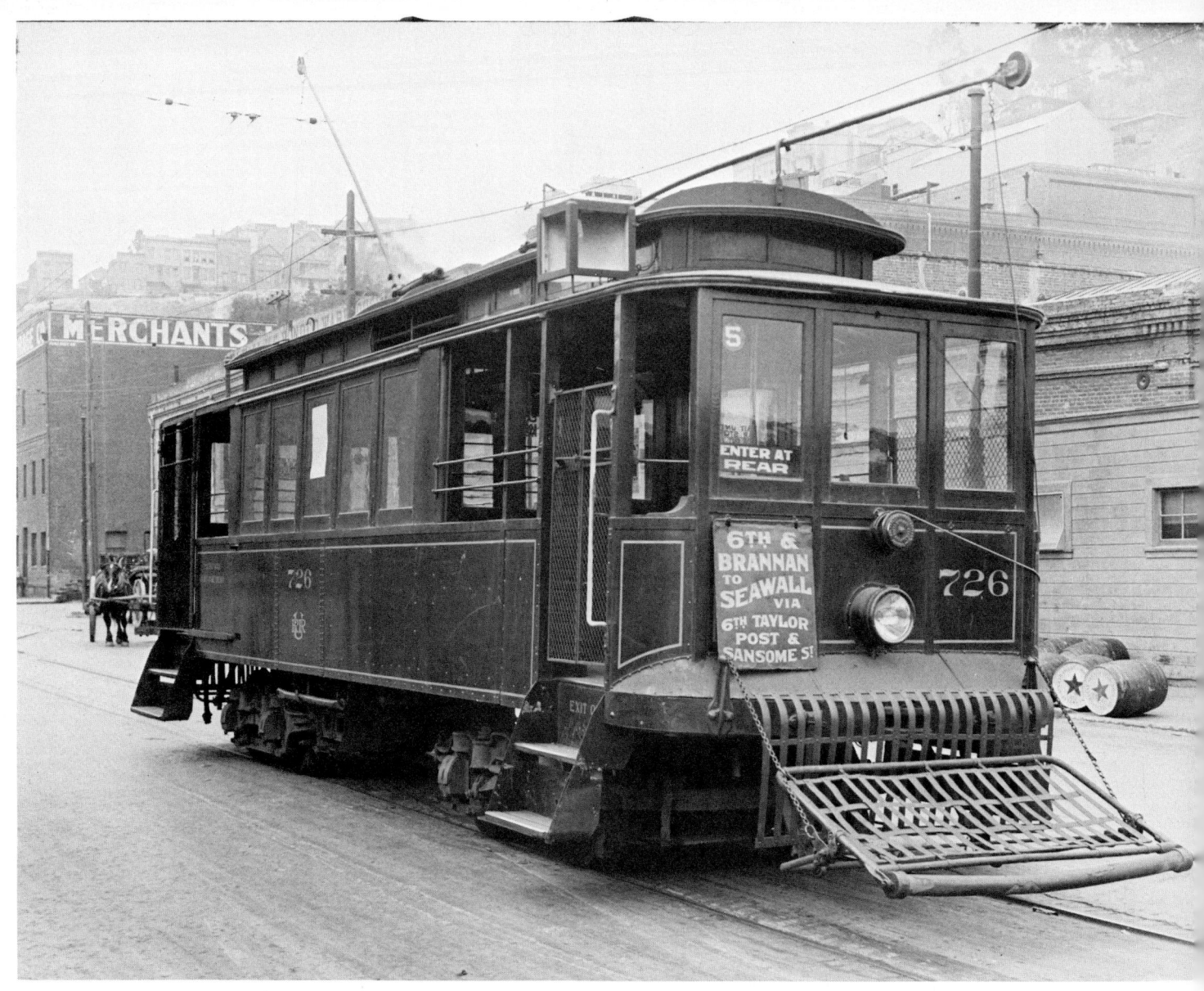

THESE TWO ODD CARS, 725 and 726, were rebuilt from Visitacion line one-man cars 1023 and 1024 following the tragic accident in Visitacion Valley on July 13, 1918, in which the third member of this class, 1022, was destroyed. **United Railroads**

Cars 725—726

Here are two odd cars that saw little use on Market Street Railway. Formerly cars 1023 and 1024, pioneer 1894 Mission St. cars that (along with car 1022) were rebuilt into one-man PAYE type for the Visitacion line in 1914.

Following a bad accident on that line in 1918 involving car 1022, which was destroyed, one-man car operation ceased; the remaining two were rebuilt into two-man PAYE cars and renumbered 725 and 726.

Both operated on the #34 line for a few years and subsequently were removed from service. They were retired in 1922.

However, 725 and 726 rose again; the old body of 725 was scrapped on December 19, 1922, and a new body was constructed. The new 725 (in which the old 725's motors, trucks, controls, etc., were incorporated) was ready for service on March 25, 1923, but was renumbered 784 shortly thereafter. Old 726 was scrapped on March 8, 1923, but a new body emerged on May 2, 1923, as 726; the new 726 was renumbered 785 on December 18, 1923.

Subsequent histories of the resurrected 725 and 726 are to be found on another page.

Cars 725—726

IN TWO "LIVES": (TOP) Newly rebuilt 1023 shows off its one-man body at Elkton Yard in June 1914. (ABOVE) Built as second 726, as shown on the page at left, this car utilized a new body and the equipment from the old 726. This photo was taken when it was renumbered to 785, in late 1923.
TOP: United Railroads
BOTTOM: Market Street Railway

General Specifications, Cars 725, 726

Body type	California, deck roof, flush platforms, PAYE
Builder	Hammond Car Company
Date built	1895
Weight	35,840 lbs.
Seats	30
Length over buffers	33'8"
Length closed section	15'1"
Length open section	9'3½"
Width over steps	9'3"
Width over drips	9'3"
Truck centers	17'0"
Controller	K-12
Motors	4 GE 1000, 35 hp.
Gear ratio	17:67
Compressor	AA-1
Trucks	Peckham 14-B3-S
Motors hung	Outside
Truck wheelbase	4'1"
Wheels	30" Cast Iron

A RARE VIEW OF a 727-class car (lower right). It is ready to leave the Ferry Building for the Southern Pacific depot on the 28 Line. The view was taken in May 1922. **Vernon J. Sappers**

Cars 727—730

These four cars were rebuilt by United Railroads at Elkton Shops in 1919 into PAYE cars from old South San Francisco California type cars 44, 46-48. As such they were the smallest double truck PAYE cars to ever operate in San Francisco, being but 28 feet long over bumpers.

They originally were part of a 10-car order, built by Hammond Car Company in 1900 for the pioneer *San Francisco & San Mateo Electric Railway Company*.

The cars saw little use on MSR and were early placed in storage inside the Third Street Car House. All were scrapped in 1927.

Cars 727—730

United Railroads Rebuilds

ONE OF THE four Pay As You Enter rebuilds, car 730, is shown at Sansome and Chestnut in October 1919.
United Railroads

General Specifications, Cars 727—730

Body type	Closed, railroad roof, flush platforms, PAYE, two sections
Builder	Hammond Car Company
Date built	1900
Weight	32,720 lbs.
Seats	33
Length over buffers	29'6"
Length closed section	14'0" (two)
Width over steps	9'3"
Width over drips	9'0"
Truck centers	15'6"
Controller	K-12
Motors	4 GE 1000, 35 hp.
Gear ratio	17:67
Compressor	MW-7
Trucks	Brill 27-G
Motors hung	Outside
Truck wheelbase	4'0"
Wheels	30" Cast Iron

ORIGINAL APPEARANCE of cars 731-745 is illustrated by 740 at 24th and Utah Car House in August 1915.   **United Railroads**

Cars 731—745

Here we have the original California-type cars built in 1895 by the W.L. Holman Car Company of San Francisco for Adolph Sutro's electric line on Clement St. from Sutter and Presidio Ave. to the Cliff House and his Sutro Baths and Museum. United Railroads obtained these cars when it purchased the *Sutter Street Railway* cable road in 1902; Sutro had sold his electric line to the cable road about 1900, which, incidentally, is a rare instance of a cable railway's controlling an electric road.

These cars continued running in their original conditi[on] until 1915-16, when URR brought them to its Elkton Sho[ps] and rebuilt them into a rather attractive California-ty[pe] PAYE car.

Having flush platforms, they faced an early demise wh[en] the new car construction program began. However, they r[an] up to the mid-1920s.

Cars 731—745

General Specifications, Cars 731—745

```
Body type..........California, deck roof, flush platforms, PAYE
Builder..........................W.L. Holman Car Company
Date built...............................................1895
Weight............................................37,600 lbs.
Seats.....................................................44
Length over buffers....................................42'2"
Length closed section..................................16'0"
Length open section....................................13'1"
Width over steps........................................9'8"
Width over drips........................................8'6"
Truck centers..........................................21'0"
Controller..............................................K-12
Motors.......................................4 GE 1000, 35 hp.
Gear Ratio..............................................17:67
Compressor..............................................MW-7
Trucks........................................Peckham 14-B3-S
Motors hung..........................................Outside
Truck wheelbase........................................4'1"
Wheels.......................................30" Cast Iron
```

AS REBUILT, car 732 shows an utterly different appearance. This 24th and Utah view was taken in November 1915.
United Railroads

PARLOR CAR "HERMOSA", seen in 1904, emerged from Elkton Shop on October 10, 1919, rebuilt into car 746. No photo has been found of 746 bearing that number.
United Railroads

Car 746

This car was built in 1896 by St. Louis Car Company as a private parlor car and was named HERMOSA. Originally having but a single truck, the car received double trucks before the turn of the century to improve its riding qualities.

By 1918 there was little need for such a car on the system, so it underwent rebuilding at Elkton Shops in that year (along with the 727-730 class, with which car 746 was generally used). The 746 emerged as a small Pay As You Enter car.

This car was little used by Market Street Railway; after the customary period of storage, it was scrapped in 1927.

General Specifications, Car 746

Body type	Closed, deck roof, PAYE
Builder	St. Louis Car Company, 1896
Date built	1896
Weight	36,300 lbs.
Seats	29
Length over buffers	32'6"
Trucks	Brill 27-G
Truck wheelbase	4'0"
Wheels	30" Cast Iron
Motors	4 GE 1000, 35 hp.
Gear ratio	17:67
Compressor	CP-25
Controllers	K-12

REBUILT FROM car 1004, one of the original Hammond double-truck electric cars of 1895, car 753 pauses at Ferry Terminal in 1922. Units 751-756 never received the White Front treatment, and all were retired by 1925. In this view car 753 is assigned to Route 28, the Ferries-Southern Pacific Depot line. This is the only known photo of this class with the Market Street name affixed.

Charles Smallwood

Cars 751—756

These six flush platform, California-type Pay As You Enter cars were rebuilt by URR in 1916 from the original 1895 Mission St. electric cars of the 1000 series. In the rebuilding they received the same treatment as the 731-745 class, which series they very much resembled.

Always used on unimportant south of Market lines, the cars were all out of service and scrapped by 1926.

General Specifications, Cars 751—756

Body type	California, deck roof, flush platforms, PAYE
Builder	Hammond Car Company
Year built	1895
Weight	36,560 lbs.
Seats	46
Length over buffers	42'8"
Length closed section	14'0"
Length open section	14'4"
Width over steps	9'8"
Width over drips	8'4"
Truck centers	20'8"
Controller	K-12
Motors	4 GE 1000, 35 hp.
Gear ratio	17:67
Compressor	GE 25-C
Trucks	Peckham B-3-S
Motors hung	Outside
Truck wheelbase	4'1"
Wheels	30" Cast Iron

Cars 751—756

REBUILT FROM the 1895 cars in 1916, but gone by 1926, the 752 sits at 24th and Utah on December 27, 1916. **United Railroads**

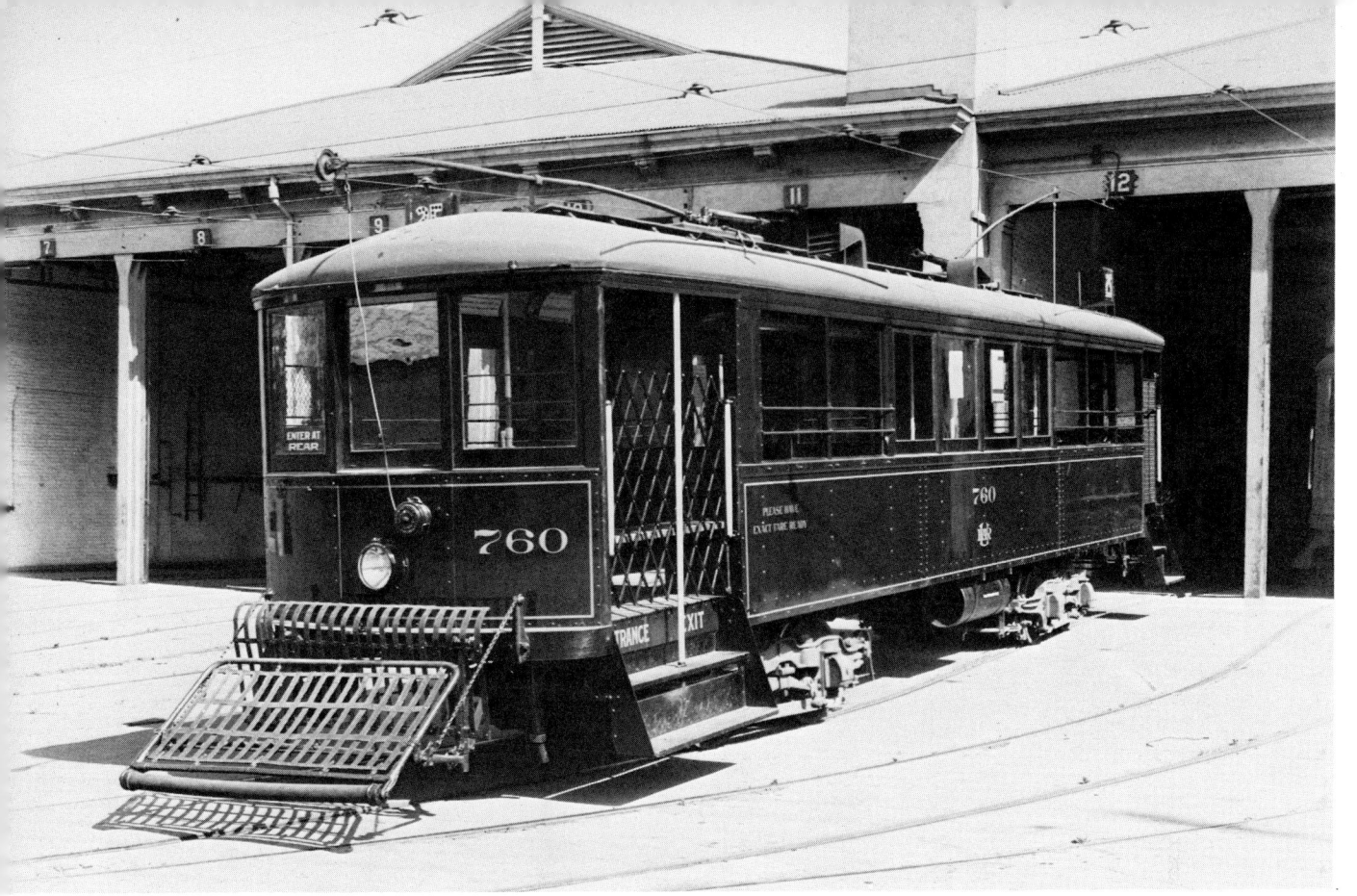

SWITCHBACK CARS: The 757-771 were standard equipment on the #33 Line until trolley coaches began operating in 1935. Car 760 was about a year old when snapped at the 24th and Utah Car House in May 1919. **United Railroads**

Cars 757—771

This class of 15 cars was built upon the underframes of some of the first double-truck electric cars used in San Fransisco—the old 1000 class "Mission St." cars built for the original Market Street Railway's pioneer Mission St. line in 1894.

The 757 class was built at Elkton Shops in 1918 and was at first used on several south of Market lines, including routes #25 and #30. In 1920 the entire class was moved to Haight St. Division for exclusive use on Line #33—18th and Park, a service they performed until the #33 line was converted to trolley coach operation in October 1935.

These cars were a flush platform, three compartment California type car but had one distinguishing feature which set them apart: they had longitudinal seats throughout, a convenience considering their long operation on the famed switchback line high on the side of Twin Peaks.

All cars of this class were scrapped in 1935. Car 765, however, had been scrapped previously, due to a collision with car 760 at the switchback in 1927. At Elkton Shops where both cars had been hauled for damage inspection on September 3, 1927, it was determined that while 760 could be repaired, 765 was too badly damaged; the unfortunate car was then scrapped three days later.

This class had a three-compartment body. Although originally built with open and closed sections, the cars were later totally enclosed. All three compartments had the longitudinal seat, obviously so no one would have to ride backwards during a portion of the journey, during which the car changed ends as a consequence of availing itself of the switchback to gain altitude. The curious seating arrangement also militated in keeping this class on the #33 Line throughout its life.

Although small by ordinary standards, the 757s must have seemed palatial to patrons of the #33 Line in 1920, for this class succeeded small, single truck cars on the hilly line.

General Specifications, Cars 757—771

Body type	California, arch roof, flush platforms, PAYE
Builder	United Railroads of San Francisco
Years built	1918 and 1919
Weight	37,060 lbs.
Seats	44
Length over buffers	42'9"
Length closed section	12'6"
Length open section	13'8"
Width over steps	9'4"
Width over drips	8'3"
Truck centers	20'8"
Controller	K-12
Motors	4 GE 1000, 35 hp.
Gear ratio	17:67
Compressor	AA-1
Trucks	Peckham 14-B3-S
Motors hung	Outside
Truck wheelbase	4'1"
Wheels	30" Cast Iron

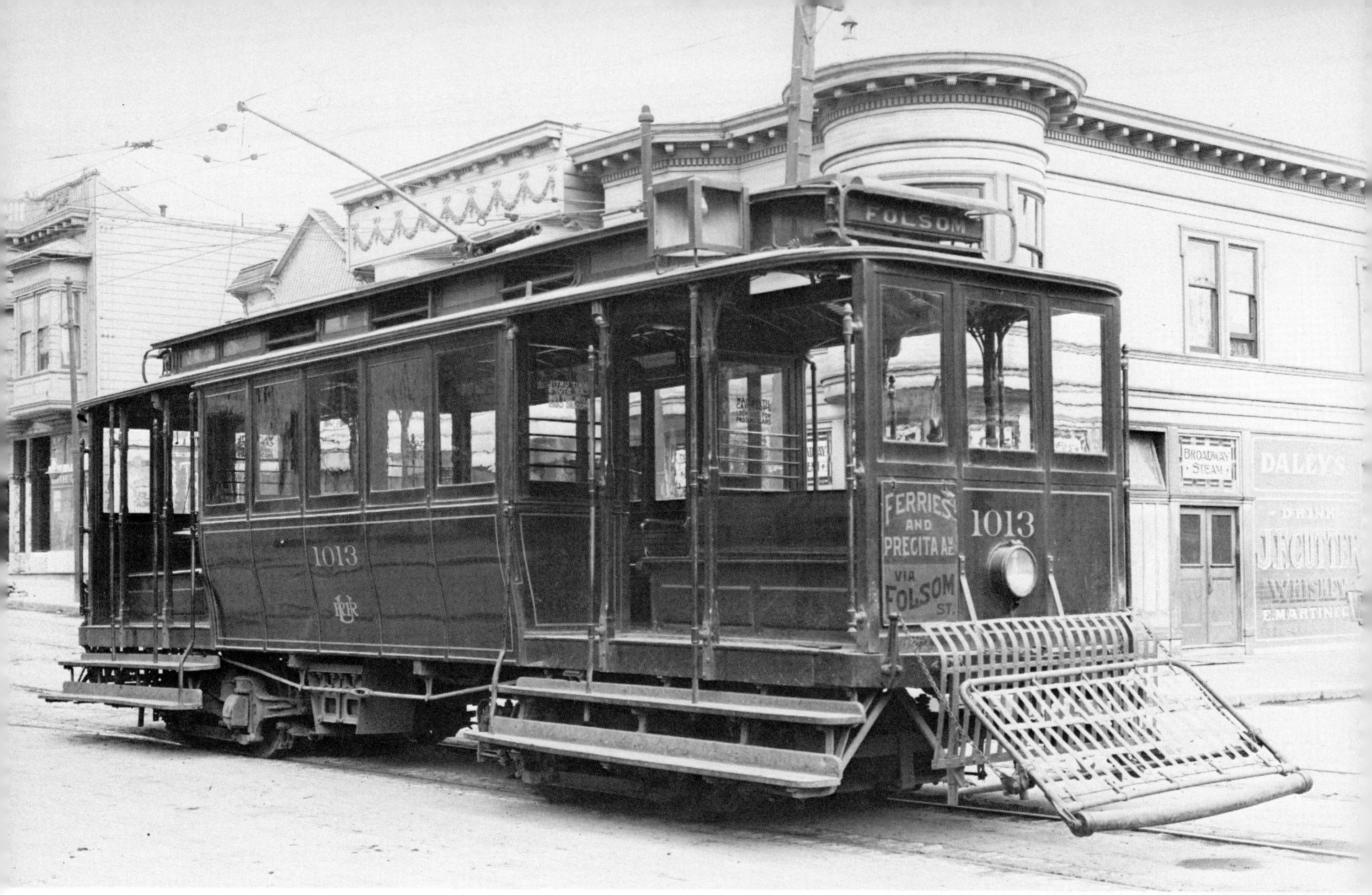

DIRECT ANCESTOR of the 757 class was the old 1000 class, of which 1013 is seen (ABOVE) at 24th and Utah in June 1914. **United Railroads** (BELOW) **CAR 758** is at 8th and Harrison, circa 1933. This class spent its entire service life on the unique switchback line. Note the ancient Peckham trucks.   **TOP: United Railroads**   **BOTTOM: Charles Smallwood**

(ABOVE) **AT THE SWITCHBACK** on upper Market Street; here is 757 in 1933. **Charles Smallwood** (BELOW) **INTERIOR OF** the 757-771 class. Longitudinal seats throughout were unique but highly practical, inasmuch as no passengers had to ride backwards after cars changed ends at the switchback.　　　　　　　　　　　　　　　　　　　　S.F. Public Utilities Commission

Cars 757—771

Cars 757—771

THE APPEARANCE of this class was considerably changed by the enclosing of the open sections. Car 761 is at Haight and Stanyan in 1930.

Market Street Railway

THIS 1932 PHOTO shows car 767 on Waller Street approaching Golden Gate Park, the western terminus of the #33 Line.

Charles Smallwood

THE MOTORMAN changes trolleys at the 8th and Harrison end of the line, in 1933.

Charles Smallwood

Cars 772—778

During September 1919, United Railroads built seven car bodies on old 40-foot underframes which came from the former *Omnibus Cable Company* cars that were rebuilt for electric service in 1898-1900. These seven cars were of the flush platform type with arch roofs. Bodywise they were of unique construction, inasmuch as they appeared to be closed-cars with glassed-in windows throughout; however, they turned out to be anything but closed, as they merely were two ends and two sides with but a single partition which was placed in the middle of the car. With the exceptions of the four rebuilt 727 class cars and car 746 (ex-HERMOSA), these cars were the only deviation from the California type that Elkton Shops ever made in any of its rebuilding or new construction.

Due to this single partition feature, the cars were extremely drafty and practically impossible to keep warm; they were very unpopular with both the riding public and crews and soon earned the nickname, "Pneumonia Specials."

Externally they were an extremely handsome car but it should come as no surprise that because of their poor interior design they fell early victims to the scrapper's torch; they were disposed of during the middle months of 1928.

General Specifications, Cars 772—778

Body type	Closed, arch roof, flush platform, PAYE
Builder	United Railroads of San Francisco
Date built	1919-20
Weight	37,160 lbs.
Seats	44
Length over buffers	42'6"
Length closed section	20'0" (two)
Width over steps	9'3"
Width over drips	8'6"
Truck centers	21'9"
Controllers	K-12
Motors	4 GE 1000, 35 hp.
Gear ratio	17:67
Compressor	AA-1
Trucks	Brill 27-G
Truck wheelbase	4'0"
Wheels	30" Cast Iron

"**PNEUMONIA SPECIALS**" was the nickname earned by the drafty 772-778 series. Here, 773 poses at 24th and Utah Car House in August 1920. **United Railroads**

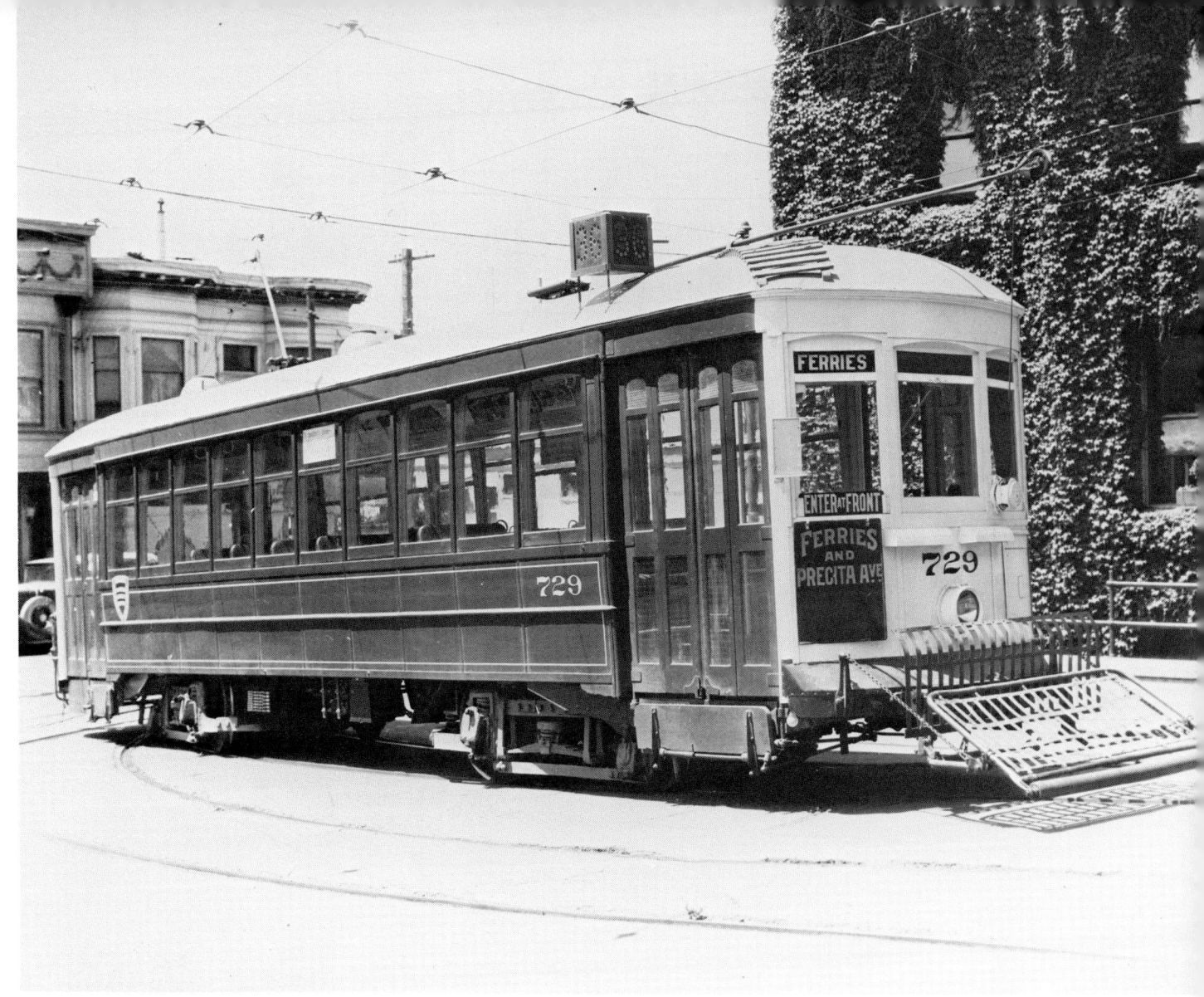

SECOND-HAND from Williamsport, Pennsylvania, (2nd) 725-734 were especially neat and trim, as 729 shows at 24th Street Car House in 1936.
Market Street Railway

Cars 725—734 (II)

These 10 cars were purchased second-hand from the *Williamsport Railway* of Williamsport, Pa., in June 1935. They were of the J.G. Brill Company's semi-convertible design and were built in the 1912 era. They had Brill maximum traction trucks—unusual in San Francisco—a feature which caused much comment among employees and patrons. The company made a good buy on these cars as they were, although of an older design, in very good condition. A minimum of work was required to put them in service; it consisted merely of applying standard Eclipse fenders, route number boxes and a coat or two of MSR paint. The cars gave the company good service while they were able to be operated one-man. After the one-man operation was outlawed in 1939, all cars of this class were put into dead storage; they were scrapped in July 1941.

General Specifications, Cars (II)725-(II)734

Body type	Closed, arch roof, drop platform, one-man
Builder	J.G. Brill Company, Philadelphia
Date built	—
Weight	38,100 lbs.
Seats	40
Length over buffers	42'6"
Length closed section	28'1"
Length of platform	5'6"
Width over steps	9'1"
Width over drips	8'5"
Truck centers	19'4"
Controller	K-36-J
Motors	2 West. 306, 60 hp.
Gear ratio	15:69
Compressor	CP-27
Trucks	Brill 39-E "Maximum Traction"
Motors hung	Outside
Truck wheelbase	4'8"
Wheels	33" steel drivers, 21" steel idlers

A FOGGY MORN in 1935 witnessed this scene: a string of flatcars shunted into a siding at Elkton Shops, with a cargo of second-hand streetcars from Williamsport, Pennsylvania. (BELOW) **A CLOSEUP** of one of the Williamsport cars, about to enter a new life in the city by the Golden Gate.

BOTH: Charles Smallwood

BEFORE AND AFTER receiving the White Front treatment. (ABOVE) Williamsport car 53 is shown prior to its shipment to Market Street Railway, while (BELOW) the same car is now MSR 732. It is seen at Six Mile House in 1937 while in service on the Visitacion Valley line.
TOP: C.W. Yingling; BOTTOM: Charles Smallwood

(ABOVE) **THE ONLY KNOWN** picture of this type on the South San Francisco local line was taken at Grand Avenue, South City, in 1935. **Charles Smallwood** (BELOW) **THE BARREL-LIKE** construction of the interior is typical of Brill's semi-convertible design.

Market Street Railway

(ABOVE) **VISITACION LINE'S 732** is seen below at the Southern Pacific shops on Bayshore Blvd., in 1936. (BELOW) **SIX MILE HOUSE** was the joint terminus of the #16-Third Street main line and of the Visitacion Valley Line. Here, in a 1937 scene, car 732 of the latter route and a San Francisco standard lay over pending their respective departure times. **BOTH: Charles Smallwood**

(ABOVE) **THE OPERATOR** changes ends as 725 prepares to return to the Ferry Building from the Southern Pacific station terminus of the #28 Line in September 1937. (BELOW) **HER EVERY LINE** characteristic of Brill ancestry, car 727 is shown, also at Third and Townsend (SP depot), but a year earlier. Note the Brill "Maximum Traction" trucks. **BOTH: Charles Smallwood**

Cars 725—734 (II)

Cars 735—736 (II)

Cars (II)735 and (II)736 were purchased used from the *Williamsport* (Pa.) *Railways* in 1935, whose numbers 42 and 43 they were. Typical Brill semi-convertibles of the 1905 era, they reportedly sported steam coach roofs originally; these became deck roofs when the pair was converted to one-man operation in 1918.

The twins were placed in service on July 16, 1935, on the Visitacion Line, operating there until the line was converted to motor coaches on July 31, 1937. Thus their total life operating span in San Francisco was but two years, all of which was spent on that quite minor cross-country line.

Ironically, these two cars, among the oldest in Market Street Railway's fleet, were still in storage in 1944 and passed into Municipal Railway ownership on September 29 of that year. Muni never used them and sold them for scrap a few years later.

General Specifications, Cars (II)735, (II)736

Body type	Closed, deck roof, drop platforms, one-man
Builder	J.G. Brill Company, Philadelphia
Date built	—
Weight	41,490 lbs.
Seats	40
Length over buffers	43'9"
Length closed section	28'0"
Length of platform	5'11"
Width over steps	8'11"
Width over drips	8'3"
Truck centers	16'0"
Controller	K-36-J
Motors	2 GE 80, 40 hp,—Car 735
	4 GE 80, 40 hp,—Car 736
Gear ratio	15:71
Compressor	CP-27
Trucks	Brill 27-G
Motors hung	Outside
Truck wheelbase	4'0"
Wheels	33" Steel

(ABOVE) **WILLIAMSPORT RAILWAY'S** cars 42 and 43 are seen above in that Pennsylvania city prior to their shipment to MSR, in 1935. These became MSR 735 and 736. **C.W. Yingling** (BELOW) **THE TWO** Williamsport deck-roofers are shown below in Elkton Yard upon their arrival in 1935. **Charles Smallwood**

Cars 735—736 (II)

(ABOVE) **PROOF IT IS** definitely in one-man service is the MSR shield mounted on the blocked rear doors on car 735, seen at Schwerin and Wallbridge, on the Visitacion line in 1937. (BELOW) **CAR 735** takes on a few passengers at Six Mile House in 1937. **BOTH: Charles Smallwood**

A LINEUP of the ''Long'' East St. Louis Cars (755-759 series) as they appeared (ABOVE) upon arrival at Elkton Yard in 1936. (BELOW) **FOR ABOUT FIVE YEARS** the 740 class was a familiar sight at the Ferry. Unit 743 is seen on the #36 Line in 1936. **BOTH: Charles Smallwood**

"SHORT ST. LOUIS" car 748 was assigned to the Richland Shuttle when this 1936 photo was snapped; the cars lay over at Richland Avenue and Andover Street. No destination signs are in evidence. (The "Short" cars of this service had 10 side windows, the "Long" cars had 12.)

Charles Smallwood

Cars 740—754 • 755-759 (II)

The 20 cars (II)740—(II)754 and (II)755—(II)759 were purchased used from *East St. Louis & Suburban Railway* in April 1936—a product of MSR's nationwide search for one-man cars. Built by St. Louis Car Company in 1918, these cars (together with nine other cars bought from the East St. Louis Company) were among the finest cars MSR ever owned. They comprised two groups, both groups being identical in every particular except for length: cars 740-754 were 10 windows long, while 755-759 had 12 windows to the side.

After some modification at Elkton Shops these cars were placed in service on lines operating south of Market St., and operated out of the Third St. and 24th and Utah Divisions. The cars were fairly fast and very comfortable; they actually increased riding on lines on which they ran.

When one-man operation ceased on MSR in February 1939, cars 740, 741, 743, 745, 750 and 751 were rebuilt into two-man cars, mainly because of the traffic hopefully to be generated by the 1939 World's Fair, held on Treasure Island. Remaining cars of this class were put into dead storage. Modifications made on the six cars retained in service consisted of removing the treadle-operated exit doors from each end and substituting folding pantagraph gates of the type used on standard MSR two-man cars. To lessen drafts through the cars, double sliding door bulkheads were installed at each end of the body; the bulkheads came from scrapped cars of 1550-1749 class.

When traffic returned to normal at the close of the fair, these cars were rendered surplus and were also placed in storage.

Renumbering Data

MSR	St. L. No.	Arrived
740	311	4-25-36
741	312	4-24-36
742	313	4-25-36
743	314	4-21-36
744	315	4-21-36
745	321	4-25-36
746	322	4-24-36
747	323	4-25-36
748	324	4-24-36
749	325	4-25-36
MSR	St. L. No.	Arrived
750	316	4-22-36
751	317	4-22-36
752	318	4-22-36
753	319	4-22-36
754	320	4-25-36
755	300	4-25-36
756	301	4-25-36
757	302	4-23-36
758	303	4-25-36
759	304	4-23-36

These cars were scrapped at Elkton in 1941.

EAST ST. LOUIS car 300 is seen (ABOVE) on the Illinois side of the Eads Bridge in July 1932. An extremely attractive type, the five long cars were the company's finest except for the Rail Sedans, one of which (BELOW) is passed by 301 near the site of today's famed Peace Arch, also in July 1932.
BOTH: R.V. Mehlenbeck

Cars 740—754 • 755-759 (II)

"Short" Cars From East St. Louis

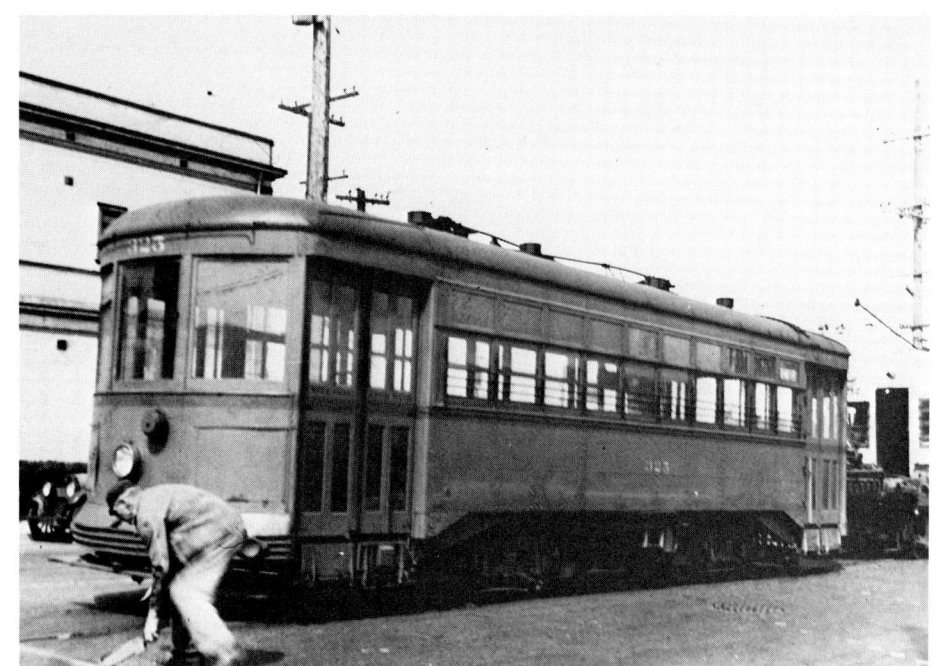

(LEFT) **SHOPMEN SWITCH** newly arrived "short" (10-window) East St. Louis Car 325 into Elkton Shops in 1935 with the aid of 0507.

(BELOW) **CAR 325 EMERGED** from the shops as a quite attractive MSR vehicle. Renumbered 749, it is seen at 24th and Utah Barn in 1937. It was assigned to the #27 Line, whose short-lived extension from 26th and Mission to Richland and Andover enabled the former #27 Line to be replaced by one-man cars.

BOTH: Charles Smallwood

FOUR TRACKS, but along this portion of Second Street the outer tracks belonged to Southern Pacific! Car 750, nearing Townsend, in 1939, was a two-man car at this time. A Bay Bridge highway approach crosses overhead.   **Charles Smallwood**

General Specifications, Cars 740—749

Body type	Closed, arch roof, drop platforms, one-man
Builder	St. Louis Car Company
Date built	1918
Weight	42,050 lbs.
Seats	40
Length over buffers	41'9"
Length closed section	26'4"
Length of platform	7'4"
Width over steps	——
Width over drips	8'8"
Truck centers	15'2"
Controller	K-28
Motors	4 GE 200 E, 40 hp.
Gear ratio	14:67
Compressor	CP-27
Trucks	Brill 27-GE1
Motors hung	Outside
Truck wheelbase	4'6"
Wheels	33" Steel

General Specifications, Cars 750—754

Body type	Closed, arch roof, drop platforms, one-man
Builder	St. Louis Car Company
Date built	1918
Weight	37,400 lbs.
Seats	40
Length over buffers	41'0"
Length closed section	26'4"
Length of platform	7'4"
Width over steps	——
Width over drips	8'8"
Truck centers	15'2"
Controller	K-75
Motors	4 GE 264-B, 25 hp.
Gear ratio	16:97
Compressor	CP-27
Trucks	Brill 27-GE
Motors hung	Outside
Truck wheelbase	4'6"
Wheels	33" Steel

General Specifications, Cars 755—759

Body type	Closed, arch roof, drop platform, one-man
Builder	St. Louis Car Company
Date built	1918
Weight	44,380 lbs.
Seats	48
Length over buffers	46'4"
Length closed section	31'8"
Length of platform	7'4"
Width over steps	——
Width over drips	8'8"
Truck centers	21'9½"
Controller	K-28
Motors	4 GE 203-P, 50 hp.
Gear ratio	17:67
Compressor	CP-27
Trucks	Brill GE-1
Motors hung	Outside
Truck wheelbase	4'6"
Wheels	33" Steel

TURNING THE AROMATIC corner of 2nd and Folsom in 1939, 740 passes the Schilling spice works. The car had been rebuilt for two-man service (note fixed rear step). **Charles Smallwood**

(BELOW) **ONE-MAN** ''short'' #742 poses at 22nd and Folsom, in 1936. **Charles Smallwood**

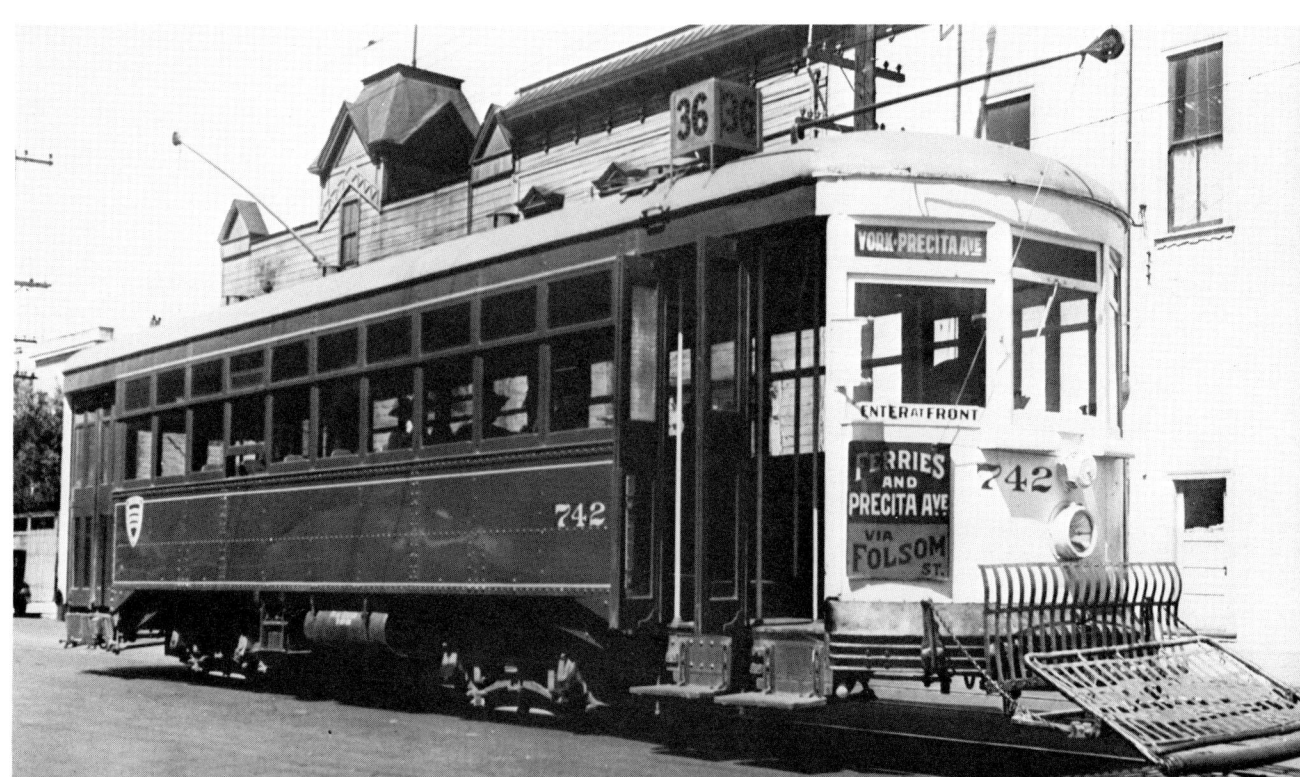

Cars 740—754 • 755-759 (II)

(BELOW) **CRESTING THE GRADE** at 24th and Rhode Island, (II)759, one of the five "Long St. Louis" vehicles, lays over at this terminus of the Howard Street Line in 1936. These cars gave an exceptionally smooth ride. (BELOW) **LEAVING 24th STREET** Car House in 1937, 757 heads out for a San Bruno run. **BOTH: Charles Smallwood**

WAITING FOR THE game to end, 758 waits on Bryant Street, near 16th Street, in 1936 . . . it was a baseball tripper to Seals Stadium.

Charles Smallwood

AT THE FERRY BUILDING 756 is in service as a one-man car on the #36 Line, in 1936.

Charles Smallwood

Cars 740—754 • 755-759 (II)

AS BUILT, 1230 was part of the original rolling stock for the San Mateo interurban line. This view was taken when it was new, in 1903.
United Railroads

INTERIM REBUILDING: (BELOW)   1225 is seen after a rebuilding, at Geneva and San Jose in July 1918. Note the short open section and short vestibules. Those big trucks are Brill model 27-E.
United Railroads

FINAL MODIFICATIONS: When placed back on the San Mateo interurban line in 1923, the 1200s had once again been rebuilt (see earlier versions on page at left). Lengthened platforms and improved seating were among the improvements for operation and passenger comfort. 1242 poses on a slight downgrade on San Jose and Geneva.   **Market Street Railway**

Cars 1225—1244

These 20 interurban-type cars, built in 1903 by Laclede Car Company of St. Louis, were perhaps among the most interesting electric cars ever to run in San Francisco. Large, commodious and delightfully fast and smooth-riding, these cars were the original equipment on the 20-mile interurban line to San Mateo.

In 1906 the 1225 class was superceded on the San Mateo run by the 12 P&W cars (see 1-12). However, the 1225s continued to run to San Mateo on occasion as extra cars and trippers. During the years of the P&W reign, the 1225 class served Route #14 which during those years ran from the Ferry Building to Holy Cross Cemetery.

The year 1923 saw the massive P&W cars removed from service as an economy measure. Thereupon, the 1225 class returned to its former interurban status. For the new lease on interurban life, certain modifications were made in the 1225s: platforms were lengthened to permit Pay As You Enter operation, deeply cushioned leather seats replaced the former cane-covered seats, electric heaters were installed, and partitions were constructed which made a three compartment car out of them. Control equipment was changed from the cumbersome K-14 type to the K-28. Platforms were also enclosed with glass doors replacing the former wire gates.

Cars 1225-1244 continued to serve the San Mateo interurban line until abandonment of that service in January 1949.

These cars were well-liked by the riding public, so much so that they were greatly responsible for the excellent patronage, even during the depression years of the 1930s, which the San Mateo Line enjoyed despite severe bus and train competition.

Up to the end the public was reluctant to see these remarkable cars leave the Peninsula transportation scene. They were indeed a credit to their builder. After nearly a half century of service they were by no means worn out and could have continued to carry their satisfied riders swiftly and comfortably. But now they simply had no place to go.

Cars 1225—1244

WELL SPRUNG TRUCKS and deeply cushioned leather seats made the 1200 Class cars smooth riding and comfortable. This 1928 photo shows these modern seats, replete with arms, and also shows other interesting things: an Ohmer fare register and a big sign offering a reward to anyone catching a seat slasher at work.
S.F. Public Utilities Commission

ELECTRIC HEATERS were found under the seats. Other improvements in the 1926 upgrading included enclosed smoking sections at both ends, electric signal bells which rang on both platforms simultaneously, and air-operated gongs, controlled by a small key on the air brake pedestal. **Charles Smallwood**

General Specifications, Cars 1225—1244

Body type	Closed body, deck roof, drop platforms, interurban
Builder	Laclede Car Company
Year built	1903
Weight	56,138 lbs.
Seats	40
Length over buffers	48′ 1″
Length closed section	—
Length of platform	6′ 1½″
Width over steps	9′ 6″
Width over drips	9′ 6″
Truck centers	23′ 0″
Controller	K-28B
Motors	4 GE 57, 50 hp.
Gear ratio	22:63
Compressor	A-4
Trucks	Brill 27 E
Motors hung	Inside
Truck wheelbase	6′ 0″
Wheels	33″ Steel

Cars 1225—1244

NORTHBOUND 1233 still sported ribbed sides when this 1934 photo was taken at Burlingame Station. A few months later the car was shopped and emerged with straight steel sides.
Charles Smallwood

SPEEDING THROUGH Euclid Station in 1934, northbound school tripper 1239 has some impromptu art work on its side.
Charles Smallwood

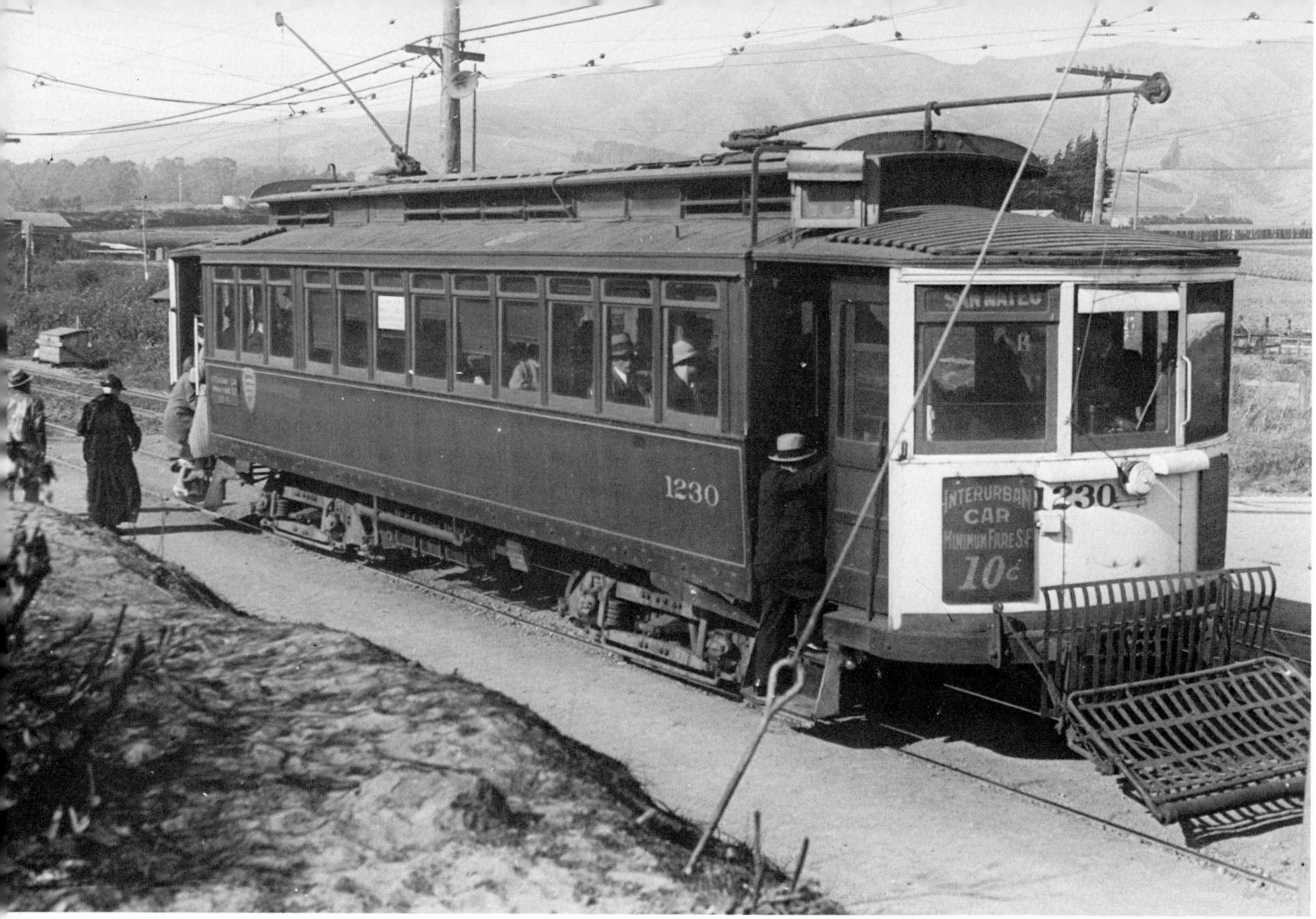

(ABOVE) **SOUTHBOUND TO SAN MATEO,** 1230 stops to pick up passengers at Leipsic Junction in March 1935. (BELOW) **INTER-URBAN CAR 1232** is seen at San Bruno in 1936. The drop platform is well illustrated here. **BOTH: Charles Smallwood**

Cars 1225—1244

ALTHOUGH FIXTURES on the #40—San Mateo interurban run, 1200s did serve other lines, especially in one-man car days. (ABOVE) Downgraded to a local city run, 1239 forlornly awaits departure time at the Ingleside Line's beach terminus in 1939. (BELOW) 1234, as a Balboa High School tripper, awaits the homeward-bound students' rush on Onandaga Avenue in 1936.
BOTH: Charles Smallwood

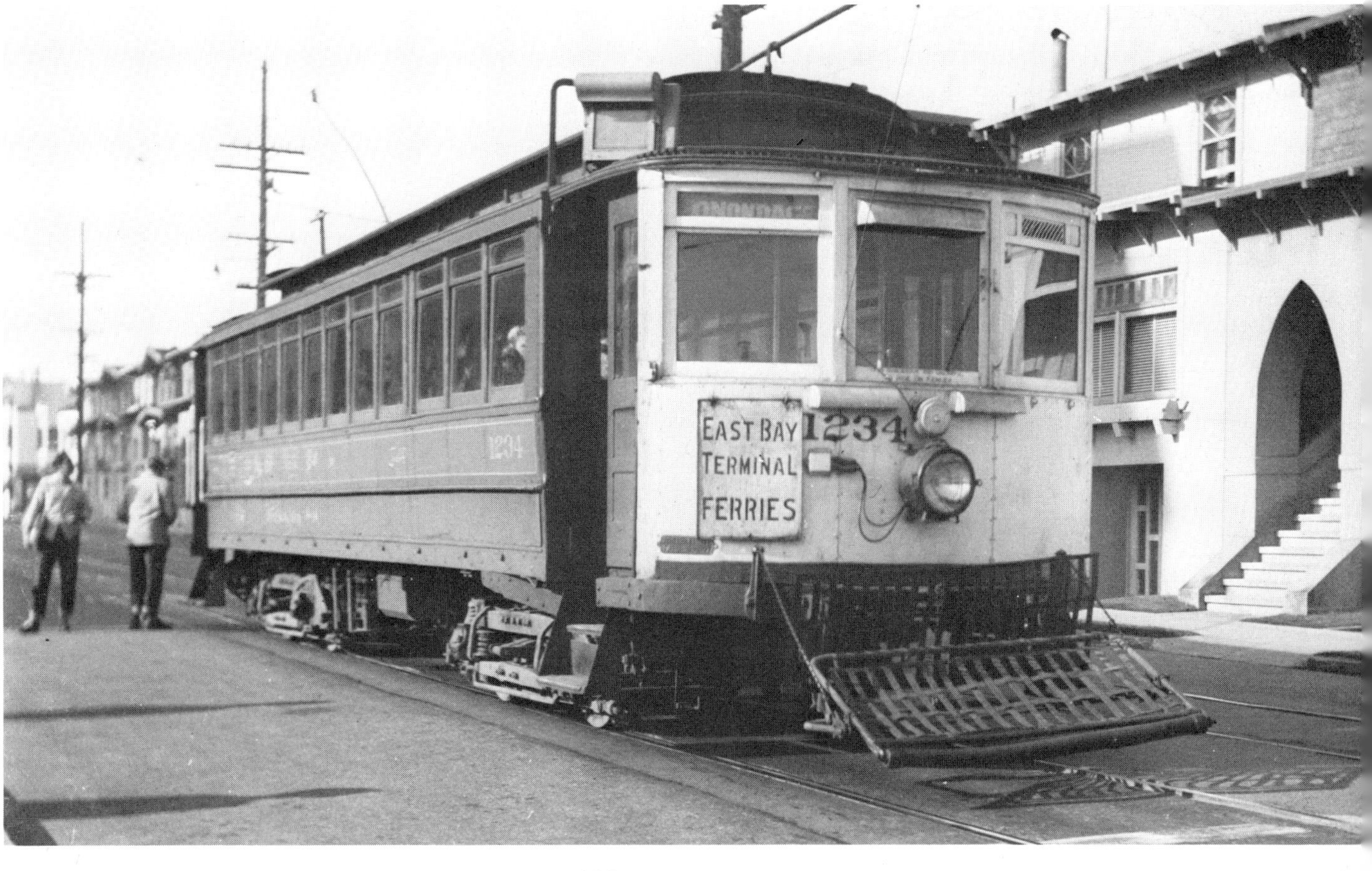

Cars 1225—1244

MEET AT HOLY CROSS: Northbound interurban 1238 has a meet with a 1600 at Colma cemetery siding, in May 1938.
Charles Smallwood

THE SAN MATEO CARS were the first to be repainted after Muni took over in 1944. Blue and gold 1243 is seen at San Mateo in 1948 with railfan-motorman Lorin Silleman in the foreground. He operated the last car on this line on January 15, 1949.
Lorin Silleman

Cars 1301—1424

THESE 125 DOUBLE-TRUCK cars, purchased between 1903 and 1905, were the first to surpass the hitherto largest city cars (like 1207, seen below, rebuilt from a cable car—these rebuilt cars were in the 950, 1000, 1100, and 1200-1215 Classes and few survived into Market Street Railway days). In the top view, brand new 1376 is seen at Land's End in January 1906.

BOTH: United Railroads

AS ORIGINALLY CONSTRUCTED by St. Louis Car Company in 1904-05, the 1301-1374 Class appeared as above. Location of steps, handbrake levers, destination signs and slat shrouding were typically San Francisco. **United Railroads**   (BELOW) 1353 in a broadside portrait at Steiner and Turk. **United Railroads**

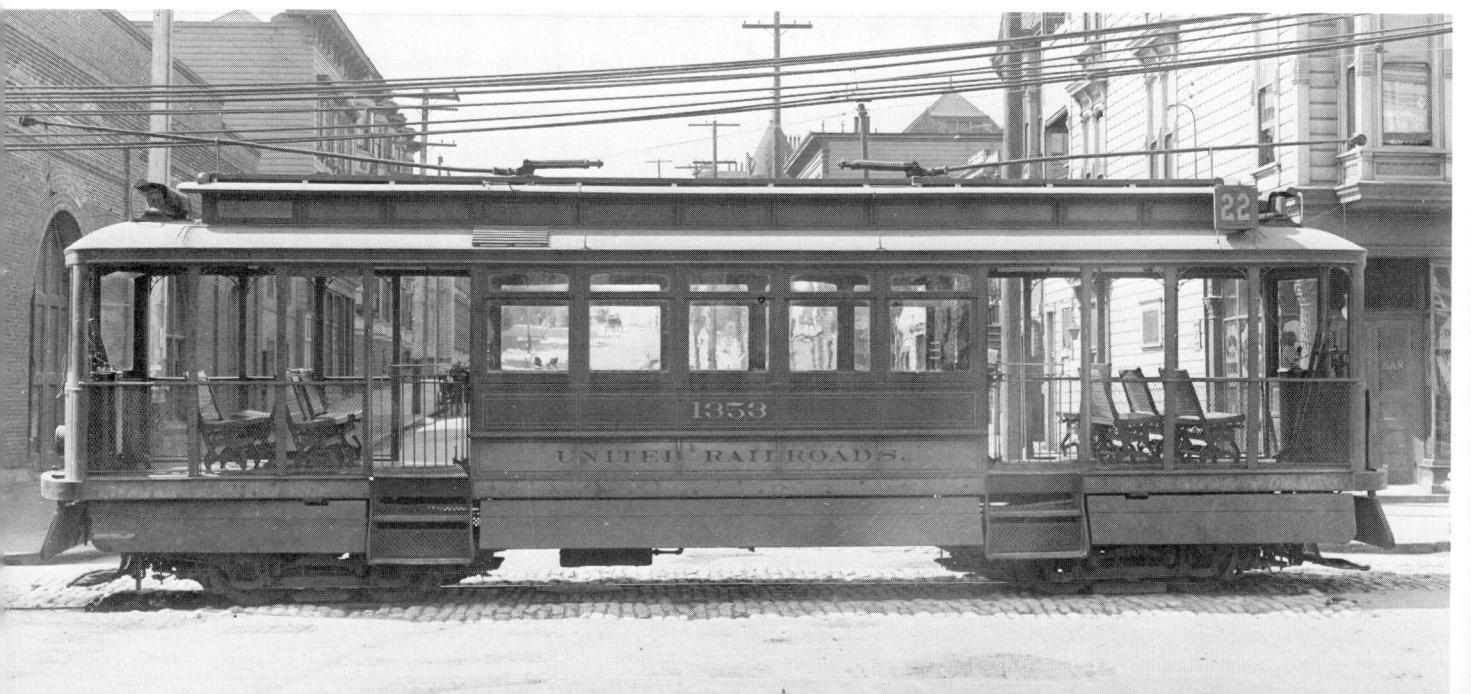

Cars 1301—1424

Between 1903 and 1905 United Railroads purchased a total of 125 large double-truck cars of a modified California type. In place of the longitudinal benches facing outward as in the traditional manner up to that time, the new cars had their open sections screened up to the belt rail (bottom of windows), and utilized reversible cross seats in place of the benches. Entrance and exit were through doorways located next to the closed section. These were San Francisco's first city cars to be equipped with air brakes; at that time only the 1225 class interurban cars were so equipped.

This class fell into three subclasses, each having minor differences:

1300-1349: Five window closed section; built 1903-04.

1350-1374: Five window closed section; built 1904. Same dimensions as 1300-1349 but somewhat more finished looking.

1375-1424: Four window closed section; built 1905. Also slight difference in design from the above two groups.

All were built by St. Louis Car Company. Their design was widely copied by other California streetcar companies, both in their original form and after URR lengthened and rebuilt them for Pay As You Enter operation. Cars of almost identical design were purchased by Sacramento, Stockton, San Jose, Fresno, Los Angeles area, Bakersfield and Phoenix—some for Sacramento and Bakersfield being built as late as 1914.

These cars were used throughout the city with the exception of lines operating on Market St.; flush platform cars were barred from that thoroughfare due to their extremely protruding steps, considered a hazard to cars operating on the inside tracks of the four-track street.

When Market Street Railway embarked on its car building program in the early 1920s, it quite naturally adopted a type of car with the low drop platform design. This necessitated the gradual phasing out of the flush platform type of car in San Francisco. Beginning in 1927, the 1301-1424 class began to disappear, the last being scrapped in December 1935. Trucks, motors and controls were used in many of the new cars turned out by Elkton Shops.

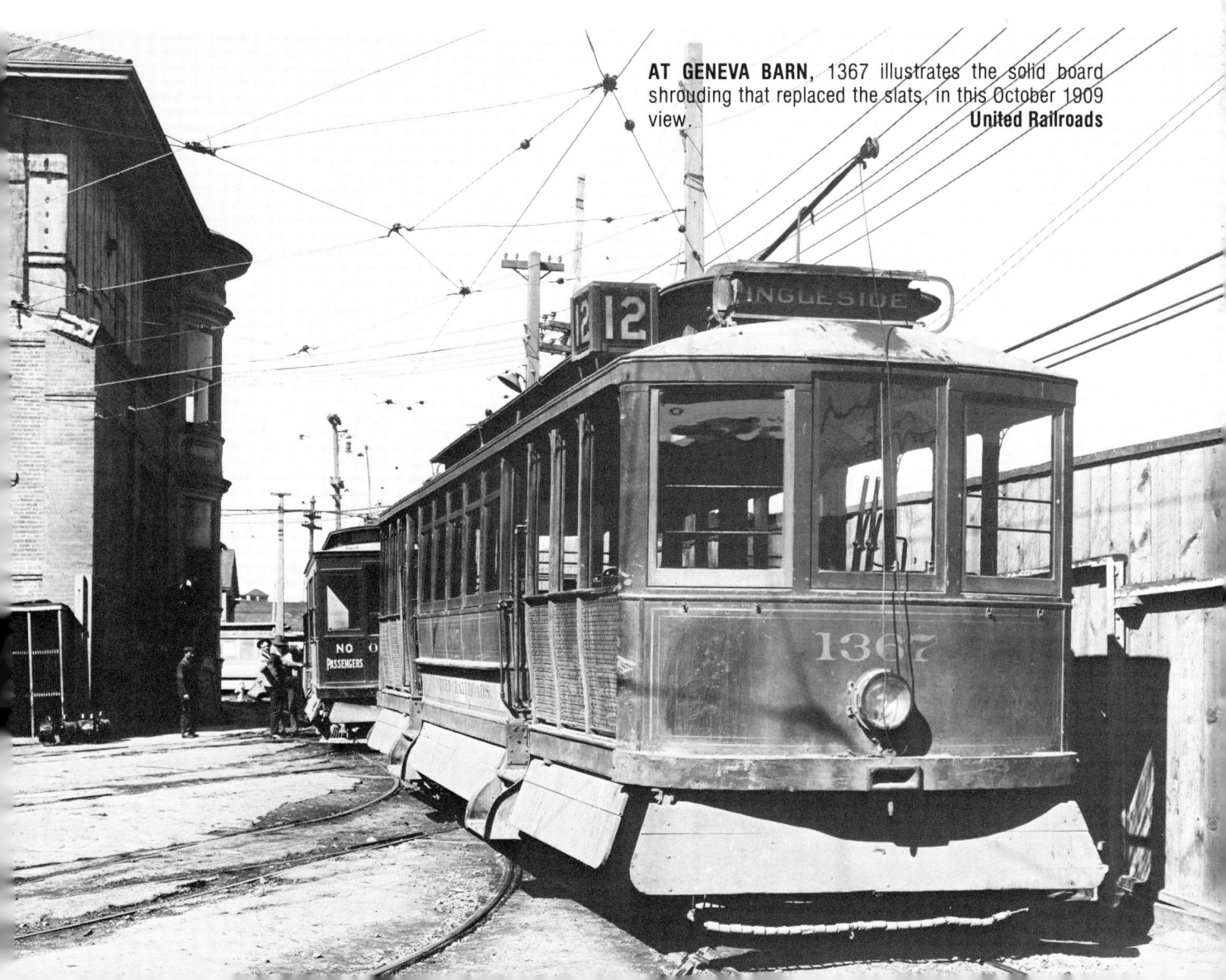

AT GENEVA BARN, 1367 illustrates the solid board shrouding that replaced the slats, in this October 1909 view. **United Railroads**

1300s and 1400s—The Original Design

WHAT A CONTRAST! Compare this view of 1324 in original condition with that of 1422 on the page at right after the 1911-12 rebuilding. United Railroad colors for the car in the March 1909 view at Sutro Barn were red and buff with tan roof.

United Railroads

INTERIOR APPOINTMENTS of the 1375 Class were similar to other MSR cars. Note the cane longitudinal seats in the center section in this 1928 view. **S.F. Public Utilities Commission**

As Rebuilt For Pay-As-You-Enter Operation

CAR 1422 of the third order of the class illustrates the 1911-12 program to modify them for Pay-As-You-Enter operation. Obvious differences are installation of solid siding to the end sections, relocation of doors to extreme corners, and removal of roof destination sign boxes. This car, seen on Turk Street near Steiner in October 1915, also shows the four-window center section of the third order, a contrast from the other cars' five-window design. **Charles Smallwood** (BELOW) **SIDE DETAILS** of 1409 are seen in this 1922 view at Turk and Fillmore Barn. **United Railroads**

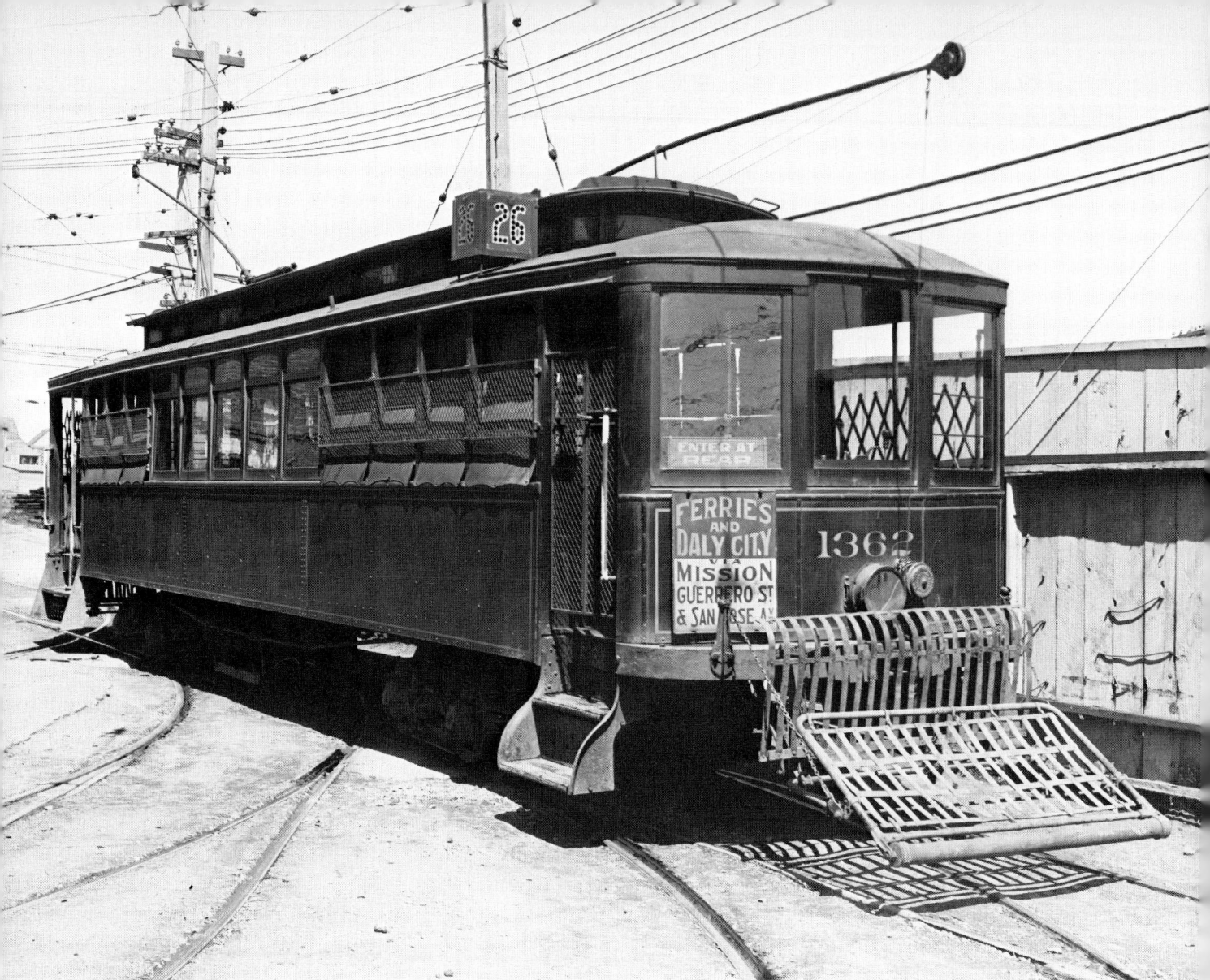

FOR THOSE DAMP San Francisco mornings, car curtains could be secured to the outside belt rail, as shown in this company view of 1362 at Geneva Barn in 1920.
United Railroads

1301 Class Miscellany

Roof number boxes were added in 1908, as were also Eclipse fenders.

In 1911-12, cars were lengthened and changed to Pay-As-You-Enter operation. Included: enclosing open ends to the belt rail, moving doors to extreme ends, and eliminating slat skirting.

Open sections were given glass windows starting in 1926, when one side of each section received windows. A year later the other side was given windows, resulting in a very different appearance.

First 1310 was burned at 19th and Guerrero in the April 18, 1906, disaster. 1300 became Second 1310.

Cars 1417 and up were assigned to South San Francisco. As the class began to be scrapped, Elkton Shops would receive one in exceptionally good shape; a bad South San Francisco car would then be scrapped in its place, after trading numbers —all entirely unofficial. This happened numerous times.

General Specifications, Cars 1301—1349

Body type	California, deck roof, flush platforms, PAYE
Builder	St. Louis Car Company
Year built	1903
Weight	42,290 lbs.
Seats	52
Length over buffers	44' 11"
Length closed section	14' 8"
Length open section	15' 1½"
Width over steps	9' 6"
Width over drips	8' 6"
Truck centers	23' 0"
Controller	K-12
Motors	4 GE 1000, 35 hp.
Gear ratio	17:67
Compressor	AA-1
Trucks	Peckham 14-B3-S
Motors hung	Outside
Truck wheelbase	4' 1"
Wheels	30" Cast Iron

Cars 1301—1424

THOSE PROTRUDING STEPS kept this series off four-track Market Street, where they would have maimed many pedestrians' legs. The omission of "unlucky" route 13 did not prevent the presence of a car 1313, which never lived up to its potential as a "jinxed" car.
United Railroads

General Specifications, Cars 1350—1374

Body type	California, deck roof, flush platforms, PAYE
Builder	St. Louis Car Company
Year built	1904
Weight	43,510 lbs.
Seats	52
Length over buffers	45'5"
Length closed section	14'8"
Length open section	15'4½"
Width over steps	9'6"
Width over drips	8'6"
Truck centers	23'0"
Controller	K-12
Motors	4 GE 1000, 35 hp.
Gear ratio	17:67
Compressor	AA-1
Trucks	Peckham 14-B3-S
Motors hung	Outside
Truck wheelbase	4'1"
Wheels	30" Cast Iron

General Specifications, Cars 1375—1423

Body type	California, deck roof, flush platforms, PAYE
Builder	St. Louis Car Company
Year built	1905
Weight	44,780 lbs.
Seats	48
Length over buffers	45'11"
Length closed section	13'2"
Length open section	16'4½"
Width over steps	9'6"
Width over drips	8'6"
Truck centers	23'6"
Controller	K-12
Motors	4 GE 1000, 35 hp.
Gear ratio	17:67
Compressor	AA-1
Trucks	Peckham 14-B3-S
Motors hung	Outside
Truck wheelbase	4'1"
Wheels	30" Cast Iron

CARS 1419-1423 were equipped with Brill 27-G trucks from 1919 to 1934 so railroad tread wheels and flanges could be used. These cars were restricted to Mission Street and the South San Francisco and Visitacion Valley lines during this period. (ABOVE) In 1915 car 1396, shown on Turk Street and Fillmore, still rolled on Peckham trucks, while (BELOW) car 1423 shows off its Brills at Geneva Barn, in 1920. **BOTH: United Railroads**

Cars 1301—1424

FLUSH PLATFORM CARS like the 1300-1400 Class, did not fit into Market Street Railway's plans, and two years after this 1925 view (ABOVE) of 1378 at Geneva Barn, their numbers began dwindling. **Market Street Railway** (BELOW) **TESTING TRUCKS** was 1367's forte. It is seen at Elkton Shops in April 1914 on a pair of low-floor trucks borrowed from the Pittsburgh, Pennsylvania, system; these later went under car 301. Later this car briefly received cut-down Peckham trucks. **United Railroads**

BAY WINDOWS are typical of San Francisco neighborhoods served by MSR 1300s, like 1327 (ABOVE) seen on Coleridge Avenue in back of the 29th Street Barn in 1916. Note the Peckham trucks. **United Railroads** (BELOW) Car 1396's conductor poses as the car rests at Fillmore and Broadway about 1922. **Market Street Railway**

Cars 1301—1424

Crunch!

EVEN A SLIGHT altercation would result in damage to those protruding steps on the 1300-1400s. The arc headlight seen in this accident photo was necessary for South San Francisco interurban service. It originally came from a San Mateo "Big Sub" (see cars 1-12).
Market Street Railway

Finale

WHITE FRONTS came in as the 1300-1400 series went out. Things look bad for 1347 (ABOVE) as it sits out back of Elkton Shops, while 1421 (BELOW) stands shorn of dash lights and company insignia in Elkton Shops prior to scrapping, in December 1935. Her trucks and equipment, however, would live far into the future under a new body (see cars 266-305 —778-994). **Charles Smallwood**

Home Built . . . . . Long Lived

MARKET STREET RAILWAY'S first venture into the car building field resulted in car (2nd) 1424, seen in its builder's photo, taken in Geneva Yard in 1923. Note the double headlights (one atop the other) required by the joint city-interurban service on the South San Francisco Line, on which the car entered service on January 22, 1923.
                                                                                                              Market Street Railway

Car 1424 (II)

This car was Market Street Railway's first venture into the field of car building at Elkton Shops. It left the shops on January 22, 1924, and entered service on the South San Francisco local line, replacing California type car 1421 which had previously been demolished in a collision with a steam train at Leipsic Junction.

For the South San Francisco service 1424 was fitted up with entrance and exit doors of the type used by interurban cars 1225-1244. The car also had wide tread wheels, required on the South San Francisco line owing to some operation over steam road trackage. It also had interurban headlights for rural use.

The 1424 continued in South San Francisco service un the line was converted to one-man operation on May 2 1934, when it was replaced by rebuilt cars 284 and 285. C 1424 was thereupon assigned to the Visitacion Valley line an ran there until again ousted by conversion to one-man oper tion. Ex-Williamsport cars 735 and 736 took over on that li on July 16, 1935.

The car was then taken to Elkton Shops and rebuilt into standard one-man, two-man car of the MSR 265 type ar renumbered 778; it was still running at the time of the 19 consolidation and was the only 700 type car still in service in the Muni era. The car was finally scrapped in 1948.

General Specifications, Car 1424 (II)

Body type	California, arch roof, drop platforms PAYE, enclosed platforms
Builder	Market Street Railway Company, San Francisco
Year built	1923
Weight	38,948 lbs.
Seats	44
Length over buffers	47′0″
Length closed section	15′6½″
Length open section	14′11″
Width over steps	8′9″
Width over drips	9′3″
Truck centers	20′10″
Controller	K-12
Motors	4 GE 247, 40 hp.
Gear ratio	15:63
Compressor	AA-1
Trucks	Brill 27 G
Motors hung	Outside
Truck wheelbase	4′0″
Wheels	30″ Cast Iron

Another One of a Kind

IN MAY 1934, car (2nd) 1424 was replaced in South San Francisco service by one-man cars, and it then did a brief stint on the Visitacion Line. In a few months it was again replaced by one-man cars. Car 1424 then entered Elkton shops for rebuilding; emerging as a one-man, two-man car, renumbered (2nd) 778. **Charles Smallwood**

HAD THE EARTHQUAKE and fire not struck San Francisco in 1906, the 50 1500-Class cars would have been delivered to their intended owner, the Chicago City Railway. (ABOVE) Car 1529 shows off its massive McGuire 10-A trucks at 28th and Valencia Barn in March 1909. **United Railroads** (BELOW) Similar car 5091 in Chicago shows how the 1500s would have looked had not fate intervened. **Charles Smallwood**

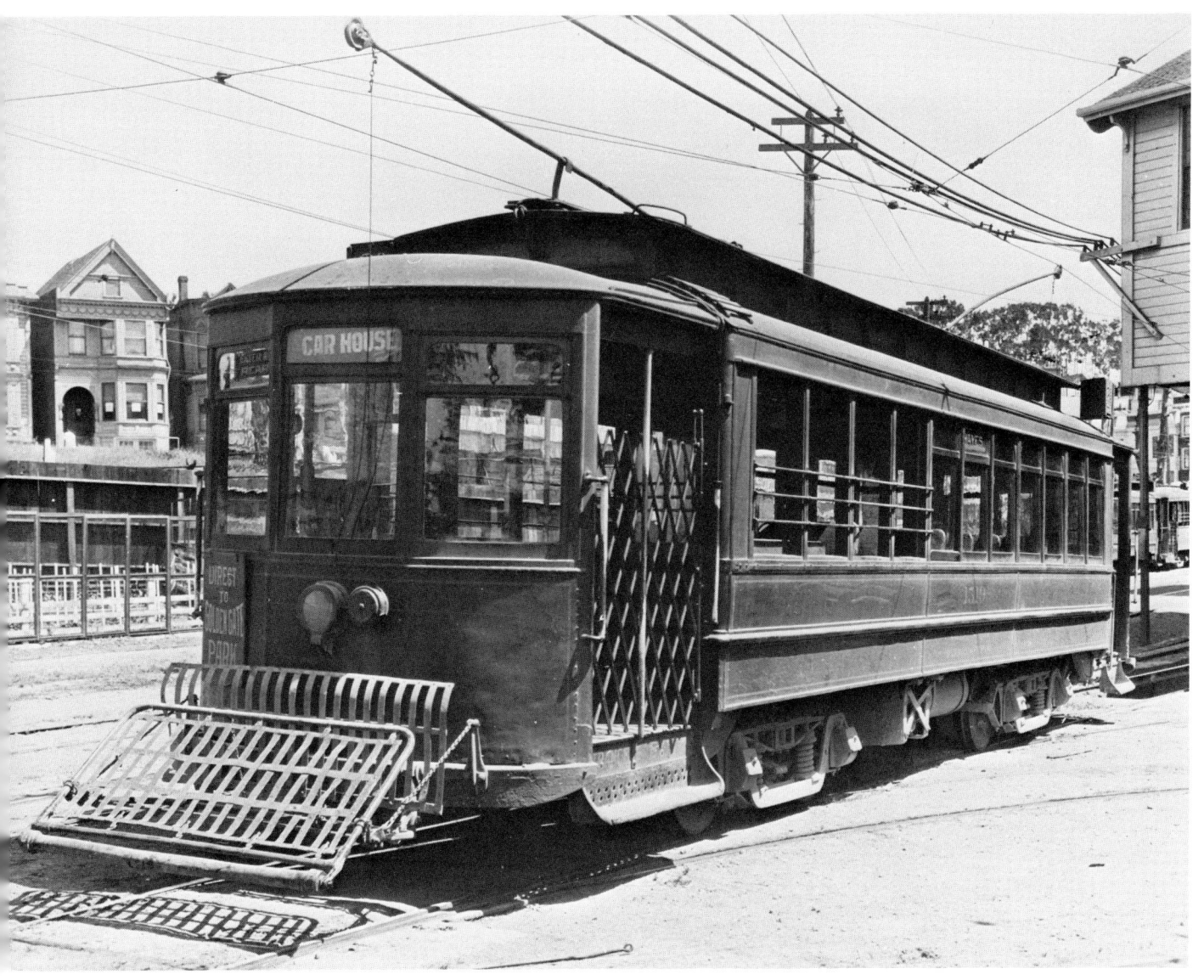

ADDITION OF AN OPEN SECTION for smokers is evident in this 1922 view of 1519 at McAllister Car House. Other notable changes were locations of headlight and retriever.
Market Street Railway

Cars 1500—1549

These 50 cars were built by American Car Co. of St. Louis in 1906 for the *Chicago City Railway* and were the first of an order of some 200 cars of this type for Chicago. Following the 1906 disaster in which URR was badly hurt and had to obtain replacement cars in a hurry, URR President Patrick Calhoun made a trip to the St. Louis area car builders in a desperate search for any available rolling stock. These 50 cars were completed and ready to be shipped to Chicago, but Calhoun's plea for them was graciously received (there was an abundance of sympathy around the nation for San Francisco at the time) and the Chicago company allowed Calhoun to purchase the cars.

The 1500 class cars were closed, single compartment cars, incorporating a popular Chicago feature, that of removable window sashes; in summer these cars could be an airy open vehicle, and in winter they were snug and warm with windows again in place. Needless to say, this feature would have been anything but popular in the San Francisco climate, so the windows were never removed throughout all the years they operated.

As built, this class was of the non-prepayment type, with a passenger boarding at either the front or rear and paying the conductor after selecting his seat; the conductor then rang up the fare on a register. In 1911-12 all 50 cars were converted to Pay As You Enter operation.

When these cars arrived in San Francisco in May 1906, cars 5200-5212 had Chicago City Railway numbers and insignia, plus folding doors on all four corners. Cars 1516-1549 were lettered and numbered for United Railroads at American Car Company's plant in St. Louis; these had no doors but had pantograph gates installed on all four corners in St. Louis. Their Chicago paint scheme of medium dark green body, tile red window sash and roof, with striping and lettering in golden yellow was well received by San Franciscans; URR had intended to repaint the cars in its standard maroon and cream as soon as the pressing need for cars passed, but owing to the

ALTHOUGH EQUIPPED with removable window sash, specified for their intended role in Chicago, the transplanted cars ran with windows in place year-'round in cool San Francisco. Car 1537 poses at McAllister Barn in 1915; note the sliding gate at front which replaced the original pantograph gates. **United Railroads**

(BELOW) **THE RATTAN SEAT-EQUIPPED** interior of a ''Chicago'' 1500. **Charles Smallwood**

Cars 1500—1549

popularity of the Chicago paint job, it decided to adopt Chicago City Railway's paint scheme as its own. This occurred, and green remained the basic color of equipment throughout the life of the system under private ownership.

During subsequent years of operation, three cars of this class fell on evil days when they were severely damaged in runaway accidents. Ironically, these accidents all took place at the same location: Hayes and Stanyan streets; all three were smashed up by crashing into the same power pole and the same building! At the time of these mishaps the cars were running on the Hayes and Ellis line, which in those days terminated at Stanyan and Fulton streets. Stanyan St. between Fulton and Hayes is a very steep grade. At the base of the grade the line made a sharp left turn into Hayes St., and it was at this curve that the three runaways came to grief.

The first of these accidents occurred on the evening of March 21, 1913, when car 1504 slipped its brakes while descending the Stanyan grade, failed to make the curve at the bottom and slammed into the building on the southeast corner, also snapping off a large power pole that was in the way. Less than two months later, car 1502, on May 18, and under the same ill-fated circumstances, crashed into the same house and power pole. Again, less than two years after 1502's wild flight, disaster struck again at the same location when, on April 28, 1915, car 1508 was almost totally destroyed at the same spot. The same house and the same power pole again got in the way.

Cars 1502 and 1504 required complete rebuilding and emerged from the repair shops with a greatly changed design from the rest of the 1500 class; for one thing, the rather short platforms of the 1500s were extended several feet in the rebuilding, an improvement recommended by the eminent Chicago traction engineer Bion J. Arnold, for this series of cars when he conducted a survey of San Francisco street railway companies in 1912. Incidentally, these were the only cars of the 1500 class to receive the recommended extended platforms; the remainder of this class retained their original short platforms until retirement.

Car 1508 was considered to have been too badly damaged to be rebuilt at all, so a new body was built for it; this new body generally followed the lines of the 201-265 class. The new car retained the number—1508—and always worked with the 1500 class, although inevitably regarded as somewhat of a misfit in that class.

It is worthy of mention that yet a fourth car received the coup de grace at the same infamous corner when on August 30, 1942, car 123 met its fate there; it never was repaired. Happily enough, none of the four accidents resulted in any loss of life.

In the early years of operation of the 1500s in San Francisco, the Chicago cars saw much service on the relatively unimportant lines south of Market St. The reason for using such excellent cars on such minor lines, especially when URR owned so many older cars which then were assigned to the im-

A "Chicago" Loops at the Ferry

THE LOW 1500s were still the mainstays of the #21—Hayes Line when this Fourth of July 1935 view was taken of 1530 on the Ferry Loop. Note that this car, as well as all but one of the 1500-1549 series, had lost its midsection rub rail. **Charles Smallwood**

Cars 1500—1549

portant Market St. group of lines was this: the Market St. group had just been electrified from cable operation and much of the trackage, both on Market St. itself and on other important streets these lines traversed was of the light type of construction characteristic of cable trackage. The heavy Chicago cars would have pounded the light rail unmercifully. As the company relaid these Market lines with heavier rail, the Chicagos were brought over to work the rebuilt lines.

In 1914 the 1500 class was assigned to McAllister Division and for many years they were the mainstays on the important #5—McAllister and #21—Hayes lines. In the late 1920s they began to be replaced on the #5 line by new cars of the 800 class; however, the 1500s remained on the #21 line as the trackage on that route was considered too rough for the lightweight 800s. The Chicago cars ousted from the #5 line by the 800s were once again assigned to the 24th and Utah Division for south of Market service; eventually the entire 50 cars ended up at 24th and Utah when rebuilt cars of the 1550 class replaced the remaining McAllister Division cars used on the #21 line. The Chicagos held down south of Market assignments until replaced by one-man cars on those routes in 1935-36; at that time some 1500s were sent to the 29th and Mission Division for service on lines #23 and #24 while others returned to McAllister Division for #21 line service.

General Specifications, Cars 1500-1507, 1509-1549

Body type	Closed, deck roof, drop platforms, PAYE
Builder	American Car Company, St. Louis
Year built	1906
Weight	50,990 lbs.
Seats	44
Length over buffers	45′9″
Length closed section	32′4″
Length of platform	6′8½″
Width over steps	9′0″
Width over drips	9′0″
Controller	K-28-J and K-28-E
Motors	4 GE 80, 50 hp., and 4 GE 90, 50 hp.
Gear ratio	19:67 and 15:71 respectively
Compressor	AA-4
Trucks	McGuire 10-A
Motors hung	Inside
Truck wheelbase	6′0″
Wheels	33″ Cast Iron

After a few months the cars assigned to 29th and Mission Division were placed in storage when that division was closed on June 15, 1935.

The Chicagos continued to hold down the #21 line service with some help from the 1550 class until the late 1930s when cars of the 101-180 class took over the #21 line. The Chicago cars were then placed in storage, and all were scrapped at Elkton Shops between 1935 and 1940.

Longer Platforms

TWO CARS, 1502 and 1504, had their platforms lengthened and modified in 1913 after accident damage. This change was suggested by Bion J. Arnold, famed Chicago traction expert in his 1912 survey of San Francisco street railways. Arnold urged changing platforms on all 1500, 1600 and 1700 Class cars, but only 1502 and 1504 were modified. Car 1502, shown at Eighth and Clement in 1936, was the only car in its class to retain the rub rail.
Charles Smallwood

TIME RUNS SHORT for the Chicago 1500s as 1509, a rare sight on the #8 Line, begins leaving the Ferry loop for a spin out Castro Street in 1937. (BELOW) **DISPLACED BY ONE-MAN CARS**, three of the proud Chicagos . . . forlorn and weary after three decades of service . . . await their sad fate on the funeral pyre. Location here is the rear of 29th and Mission Car House, in 1937. **BOTH: Charles Smallwood**

Cars 1500—1549

(ABOVE) **SOME TRUCK SWAPPING** in the mid-1920s resulted in 1512, 1513, and 1518 (the last car seen with poles down at McAllister Yard in 1936) receiving Brill 27-G trucks from 1700 Class San Mateo cars. (BELOW) **ANOTHER RUN COMPLETED** out the Hayes Street Line, 1520 met the camera at its 8th Avenue terminus in this 1936 photo study. **BOTH: Charles Smallwood**

The End of (1)1508

THE FIRST 1508 ended its useful life by literally wrapping itself around a pole at Hayes and Stanyan, on April 28, 1915. Seeing the major structural damage, shop officials concluded it would be cheaper to construct an entirely new body than to repair this one. **United Railroads**

The Second 1508

A NEW, home-built body was combined with equipment off the wrecked 1508, and by June 18, 1915, a company photographer could record its considerably changed lines, which closely resembled the 200 Class. (2nd) 1508 poses at Masonic and Fulton. **United Railroads**

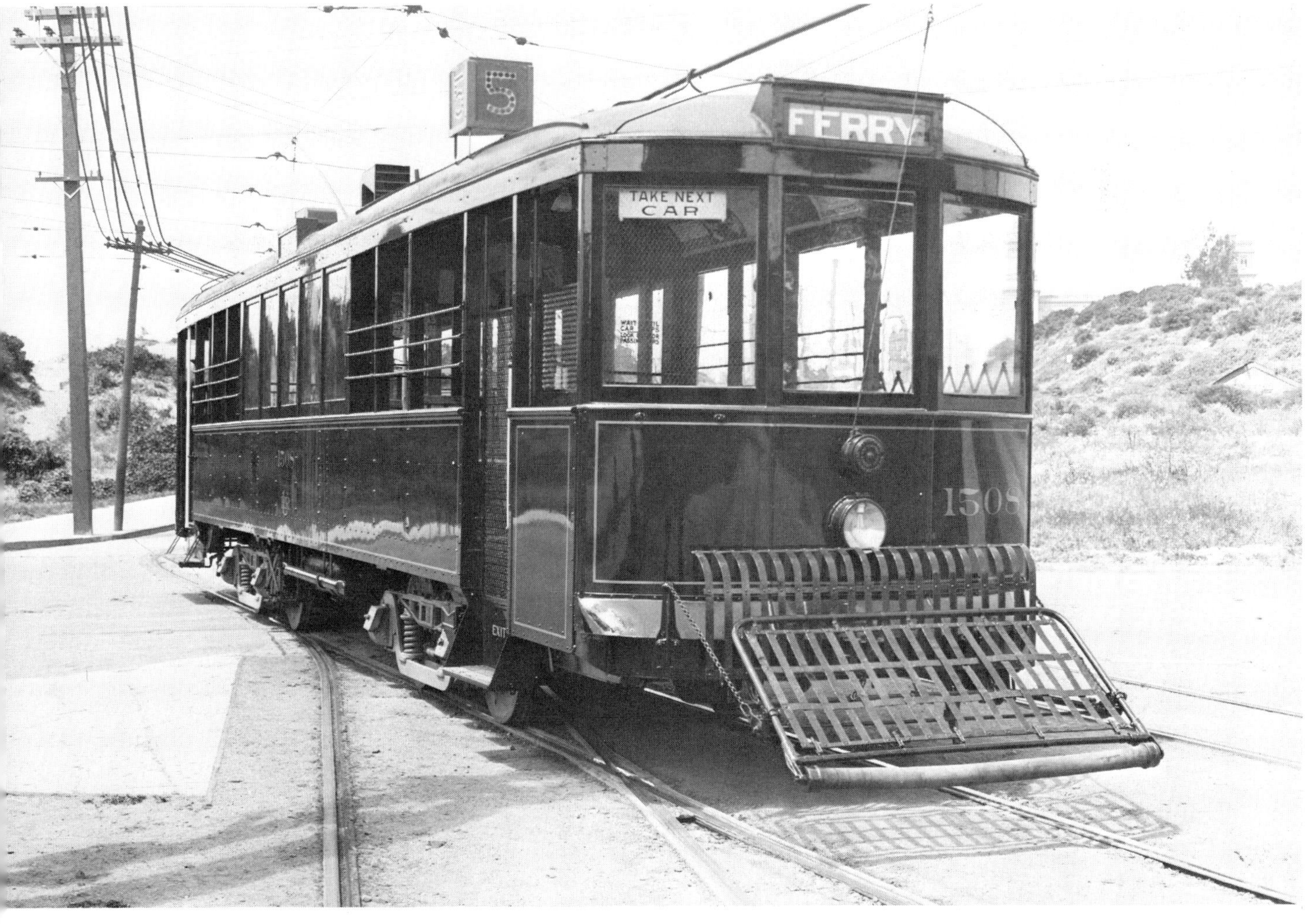

INTERIOR APPOINTMENTS of the new 1508 were quite spartan, with the same seating pattern as the 200s built in 1913.
United Railroads

THE ODD 1500 was in dead storage at the Lincoln Way boneyard when this photo was snapped in 1939.
Warren K. Miller

General Specifications, Car 1508 (II)

Body type	California, arch roof, drop platforms, PAYE
Builder	United Railroads of San Francisco
Year built	1915
Weight	—
Seats	50
Length over buffers	47′ 0″
Length closed section	14′ 2″
Length open section	14′ 5″
Width over steps	9′ 3″
Width over drips	8′ 6″
Truck centers	20′ 5″
Controller	K-28-E
Motors	4 GE 80, 50 hp.
Gear ratio	19:67
Compressor	AA-4
Trucks	McGuire 10-A
Motors hung	Inside
Truck wheelbase	6′ 0″
Wheels	33″ Steel

SIDESWIPED AND GOUGED (see ''wound'' above right-hand truck), the arch-roof 1508 pulls into the ladder tracks at Elkton Shops for repairs. **Market Street Railway**

A BROADSIDE ''BUILDER'S PHOTO'' of the second 1508, at Masonic and Fulton upon its completion on June 18, 1915.
United Railroads

Car 1508

THE YEARS MADE CHANGES in the 1550s, a mighty group of 200 cars purchased in 1906-1907. (ABOVE) This class is seen as originally constructed. Car 1646 is at 29th and Noe streets, terminal of the Valencia Line, in 1909. (BELOW) Third Street Division car 1625 shows the open smoking section received by more than half the cars of this class between 1916 and 1918.

TOP: Charles Smallwood
BOTTOM: United Railroads

THE 1550 CLASS gave an instant impression of strength and solidness. The wide deck roof, thick underframe and lowness on trucks all contributed to this aura. Here is 1680 at the Third Street Barn in December 1914. **United Railroads**

Cars 1550—1749

This group of 200 cars purchased from St. Louis Car Company in 1906-07 was the largest single order of cars bought from a car builder ever to operate in San Francisco. Like cars of the 1500-1549 class (received from eastern builders the previous year) these cars deviated from the traditional California type, so long a favorite in the city; these cars were all closed.

Familiarly known as "The 1600s" among company employees, these cars were of extremely heavy construction.

As built, the 1600s closely followed St. Louis Car Company's well-known design known as the "Robertson Type" which was a style of car employing a closed body whose side and end windows could, when weather waxed warm, be dropped down out of sight into the car side, thus giving the effect of an open car.

A contemporary San Francisco magazine article described the new cars' interior thusly:

> The interior finish is of mahogany, highly polished, and ornamented with marquetry; the seats are reversible, with automatic foot rests, have extra-high backs with rolling top and corner grab handles.

However, longitudinal seats were provided for half the seated passengers, cross seats being used opposite them; at mid-car, the seating types reversed. All seats were spring cushioned and upholstered in rattan. Each end bulkhead incorporated double sliding doors.

The 1600s were mounted on Brill 27-G trucks, had General Electric #90 motors (50 hp.) with K-28 control; the air brakes were of the National Brake & Electric Company's construction.

As originally built, these cars were equipped with two air valves in each motorman's compartment; one was to operate the standard wheel brakes, while the other operated wooden block brake shoes, two to each truck (of the same type as is presently used on San Francisco's cable cars). This auxiliary wooden shoe brake, intended for use on steep grades, was found to be superfluous; it was removed from all these cars by 1909.

Another unusual feature was the large headlight—mounted in the center of the dash; it was a combination arc and incandescent lamp; the arc gave out a brilliant light which proved to be too bright for other traffic, tending to blind team drivers and early motorists. After numerous complaints had been received, the use of the arc was discontinued.

These cars were very smooth-riding and comfortable and, in the opinion of many, were the finest-riding city cars ever to roll in San Francisco. This high regard was buttressed when the company installed leather-cushioned cross seats in many of them in the 1920s. With their wide window sills (just right for comfortable elbow resting) and mellow motor hum, many a late worker on his way home after a hard period of toiling dozed off and rode past his intended stop.

A STUDY IN INTERIORS of the 1500 Class: (ABOVE) The Sterling-Meeker fare register was a relic of pay-within days. After conversion to PAYE, in 1911, it was thereafter used only to ring up school tickets. (BELOW) This view of 1732 shows its interior partition.
BOTH: Charles Smallwood

Cars 1550—1749

These fine cars from their introduction were used on some of the most important lines of the company. For decades they were encountered everywhere in the city. At one time or another they ran on almost every one of the numerous electric lines of the company. Until the advent of home-built cars in the 1920s, the 1600s were always used to illustrate any company advertising, although they predated cars of the 100 and 200 classes by several years.

Beginning in 1915, about 75 percent of the 1600 fleet was converted into two-compartment cars. The Number One bulkhead was moved back four windows to form a smoking section; windows in this section were removed. In the late 1920s, these windows were put back in the open section, as was done with all MSR cars with open sections at that time.

Between 1915 and 1918 three of this class: 1690, 1722 and 1745, were damaged in accidents and were beyond resonable repair. Three new car bodies were thereupon constructed at Elkton Shops to replace the wrecked ones, and trucks, motors, controls, etc., of the original cars were installed. These new bodies closely resembled the one built in early 1915 to replace wrecked Chicago car 1508. All were patterned after the very successful 200 class of 1914.

These same three cars were extensively rebuilt for use on the upgraded San Mateo interurban line in 1923-24. They received McGuire swing bolster trucks in a swap with three of the Chicago cars, as well as interurban type of seats, large headlights, whistles, and enclosed platforms. At this time cars 1690 and 1745 were renumbered 1715 and 1716 to bring numbers of cars assigned to Geneva Car House into conformity.

In the late 1920s, several of the top-numbered cars in this class (which had remained single-compartment cars) were rebuilt into three-section, or California, type cars by installing a three-window smoking section at either side of the central closed section. These rebuilt California-type 1600s saw most of their service on the #21—Hayes St. Line.

The year 1930 saw the beginning of the end for the 1600s. In that year, on November 26th, car 1711 was scrapped; its motors, trucks and controls were used on a new 900 class car constructed at Elkton Shops. Despite continued scrapping in the following decade, the 1600 class was destined to trundle over San Francisco streets for almost two more decades.

The mighty 1600 class was scrapped as follows:

1930:	1 car	1934:	0	1938:	6
1931:	20	1935:	6	1939:	14
1932:	21	1936:	0	1940:	25
1933:	8	1937:	6	1941:	84

The Market Street Railway Company scrapped a total of 191 of this class. In 1944, nine of the class (including rebuilds 1715, 1716 and 1722) passed into Municipal ownership; most of these remained in use until January of 1949; shortly after, the survivors were scrapped.

THE CLOCK TOWER of the Ferry Building is the background for this typical scene at the Mission Street Terminal, in 1937, where cars of the 1550-1749 Class were a familiar sight for more than 30 years.
                                                                                                    Charles Smallwood

RARE ROUTE NUMBERS—one for real, one for fun. (ABOVE) A rare sight was a 1600 on the relatively unimportant Folsom Street Line. This unusual assignment in 1937 was due to forced discontinuance of one-man cars on this route. (BELOW) Car 1599, photographed in Geneva Yard in 1941, was signed for long-abandoned Route 32 on the occasion of a railfan excursion.

BOTH: Charles Smallwood

Cars 1550—1749

Thus passed from the transit scene San Francisco's most numerous single car type.

The 1600s suffered from the stigma of excessive weight. Built in a period when the optimum weight of a city car was about 48,000 pounds (dropped to 15,000 pounds in the most modern cars), the 1600s' weight of 56,000 pounds was undoubtedly excessive. The weight of these cars came under the unfavorable scrutiny of the noted Chicago traction engineer, Bion J. Arnold; in a report he made on San Francisco's street railways in 1913, Arnold recommended that motors, controls, etc., of the 1600s be salvaged and used in new lighter car bodies. Especially unfortunate, in Arnold's opinion, was the fact that the 1600s were used on lines having severe grades, making their normally heavy consumption of power all the more severe. For the time being, the company did attempt to assign the 1600s to those lines having light grades; eventually lighter bodies did appear which used many of the 1600s' components.

General Specifications, Cars 1550—1714, 1717—1721, 1723—1749

Body type	Closed, deck roof, drop platforms, PAYE
Builder	St. Louis Car Company
Year built	1907
Weight	54,420 lbs.
Seats	44
Length over buffers	45'4"
Length closed section	32'4"
Length of platform	6'6"
Width over steps	8'9"
Width over drips	9'2"
Truck centers	21'6"
Motors	4 GE 90, 50 hp.
Gear ratio	19:67 and 15:71
Controller	K-28-J
Compressor	A-4
Trucks	Brill 27-G-E2
Motors hung	Outside
Truck wheelbase	4'4"
Wheels	33" Cast Iron

INGLESIDE LINE CAR 1733 received cane-covered seats from 1200 Class interurban cars when the latter were upgraded with leather-cushioned seats in the mid-1920s. This view of 1733 was taken in October 1928. **S.F. Public Utilities Commission**

CAR 1553 operates on the #8 Market and Castro Line in 1938, after that line had been extended to 18th and Caselli. **Charles Smallwood**

WITH TWO HUNDRED CARS within its boundaries, the 1550 Class was Market Street Railway's largest group of factory-built cars. Car 1581 (ABOVE) models this design well as it poses at 28th and Valencia streets in 1937. (BELOW) Car 1610, a veteran Valencia Division car, waits for motor repairs at Elkton, also in 1937. **BOTH: Charles Smallwood**

TWO NOTABLE 1550s: (ABOVE) Only one 1550 received Municipal Railway's paint job. Car 1553 is shown in front of Geneva Barn in 1948. There were less than a dozen 1500 Class cars at the time of the 1944 Merger. (BELOW) The top-numbered of all 200 1550s was 1749, seen here at the 8th Avenue terminus of the Hayes Street Line in 1935.   **BOTH: Charles Smallwood**

A RAILFAN EXCURSION in 1942 was the occasion for these two Peninsula views. (ABOVE) Car 1731 poses in the town of Burlingame on the San Mateo interurban line. (The ''Pacific City'' on the dash sign was a short-lived amusement park built in the 1920s on this line; it first generated heavy traffic causing several 1700s to be fitted up for interurban service). (BELOW) The same excursion car also traveled to the San Mateo terminus, at the Southern Pacific depot in that city, of the 40 Line, with a 1200 Class car in regular service at rear.

BOTH: Charles Smallwood

(ABOVE) **AS A SOUTHERN PACIFIC** train streaks by, excursion car 1731 pauses near Burlingame (see also photos on preceding page). (BELOW) **A SCENE AT HOLY CROSS** terminal on Memorial Day, 1937. Streetcar travel to the city's cemeteries (in Colma) was fantastic on this day, even up to the last year of May service in 1948. **BOTH: Charles Smallwood**

NEW BODY, NEW LIFE: Car 1722 was one of three 1550s rebodied after bad wrecks. (ABOVE) The original 1722 was struck by Big Sub 12 at Richland and Mission on March 31, 1918. One person was killed and several were injured. It was decided to build a new body for this car, with the result (BELOW) at Geneva Barn, less than six months later, on August 14 of that year.

United Railroads

Cars 1550—1749

ANOTHER 1550 REBUILD was 1690, later renumbered 1716. This Elkton-built body has the lines of the handsome 200 Class. (ABOVE) This photo was taken at 28th and Valencia Barn in April 1918. **United Railroads** (BELOW) Now numbered 1716, this car still had MCB trucks and large headlights from its San Mateo days when viewed at the Ferry in 1935. **Charles Smallwood**

General Specifications, Cars 1715, 1716, 1722 (II)

Body type	California, arch roof, drop platforms, PAYE
Builder	United Railroads of San Francisco
Year built	1918
Weight	—
Seats	44
Length over buffers	46′6″
Length closed section	15′0″
Length open section	14′0″
Width over steps	8′10½″
Width over drips	9′0″
Truck centers	21′6″
Controller	K-28-B
Motors	4 GE 57, 50 hp.
Gear ratio	22:63
Compressor	A-4
Trucks	McGuire 10-A
Motors hung	Inside
Truck wheelbase	6′0″
Wheels	33″ Steel

THE WRECK OF 1745 resulted in the third rebuilding of a 1550. (ABOVE) Second 1745 appeared at 28th and Valencia Barn in November 1915 with this new arch-roof California style body. **United Railroads** (BELOW) Rebuilt again, for San Mateo service, the car has become Second 1715. View is at Geneva Yard in 1924. **Emanuel Mohr**

Cars 1550—1749

(ABOVE) **THE THREE 1550** Class rebuilds survived the rest of the class. All but nine were gone by 1941, but 1715 lasted until 1948, while 1716 and 1722 (the latter car shown at Ocean Beach terminal of the 12 Line in 1936) went to the torch in 1949.
Lorin Silliman

SAFETY MISSION: Back in 1928 car 1581 brought the boys from 28th and Valencia Barn over to Sutro Division to pick up the Safety Award.
Charles Smallwood

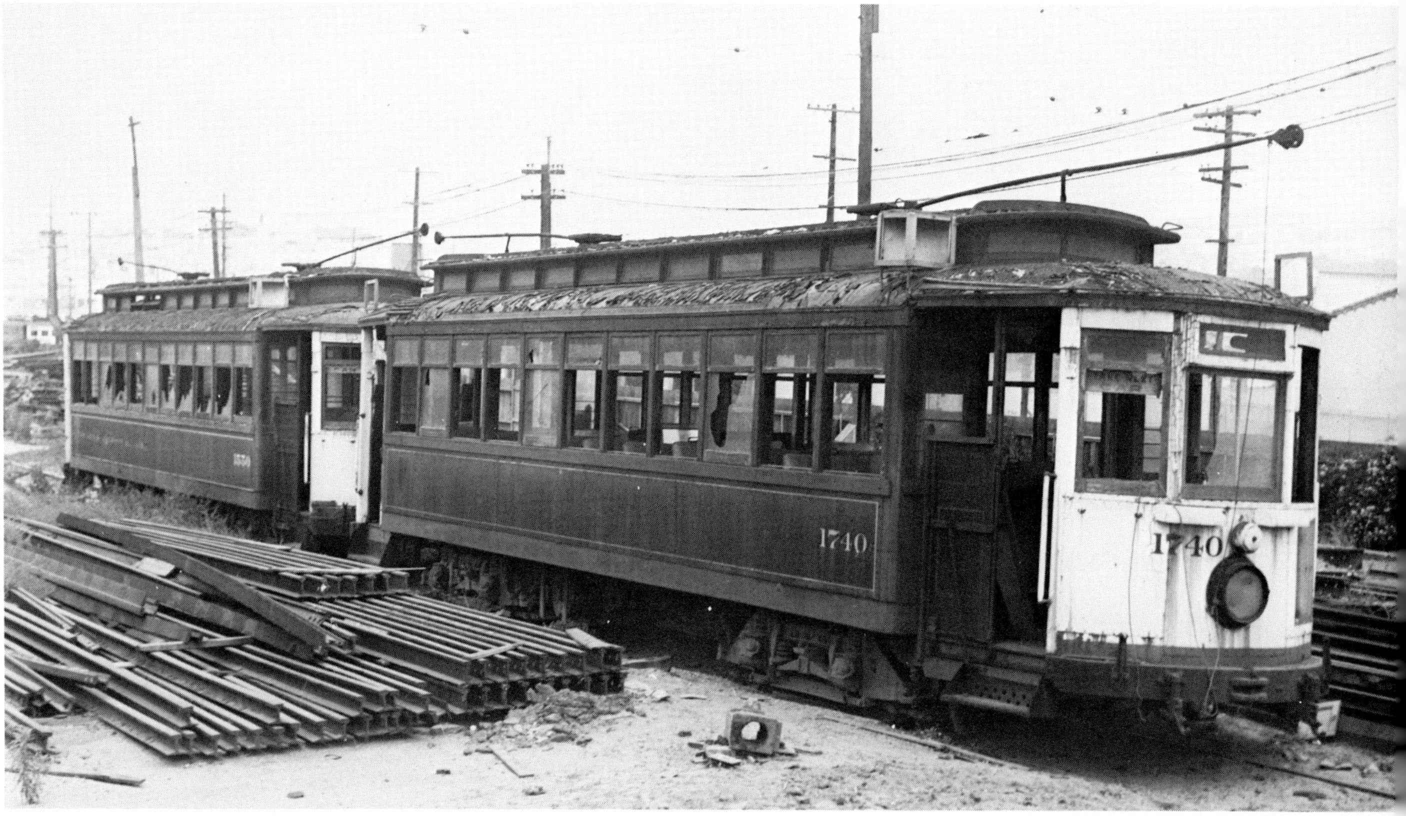

Cars 1550—1749

END OF THE LINE: While we have not dwelled on views of burning and scrapping each class, these two illustrations of the passenger fleet show that it was done. (ABOVE) Cars 1740 and 1550 await ''cremation'' at Elkton Yard in August 1941. (BELOW) The immolation of 1713 at Elkton Yard on May 28, 1931.

TOP: Charles Smallwood
BOTTOM: Market Street Railway

Commercially Built Cars

This table summarizes building data on United Railroads and Market Street Railway cars purchased commercially. It excludes the early cars of predecessor companies built locally by such firms as Hammond and Holman.

Table prepared by P. Allen Copeland

Car Numbers	Builder	Lot Number	Order Date	Remarks
1-12	St. Louis	580	July 1905	Built as P&W 1-12 (cancelled order)
101-180	Jewett	?	1911	
201-265	American	968	1-5-13	
402-406	St. Louis	1451	5-24-27	Ex-EStL&S 350-354
407-410	St. Louis	1325	11-22-23	Ex-EStL&S 600-663
681-697	St. Louis	186	3-20-01	Ex-SF&SM 51-60,62-66,68-70
746	St. Louis	—	1896	HERMOSA
725-730	Brill	18930	4-10-13	Ex-Williamsport Ry. 50-55; 9-14
731-734	Brill	20193	1-24-17	Ex-Williamsport Ry. 56-59; 15-18
735-736	Brill	14265	3-9-05	Ex-Williamsport Ry. 42-43; 2-3
740-749	American	1090	8-3-17	Ex-EStL&S 315-324,325-329,310-314; orig. from 600-644 series.
750-754	St. Louis	—	1918	
755-759	St. Louis	—	1918	ExEStL&S 300-304
1225-1244	Laclede	567	1903	
1300-1349	St. Louis	390	1903	
1350	Pressed Steel	—	1905	Later 1394
1351-1374	St. Louis	478	7-21-04	
1375-1424	St. Louis	556	5-24-05	
(1425-1524)?	St. Louis	585	5-8-05	Order cancelled
1500-1549	American	641	1906	Div. from Chicago City Rys. 5201-5250
1550-1649	St. Louis	682	1906	
1650-1749	St. Louis	697	1906	

Boneyard Brigade

The former Market Street Railway cars were retired as quickly as MSR lines were converted to bus operation. Car scrappings were:

1945: 103, 282, 290, 735, 736, 745, 808, 815, 847, 854, 895, 900, 902.

1946: 179, 276, 280, 301, 740-744, 746-749, 779-799, 835, 836, 839, 841-844, 846, 848, 865, 872, 875, 886, 888, 889, 892-894, 896, 897, 901, 905, 909, 910, 917, 919, 920.

1947: 140, 226, 252, 809, 810, 822, 852, 862, 874, 1244.

1948: 107, 114, 120, 128, 129, 141, 143, 149, 156, 159, 218, 239, 243, 250, 266, 267, 273, 275, 278, 287-289, 292, 293, 295, 297, 299, 300, 302-305, 410, 426, 431, 480, 691, 694, 696, 698, 778, 800-807, 811-814, 816-821, 823-834, 838, 840, 845, 850, 851, 853, 855-861, 863, 864, 866-871, 873, 876-885, 887, 890, 898, 899, 903, 904, 906-908, 911-913, 915, 918, 921, 922, 932, 942-949, 951, 956, 957, 963, 982, 1225, 1553, 1572, 1583, 1595, 1599, 1715, 1731, SAN FRANCISCO.

1949: 106, 108, 109, 113, 115-119, 121, 122, 125, 127, 134, 136, 138, 142, 145-148, 153, 155, 163, 169, 170, 174-178, 214-217, 219-221, 223-225, 227-234, 236, 237, 240-242, 245, 246, 248, 249, 253, 255, 256, 258, 261, 264, 268-270, 272, 279, 285, 401, 402, 404, 405, 411, 412, 424, 430, 432, 433, 435, 437, 439, 444, 450-452, 454, 457, 458, 460-462, 464-468, 471-473, 601-605, 608, 611, 612, 613, 622, 651, 654, 657, 663, 671, 674, 677, 681, 683, 684, 686, 849, 914, 923-929, 933-938, 940, 941, 950, 952-955, 958-962, 964-973, 977-981, 983-994, 1227-1238, 1241-1243, 1716, 1722.

1950: 606, 607, 609, 610, 635, 638, 644, 647, 659, 660, 662, 665, 891, 916, 930, 931, 939, 975, 976.

Saved: Car 974 was sold for preservation to Bay Area Electric Railroad Association in 1950.

Note: 400s were ex-100s; 600s were ex-200s. Only the first digit was changed.

Miscellaneous Cars

This section covers two types of special-use cars: private car (later Ambassador of Goodwill car) SAN FRANCISCO, and the Funeral Cars.

"San Francisco"

AS AN INSTRUMENT to create goodwill for Market Street Railway, the beautiful car "San Francisco" had no peer. The courtesy of this car was extended to all schools—public, parochial and private—for transportation of students to and from any points on the company's lines (including the San Mateo interurban) free of charge. **Market Street Railway**

"San Francisco"

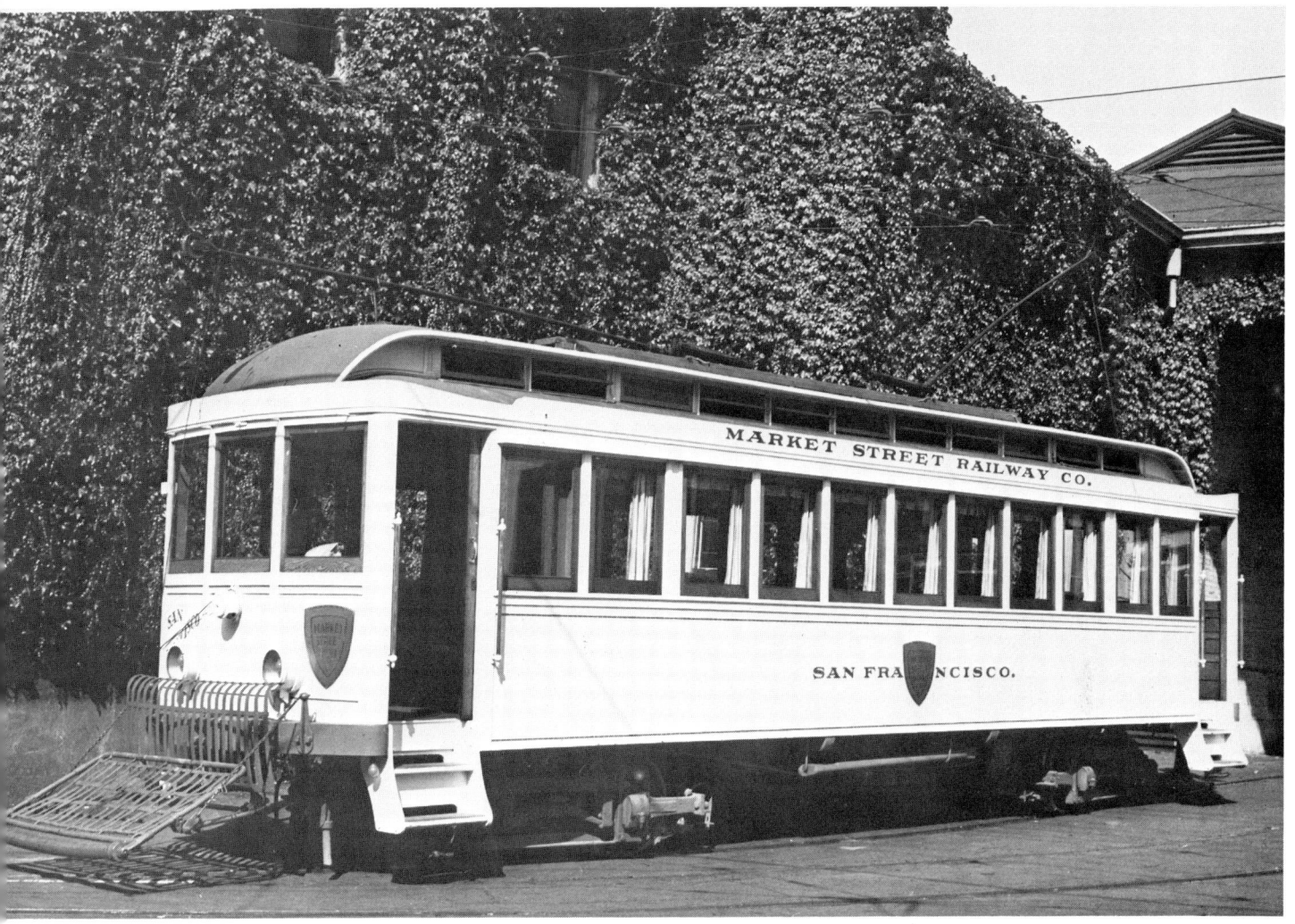

THE "SAN FRANCISCO" lays over at 24th Street Car House on a sunny morning in 1936. It is probably awaiting a passenger load of recuperating patients from nearby San Francisco General Hospital for a tour around the city.
Charles Smallwood

General Specifications, Private Car SAN FRANCISCO

Body type	Closed, railroad roof, flush platforms
Builder	St. Louis Car Company
Year built	1901
Weight	38,300 lbs.
Rebuilt	United Railroads of San Francisco, 1904
Seats	26
Length over buffers	37'0"
Length closed section	29'6"
Length of platform	4'0"
Width over steps	9'8"
Width over drips	8'10"
Truck centers	22'0"
Controller	K-12
Motors	4 GE 1000, 35 hp.
Gear ratio	22:66
Compressor	AA-1
Trucks	Brill 27-G
Motors hung	Outside
Truck wheelbase	4'0"
Wheels	30" Cast Iron

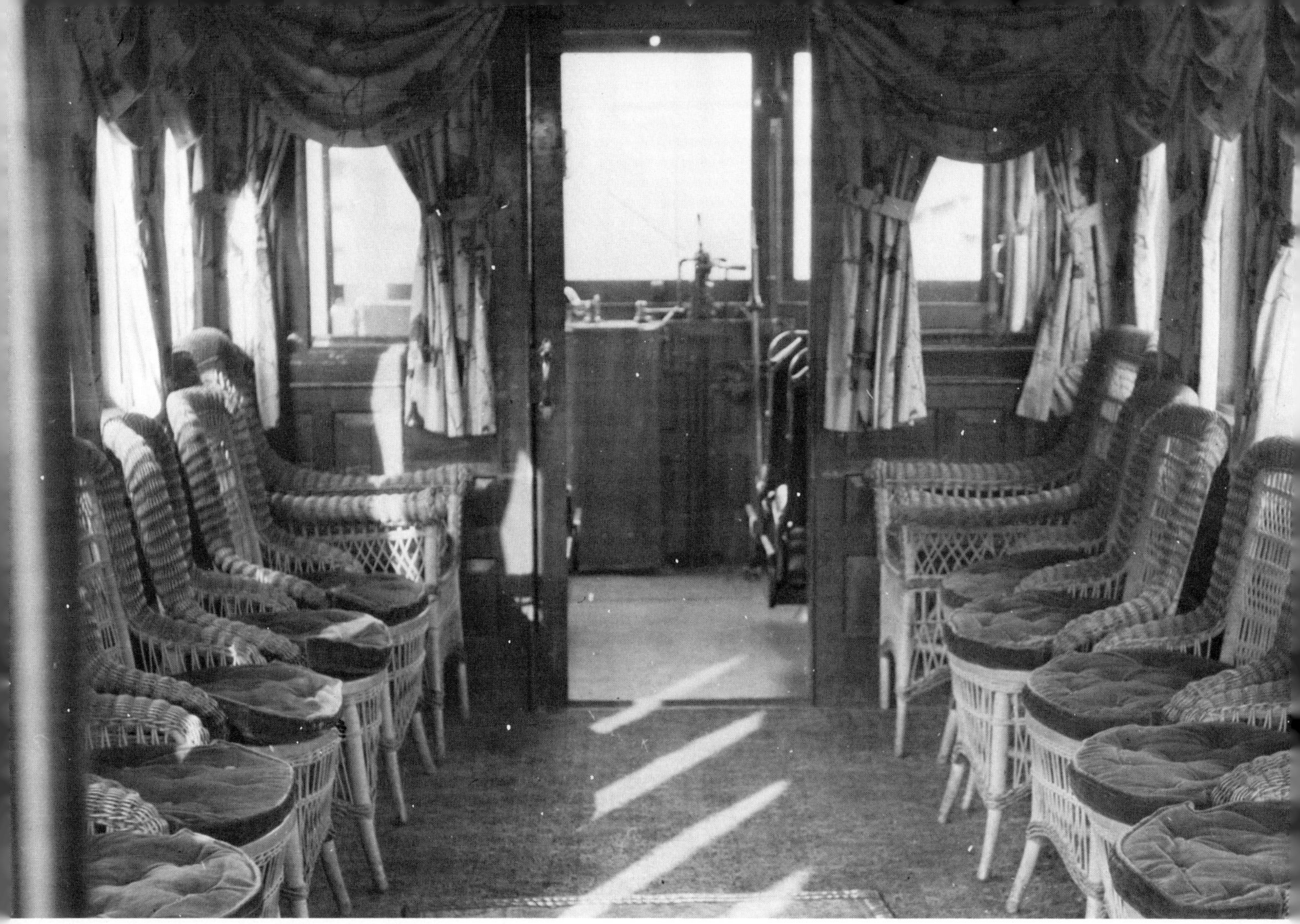

WICKER FURNITURE, window drapes and carpeted floors inside the "San Francisco" added a touch of class to company-sponsored outings. **Market Street Railway**

IN ITS ROLE as a school car, "San Francisco" carried classes to Elkton Shops on inspection tours and served shut-in children with no other means of transportation. It is shown in front of Polytechnic High School in October 1927. **Charles Smallwood**

(ABOVE) **CIVIC LEADERS** and company officials rode San Francisco on the first trip over the new electric line on Market Street after the earthquake and fire of April 18, 1906. The party included Mayor Eugene Schmitz and wife, URR President Patrick Calhoun, supervisors and other officials. This photo was taken at the Ferry on May 3, 1906. **United Railroads**

(BELOW) **THE HOLIDAY SEASON** of 1936 found the Market Street Railway wishing the city the season's best by way of a gaily decorated San Francisco. Christmas music was played. It is pictured on Second Street, at Market, on the day before Christmas. **Market Street Railway**

Mt. Olivet's Ca

(ABOVE) **THE MOURNER'S CA**
originally a 670-Class car on Unite
Railroads, entered Mt. Olivet servic
in 1907 after old Number 1—an o
horsecar mounted on a Bemis truck
burned up. These pictures were ta
en in 1925.

**MT. OLIVET CEMETERY ASSOCI
TION'S** private car line, though sho
traversed a picturesque route. Here
the lone car (LEFT) descending t
grade en route to the cemetery gat
where connection was made with t
interurban line to either San Franci
co or San Mateo.

BOTH: Mt. Oli
Cemetery Ass

THE FUNERAL CARS were elegant and immaculate. The three cars assigned to this funeral service were painted Brewster green with tile red roofs, gold letters and numbers, and golden oak window sash. (BELOW) Funeral car 3 is seen at Cypress Lawn Cemetery in July 1911.
United Railroads

KEPT FOR A SPARE in case the Mt. Olivet Cemetery car broke down, car 45 is seen at Geneva Yard in the early 1900s.

United Railroads

Funeral Cars

(NOTE: This special service is fully described in a "Special Revenue Cars" section of the "Coming of the White Front Cars" chapter.)

General Specifications, Funeral Cars 1, 2, 3

Body type	Three compartment
Builder	United Railroads
Dates built	1903, 1904
Weight	45,260 lbs.
Seats	32
Length over buffers	45'0"
Length main section	35'0"
Length of platform	5'0"
Width over steps	9'6"
Width over drips	9'0"
Truck centers	23'6"
Motors	4 GE 58, 35 hp.
Gear ratio	17:67
Trucks	Peckham 14-B3-S
Truck wheelbase	4'1"
Controller	K-12
Compressor	AA-1
Wheels	30" Cast Iron
Scrapped	#1, February 11, 1926
	#2, February 17, 1926
	#3, March 12, 1926

Car 45

Car 45 was an oddity in MSR's car fleet inasmuch as it remained throughout its service life in its original condition: California car with outward facing longitudinal benches in its open sections. It began life in a group of cars built in 1900 for *The San Francisco & San Mateo Electric Railway*; the 10 cars were numbered 41-50. When the San Mateo line was taken over, these cars became URR's 671-680.

In 1904 three were again renumbered, 1-3, and lettered for the *South San Francisco Railway & Power Company*. Between 1905 and 1907, another car of this class was sold to the *Reno Traction Company*, yet another was sold to the *Mt. Olivet Cemetery Association* (it became Mt. Olivet's #2). In 190_ two of the series were rebuilt into closed pouch U.S. Mail cars "D" and "E" and were used to shuttle mail matter from the main post office at 7th and Mission streets to the Ferry Annex Post Office. Cars "D" and "E" had a short-lived career however, as both were lost by fire on lower Mission Street during the 1906 disaster. A fifth car was rebuilt into line car 030 during the period.

Around 1908 the five remaining in passenger service on United Railroads were again renumbered, becoming 44-4_ Cars 44 and 45 were lettered for URR, while 46-48 bore the legend of the *South San Francisco Railway & Power Company*.

Cars 44, 46, 47 and 48 were rebuilt into Pay As You Enter cars in 1919—but car 45 remained in its original condition.

Car 45 was the last double-truck California car in its original condition to run in San Francisco. It was based at Geneva Car House and occasionally relieved Mt. Olivet #2 when that car was due to be brought in for maintenance. Car 45 was scrapped on January 19, 1926.

See cars 727-730 for the later history of the remainder of this class.

ALL THOSE INITIALS on tiny car 3 stand for "South San Francisco Railroad & Power Company." It is seen at Holy Cross Cemetery in 1905. At this time the SSF cars went along the county road to Holy Cross Cemetery from Leipsic Junction. **Charles Smallwood**

General Specifications, Car 45

Body type	California, railroad roof, flush platforms
Builder	Hammond Car Company
Date built	1900
Weight	32,720 lbs.
Seats	30
Length over buffers	29'6"
Length closed section	11'3"
Length open section	9'1½"
Width over steps	9'8"
Width over drips	8'10"
Truck centers	15'6"
Controller	K-12
Motors	4 GE 1000, 35 hp.
Gear ratio	17:67
Compressor	MW 7
Trucks	Brill 27-G
Motors hung	Outside
Truck wheelbase	4'0"
Wheels	30" Cast Iron

Funeral Cars

Purely Functional

BITUMEN CAR 0116 was perhaps the ultimate example of the homely-but-highly-useful service (or work) car fleet of the Market Street Railway. Some were not quite so plain, and basic, as this little car; but 0116's function of transporting boxes of hot bitumen paving to track jobs made it as valuable as one of the California Comfort Cars. Seen in 1907, it lasted well into the 1930s, when finally supplanted by motor trucks. **United Railroads**

Service Cars

THE WORK CARS of Market Street Railway constituted a heterogeneous fleet as was customary for a large traction company. Many of the cars used in this service were rebuilt from obsolete passenger cars; many others were purchased new for the specialized jobs they were required to perform.

Despite a very large number of units, Market Street Railway established and adhered to an orderly numbering scheme for its fleet of service cars; the numbering series indicated the department or service to which the unit was assigned. All work cars' numbers were prefixed by "0" so as to differentiate them from passenger cars' numbering series.

Series numbers were assigned as follows:

    01: Miscellaneous equipment
 0100: Engineering Department
 0200: Stores Department
 0300: Overhead Lines Department
 0400: Street sweeping service
 0500: Equipment Department Wreckers
 0600: Transportation Dept. Sand Cars
 0700: Not Assigned
 0800: Not Assigned
 0900: Construction Department
  1-3: Rock crushers

Each of these classes is examined separately in this chapter.

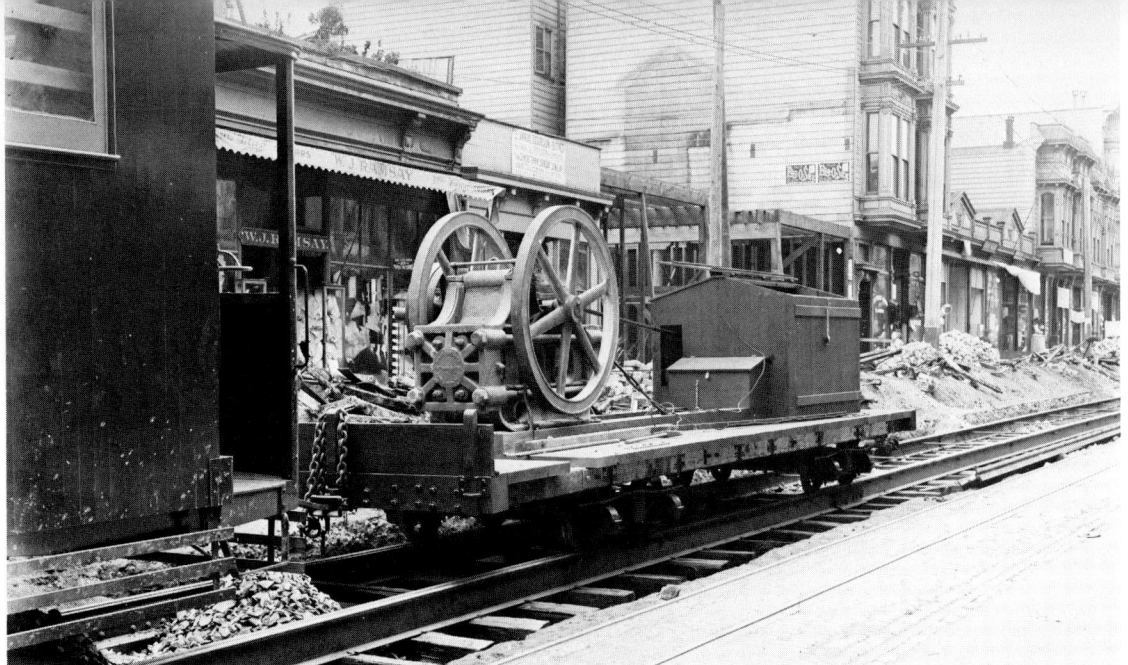

ONE OF THREE rock crushers (numbered 1, 2 and 3) works on Hayes Street pulling cable yokes in July 1906. Car at left appears to be Horse Car 0901. These flat cars went to scrap November 15, 1937.
United Railroads

01 Class

Cars 01-010 were used for odd jobs and did not fit in with any of the main categories. The only way to describe the 10 cars in this class is to consider each individually.

- **01:** Skeleton car, used to instruct trainmen at 29th and Mission Car House.

- **02:** Fillmore St. hill balance dummy.

- **03:** Single truck sand trailer.

- **04:** Flat car for transporting narrow and wide gauge cable cars to and from Elkton Shops.

- **05:** Tool car at Sunset District sand lot; formerly it was the Tanforan Race Track horse car, #0910.

- **06:** Electric shovel at 3rd St. Division.

- **07:** Single truck flat car fitted with tank filled with black paint in which fenders were dipped.

- **08:** Single truck electric car from 600 class fitted up with the necessary equipment for spray painting of car houses and other buildings.

- **09:** Single truck electric car of 600 class fitted up for cleaning car houses, washing windows, etc.

- **010:** Four-wheel tractor fitted with flanged wheels for 3'6" gauge and Ford Model A gas engine; used as cable car shunter at Washington and Mason Car House.

All but 04 and 010 were gone by the time the Municipal Railway succeeded to ownership in 1944. Flat car 04 was discarded circa 1950 when electric railway connection to Washington and Mason cable car barn was discontinued. The sole remaining unit of this class is the tractor 010, still in service at the cable car barn.

SAND TRAILER 03 served 24th Street Division. Note the early Bemis trucks from a San Francisco & San Mateo Railway car of 1891.
Charles Smallwood

ELECTRIC SHOVEL 06 is at work on the Cliff line in December 1907.
United Railroads

FENDER DIPPER 07 was periodically towed to the various car houses for the purpose of painting the protruding Eclipse fenders used on the cars. Fenders were dipped in the vat of black paint seen in the middle of the car. **Charles Smallwood**

(LEFT) **PAINT SPRAY CAR 08** was originally passenger car 1056, which was renumbered to 636 on July 22, 1911, withdrawn from passenger use December 18, 1929, and rebuilt for this use. It was scrapped June 11, 1937. (RIGHT) **WASH CAR 09'S** task was to clean the windows and tidy up MSR's many car houses and other buildings. **BOTH: Charles Smallwood**

Cable Car Shunter

FORD TRACTOR 010 has been a cable car shunter for many years at Washington and Mason Barn.
Charles Smallwood

STORES DEPARTMENT CAR 0102 poses for an official company portrait. Charles Smallwood

SUTRO DIVISION WRECKER 0103 carried gear to patch up disabled passenger cars. It was one of many single-truck cars converted to work service. **Charles Smallwood**

Plow Car 0104 began life as an ordinary double-cab flatbed work motor. In 1921 it was rebuilt at Elkton to make it suitable for plowing up the right-of-way. One of the cabs was removed and in its place were mounted a winch with its accessories and a derrick. Car 0104 proved to be a complete success in plowing and rooting out ties and concrete. It could make a furrow 11 feet outside the rails.

The plow was drawn by a cable running from a three-ton, one-drum winch powered by an old streetcar motor—a GE 1000 with an ordinary K type controller. The cable which pulled the plow passed between guide sheaves at the center of the car's rear end; additional sheaves were also provided on either corner, so that the pulling effort could be readily offset further when so desired. The car was used on a temporary portable T-rail track alongside the track trench being plowed. The plow was lifted off the ground by a derrick powered by air.

(RIGHT) PLOW CAR 0104 had a very ingenious power-assisted track removing device—a plow. It is seen in 1921.
Charles Smallwood

(BELOW) **A TRADE JOURNAL** illustration shows 0104 in action.

(TOP) **SUPPLY CAR 0106** is seen at McAllister Barn in December 1938. **Ted Wurm**

RAIL GRINDER 0107 posed for this photo in September 1939. **Ted Wurm**

RAIL GRINDER 0110 shows off its big Peckham truck. **Charles Smallwood**

RAIL GRINDER 0109 is seen at the Third Street Viaduct in 1942.   **Charles Smallwood**

THE SAME CAR was still hard at work on the Municipal Railway in 1970. Here it is next to the venerable Geneva headquarters building. Car 0109 is now at the California Railway Museum at Rio Vista Junction, California. **Charles Smallwood**

BITUMEN CAR 0122 was once a familiar sight hurrying around the MSR system with bins of hot asphalt from the Market and Valencia Paving Plant.

Charles Smallwood

0100 Class

This class was used in track and right-of-way maintenance and included both single and double truck cars. In this group were the track grinders, the crane and derrick cars, the delivery car of the Stores Department and some motor flat cars. The crane car and the derrick car, the delivery car and a track grinder were still on the property when taken over by Municipal Railway in 1944. Surviving into the 1970s were the crane car, #0130, and grinder #0109.

A unique and highly interesting endless bucket type of sand elevator, #0119, used at the company's sand lot on 21st Avenue was also included in this class.

0200 Class

This class contained but one car: a double-truck electrically powered tank car originally used to transport fuel oil to Market Street Railway power houses. Municipal Railway succeeded to ownership of this car on September 29, 1944, and kept it on the property until 1951. Its last job was to spray weed killer along the private right-of-way of the M Line.

THERE WAS A TIME when traction companies were required to sprinkle dirt streets as a condition of their franchise. A sprinkler car like MSR's 0201 was inevitably one of the most important work cars on the company roster.

Market Street Railway

Tanking Up

FILLING UP THE TANK of Sprinkler Car 0201, shown in this early view, seemed to be very labor intensive. Could be that some of the folks found out a camera would record this particular day's operation.
                                Market Street Railway

DISCHARGE OF WATER, when 0201 was used for wetting down unpaved streets, was through these perforated pipes.   **Market Street Railway**

(BELOW) **BUILT AT THE TURN** of the century, Tank Car 0201 lasted well into the era of Municipal Railway. It was, in succession, a street sprinkler, a bulk oil carrier, and finally a weed killer for rights-of-way. It was last used in 1949 to spray weeds along Muni's M line, and was scrapped at Elkton Yard soon after.
                                Charles Smallwood

THRONGS GATHERED on October 27, 1927, to watch MSR Crane 0130 lift pie wagon horse "Jerry" from the basement of the famed Fly Trap Restaurant, at Sutter and Montgomery streets. The animal had fallen through the steel sidewalk trap doors. Market Street Railway and the San Francisco Society for the Preservation of Cruelty to Animals kept a special sling in readiness for many years to be used in lifting fallen horses from ditches and holes. MSR made no charge for this service.
Market Street Railway

(LEFT) **A MORE COMMON** burden for Crane Car 0130 was rails, in this case those of the abandoned 34—Sixth and Sansome Line, on Post Street. This car was built on the underframe and trucks of passenger car 1310, which was lost at 19th and Guerrero streets during the 1906 earthquake and fire. Car 0130 passed to Municipal Railway in 1944 and ran until 1975, when it was taken to the California Railway Museum, at Rio Vista Junction.
Charles Smallwood

(ABOVE) **LINE CAR 0304** crosses the Southern Pacific branch line on Ocean Avenue, at the Elkton Shops, in 1935. This car, much rebuilt, was still in use on the Municipal Railway in 1978. (BELOW) **LINE CAR 0306** was sometimes rented to Muni to string trolley wire on new lines. The last such job was on Muni's N Line in 1928.

Charles Smallwood

0300 Class

Assigned to the Overhead Line Department, cars in this class included MSR's two line cars, #0304 and #0306. A single-truck double-cab flat car, #0305, was also assigned to the Line Department and was used for transporting poles over the system; when motor trucks took over this responsibility in the 1920s, 0305 was fitted out as a track grinder but retained its original number. Line car 0306 was frequently rented to Municipal Railway for the purpose of stringing trolley wire on newly constructed lines. The coming of auto trucks to overhead work relegated 0306 to secondary status; while under MSR ownership it probably did as much work for the city-owned system as it performed for its parent company.

Car 0304 was still in use in the 1970s as Municipal's line car. It had been extensively altered for use in Twin Peaks and Sunset tunnels.

LITTLE USED by Market Street Railway, single truck Line Car 0301 was scrapped on April 13, 1924.
United Railroads

(BELOW) **THIS FAGEOL** wrecker truck was one of the motor vehicles which augmented MSR's rail fleet of work cars. Truck and crew are seen, circa 1929; the vehicle was painted red and equipped with a siren and red lights. **Market Street Railway**

Division Wreckers

THE 24th STREET Division Wrecker, 0501.
Charles Smallwood

THIRD STREET Division Wrecker, 0503.
Charles Smallwood

28th AND VALENCIA Division Wrecker 0505. This is a very rare photo of this car on the job, as it saw little use after 1920. It is seen here on Cortland Avenue in 1933.
Charles Smallwood

FORMER SUTRO DIVISION Wrecker 0506 is shown at Elkton Shops prior to scrapping in March 1939. Wrecker 0103 was its replacement at Sutro.
Charles Smallwood

0400 Class

The two cars in this class, 0401 and 0402, were unusual among MSR's fleet of work cars in that they were once carried on the books as revenue equipment—a highly interesting tale (for which see Special Revenue Cars).

0500 Class

MSR's wreckers were made up entirely of old single- and double-truck California type passenger cars—an admirable type for this service due to the ease of obtaining a large open area at both ends simply by removing seats in the former open sections. Here were carried jack blocks, broken axle dollies and other paraphernalia used in wrecker service.

Each division was provided with one of these cars for whenever an emergency arose.

Prior to 1927 the 24th and Utah, Kentucky (3rd St.) a Geneva Divisions were equipped with large double-truck c for this purpose; after that year only Geneva retained a la wrecker, the other two divisions being provided with a sing trucker rebuilt from 600 class passenger cars.

GENEVA DIVISION Wrecker 0507 performed most of Market Street Railway's heavy wrecker work. (ABOVE) It poses at Geneva Yard. **Charles Smallwood** (BELOW) It pushes a disabled car into Elkton Shops, at San Jose Avenue and Geneva, circa 1942. **Randolph Brandt**

ONCE A PASSENGER CAR in the 600 series, this tiny car became the McAllister Wrecker.   **Charles Smallwood**

Geneva Division was always the main wrecker facility, and was equipped with the heaviest wrecking car on the system. Principal reason for this was that this division had the San Mateo interurban line under its wing; it was also just across the street from the Elkton Shops. This wrecker, 0507, always appeared at all major accidents; if damage to a car was sufficiently serious, this wrecker would tow the unfortunate directly to Elkton Shops. To this day a rail wrecker is assigned to Geneva Division by Municipal Railway; old 0507 is now gone, and was replaced by rebuilt Muni car #130 of its "B" type. Car 0507 was retired on June 15, 1956.

MSR maintained its wrecking car fleet to the very end of its operations, 1944, except that Fillmore Division wrecker was replaced by a motor truck in April 1924, and another wrecker truck was purchased about the same time and was stationed at the ferry.

Doubtless motor wrecker trucks could have supplanted the single-truck rail wrecker cars at all divisions except Geneva in the cause of efficiency, but MSR, always keeping a prudent eye on the dollar, couldn't see investing money in new equipment for such infrequent use when what it already had on hand was doing the job and was already paid for.

0600 Class

MSR's sand cars were all rebuilds of former single-truck California type passenger cars. Here again the seats were removed from the end sections and sand bins installed in the center closed section.

Sand cars were operated by the Transportation Department. Regular motormen and conductors were assigned to take the sand cars over certain hilly routes, usually before the first car of the day. The purpose was to sprinkle sand on the rails at steep downgrades to insure good braking for the early morning runs.

No sand car survives as such today, although car #0601 formerly the Geneva Division sand car, has been beautifully restored by Municipal Railway to its original passenger car appearance; it has been painted in its original 1895 colors as car #578 of the Ellis and O'Farrell streets line and is now among the collection of historic railway equipment at the California Railway Museum, Rio Vista Junction.

(RIGHT & BELOW) **GENEVA DIVISION** Sand Car 0601 poses on its home ground. In 1956 this car was restored to its 1895 original appearance by Municipal Railway and was used in a Market Street parade commemorating the 50th anniversary of the disastrous earthquake and fire. In its restored appearance and number (Muni 578) this car is seen at East Bay Terminal in April 1956. In 1978 it was carrying visitors at the California Railway Museum at Rio Vista Junction. **Charles Smallwood**

(RIGHT) **THIRD STREET DIVISION** Sand Car 0602, another ex-single-truck passenger car, suns itself in May 1941. **Charles Smallwood**

OAK AND BRODERICK Sand Car 0603, at Funston Yard.
Charles Smallwood

SUTRO Division Sand Car 0606 saw little service after the 1920s and never received the White Front treatment. **Charles Smallwood**

24th STREET Division Sand Car 0607. **Charles Smallwood**

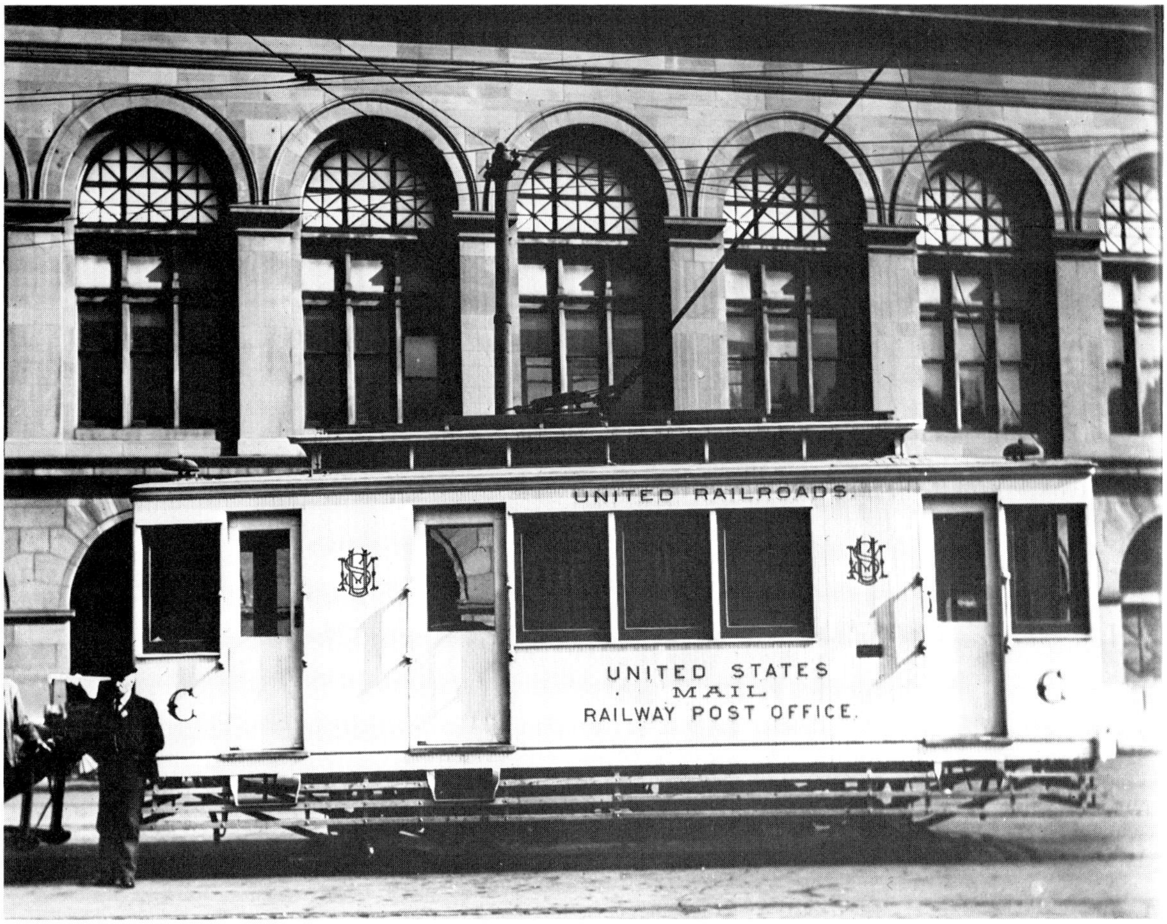

THE MISSION STREET Mail Car "C" is seen above at the Ferry Building in 1904. The car later became Money Car 0902 (BELOW) and received a pair of Brill 27-G trucks, in which configuration it is seen, in 1927, at Elkton Yards. Note the mail slot was still very much in evidence.

United Railroads

MONEY CAR 0902, formerly U.S. Railway Post Office Mail Car "C" (see "Special Revenue Cars" in Chapter Two) shows off its White Front in 1929. It was at one time used to pay employees at the carbarns and was said to be the most popular car on the system (at least on paydays!). When payrolls went from cash to check, 0902 was relegated to visiting each car house every morning to pick up the previous day's receipts; these were carried to the MSR main office at 68 Sutter Street.

Market Street Railway

COMPRESSOR CAR 0918 performed the important task of providing compressed air for pneumatic tools. It is seen at work on Mission Street during a 1933 track relaying job.

Charles Smallwood

(ABOVE) **COMPRESSOR CAR 0918** is again seen at work, in 1935, on a Mission Street track construction project.

(RIGHT) Neglected and virtually forgotten, former Horse Car 05 (for its better days, see the "Special Revenue Cars" section of Chapter 2) lies rotting at the 19th and Pacheco sand lot in 1933.

BOTH: Charles Smallwood

0700—0800 Classes

These numbering designations were not used in later years. The only car to be numbered in the 0700 Series was #0701, called the "Air Brake Instruction Car." It was a single-truck passenger car used to instruct student motormen in the proper use of air brakes. In the early years it was brought to a division which had only hand brake equipment to acquaint the operating personnel on the handling of air brakes on future series of cars so equipped which were tabbed for assignment to that division. It early outlived its usefulness and was scrapped on February 5, 1913.

The 0800 Series consisted of a few single-truck work cars which disappeared in early years. One exception was car 0801, the Fillmore Hill balance dummy which was in later years renumbered #02.

0900 Class

In this category were found the heavy construction work horses of the system. One notable exception to this, however, was car #0902, the "Money Car," formerly U.S. Railway Post Office car "C". As 0902 the car visited each division daily to pick up the previous day's receipts and transport them to the company's main office. The bulk of the 0900 class was, however, either center or end cab dump cars.

The finest work car equipment MSR ever owned was represented in this class by cars 0929-0932; these four all-steel automatic side dump cars were built for MSR in 1923 by Differential Steel Car Company.

A few of the older 0900 Series cars, as well as the four steel automatic dump cars, were turned over to Municipal Railway in 1944; all were gone by the early 1950s.

MARKET STREET RAILWAY'S work motors performed many varied tasks, each necessary to keep the busy street railway system functioning. (ABOVE) Center Cab motor 0920 provides an excellent view of the very heavy MCB type trucks used by this class. (BELOW) Trash Car 0921 unloads garbage from the car houses at the dump in the rear of Third Street Car House, 1938.

BOTH: Charles Smallwood

(ABOVE) **CENTER CAB WORK MOTOR 0922** was awaiting the scrappers' torch at Elkton Shops when this photo was taken in 1941. **Lorin Silliman** (BELOW) **SWITCHER 0925** in its native habitat, Elkton Shops, where for many years it switched freight cars from the Southern Pacific interchange track. The load of old wheels was to give added traction. **Charles Smallwood**

(ABOVE) **HEAVY DUTY** Flat Car 0928 was constructed primarily to move heavy electric generating machinery around the system.
Charles Smallwood

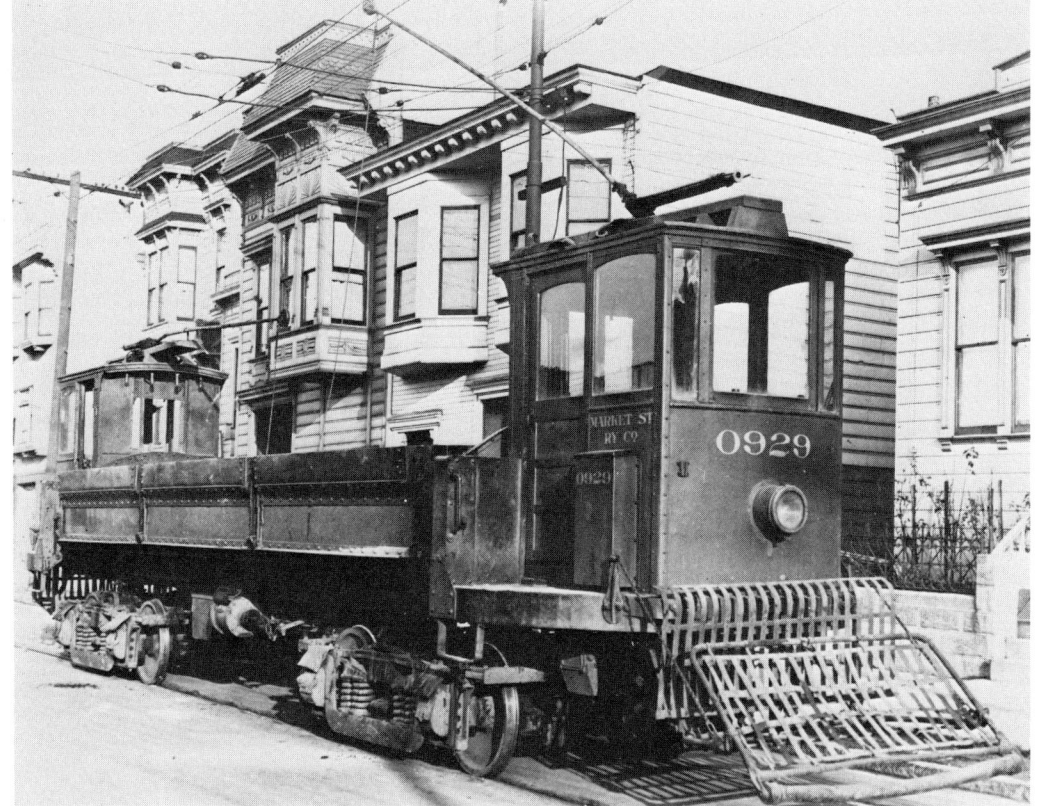

(LEFT) **DIFFERENTIAL** Dump Car 0929 posed for this photo when it was brand new, in 1923.
Market Street Railway

(RIGHT) A CLOSEUP of the massive St. Louis 23-C truck used under MSR's heaviest work cars. The quadruple coil springs were rare in this truck. **Market Street Railway**

TWO VIEWS of busy Differential Dump 0130: (ABOVE) On the scene during track relaying on Sutter Street, between Powell and Stockton, in 1930, it switches onto temporary trackwork. **Market Street Railway** (BELOW) At rest, with sister dump 0932, at the Market and Valencia Paving Plant in October 1941. **Charles Smallwood**

(ABOVE) **SAND SCOOP 0119** has just dredged up a load into Differential Dump Car 0932 at the 21st and Pacheco Sand Lot in 1937.
Charles Smallwood

(BELOW) **RUNNING EMPTY,** 0932 was busily engaged in an errand when photographed on Third Street in 1938.
Charles Smallwood

NON-REVENUE ROLLING STOCK — AUGUST 1921

TYPE OF CAR	SERIAL NUMBER	WEIGHT CAPACITY	LENGTH OVER BUMPERS	WIDTH OVER SILLS	TRUCK CENTERS	BRAKES	COMPR. BRAKES	CONTROLLER	TYPE OF MOTORS	TROLLEY BASE BOTTOM SWING	HOOD OR CAR OUTSIDE HUNG	TYPE OF TRUCK	WHEEL BASE	WHEEL DIA.	REMARKS
Geneva Wrecker	0507		37'-8"	8'-8"	21'-6"	Air	F-1	Two K-12	4-G.E. 80	B.S.	Inside	Brill 27-6.E.2	4'-4"	33" C.I.	Closed Body. No vestibule.
Geneva Sand Car	0601		26'-2"	8'-0"		Hand		Two K-10	2-G.E. 58	B.S.	Inside	Peckham Single	7'-0"	30" C.I.	Vestibule ends. Closed body.
Sutro Wrecker	0506		26'-6"	7'-4"		Hand									
Sutro Sand Car.	0606		27'-6"	7'-4"		Hand		Two K	2-G.E. 1000	B.S.	Inside	Peckham Single	7'-0"	30" C.I.	Vestibule ends. Closed body.
Oak & Broderick Wrecker	0103		26'-10"	7'-3"		Hand		Two K-10	2-G.E. 1000	B.S.	Inside	Peckham Single	7'-0"	30" GI.	Vestibule ends. Closed body.
Oak & Broderick Sand Car	0603		27'-6"	6'-8"		Hand		Two K	2-G.E. 1000	T.B.	Inside	Peckham Single	7'-0"	30" C.I.	Vestibule ends. Closed body.
Kentucky Wrecker	0503		26'-10"	7'-3"		Hand		Two K	2-G.E. 1000	B.S.	Inside	Peckham Single	7'-0"	30" C.I.	Vestibule ends. Closed body.
Kentucky Sand Car.	0602		27'-0"	7'-4"		Hand		Two K	2-G.E. 58	T.S.	Inside	Brill Simple	7'-0"	30" C.I.	Vestibule ends. Closed body.
28th St. Wrecker	0505		28'-0"	7'-4"		Hand		Two K	2-G.E. 58	T.S.	Inside	Peckham Simple	7'-0"	30" C.I.	Vestibule ends. Closed body.
29th St. Sand Car.	0604		25'-0"	7'-4"		Hand		Two K	4-G.E. 800	B.S.	Inside	Brill Simple	7'-0"	30" C.I.	Vestibule ends. Closed body.
29th St. Instruction Car.	01		40'-0"	8'-6"	20'-0"	Air	AH-1	One B-18		T.S.	Outside	Brill 27-6	4'-0"	30" C.I.	Bottom & Side framing only.
Turk & Fillmore Sand Car.	0608		26'-10"	7'-4"		Hand		Two K-10	2-G.E. 1000	T.S.	Inside	Peckham Single	7'-0"	30" C.I.	Vestibule ends. Closed body.
Turk & Fillmore Balance Car.	02		18'-0"	6'-8"		Hand						Brill Simple	7'-0"	30" C.I.	No Cabs.
24th St. Wrecker	0501		26'-10"	7'-3"		Hand		Two K-10	2-G.E. 1000	B.S.	Inside	Peckham Single	7'-0"	30" C.I.	Vestibule ends. Closed body.
24th St. Sand Car	0607		27'-0"	7'-4"		Hand		Two K	2-G.E. 58	T.S.	Inside	Peckham Single	7'-0"	30" C.I.	Vestibule ends. Closed body.
24th St. Sand Car	03		14'-3"	6'-3½"		Hand						Market St. R.R.	4'-0"	30" C.I.	Box. 14'-0" x 6'-6" x 4'-9".
McAllister Sand & Wrecker	0508		27'-6"	7'-4"		Hand		Two K-10	2-G.E. 1000	T.S.	Inside	Peckham Single	7'-0"	30" C.I.	Vestibule ends. Closed body.
Switching Car. Elkton Yards.	0925		38'-8"	8'-4"	23'-8"	Air	A-4	One K 28-J	4-G.E. 90	B.S.	Outside	Brill 27-6.E. 2	4'-4"	33" C.I.	Flat Car. One cab in centre.
Switching Car. Elkton Shops	0927		39'-2"	8'-2"	23'-0"	Air	AA-4	One K-28-A	4-G.E. 90	B.S.	Outside	Peckham Single	4'-0"	30" C.I.	Flat Car. One cab in centre.
Switching Car. Elkton Shops.	0108		26'-0"	7'-5"	23'-0"	Air	AH-1	Two K-12	2-G.E. 1000	B.S.	Outside	Peckham Single	7'-0"	30" C.I.	Flat Car. with Derrick no cab.
Delivery Car.	0106		30'-3"	7'-11"	19'-6"	Air		Two K-10	4-G.E. 1000	T.S.	Inside	Peckham 14.B.3-X	4'-9"	30" C.I.	Flat Car. One cab in centre.
Trailer Flat Car. Elkton Shops	04		33'-7"	8'-5"	23'-7½"	Hand						Market St. R.R.	3'-6"	22" C.I.	Car equipped with air brake connections.
Trailer Flat Car. Elkton Shops	0928											McGuire 10-A	6'-0"	30 C.I.	Flat Car.
Fender paint Car	07											Peckham Single	7'-6"		Flat Car & small derrick
Two Cabs. Flat.	0102		40'-0"	8'-0"	25'-0"	Air	AA-1	Two K-12	4-G.E. 59	B.S.	Outside	Peckham 14.B.3-X	4'-0"	30" C.I.	Two Cabs. Two boxes hinged.
One Cab. Plow Car.	0104		40'-0"	8'-0"	25'-0"	Air	A-4	Two K-10	2-G.E. 58	T.S.	Outside	Peckham 14.B.3-X	4'-0"	30" C.I.	One Cab. Plow Car.
Rail Grinding Car	0107		26'-10"	7'-3"		Hand		Two K-12	2-G.E. 90	B.S.	Inside	Peckham Single	7'-0"	33"Steel	Two Cabs.
Paint car	08		26'-10"	7'-3"		Hand		Two K-10	2-G.E. 800	T.S.	Inside	Peckham Single	7'-0"	30" C.I.	Equipped with air compressor & tanks for spraying apparatus.
Rail Grinding Car	0109		26'-10"	7'-3"		Air	AA1	Two K-10	4-G.E. 90	B.S.	Inside	Peckham Single	7'-0"	39"Steel	Closed body.
Rail Grinding Car.	0110		26'-2"	7'-4"		Air	AA1	Two K-10	4-G.E. 90	B.S.	Inside	Peckham Single	7'-0"	33" C.I.	Two Cabs.
Rail Grinding Car	0111		24'-6"	7'-4"	21'-3"	Air	A-4	One K-12	4-G.E. 58	T.S.	Outside	Peckham Single	7'-0"	33" C.I.	Box Car body.
Switching Car Elkton Shops	0115		27'-0"	6'-4"		Air	A-4	One K-28-A	4-G.E. 1000	B.S.	Outside	Peckham 14.B.3-X	4'-4"	30" C.I.	No Cab. Small Derrick
Bitumen Car.	0116					Hand				B.S.	Inside	Peckham Single	7'-0"	30" C.I.	No Cabs. Small Derrick.
Sand Elevator	0119		27'-0"	7'-6"	25'-0"	Air	A-4	Two K	2-G.E. 1000	T.S.	Inside	Brill Simple	4'-0"	30" C.I.	Sand Elevator Equipment.
Wash Car	09		26'-10"	7'-9"	25'-0"	Hand		Two K-10	2-G.E. 800	B.S.	Inside	Peckham Single	7'-0"	30" C.I.	Equipped with car washing material.
Tractor W.&M. Car House	010	4,000	6'-8"	4'-4"		Hand			Ford 4 Cyl.				3'-6"	22" C.I.	
Bitumen Car	0122		27'-0"	6'-4"	23'-0"	Hand		Two K-10	2-G.E. 90	B.S.	Inside	Peckham Single	7'-0"	31"Steel	No Cab. Small Derrick.
Oil Tank Car.	0201		40'-2"	8'-2"	21'-0"	Air	A-4	Two K-28-A	4-G.E. 90	B.S.	Outside	Brill 27-G	7'-0"	33" C.I.	Two Cabs. Tank capacity 4410 Gal.
Two Cabs	09/18-9912		40'-8"	8'-2"	27'-1"	Air	A-4	Two K-28-A	4-G.E. 90	B.S.	Outside	St.Louis 23-B-3.	4'-4"	33"Steel	Differential Bumpers.
Two Cabs.	0813-0917		42'-8"	8'-10"	25'-0"	Air	A-4	Two K-28-F	4-G.E. 59-3	B.S.	Inside	St.Louis 23-B-3	6'-0"	55"Steel	Two Cabs. Two boxes hinged.
Two Cabs.	09/18-0919		42'-8"	8'-10"	25'-0"	Air	A-4	Two K-28-J	4-G.E. 59	T.S.	Inside	Brill 27-G.E.2.	6'-0"	30" C.I.	Two Cabs. Two boxes hinged.
One Centre Cab.	0920-0921		42'-8"	8'-10"	25'-0"	Air	A-4	One K-28-J	4-G.E. 90	B.S.	Inside	St.Louis 23-B-3	6'-0"	31"Steel	One Cab. Two boxes hinged.
One Centre Cab.	0922		49'-8"	8'-8"	29'-4"	Air	A-4	One K-28-J	4-G.E. 90	B.S.	Inside	St.Louis 23-B-3.	6'-0"	31"Steel	Two Cabs. Two boxes hinged.
Two Cabs.	0929-0930		40'-8"	8'-8"	25'-0"	Air	A-4	Two K-28-A	4-G.E. 90	B.S.	Inside	Peckham 14-B.3-X	4'-4"	30" Steel	Differential Bumpers.
Crane Car	0130		29'-10"	7'-2"	15'-4"	Air	A-4	Two K-28-A	4-G.E. 1000	B.S.	Outside	Peckham 14-B.3-X	4'-4"	31"Steel	5-Ton Crane at 20' Radius.
Derrick Car.	05		47'-0"	8'-10"	26'-0"	Hand						Brill 27-G.	4'-0"	30" C.I.	Box Car.
Tamaron Horse Car.	1-2-3		35' 3½"	7'-9"	14'-6"	Hand						McGuire 59-A.	3'-7"	20" C.I.	Flat.
Rock Crashers.	06		14'-6"	9'-4"	16'-6"	Drum			1-Motor 75H.P.			Market St.R.R.	6'-0"	20" C.I.	4¼ Kentucky Dump.
Elect.Barker Gunnerty Elec.Shovel.															
Tower Car.	0305		36'-0"	8'-0"		Air		Two K-12	4-G.E. 58	T.S.	Outside	Brill 27-G.	4'-4"	33" C.I.	Two Cabs. Tower Air operated.
Pump Car.	0804		31'-0"	8'-8"		Air		Two K-28-A	4-G.E. 90	B.S.	Outside	Brill 27-G.E.2.	4'-4"	30" C.I.	Two Cabs. Tower Air. Hand operated.
Tool Car. 8	0905		27'-0"	7'-6"		Air		Two K-10	2-G.E. 800	T.S.	Inside	Brill Simple	7'-0"	30" C.I.	Two Cabs & Roof, no body.

MARKET STREET RAILWAY COMPANY
EQUIPMENT DEPARTMENT
Schedule of Non-Revenue Rolling Stock

DRAWING NO. M.M. 2005
SCALE None
DRAWN BY W.B. Farlow 8-17-21 Compiled by C.D. Miller
CHECKED BY
APPROVED BY _____ MASTER MECHANIC

M.M. 2005

THE TOURIST'S VIEW of Powell and Market was thus in the late 1930s. By the late 1970s, only the ownership had changed for the city's famed hill-climbing cable cars, which still revolved on this turntable. Building facades and street furniture have been updated, of course. **Randolph Brandt**

Cables

MUCH HAS BEEN and is being written about San Francisco's doughty little cable cars; this volume will confine itself generally to the cable system as it was operated during the days of Market Street Railway's ownership. However, a few words pertaining to that portion of the MSR cable system which remains today would not be amiss.

Today the bossy little cars still ply up and down Powell St., their stronghold since 1887—fussily scolding anyone or anything which might attempt to interfere with their clanging progress. Much maligned as archaic three decades ago, the jaunty little cars have weathered criticism as well as economical and progressive change and have clattered on their way to become the proud symbol of a great American city.

Much of the credit for the far-sighted retention of this amazingly popular tourist attraction must go to Mrs. Hans Klussmann, socialite and civic leader, who, almost single-handedly through tireless campaigning, awakened the populace to the desirability of perpetuating this priceless heritage.

Today the cable lines are protected by the city charter. They have been designated a national landmark. A sympathetic city administration has refurbished the old car barn at Washington and Mason streets. A cable car museum has been established within its massive walls. Most surprising of all, a plan has been put forward to actually extend the Powell-Mason Line three blocks from Bay St. to Jefferson St. and Fisherman's Wharf; when the line was constructed in 1887, Bay St. was the waterfront.

The cable railway system taken over by the Market Street Railway Company from United Railroads in 1921 consisted of 14.7 miles of track. Route mileage was approximately 8.25. The longest lines were the Washington and Jackson and the Sacramento and Clay streets routes, each about 2.25 miles long. In terms of importance, the heaviest traveled lines were the two on Powell Street, the Powell-Mason and Washington routes. Next in importance was the Sacramento-Clay (a portion of whose route was over the world's first cable line), followed by the Castro St. line (an extension of the outer end of the #8—Market St. electric line). The Pacific Ave. line brought up the rear—a very poor fourth.

Three different track gauges were represented in this cable network: the Powell St. and the Sacramento-Clay routes had a track width of 3'6"; Castro St. was standard gauge (4'8½"); Pacific Ave. had a gauge of five feet. An interesting method was used to transport the narrow and wide gauge cars to and from Elkton Shops for repairs; a special flat car with dual gauge rails mounted on its bed and hauled by an electric work car would carry the cable car in piggyback fashion. Castro St. cable cars, being standard gauge, were towed by an electric car to and from the shops on their own wheels. There were standard gauge electric spur tracks from adjacent electric trolley lines into both the Castro and the Washington and Mason cable barns; Pacific Ave. cars were loaded onto the flat car at the nearby #19 line on Polk St.

The power house at Washington and Mason barn, largest on the system, was originally operated by steam, but was converted to electricity in 1912. At that time, a 900-horsepower, 600-volt direct current motor was used in this conversion, the plant receiving power by means of tapping off the feeder of the nearby Kearny St. trolley line. The original steam power plant remained, however, until 1926 when it was dismantled.

This plant supplied power to propel the cable for the tw Powell St. lines and the Sacramento-Clay route.

The Castro cable received power from a small electric plan located in one section of the car house at Castro and Jerse streets. Power to feed the motor came from the #11 streetca line which ran on 24th St., one block north of the car barn

The Pacific Ave. cable was propelled by an ordinar 600-volt D.C. traction motor of the type used on some of th company's electric cars. This motor was geared to the driv machinery in a very low ratio, making the cable speed on th line the slowest of any cable line in the city. The car barn an power station of this line was located on the north side c Pacific Ave. between Van Ness Ave. and Polk St.

The Pacific Ave. cable was never anything but a money losing proposition. When originally built, this line was th outer portion of the four-mile-long Pacific-Polk-Larkin-9t St. crosstown cable line built by *Sutter Street Railway Com pany* in the 1880s. At the time of the earthquake and fire c April 18, 1906, that part of the route on Polk, Larkin and 9 St. was under reconstruction as an electric line; the outer le of this line on Pacific Ave. between Polk and Divisader streets was not included in the electrification—not becaus the grades were too steep for electric traction, in fact the were quite gentle, but because of persistent opposition

GRIPMAN AND CONDUCTOR combine strength to turn Cable Car 514, and passengers, on the Powell and Market turntable.
Randolph Brandt

electric cars by influential citizens who resided on that street. In 1909 the remaining cable portion of the line was reopened using the original open grip car-closed trailer trains. This very short cable line was hopeless from the revenue standpoint, and fell an early victim to the depression, making its last run on November 17, 1929.

For the next dozen years the cable mileage remained constant. After a series of fare raises on MSR between 1937 and 1939, the Sacramento-Clay line, once very profitable, began to suffer a sharp downward trend in revenue—brought about by the competition of the California St. route of the *California Street Cable Railroad Company* which paralleled the Sacramento-Clay route for its entire distance one block to the south. The California Street company provided a frequent headway with a five-cent fare which caused many passengers to desert MSR's line. With little or no hope of improvement in view, the company substituted motor coaches on the line on February 15, 1942.

Time ran out for the isolated Castro St. cable line when MSR inaugurated a new north-south crosstown bus line on April 5, 1941. This new bus line gobbled up the unique Fillmore Hill cable-electric line and the #24—Divisadero St. trolley cars as well as the Castro cable.

The hardy and indestructible Powell St. cables continued on. But the company had plans for these, too. The success of the 1935 trolley coach installation on the #33 line indicated that this would be the answer for the Powell St. lines. What the company did not have was the money to implement this plan. From the company's point of view cable operation on these lines was costly; the substitution of trolley coaches would have resulted in financial savings. However, this inability to make the change sparked the almost unbelievable chain of happenings which finally culminated in the perpetuation of cable traction on the Powell St. routes.

It is interesting to note that the Powell-Mason cable line has provided service from terminal to terminal over the same route, using the same method of propulsion and operated by the same cars, for more than 90 years! Certainly, this must be a world's record for city transit.

BACK IN 1880, a well-dressed group posed aboard a train of the Clay Street Hill Railroad Co., at Clay and Van Ness. The open bench grip car tows a "muzzle loading" or "bobtail" trailer. **Charles Smallwood**

THE THREE TYPES of cable cars used on Powell Street by Market Street Railway are shown on this and the next page: (ABOVE) Car 504 was rebuilt from an open car of 1887 vintage at Washington and Mason Barn by the Powell Street Railway Company. (BELOW) Car 510 shows the 1893 type built by Carter Brothers. **BOTH: Charles Smallwood**

ONE OF THE original Mahoney Brothers cars, 524, is seen at Bay and Taylor turntable.

Charles Smallwood

(BELOW) **PRIOR TO ABANDONMENT** of trolley lines in the North Beach area, Powell cable cars used to ride piggyback to and from Elkton Shops on the work train shown here. Flat car 04 had 3' 6" gauge rails laid on its bed to carry cable cars. The scene is on Broadway near Mason Street, 1936.

Market Street Railway

Market Street Railway
Cable Car Roster — 1921-1944
Powell Street Cars

Car No.	Builder and Date	Remarks
501	Mahoney Bros. 1887	Formerly open car 544. Rebuilt URR 12-13-12
502	Carter Bros. 1891	
503	Carter Bros. 1891	
504	Mahoney Bros. 1887	Formerly open car 543. Rebuilt URR 11-15-15
505	Carter Bros. 1891	
506	Carter Bros. 1891	
507	Carter Bros. 1891	
508	Carter Bros. 1891	
509	Mahoney Bros. 1887	Formerly open car 542. Rebuilt MSR 1-31-23
510	Carter Bros. 1891	
511	Carter Bros. 1891	
512	Carter Bros. 1891	
513	Carter Bros. 1891	
514	Mahoney Bros. 1887	Formerly 528. Renumbered 12-13-29
515	Carter Bros. 1891	
516	Carter Bros. 1891	
517	Mahoney Bros. 1887	Formerly 532. Renumbered 12-13-29
518	Carter Bros. 1891	
519	Carter Bros. 1891	
520	Carter Bros. 1891	
521	Mahoney Bros. 1887	Formerly 533. Renumbered 12-16-29
522	Mahoney Bros. 1887	
523	Ferries & Cliff House Ry. Co. 1888-90	
524	Mahoney Bros. 1887	Formerly 534. Renumbered 12-16-29
525	Ferries & Cliff House Ry. Co. 1888-90	
526	Ferries & Cliff House Ry. Co. 1888-90	
527	Mahoney Bros. 1887	

Notes: Cars built by *Ferries & Cliff House Ry. Co.* were constructed at Washington and Mason Car House between 1888 and 1890. They were exact duplicates of the Mahoney Bros. combination cars with but one difference: the company-built cars had wooden underframes instead of steel. The company built six of these cars. In 1918 car 533 (later 521) was rebuilt with straight sides after being badly damaged in an accident with a runaway auto.

This heterogeneous fleet of 27 cars owes its existence today to the fact that 24 of these cars were stored at the Sacramento St. Car House instead of at Washington and Mason barn when the latter was destroyed with its entire contents in the 1906 disaster. The Sacramento St. barn was located on the south side of that street between Presidio Ave. and Walnut St. and, at that time, was the western terminus of the Sacramento-Clay cable line.

The remaining three cars saved were the open cars 542, 543 and 544. These were housed in a small car house located around the corner on Presidio Ave. Both of these houses were well out of the fire zone.

Some of these cars were originally Powell St. cars while others were built in 1891 for the Sacramento-Clay line when it was extended to 6th Ave. and Fulton St. to accommodate crowds of the Mid-Winter Fair, soon to be held in Golden Gate Park. Their numbering in the 500 series was a holdover from the original *Market Street Railway* practice of assigning a certain group of numbers to each individual line. United Railroads continued this numbering system on cable lines only, as the practice was abolished on electric car lines after 1902. Prior to 1906, cars working Powell and Mason line were assigned numbers starting with 400; 450 began the Powell-Washington-Jackson line, and 500 the Sacramento-Clay route.

During the months following the earthquake and fire of 1906, the rubble of the destroyed Washington and Mason car barn and power house was cleaned away and reconstruction of the facilities commenced. First to be put back into use was the steam-operated cable driving machinery—even before work on reconstructing the car house started. Service on a limited scale resumed early in 1907. The 500 class cars were brought to Washington and Mason and, while the building was being rebuilt, were stored outside on unused tracks on Mason Street. Only enough cars were brought over at first to work that portion of the lines which were operating, but as reconstruction of the lines and building progressed, the remainder of the surviving cars was placed in service.

During Market Street Railway's ownership, these cars were little changed. The last open car, 542, was rebuilt into combination open and closed car 509 in 1923. During the 1920s a heavy flat steel reinforcing plate was attached to the outside bottom of the sides of each car to strengthen the body. The standard MSR white front paint job was applied during 1926-27, but without the lights.

All cars in the Powell St. fleet were in service on September 29, 1944, when the property was turned over to the city's Municipal Railway.

THE SACRAMENTO-CLAY cable line traversed the swanky Pacific Heights section of San Francisco. Here is outbound car 19 passing stately mansions at Sacramento and Laguna.

Charles Smallwood

Sacramento-Clay Cars

15-24, 27, 28

These 12 large double end combination open and closed cable cars were rebuilt in 1907-08 at Elkton Shops from original open Market St. cable cars of 1880 vintage. They were built to the same plans as Castro cables 2-6.

Weighing 14,000 pounds, they were the heaviest cable cars operating in the city as well as the largest.

The odd gap in the numbering was closed when on December 13, 1929, cars 27 and 28 were renumbered 25 and 26, thus making numbers consecutive.

Car #20 was shortened somewhat and rebuilt with an arch roof after having been almost demolished in a collision with Kearny St. electric car 1747 on January 28, 1915, at Clay and Kearny streets.

Although Sacramento-Clay cable service was ended on February 15, 1942, cars remained on the property at the Washington and Mason barn until taken over by Municipal Railway in 1944; they were disposed of by the city-owned line shortly thereafter.

In 1967 car #19 was returned to Washington and Mason car barn, restored, and placed on exhibit with Municipal Railway's historical cars.

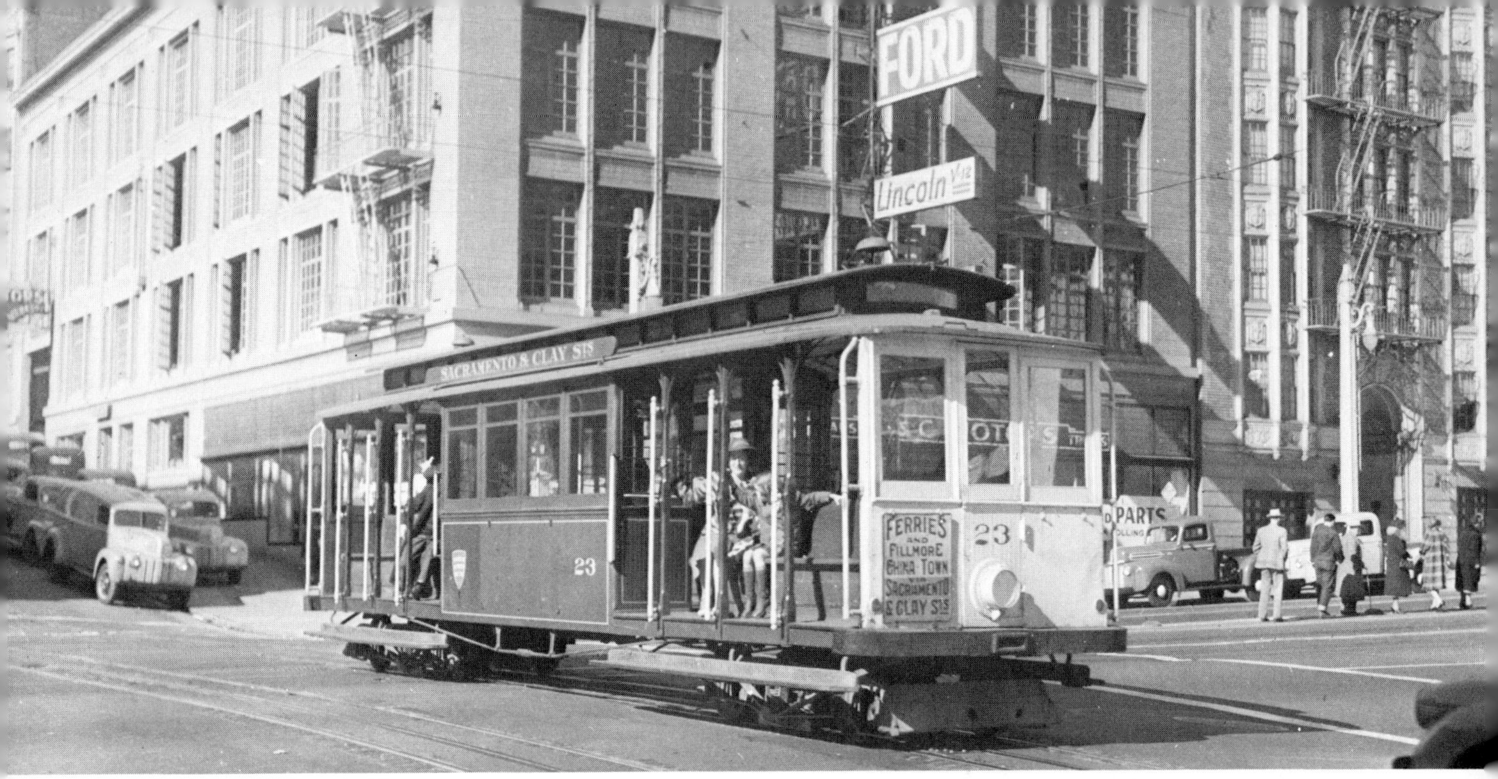

OUTBOUND SACRAMENTO-CLAY cable car 23 crosses busy Van Ness Ave. on February 8, 1942, a week before abandonment.
Charles Smallwood

RARELY PHOTOGRAPHED on the line, Sacramento-Clay car 20 was the only arch roof type in the fleet. It was removed from service shortly after this 1934 view, at the Sacramento and Fillmore terminus.
Charles Smallwood

ON THE EMBARCADERO, Sacramento-Clay cable car 21 awaits patrons at the Ferry Building terminal. The route's trackage was intertwined with the Market Street loop.
Charles Smallwood

NO STRANGER to steep climbs was Sacramento-Clay #16. The car is shown in its last, and steepest, climb (straight up!) as it is hoisted to the roof of The Emporium department store on April 6, 1948, to become part of the store's Kiddieland complex.

Randolph Brandt

IT IS THE LAST DAY of operation for the Castro cable line (April 5, 1941) as northbound car 6 approaches 20th Street.
Charles Smallwood

Castro Street Cars

Car No.	Builder	Remarks
1	J. Hammond	Ex-Omnibus Cable Co. open car. Rebuilt URR 1907
2	Central Pacific	Ex-Market St. cable open car. Rebuilt URR 1907
3	Central Pacific	Ex-Market St. cable open car. Rebuilt URR 1907
4	Central Pacific	Ex-Market St. cable open car. Rebuilt URR 1907
5	Central Pacific	Ex-Market St. cable open car. Rebuilt URR 1907
6	Central Pacific	Ex-Market St. cable open car. Rebuilt URR 1907
7	J. Hammond	Ex-Omnibus Cable Co. open car. Rebuilt URR 1907

Notes: Cars 1, 2, 3, 4, 5, and 6 rebuilt to combination open and closed California type double end by URR 1907. Car 7 remained the sole open car on Castro St.; rebuilt with longitudinal seats facing outward by URR 1907. Car 1 was shorter than the others, having three windows in closed section instead of four. The original open cars of Market Street Cable Railroad Company were built in the Sacramento shops of Central Pacific Railroad in the 1880s.

In 1925 car #2 was equipped with an experimental air-operated grip and air-operated wheel brakes. The track brake was not changed and still remained operated by the usual hand lever. To supply air to the four tanks mounted under the car, a compressor and large tank were installed at the car barn to supply the initial charge of air to the car before it started its run; to maintain pressure while on the road, a continuous acting compressor was mounted beneath the car, driven by a belt to one of the axles. Experiments with this method began July 2, 1925, and were abandoned after a short period. It was said that while the air-operated grip started the car very smoothly after gripmen became accustomed to it, it also caused excessive wear on the cable.

Cars 1, 3, 4, 5, 6 and 7 were equipped with new bodies in 1926-27. An arch roof and rounded ends were marked differences with all but #1, which kept its shorter three-window closed section and flat ends. Cars 3, 4, 5 and 6 were shortened by approximately three feet and, like #1, came with a three-window closed section instead of the former four-window. Open car #7 likewise was rebuilt into a shorter combination open and closed car. Weight of the cars after this rebuilding was 12,700 pounds.

Car #2 was not rebuilt and retained its original form until the end of service, but was no longer used after 1927.

(ABOVE) **SMALL FRY** give the crew a hand pushing car 4 off the table at 26th and Castro on the last day of cable operation.
Charles Smallwood

(RIGHT) **LOOKING OVER** the 26th and Castro turntable in 1937. Although single-end cable cars used on Castro prior to 1906 made the table necessary, it was retained after 1906 to switch double-end cars from the outbound to the inbound track.   **Market Street Railway**

(ABOVE) **AT THE INNER TERMINAL** of the Castro line, 18th and Castro, cable car 7 is seen in black mourning crepe on the final day of service, April 5, 1941.
Charles Smallwood

(BELOW) **CASTRO CAR 2** was the same type as used on the Sacramento-Clay line. Here it is being removed from Castro Barn to be towed to Elkton Yard for scrapping, in April 1941.
Charles Smallwood

Market Street Railway Castro Cable Car 133

MENTION MUST BE MADE of one cable car owned by Market Street Railway that, although never used in revenue service by MSR, is nevertheless of much interest. This is car 133, an original Market and Castro single-end car in use on this line up to the time of the earthquake and fire of April 18, 1906. This car, in its original Castro Street line colors of buff and white and in perfect condition even down to the wooden shutters on the windows, reposed in the Castro barn from 1906 until the facility was closed in 1941. The historic car was then towed to Elkton Shops. Officials of the MSR made an earnest effort to present the car to any organization or individual which would preserve it—but with no success. Everyone contacted thought that the old car should be saved, but no one wanted to take the responsibility. At that time MSR had a serious space problem, so the decision was reluctantly made to scrap the car . . . it was destroyed on May 8, 1941. This view was taken two days before the end. Thus a priceless relic of San Francisco's glorious past was lost forever. **Charles Smallwood**

Sad Last Journey

HISTORIC CABLE CAR 133 was moved from Castro Street Car House to Elkton Yard for scrapping. (ABOVE) A shopman places rerailer while the foreman looks on. **Bert Ward** (BELOW) The Geneva wrecker tows the venerable old car down Dolores, between 24th and 23rd. Note the conductor sitting on the wrecker's fender pouring sand on the rails for adhesion. The sad trip was made in April 1941.
Charles Smallwood

Cable Train

A DUMMY GRIP CAR and Trailer 52 stand at the end of the line on Pacific Avenue in the later 1920s; time was growing short for this cable route.
                                                  S.F. Public Utilities Commission

Pacific Ave. Cars

Five two-car cable trains consisting of open grip (or dummy) cars and closed trailers were retained by United Railroads for service on the shortened Pacific Ave. cable line. Cars for these five trains were picked at random from the large fleet made surplus by the electrification of the Sutter and Polk-Larkin lines at the time of the 1906 disaster; the cars kept for Pacific Ave. service retained their scattered numbering throughout their existence.

Cars used on this line until its closing in 1929 were grip cars numbered 33, 46, 51, 61—and trailers 52, 54, 56, 61 and 77.

In 1915 another grip car, #55, was fitted up as a one-man Pay As You Enter cable car but was not a success and was discarded after a very short time.

All cars used in this service were built in the early 1880s by *Sutter Street Railway Company* at its car barn located at Sutter and Polk streets.

Most of the old cars were either sold or given away by MSR when the line quit in 1929. Two exceptions were one dummy grip car which had been damaged in a collision with a Van Ness Ave. trolley car a short time before abandonment (it was scrapped) and one train consisting of grip car #46 and trailer 54 which was retained by the company for historical purposes; today the train is on display at the Washington and Mason cable barn, after having been restored to its former *Sutter Street Railway* livery.

CABLE TRAILER 61, from the Pacific Avenue route, was in storage at Elkton Yard in 1935 when this view was taken.
                    Charles Smallwood

PACIFIC HEIGHTS RESIDENTS turned out en masse for the last day of the Pacific Avenue cable line, November 17, 1929. Celebrants pack a train at Pacific Avenue and Divisadero Street.
Charles Smallwood

THIS OLD PACIFIC AVE. cable train was restored by MSR to pre-1900 style for the 1939 Treasure Island Fair. The train is now on exhibit at the Washington and Mason cable barn museum.
Charles Smallwood

BACK IN THE GOOD OLD DAYS when the cables reigned supreme: the finely detailed livery and lettering scheme complement the beautiful lines of this Powell Street Railway Company car, seen at Bay and Taylor in the 1880s.
C.D. Miller

IN 1928, the Washington and Mason Car House depended upon this Ford Model T truck for its wrecking work. Note the cable car gong on its roof.
S.F. Public Utilities Commission

WASHINGTON AND MASON car barn and power house was a striking edifice in the 1890s (ABOVE) but was totally destroyed (including its rolling stock) in the 1906 earthquake and fire. (BELOW) The bricks from the destroyed building were used to construct the present structure (which is one story shorter) on that site. **TOP: Richard Schlaich; BOTTOM: United Railroads**

POWELL AND MARKET TURNTABLE was busy in the 1890s turning cars of the Ferries and Cliff House Railway, like car 6, seen with its crew and passengers. **Richard Schlaich**

(BELOW) **THIS WAS JACKSON STREET** and Central Ave. in the early 1890s. At this time these Powell Street Railways Washington and Jackson cable cars terminated at Central (now Presidio) Ave. and California Street.
Charles Smallwood

(RIGHT) **WHEN THE MARKET STREET** cable cars were made surplus by the electrifications following the earthquake and fire several were sold as dwellings for the many refugees made homeless by the disaster. This group of such cars was located on the Richmond District block bounded by California, Cornwall, 5th and 6th Aves.
Charles Smallwood

Street Car Replacements

SOMETHING NEW was coming to the Polk Street route in June 1939, as buses 30 to 41 lined up for a publicity parade. The entry of ''White Front Buses'' on this line was the first in a series of pre-World War II conversions from rail to rubber. **Warren K. Miller**

The Bus Gets a Foothold

THE BUS CAME TO Market Street Railway in 1926 not to conquer, but to supplement. It was on April 6 of that year that a pair of Fageols opened the new Excelsior motor coach line.

But the picture had changed by the time Municipal Railway took over on September 29, 1944. Those two buses had grown to a fleet of 125 coaches—and they were operating not only on lines which were established as bus operations but on former streetcar and cable lines as well.

Indeed, it is asserted that had it not been for monetary problems, Market Street Railway planned to convert every one of its cable lines to buses, as well as changing over all but the most robust of its trolley car routes.

Why was MSR's management so enamored of buses? Probably the most persuasive reason was that the bus could legally be operated by a one-man crew, whereas steadfast and bitter opposition to the operation of streetcars by one-man crews had prevailed in court. Market Street Railway could not operate its marginal car lines with one-man cars, but it could operate the same lines with one-man buses. Small wonder that the bus began to appear with ever-increasing regularity on lines of MSR after 1935.

Market Street Railway's bus lines may be said to have fallen into three categories: (1) original bus routes; (2) converted lines; and (3) wartime bus lines. Considering each in turn:

Original Bus Routes

These were lines which, from their inception, were operated by buses. Chief characteristic of such lines was that they were feeders, pure and simple, operating from major car lines into areas of sparse population. Their riders had to transfer to get to the downtown area. There were five lines in this category: Silver Avenue (Mission and San Bruno), Excelsior, Crocker-Amazon, Southern Heights, and Sunset.

First to be established was Crocker-Amazon which was opened on April 6, 1926, followed immediately by the Excelsior Line. Next came Silver Avenue, opened on October 7, 1927. Southern Heights began operating on February 10,

1932; and the last, Sunset District, started service on February 12, 1932. All used Fageols at first.

#50—CROCKER-AMAZON: From Mission and Geneva via Mission, Amazon, Moscow, Geneva, South Hill Blvd., Baltimore, Cordova, Geneva to Mission.

#51—SILVER AVENUE: This line originally operated on Silver Ave. from Mission St. to San Bruno Ave., making a rather large loop via Felton St. and Bowdoin St. and then returning to Mission St. In 1937 this line was extended on Silver Ave. to Third and Palou. On March 22, 1943, it was still further extended to Hunter's Point, giving the line a length of 10.2 miles. Operated from Utah Division.

#52—EXCELSIOR: This line traversed an irregular loop starting at Mission and Excelsior; it then ran via Excelsior, Brazil, Prague, Russia, Moscow, Italy, Naples and Brazil back to Mission St. Lest the reader think this was the world's longest bus line, these are all good San Francisco street names. It was actually about 2.5 miles long. Ran from Utah Division.

#53—SOUTHERN HEIGHTS: This line started at 16th and Bryant (Seals Stadium), thence via 16th, San Bruno, 19th, Vermont, 20th, Rhode Island, 21st and 22nd to 23rd and Wisconsin—later extended to 25th and Connecticut, about 3.5 miles. This line also operated from the Utah Division.

#54—SUNSET: From Lincoln Way and 20th Ave., via 20th, Irving St., 25th Ave., Noriega St., 27th Ave., Moraga St., 25th Ave., Irving, 21st Ave., and Lincoln Way to 20th Ave. This line operated only in the morning and evening rush hours as of 1932.

Converted Lines

In this category are former rail lines which MSR converted to bus operation, largely because of its unsuccessful efforts to use one-man cars on light lines. Lines thus converted and dates of conversion are:

#50—	Visitacion Valley	8-1-37
#19—	9th and Polk Streets	6-25-39 (Partial)
#35—	Howard Street	11-5-39
#27—	Bryant Street	1-28-40 (Partial)
#36—	Folsom Street	1-28-40 (Partial)
#28—	Ferries and S.P. Depot	4-1-40
#12—	Ingleside	6-23-40 (Partial)
#15—	Third and Kearny	6-23-40 (Partial)
#24—	16th and Divisadero	4-6-41
	Castro Cable	4-6-41
	Fillmore Hill	4-6-41
#55—	Sacramento Cable	2-15-42

These bus substitutions have been described in the chapter devoted to rail lines and this data will not be repeated here. For the most part, the conversions were on a direct replacement basis with buses following rail routes closely except for the required loops at ends of lines.

However, rail line #50—Visitacion Valley was absorbed into an existing bus line, Crocker-Amazon. And new bus line #24—Castro-Divisadero-Fillmore Hill absorbed three rail lines in one fell swoop.

IT WAS A BIG DAY for residents of the Crocker-Amazon and Excelsior districts when Market Street Railway opened its first motor coach line on April 6, 1926. Here, bus number 2 leads the big parade of celebrants on that festive day. **Paul Ward**

THE BUS OPERATIONS of Market Street Railway were centered at the 24th & Utah bus garage, shown above circa 1940. The maintenance of successor Municipal Railway buses was performed there into the 1970s. (BELOW) An interior view of the same garage shows the bus washing machine.   **UPPER: Warren K. Miller; LOWER: Charles Smallwood**

Wartime Lines

World War II hit San Francisco with the same total impact felt in the rest of California. Defense industries sprang up (notably shipbuilding) almost overnight, and their workers had to be transported. Wartime gasoline and rubber rationing severely cut down the use of private transportation. Production of new transit vehicles was under government control and new cars and buses were assigned by the Office of Defense Transportation only after careful study of the need and the lack of other transportation to meet that need. Market Street Railway was perhaps more fortunate than many electric railway companies in that it not only had not gotten around to scrapping cars and rails of lines recently converted, but had a comparatively new bus fleet capable of confronting the emergency with optimum efficiency.

Two major rail lines which had been converted, Third St. and Polk St., again received cars on a part-time basis. Sixteen large new diesel buses, taken over at the factory by ODT from Third Avenue Railway of New York City, were diverted to MSR. It thus became possible to secure rolling stock to serve the newly created wartime lines.

Line #54—Hunters Point began operating on December 12, 1940, running from Third and Evans to Hunters Point. On September 13, 1943, the line was extended to 26th and Castro via Third and Army streets, giving a total length of 10.40 miles.

Bus line #57, also serving Hunters Point, was established on March 16, 1942. It ran from Brazil and Mission and Geneva and Mission to take workers to Hunters Point.

Aiding greatly in the operation of these wartime lines were 16 large 45-seat Yellow TD-4505 buses which were rented to MSR by the U.S. Navy. Municipal Railway continued to rent these after the 1944 merger.

Maximum use of buses was achieved by operating them in evenings, Saturdays and Sundays on certain rail lines. MSR thus, under wartime emergency conditions, achieved one-man operation to a modest degree.

With the merger of September 29, 1944, buses of Market Street Railway were integrated into Municipal Railway. At that time Muni was purchasing only White gasoline buses and, since all but four ex-MSR buses were Yellows, Muni did not feel constrained to keep them; in the interests of stand-dardization and economy Muni sold off its ex-MSR buses as soon as possible—some, but eight years old, going for as little as $35 each (buses 63-65, 75, 76). By 1952 there was not a single former Market Street Railway bus remaining on the property.

General Specifications, MSR Motor Coaches

Numbers	Builder and Date	Units	Weight	Seats	Model/Serial	Length	Width	Height	Wheelbase	HP	Cu. In.
1-3	Fageol 1926[1]	3			Safety Coach						
4-6	Fageol 1927[1]	3			Safety Coach						
7-8	Fageol 1932[1]	2	16,380	30	Safety Coach	23'9"	8'3"	9'1"	19'6"	105	468
9	Fageol 1927[2]	1			S-C/20499						
21	GM 1932	1	7,120	17	T-26C/711	14'1"	7'5"	8'10"	13'11"	76	267
25-26	Twin Coach 1937	2	9,465	23	23R	22'9"	7'11"	8'1"	14'10"	110	404
27-28	Twin Coach 1938	2	9,465	23	23R	22'9"	7'11"	8'1"	14'10"	110	404
30-41	Yellow 1939	12	10,600	25	739	24'2"	7'11"	9'1"	14'3"	110	400
60-73	Yellow 1939	14	10,600	27	739	24'2"	7'11"	9'1"	14'3"	110	400
74-76	Yellow 1940	3	10,600	27	739	24'2"	7'11"	9'1"	14'3"	110	400
101-110	Yellow 1939	10	16,200	36	731/502-511	30'10"	8'0"	8'10"	17'11"	158	529
111-120	Yellow 1940	10	16,200	36	731/512-521	30'10"	8'0"	8'10"	17'11"	158	529
121-122	Yellow 1940	2	14,280	36	TG3601/002-003	30'5"	7'11"	9'3"	17'6"	158	529
151-159	Yellow 1941	9	15,200	36	TG3601/013-021	30'5"	7'11"	9'3"	17'6"	170	707
160-165	Yellow 1942	6	16,480	36	TG3605/055-060	30'5"	7'11"	9'3"	17'6"	170	707
166	Yellow 1942	1	16,600	36	TG3605/043	30'5"	7'11"	9'3"	17'6"	170	707
201-207	Yellow 1940	7	12,340	32	TG3201/029-035	28'0"	7'11"	9'3"	15'1"	145	426
301-311	Yellow 1930	11	14,740	36	TD3601/006-016	30'5"	7'11"	9'3"	17'6"	165	426
1-16	Yellow 1942	16		45	TD4505/note 3						
401-430	Yellow 1941	30	15,820	37	TG4502/006-035	34'10"	7'11"	9'3"	21'9"	158	529
431-433	Yellow 1942	3	17,080	37	TG4505/002-004	34'10"	7'11"	9'3"	21'9"	158	529

NOTES: (1) California Motor Coach bodies. (2) Ex-San Francisco Muni 025, 1938. (3) Serials are: 249-250, 228, 224, 236, 240, 233, 232, 238, 225, 227, 219-220, 226, 251. Purchased by Muni 1946, renumbered 312-327. All these 16 buses were leased from the U.S. Navy; other leased USN buses: 17-19, International Schultz bodies; 42-52, pur. 1942, Yellow TG3606; 77-84, International, bus 77 had Superior body, others had Gillig bodies.

(Roster: Eli Ba...)

Description of MSR Motor Coaches

FIRST CAME the Fageols. Top photo is of #6, on the Geneva ladder track. Driver of bus 2 (BELOW) awaits camera click at the Silver Ave. and Mission St. layover.
TOP: Public Utilities Commission; **BOTTOM:** Richard Schlaich

1—6

Market Street Railway's pioneer buses were Fageol 20-seaters. Of that builder's famed "Safety Coach" type, they were powered by Hall-Scott gasoline engines—four cylinders for buses 1, 2 and 3 and six cylinders for 4, 5 and 6. Bodies were constructed by the California Motor Coach Co. of San Francisco. All rode on pneumatic tires.

First to arrive were units 1 and 2—entering service in April 1926, on the new Crocker-Amazon and Excelsior lines and operating out of Geneva Car House. Soon added was bus 3. These units soon proved to have insufficient power for their runs and in June 1927, six-cylinder buses 4, 5 and 6 replaced them; the later sported larger windows in the front corners and nickel radiator shells.

Coaches 1, 2 and 3 were then shifted to a new line running on Silver Ave. from Mission St. to San Bruno Ave. These half-dozen buses served for about 10 years and were retired by 1938. At least one of the pioneer buses was given its own white-front paint job although this treatment was not generally applied until the advent of the transit-type coaches of the 1930s.

MARKET STREET RAILWAY didn't have to go far to find builders for its first coaches. Here is brand-new #7 in 1932. It had chassis by Fageol, which had a plant in Oakland; body by local California Motor Coach Co.; and a power plant by Hall-Scott, located over in Berkeley. Bus is ready for its assignment on the Southern Heights line, for which it was expressly purchased. **Richard Schlaich**

7—8

Buses 7 and 8 were built by Fageol in 1932 for the new Southern Heights and Sunset District bus lines. They incorporated bodies by California Motor Coach Co. mounted on Fageol chassis with six-cylinder, 105-hp Hall-Scott power plants. Bodies were equipped with double-cushioned leather seats for 30. Four-wheel pneumatic brakes and balloon tires were other features.

Two 50-gallon gas tanks kept these buses on the job without the necessity of refueling for many hours. Windshields were of safety shatterproof glass, as were the top halves of the entrance doors; lower halves used wire glass. These two buses were retired in 1940.

(RIGHT) **WITH NEW** streamstyled paint scheme, number 8 is seen from the rear, inside the 24th & Utah garage circa 1939. **Charles Smallwood**

One of a Kind

THE LAST of the early-era buses, with engine compartment forward, was number 21.

21

Motor coach 21 was the only one of this type, and was built by General Motors on a truck chassis. It was a small 17-seater purchased to replace a large bus on the Sunset District line, first entering service on March 29, 1932. After its passenger-carrying days were over, the unit was fitted with a large magnet mounted underneath just forward of the rear wheels. The bus was then operated over streetcar lines and its magnet lifted foreign metal objects (such as bolts, nuts, etc.) from the track grooves, thus preventing chipping of the flanges of car wheels.

25—28

These were the first modern, transit-type coaches purchased by MSR. They were of the famed "pusher" type of Twin Coach with rear engine. Coaches 25 and 26 were placed in service in November 1937, with 27 and 28 following in March of 1938; all four were sold by the Muni on January 11, 1946.

ABOVE: **Market Street Railway, courtesy Mrs. C.D. Miller.** BELOW: **Charles Smallwood**

30—41

Buses 30-41 were an interesting combination of Yellow Coach's old end designs with new sides. All 12 were delivered in June 1939. Municipal Railway sold six in 1946: 30, 34, 37, 38, 39 and 41. The six remaining were sold in 1948.

TWO ANGLES of number 33 were taken by the MSR photographer at Elkton Yard when it was new.
BOTH: Market Street Railway, courtesy Mrs. C.D. Miller

60—76

The first 14 coaches were delivered in December 1939 and were basically similar to 30-41. Costing MSR $7,365.39 each, these Yellow Model 739s were followed by three identical models in early 1940 to bring this sub-class to a total of 17. The Muni lost number 72 without ever using it. This bus struck a pole at 30th and Chenery streets on January 4, 1943, and was badly damaged. It had not been repaired when Muni took over on September 29, 1944, and Muni scrapped the wreck on April 14, 1945. The remaining buses of this group were sold by Muni in 1948.

(RIGHT) **ON A NEWLY-STRIPED** bus lane, coach 63 loads at the Ferry. **Charles Smallwood**

(ABOVE) **A PUBLIC CELEBRATION** of the introduction of bus service on Polk Street took place by the Ghirhardelli chocolate factory in June 1940, and featured the 30-41 series. **Market Street Railway, courtesy Mrs. C.D. Miller** (BELOW) **BUS 104,** built in 1939 by Yellow.
Charles Smallwood

101—120

Buses 101-120 were built by Yellow Coach in late 1939 and were among the last of that builder's model 731 to be constructed. Costing $9,822.48 each, they were delivered between December 7, 1939, and January 8, 1940. All were sold by Muni in 1948.

121—122

These two coaches featured the new streamlined body design of Yellow Coach (later General Motors) which was to become the industry standard for nearly 20 years. They were of the new TG-3601 model designation and were received on June 21, 1940. They did not have the inward-slanting front windshields which were to become a feature of this type of bus in later years.

As originally delivered, coaches 121 and 122 had roof baggage racks for suburban charter use. Muni sold both in 1949.

IN THESE OFFICIAL photographs of number 122, taken in June 1940, MSR showed off the baggage racks installed for charters. **BOTH: Market Street Railway, courtesy Mrs. C.D. Miller**

151—166

This group of buses had oversize gasoline engines to enable them to operate efficiently on lines hitherto considered too steep for any vehicles other than cable cars. Coaches 151-159 (Model TG-3601) were delivered on March 17, 1941, and in fact replaced cable operation over two routes: Castro and the Fillmore Hill counterbalance which they tied into one rambling, crosstown coach line.

Coaches 160-166 were TG-3605s but were very similar to 151-159 and on February 15, 1942, replaced cable cars on the Sacramento-Clay line. All buses of this group were sold in 1951 by Muni.

(ABOVE) **COACH 157** bears an ad card noting new bus service from the Noe Valley to the Marina effective April 6, 1941. **Charles Smallwood**

201—207

Coaches 201-207 were Yellow TG-3201s, one window shorter than the previous group and were designed for lines of lighter traffic. All were received in the two weeks following June 10, 1940. Bus 201 was damaged beyond repair on April 28, 1949. The others were sold by Muni in 1951.

(BELOW) **OFFICIAL VIEW** of coach 203. **Mrs. C.D. Mill**

TWO JULY 1940 views show 36-seat coach 306.   TOP: **Charles Smallwood**; ABOVE: **Courtesy Mrs. C.D. Miller**

301—311

These 11 buses were constructed by Yellow Coach in 1940 and were that builder's model TD-3601. With a price tag of $13,000 each, they represented Market Street Railway's only purchase of diesel-powered motor coaches. With only 36 seats, the 301 class was not really suitable for heavy lines and consequently saw a considerable amount of use on the lightly patronized South-of-Market lines. All went under the Muni banner on September 29, 1944. First to be retired was 304, bowing out on December 20, 1948. The rest were gone by 1951.

(RIGHT) **LAYING OVER** on Townsend Street, coach 306 is seen in 1944.   **Ira L. Swett**

(ABOVE) **LENGTH OF THE 401** Class is emphasized in this May 1941 official photograph. **Paul Ward**

(BELOW) **COACH 406** crosses Market Street onto Third Street, circa 1944. **Ira L. Swett**

401—433

These were built by Yellow in 1941-1942 and were equipped with gasoline engines unlike most coaches of this type which were diesels. One feature was the elimination of eight aisle seats to give these coaches a seating capacity of only 37. This made them good wartime crowd-movers and they saw much service on the heavy Third Street and Hunters Point lines.

The first 30 coaches, outshopped in 1941, were Yellow's model TG-4502; the last three, built in 1942, were model TG-4505s.

After 1944 Muni repainted these coaches and they kept the same numbers until retirement of the last units in 1952.

1—16

These 16 Yellow model TD-4505s were war babies in the truest sense of the term. They were under construction for New York City's Third Avenue Railway when World War II erupted and sported the distinctive New York State Public Utilities Commission-mandated roof vents.

Fifty buses were built in this order and the federal government diverted them far and wide to serve where the need for transportation was greatest. These 16 came to MSR in 1942.

In San Francisco they operated mostly on the heavy Third Street and Polk Street lines, running through the war in their red and cream Third Avenue Railway colors. They did, however, have a white front!

After the September 29, 1944, takeover of MSR by the Muni, these coaches continued in use even though technically still the property of the War Assets Corporation. Not until February 19, 1946, were they purchased by Muni. They were gradually repainted and renumbered, becoming Muni 312-327 in order; the first to go through the shops was bus which on May 10, 1946, became Muni #313. Unit #11 was the last, becoming #322 on August 29, 1947. All were sold 1951.

(ABOVE) **DURING THE WARTIME TRAFFIC EXPLOSION,** "War Baby" number 4 shared the Third and Kearny service with the car following at top center. View is at Market Street in July 1943.
James K. Gibson

(BELOW, LEFT) **ONE OF THE** wartime buses, number 6, loads across from the S.P. Depot on Third Street as a streetcar takes the crossover at right. (BELOW, RIGHT) **SOUTHBOUND ON THIRD STREET,** near Howard, "War Baby" 2, later Municipal Railway 313, is seen in 1946.
BOTH: Ira L. Swett

Hairpin Turn

CROOKED INDEED! The best-known feature of the #33 trolley coach line was the tight turn at Clayton and Upper Market. As tricky as this operation was, it was "one up" on the streetcar line it replaced, which had to use a switchback to accomplish the reversing of direction. Coaches 55 and 56 posed for the MSR camera soon after conversion, in 1935.

Courtesy Mrs. C.D. Miller

One Very Crooked Trolley Coach Line

WHEN MARKET STREET RAILWAY decided to convert its #33—Eighteenth and Park line, it chose the trolley coach, a vehicle combining the maneuverability of a bus with the power and quiet of the modern streetcar. This was the first application of the trolley coach to a San Francisco line, and the success of the vehicle on that hilly line doubtless went far in influencing a subsequent decision to convert many additional lines to this mode of transit.

Eight trolley coaches were ordered from the J.G. Brill Company, Philadelphia, in 1935. Some specifications follow:

Type	Single Compartment
Body	Closed, of steel and aluminum
Seats	37
Length	33'0"
Width	8'0"
Wheelbase	16'3"
Weight	19,425 lbs.
Type Operation	One-man, front entrance

Motors:
- Coaches 51-54 .... GE 1154-A (two), 65 hp.
- Coaches 55-58 ..... Westinghouse 1428 CT9 (two), 65 hp.

Control:
- 51-54 .... General Electric Automatic PC
- 55-58 .... Westinghouse Automatic VA

Cost .... $13,694.00 each

THE FIRST TROLLEY COACH placed in service on the #33 line is seen on opening day, October 6, 1935.   **Market Street Railway**

No change in route was made other than the necessary loops at either end. The downtown terminal at Third and Harrison streets had an elevation of 13 feet above sea level; the trolley coaches then climbed to an elevation of 466 feet on Twin Peaks and dropped down to an elevation of 259 feet at the Waller and Stanyan streets terminal. Encountered was 619 feet of 12.3 percent grade which these trolley coaches ascended with a load of 50 passengers at a speed of 17 mph. There were also about 2,400 feet of average 9 percent grade. There was no doubt as to the excellent climbing ability of these vehicles.

Nor was there any doubt as to their brakes. A five-point electric holding brake helped to slow them on downgrades.

The trolley coaches entered service on October 6, 1935, making the 10.29-mile round trip at a schedule speed of 11.10 mph, despite the fact that the winding and/or congested streets en route gave them little opportunity of demonstrating their top speed of 37 mph.

A unique feature of these coaches when placed in service was their dual trolley wheels—a holdover from streetcar days. Although they operated well, they were replaced by the usual carbon insert slides about 1948.

A ninth similar trolley coach was added later; it w: equipped by General Electric and carried fleet number 59.

Trolley coaches 51-59 operated all through the war years c Line 33, and became the property of Municipal Railway : September 1944.

Although Muni was thoroughly convinced that troll coaches were the transit vehicle of the future in San Francisc it was not high on these particular examples of the bree Chief objection was the fact that 51-59 had two motor modern trolley coach engineering had reduced this to o: motor, and the single-motor coach was the standard of the i: dustry. Another liability of the Brills was their quite hea weight; with but 37 seats, they outweighed more mode: trolley coaches having 44 seats.

First earmarked for replacement by new Marmons in 194 the Brills nevertheless proved too durable to discard at th time. Indeed, they remained on the property until 195 when all were retired and sold for scrap.

Historians take MSR's assertion that 51-59 were the "fi: trolley coaches in California" with a grain of salt. Actual the Golden State's first trolley coaches operated in Hollywo back in 1911, running into Laurel Canyon (Bungalow Tow from a connection with the Sunset Boulevard streetcar lin

ON UPPER MARKET STREET, near the hairpin turn, coach 56's "blind side" is seen along with some of San Francisco's skyline, about 1935.
Market Street Railway

AN INTERIOR VIEW of trolley coach number 55 when new.
Market Street Railway

A "High Tide" of Passengers

THE PARADE OF CARS down Market Street culminated in this loop at the Ferry Building where passengers for the ferries to the Eastbay alighted, to be replaced in only a trice by those disembarking from the endless procession of white and orange-hued Southern Pacific and Key System boats. The camera looks south down the Embarcadero in 1930. Car 263, in foreground, is about to depart out Sutter Street to "Cliff House, Sutro Baths, Legion of Honor Palace, Public Golf Links, and Fort Miley." Balancing this dash sign is another advertising the great tenor, John McCormack, in his first "talkie," "Song O' My Heart," at Lowe's Warfield. Hard by 263's steps are the rails of the State Belt Railroad of California, and at the right is a Muni J line car, about to load its share of the downtown-bound throng.

Charles Smallwood

The Transportation Factory

IN THIS CHAPTER we will consider such items as transfers, education of platform men, safety programs, communication with platform men, special accidents, operating statistics, passes, facilities directly associated with operation, joint trackage agreements, inter-company transfers, and the innumerable other facets of day-by-day operation of the huge transportation factory which was Market Street Railway.

Transportation factory? Yes, indeed. In the 1920s at its height, MSR was manufacturing more than 750,000 rides daily for its patrons. Without its product, the business, professional and social life not only of San Francisco but of the entire bay area would have diminished greatly. The white front cars of this company were undoubtedly the single greatest factor in the continued prosperity of the community.

Attention is paid in other chapters to such auxiliaries of operation as car houses and shops. The cars themselves and the line they ran on are also examined in detail in other chapters. Here we concern ourselves first of all with the men who ran the cars; with their routine problems and the company's approved solutions; with certain statistics reflecting assignments of cars; with relations with Municipal Railway in transfers and joint trackage; with total ridership and financial rewards therefrom; with safety, the one great preoccupation of MSR's executive family; with safety's inevitable opposite, accidents; with special events which called on MSR's men to react out of their set pattern.

We must also observe those twin phenomena of San Francisco, the hectic operations at the triple loops at the Ferry Building and the unique four-track operation on Market St.

The ferry terminal operation not only featured the loops but also adjacent Mission Terminal and North Terminal— each an important operation in its own right.

As for the four-track operation on Market Street, it provided an entirely different set of operating hazards from those encountered anywhere else in the nation except on Canal St. in New Orleans. Operation of the four-track system on Canal

St. was comparatively gentlemanly; in San Francisco it was fiercely competitive. And that fact made all the difference in the world.

So, let's take a good look at MSR operations at their zenith.

Inter-Company Transfer Agreements

Throughout its entire life, MSR exchanged transfers with Municipal Railway at certain points. These inter-company transfer points were:

FILLMORE AND GEARY STREETS: (Lines 22 and 23 with Lines A, B, and C.)

DIVISADERO AND GEARY STREETS: (Lines 4 and 24 with Lines A, B, and C.)

ST. FRANCIS CIRCLE: (Line 12 and Line K, Sloat Blvd. only; this was discontinued on September 15, 1937 when Muni extended its Line L to the sea.)

4TH AND MARKET STREETS: (Line 20 with Line F to and from S.P. Depot.)

FILLMORE AND UNION STREETS: (Fillmore Hill Line with Line E only.)

CALIFORNIA STREET CABLE RAILROAD COMPANY: Presidio Ave. and California St. (Lines 1 and 2 with the California St. line.)

Some of these transfer points dated back to very early agreements with predecessor companies. Those on Geary St. were with the old *Geary St., Park & Ocean Railway* cable line, while that at Fillmore and Union streets was with the *Presidio and Ferries Railway* cable line.

MSR's predecessor, United Railroads, had an even more extensive inter-company transfer agreement with Municipal Railway; at one time, passengers were transferred between the companies at Kearny and Geary, Polk and Union, and Union and Mason streets. These transfer points were discontinued, however, as Municipal Railway gradually extended its lines into the territories involved.

Joint Trackage With Municipal Railway

MSR shared common trackage with Municipal Railway on the following streets:

Junipero Serra Blvd. and Ocean Ave. from St. Francis Circle to Ocean and Brighton Avenues.

Taraval St. from 20th Ave. to 33rd Ave., until the mid-1930s.

Market St., from Sutter St. to the Ferry Loop.

Embarcadero, from Jackson St. to the north side of Ferry Terminal.

Ferry Loops.

Duboce Ave. from Fillmore to Church streets.

Carl St., from west portal of Sunset Tunnel (Cole St.) to Stanyan St.

A MARKET STREET #12 car passes a Muni K car at Junipero Serra and Ocean in 1937. Although going in opposite directions, both cars are outbound to their terminals.
Charles Smallwood

With but three exceptions these trackage agreements were entered into with Municipal Railway by the predecessor United Railroads; these exceptions were on Duboce Ave., Carl St. (made in 1928 with Muni in connection with the opening that year of Muni's Line N—Judah St.), and the East Bay Terminal Loop (built in 1939 by Muni). A third track at the Ferry Loop was a jointly built project of MSR and Muni.

The usual rental agreement between MSR and the Municipal Railway called for the tenant company to pay a rental based on kilowatt hours used by its cars while traversing the joint trackage plus a fair share of track maintenance costs.

However, the original trackage agreement between URR and Muni came in 1917 when Muni desired to provide service to the 33rd Ave. area from its then-new tunnel under Twin Peaks. By utilizing URR's existing line on Taraval St. between 20th Ave. and 33rd Ave. instead of constructing its own line on Vicente St. from 20th Ave. to 33rd Ave., Muni saved itself about $61,700. Service was provided far sooner than would have been the case had the city built its own tracks on Vicente St.

The second trackage agreement covered Junipero Serra Blvd. and Ocean Ave. from St. Francis Circle to Ocean and Brighton Avenues, also necessary after Twin Peaks Tunnel opened. In this instance, the city paid MSR $100,000 cash, plus 7.5¢ for each mile operated by its cars over the trackage segment. MSR had to bear the total expense of maintaining tracks and overhead in first-class operating condition. An interesting postscript to this agreement was this: in the event that the city should acquire MSR, the $100,000 paid for operating rights would have been applied on the purchase price, less $7,000 for each year that would have elapsed from the date of the agreement to purchase date.

Communication With Trainmen

Market Street Railway's operations depended in great degree on a channel of communications, always open and unimpeded, between its Superintendent of Transportation and its car crews. This communication invariably was in the form of "Notices to Carmen" which were published in the company's official magazine, *The Inside Track*, and were also posted at all car houses.

As a sample of these Notices to Carmen, the following are typical:

• November 22, 1922: Until further orders it will not be necessary to flag . . . crossings of The Ocean Shore Railroad.

• December 18, 1922: During the recent storms several complaints have reached this office of cars . . . switching back at various points and passengers being compelled to stand in the rain. In the future whenever it is necessary to switch back during stormy weather, trainmen must allow passengers to wait in the car until the following car has reached a point so passengers can conveniently transfer. When instructed to switch, you must change your destination signs at once and announce your destination to passengers.

• February 25, 1924: Passengers must not be permitted to alight from the front exit of inbound cars on inner tracks at the Embarcadero and Market St., nor from the front exit of outbound cars at Sansome and Market or Geary and Market on account of the danger of being struck by the overhang of cars on the outer track taking the curve leading off Market St. At the two latter points, the front gates should not be opened until after crossing the intersection into the safety zone.

• June 28, 1924: Traffic signals have been installed at Main and Market and at Drumm and Market streets and hereafter the movement of cars will be governed by these signals during the hours of the day when in operation.

• October 18, 1924: My attention has been called recently to many complaints of passengers being passed up deliberately by cars at various points. Any employee who deliberately passes up passengers (except for good and sufficient reason) is not working for the best interests of the company and will have to seek other employment. This also includes cars turning in (which must carry passengers) and conductors will announce the destination and issue emergency transfers to passengers who desire to continue the trip.

• December 3, 1924: Running ahead of schedule time is a violation of our company's rules and will not be tolerated. Our rush hour service can be greatly improved with your cooperation, in adhering to schedules, service will be more uniform, long headways will be eliminated, cars will not be bunched, and the public will be better served if every employee will do his share of the work. THERE IS NO EXCUSE FOR RUNNING AHEAD OF TIME, and severe discipline will be administered for any future violations.

• Commencing Sunday, February 1, 1925, three loops at the Ferry Terminal will be available for car operation, to be used as follows:
 Outer Loop—1, 2, 3, A, B, C, and D cars.
 Middle Loop—4, 8, 21, 32, J, K, and L cars.
 Inner Loop—5, 6, 7, 9, and 17 cars.
When leaving the Ferry Terminal, cars on the middle loop will have the right-of-way over cars on both the inner and outer loops. Inbound cars of the 4, 8, 21 and 32 lines will take the switch from the inner track to the outer track at Spear St.

• October 28, 1925: My attention has been called to the excessive speed at which cars are operated on Market St. between First St. and the Ferry. Also to the fact that motormen are not stopping their cars at the proper place at street crossings. Such operation not only violates the rules of the company but invites accidents and shows a disregard for public safety, and must be stopped at once. Any motorman reported for making a speedway of this district will be summarily dealt with.

• December 10, 1925: The lever switch for cars inbound at the south ferry terminus has been removed and an electric switch, operated by the towerman, installed in its place. Cars will be brought to a full stop before going over this point on electric switch on either track entering the terminus. You will be governed by the towerman's signal.

• April, 1926: The practice of looping trolley ropes under the grab handle on front end of car must be discontinued at once, for the reason that the practice results in the paint being worn off the grab handles. This is particularly noticeable on the white dash cars. A hook has been placed on the window sash at each end of the car and when trolley is down you will make use of the hook to keep trolley rope from obstructing the view of the motorman.

• May, 1926: CROCKER-AMAZON PARK MOTOR COACH Operators on motor coaches will punch the space "Short Trip" on all transfers issued for cash fares and these transfers will be good in both directions on either the Visitacion or Mission lines at point of contact. Conductors receiving these transfers will treat them as "Short Trip" transfers. Passengers presenting transfers on Mission or Visitacion Lines will be entitled to the "Short Trip" transfers, good on motor coaches. For instance, inbound Mission transfers, when validated over Visitacion Line, will be good on motor coaches in either direction at Geneva Ave. and Naples. Operators on motor coaches will take up all transfers presented for fare, and will under no circumstances validate them.

• February 8, 1927: From reports and complaints received, it is very evident that many of you have paid little or no attention to notices in the past, instructing you to wait at all times for a reasonable period for transferring passengers from other cars. Nothing creates a more unfavorable impression among our patrons than to deliberately run away from them at transfer points; and it is a practice which must and shall be discontinued. You are hereby warned that no leniency will be shown offenders in such cases from now on."

• April, 1928: It has come to my attention that many of you do not exercise the proper care when passing over electric switches, par-

SAFETY IN OPERATION was constantly emphasized by Market Street Railway. Monthly safety contests were held between divisions with a trophy as the prize. Above, a victorious division arrives at predecessor champion's home to pick up its award. Incidentally, this photo also shows well the uniforms of the 1928 era.

ticularly on Market St. Frequently reports come in of motormen taking these switches at full speed. This, as you well know, is a very dangerous practice and bound to result in serious accidents. You will please comply with the long-standing rule which says, YOU MUST PASS OVER ELECTRIC SWITCHES AT GREATLY REDUCED SPEED.

Safety

Market Street Railway's concern with the topic of safety was famous. Every month the various car barns competed for the Safety Trophy on the basis of fewest accidents per 1,000 car hours. A remarkable spirit of rivalry was created, and the ceremonies attendant upon one division's surrendering the coveted trophy to the new champion was duly photographed and published in *The Inside Track,* along with spirited exhortations to losers to do better the following month.

The company cooperated with newspapers and the California State Automobile Association in carrying out safety campaigns. Every day in the school year MSR gave 80,000 children their rides to and from school; that the company performed this task safely may be deduced from the fact that in 1926 this task was carried out without injury to one single child! The safety educational campaign took the form of dramatized photos showing what might happen to youngsters if they didn't "stop, look and listen" when getting off cars.

San Francisco has plenty of wet mornings, either rain fog. This could mean grief for streetcars due to slippery rai Oil and grease from autos, combined with heavy fog, wou serve to make every rail slippery, making a careless applic tion of brakes result in helpless skidding; were this to happe on a severe downgrade, the car would be out of control f dangerous moments and an accident would be almost ine table. Motormen were warned of this hazard time and tin again: "So we've got our work mapped out for us! We've g to have our cars under control at corners; keep our gon going; keep on putting sand on the rails."

Motormen were also cautioned to permit the car to come a complete halt before opening the front gate to allow passe gers to exit. They also were warned to expect passengers wh had just alighted from opposing cars to try to cross direc from behind that car to a point directly in front of them they bore down on the unsuspecting person; such caref motormen would bring their car to a halt to avoid an ac dent, and at all times would pass opposing cars at reduc speed if the opposing cars were starting up after a stop.

Conductors had their part to play in this continuing drar of safety. They were expected to watch back steps carefull and assist the aged, crippled or infirm to mount the step They were expected to be on the alert for suitcases placed aisles where others could trip over them. They themsel were warned how not to handle a throw switch, and also h correctly to handle it so feet would not be crushed.

THERE WAS NO THRILL like being sandwiched between rapidly rolling cars on the Four Tracks. As this photo indicates, there was a little more than two feet of space between the rival cars, and long experience with the dangers inherent in such a situation enabled natives to choose their waiting spots expertly.
Charles Smallwood

DERAILING on the Sloat Blvd. right-of-way in 1939, Ingleside car #1593 caused work for the Line Department as well as the wrecking crew.
Charles Smallwood

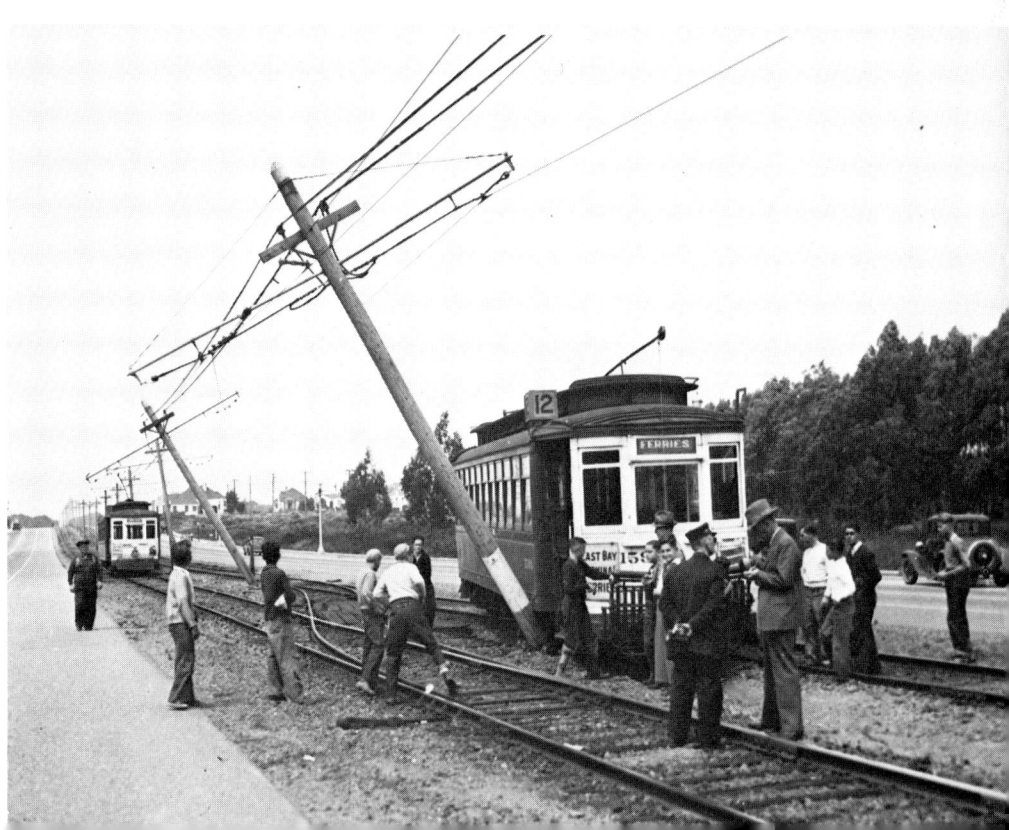

CONTESTING THE RIGHT-OF-WAY. Despite the many streetcar crossings in San Francisco, collision between cars at these points were rare. When the occasion did arise, however, the results were often spectacular!

(ABOVE) **AT HAYES AND VAN NESS,** MSR #21 car 117 jousted with a Muni "H" line vehicle. (BELOW) A 1300-class car on the #11 line got all the better of it when it argued with a Castro cable car.

BOTH: Charles Smallwood

IMMOVABLE OBJECTS, both stationary and rolling, caused grief to the cars. (ABOVE) Market Street Railway was just about six months old when Fillmore Hill car 653 broke her "wishbone" while descending steep Fillmore Hill and ran away. She came to rest smashed into a power pole between Green and Union Streets. It all took place on November 16, 1921. (BELOW) A bit of dirty work resulted from a collision between a #2 car and a garbage truck, at Sutter and Lyons, in 1935. **BOTH: Charles Smallwood**

Fill 'er Up!

EARLY ONE MORNING in June 1944, Balboa Line car 981 thought she was a motor coach, so she "drove" into a gas station at Arguello Blvd. and Balboa St., with the results shown here.
BOTH: Charles Smallwood

Education of Carmen

MSR's training school for prospective motormen and conductors was located in the 29th and Mission Barn. There a staff of veteran operators, aided by ingenious aids to education such as a skeleton car, completely operable, but which could be reduced to chaos by the mere flick of a switch by the instructor; the students would then be called upon to trace out the trouble and remedy it.

Not only fledglings but veteran carmen took advantage of the training course at 29th and Mission. Its refresher courses were open to all carmen.

In charge of the training school were a chief instructor and his staff of follow-up instructors. They planned out their puzzles with careful emphasis on those problems which might be expected to be encountered with greatest frequency, and a graduate from their rigorous program would be expected to rank high among all carmen on the system.

In addition to the skeletal car, 29th and Mission instruction hall contained a cutaway controller wired to a board with four clusters of electric lights; these gave the trainee motorman the exact effect every notch of the controller had on the car's motors. The lights represented the motors, and the flow of current was shown by their brightness or dimness.

Although the skeletal car did all its "running" while stationary, when the time finally came for it to be trundled off for scrapping the old car was able to make its last trip under its own power. The sight of the odd-appearing car coming down Mission St. must have startled all who were fortunate enough to behold its last move.

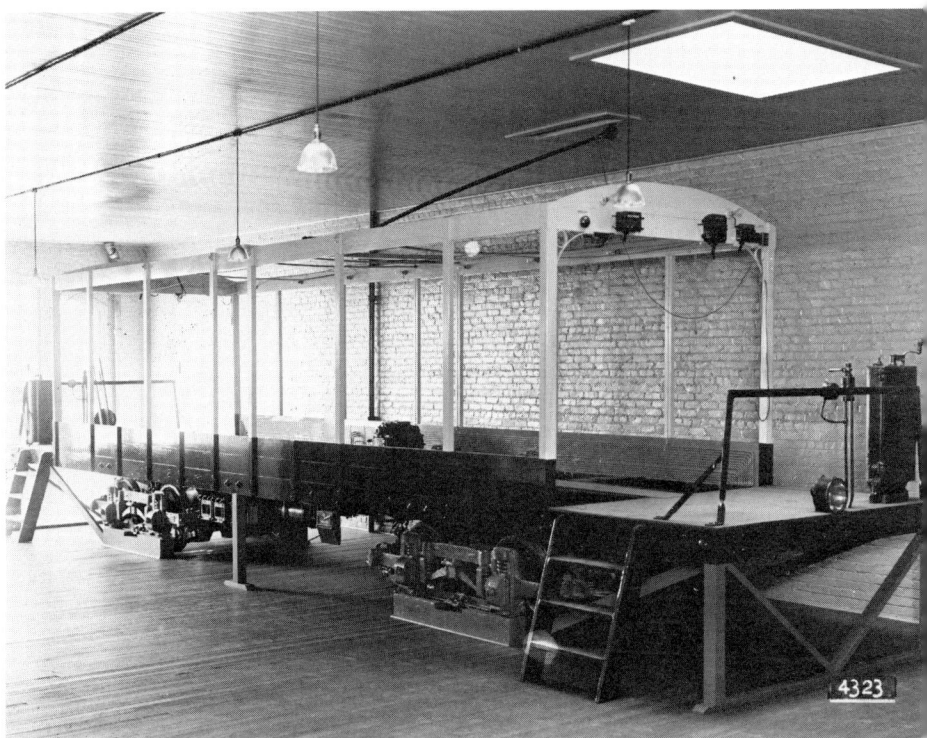

THIS SKELETON CAR was known as Instruction Car #01 and is seen at its home inside the 29th and Mission Car House in March, 1914. Countless thousands of men received their introduction to electric railway problems while undergoing training on this mockup. Car #01 went to Elkton Yard under its own power for scrapping in 1940.
United Railroads

Special Moves

From time to time, MSR was called upon to handle special movements which entailed transporting very large numbers of people. An example of this facet of operation was the Stanford-Idaho football game at newly opened Kezar Stadium on October 19, 1928.

Planning for the event took place weeks before, and on the day itself, MSR mobilized cars, equipment and crews from every one of its car houses. Making the event doubly interesting was the fact that the game was due to conclude on a Friday afternoon about five o'clock—just in time for the crowds to join the evening rush hour throngs.

About 75 extra cars were provided, of which 50 were stored at Lincoln Way and 13th Ave. yard, and 25 along the Lincoln Way main line, with temporary crossovers providing a way for the regular cars to run around them. A system of signal bells was set up, whereby a man stationed at the east end of Kezar Stadium could push a button to notify Lincoln storage yard to send more cars. This man received his cues from the luckiest MSR employee of all: an Oak and Broderick dispatcher who attended the game.

Inasmuch as five lines of Market Street Railway passed its gates, Kezar was probably one of the best-served stadia in the nation. These lines were 7, 17, 20, 32 and 33.

On days of Kezar Stadium events, MSR cars were protected by a full staff of company troubleshooters. Extra dispatchers, car repairmen, inspectors and police were on the job to move the tremendous throngs. Kezar had opened as a 30,000-seat facility, but its capacity was doubled in 1928 and that signaled MSR's greatest hours in moving crowds.

On March 13, 1931, the $1,250,000 Seals Stadium opened at 16th & Bryant, served by MSR lines 19, 22, 25, 27 and 30. Seating 25,000 for baseball and up to 50,000 for fights, the new arena was a great passenger generator for the company, which spent $20,000 on new switches and spur tracks to serve it.

Skip Stops

The industry-wide swing to skip-stop operation got its greatest impetus in World War I years when this very sensible operating aid became national in scope. In San Francisco, however, patrons expected and demanded a car stop at every street in the outlying residential districts. As a result, service was slower and more expensive than it should have been with a city of short blocks such as San Francisco.

With the coming of the depression years, MSR decided to put the skip-stop plan of operation back into service. By skipping every other street, cars saved electrical energy by going two blocks instead of one on the power required to start the car, and the speed of the car in the second block was much greater. Braking also was saved, prolonging the life of these parts. As a timesaver, the skip-stop was of inestimable value.

The skip-stop plan of operation was started in the Richmond and Sunset Districts on March 28, 1932, with lines 1, 2, 5, 7, 17 and 21 affected. The new Balboa St. line was added to the skip-stop family on May 15, 1932. On February 22, 1933, lines 16 and 29 between Islais Creek and Wilde Avenue were included in the skip-stop list; this greatly speeded service on Third St.

This brought the total of MSR car line skip-stop service to over 320 blocks, taking in most of the short block districts.

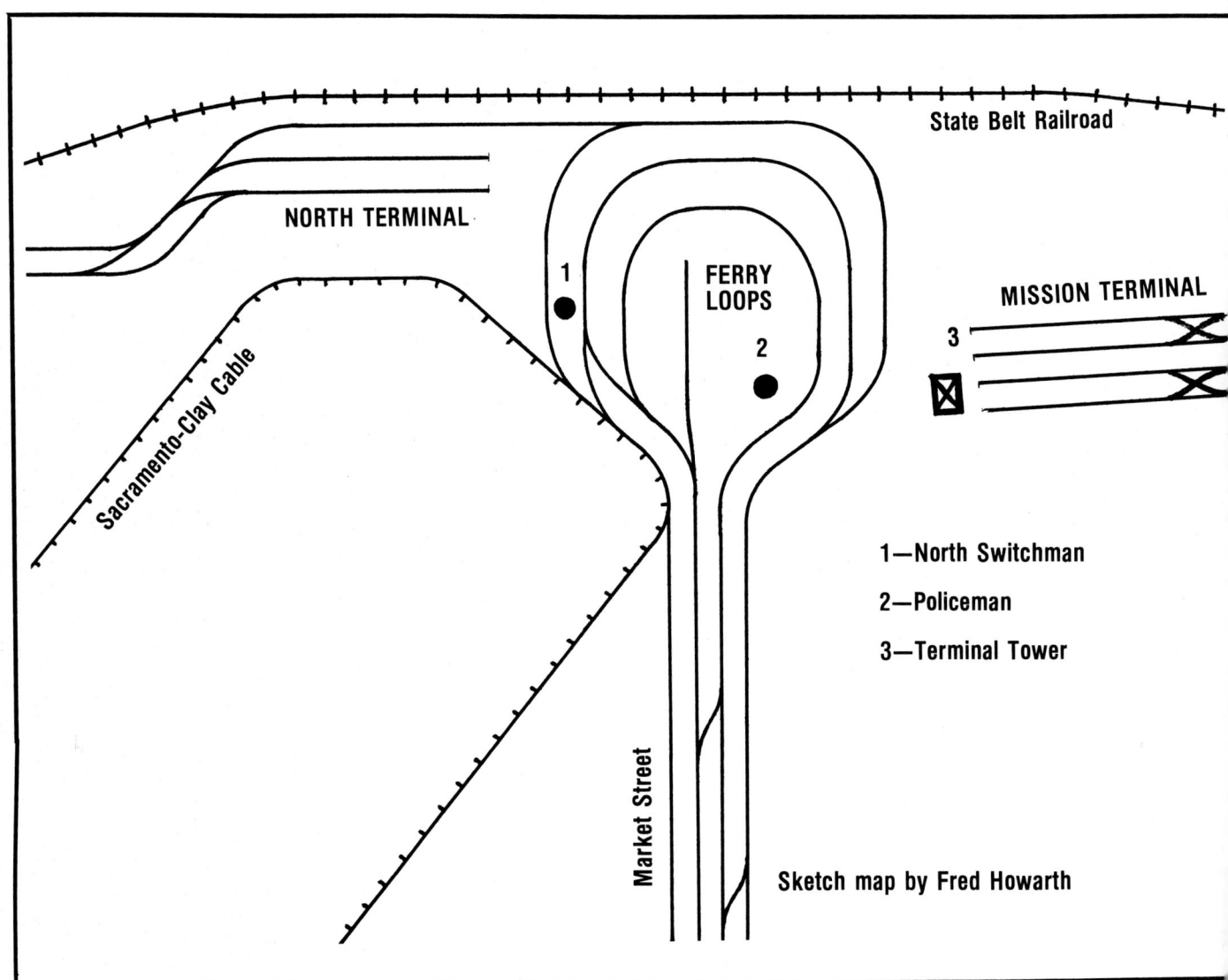

Ferry Terminal
1939

IMAGINE THE DISPATCHERS at the Ferry Building terminal keeping track of the loop and stub track operations in three directions, with departures as close as every nine seconds during the rush hour! The uses of the various tracks are described in the text on the following pages.

THE IMPRESSIVE Ferry Building and its multi-track streetcar and cable car loop terminal, in 1924. For several decades this was one of the world's busiest streetcar nerve centers. The pedestrian bridge over the north side of the Embarcadero from the terminal to Market Street (at left) became a casualty during the World War II scrap drives. **Charles Smallwood**

LOOKING NORTH at the Ferry Building Terminal from a perch near Howard Street, circa 1925, car 401 is seen at lower right.
Railway Negative Exchange

The Great Ferry Terminal

For decades the heart of San Francisco's street railway system was the ferry terminal at the foot of Market St. Here passengers to and from eastbay cities changed from cars to ferries or vice versa. It is said that at the peak of its service life, a million people weekly used the ferry terminal.

Before the 1906 disaster, car lines terminated here in stub end tracks with crossovers.

With the 1906 conversion of the Market Street car lines to electric operation, it became necessary to rearrange the trackage at the ferry to accommodate much greater patronage. A double loop was thereupon installed, which for years was ample. This was enlarged to a triple loop when cars of Municipal Railway entered the ferry scene in 1918.

Controlling the hundreds of cars which on weekdays swung around the loops was a vitally important part of the operation of a successful transit business, and how this problem was met with distinction deserves retelling.

Not only did the dispatchers at the ferry have to concern themselves with the loop alone, but also had the responsibility of controlling cars terminating on the four (originally five) stub tracks from Mission and Howard Streets to the south, as well as four (later cut to three) stub tracks serving lines to the north. Compounding all this electric operation to a point where a good dispatcher had, of necessity, to reach somewhat the same degree of traffic sophistication required of today's air traffic controllers was the fact that a cable line looped in the area and used common trackage for a short distance with the outside electric railway loop!

In 1905, United Railroads constructed a very substantial Starter's Room and placed it at the ferry loop to control the car traffic. Built of structural steel covered with heavy cast iron and ornamental galvanized iron this facility seemed quite adequate for all time. Increasing traffic, however, made it necessary later on to install a signal system to take care of increasing traffic, and the roof of the old Starter's Room was elevated and a circular-topped window placed on each of the four sides—making the structure a two-story building. Signals of various kinds, including electric switches for incoming cars, were operated from the upper floor. Still traffic increased and more signalmen were required; they were packed in the building like sardines in a box.

TWO SIGNAL TOWERS served the Ferry Building Terminal. The tiny ornate structure at right was constructed in 1905 and functioned until 1925, when the stylish, tile-roof building at left replaced it.
"Inside Track"

Increasing vehicular traffic along the Embarcadero made it prudent for the Harbor Commission to construct a subway under the Ferry Loop for autos and trucks, so more changes became necessary. Market Street Railway in 1925 built a handsome new building between the loop and the end of the Mission Terminal tracks; all signal wires, electric switch controls, telephone wires and clock wires were put underground—all controlled from the new building which also housed that all-important official, the Loop Superintendent.

The new building was also substantial: concrete foundations; one-inch stucco on outside walls; 3/8" pine veneer on all walls and ceilings; plate glass; solid brass hardware; and a real tile roof. This new building was designed and built by MSR's Engineering Department.

Trackage in the triple loop was sufficiently flexible so that dispatchers could juggle cars when necessary to keep them on schedule. A disabled car could be put on a stub track inside the loop, where mechanics (stationed at the loop permanently along with a wrecker truck) were usually able to get it functioning again.

Also prominent at the ferry loop were two other small structures. Facing Market Street was a shelter wherein one of the city's finest made his headquarters; from this vantage point he was ever available to unsnarl traffic, provide authoritative right-of-way for cars vs. autos, and, in general, lend a benevolent air to the entire proceedings. To the north was another shelter for the northside switchman, whose duty it was to guide cars to the proper track emerging from the loop.

THE MISSION TERMINAL stub tracks adjoined the signal tower at the Ferry Building terminal. View was taken in 1930.

Stubbing at the north side of the loop were the lines of both MSR and Muni from that part of the city. Muni was represented by its "E" Line whose little steel center entrance cars traversed the hilly reaches out Union Street. MSR's #16-Third St. Line also made its terminus here. And alongside, looping through the area on tracks which actually merged with those of the outer loop for a short distance, was MSR's Sacramento-Clay cable line.

At its height, the ferry loop was one of tractiana's outstanding operations. Turning back the clock to that era, let's peer into this seeming maze of cars:

The tower at the loop controlled all cars on the loop, on the Mission St. side and on the north side. A dispatcher was always on duty and cars were placed and started by a system of bell signals. Switchmen at the several switches of loops and crossovers placed the cars according to these bell signals. Loading points were marked on the pavement, and each line had its own stopping point. Open in front of the dispatcher was a run book showing the time all cars were due to leave; when cars got out of their proper order, he returned them to their place either by diverting them to another loop or by setting them on the stub track. Repairmen and oilers were regularly assigned to the loop; they inspected and lubricated cars and made needed light repairs. A wrecking crew was at one side, ready to speed to any point in the downtown area.

In front of this dispatcher was a series of telegraph senders operating the bells at seven different points; switchmen at those points responded to his signals by buzzers. The tower man, with the aid of field glasses, could inspect Market Street quite a ways up; many times he was the first to spot accidents or breakdowns and get the wrecking crew on its way. Beneath him, on the first floor, the superintendent (who was in direct charge of the ferry terminals as well as of all lines in the congested downtown district) had his office. Under the center of the loop was the large pit formerly used by cable machinery; this was utilized to store emergency and repair material as well as serving as headquarters for the terminal operating force. As of 1909, the force constantly on duty at the terminal consisted of one tower man, two starters on the ground, two switchmen, an oiler, a repairman and a wrecker attendant. At that time, 173 cars passed around the loops in rush hours of average days.

The general rearrangement of the ferry terminal in conjunction with the construction of the auto subway resulted in even more efficient operation which continued up to the fateful day, January 15, 1939, when approximately half the cars formerly terminating at the ferry were rerouted permanently to their new terminus at the Eastbay Terminal. Thereafter the crowds of hurrying commuters, so much a part of the ferry terminal scene, dwindled to virtually nothing, and cars arrived and departed with but few passengers. The three loops became two, and with the successive abandonment of former MSR car lines after the merger of September 29, 1944, even a single loop finally became superfluous. The final crusher came with the construction of the Embarcadero Freeway, whose monstrous presence today has completely obliterated the once busy and unique ferry terminal trackage.

THREE OPERATIONS used parallel tracks on the north side of the Ferry Building terminal. At left, State Belt Railroad of California locomotive #1 pushes freight cars past the building's entrance, while a Muni E car and a MSR #16 car lay over at their stub track terminal, in 1939. Gone are the trolleys and the pedestrian overpass; the steamers were replaced by diesel locomotives, and today the much-maligned Embarcadero double-deck Freeway covers this site. **Warren K. Miller**

The Ferry Building

THE MANY ARCHES of the Ferry Building enhanced this formidable structure. In this 1932 photo, the Mission Street terminal is in the foreground. Note car 1504, which bore longer platforms (along with 1502), in left center.　　　　　　　　　　　　　　　　　　　　　　　　　　　**Railway Negative Exchange**

FOR THE MANY who savored beholding streetcars in quantity, lower Market Street was ever a rare delight, as witness this photograph, taken in 1935. Imagine watching nearly 900 cars passing in both directions in a rush hour! **Paul Ward**

The Roar of the Four

THE "ROAR OF THE FOUR" was heard on Market Street as nowhere else in the land. From the Ferry to Castro Street the four tracks carried the heaviest streetcar traffic of any city in the world—Market Street Railway's White Front cars on the inner tracks, Municipal Railway's cars on the outer. This 1937 view looks down Market Street from First. **Charles Smallwood**

(ABOVE) **A SCENE** in July, 1937. (RIGHT) A view in 1937 wherein car roofs make the pavement hard to find! **BOTH: Paul Ward**

‡

The glory that was Market Street When The Roar of the Four added its obligato to the symphony of the busy city

‡

The Tower at Spear Street

FOR MANY YEARS a tiny tower (middle left) perched atop a pole at Market and Spear Streets, two blocks from the Ferry loop. The job of the man in that tower was to sort out the steady stream of streetcar traffic heading down the inside track to the Ferry and see to it that certain lines' cars were shifted to the outer track so as to be on the correct track of the three at the loop. This switching operation further slowed the already glacial procession of cars in rush hours and was the subject of spirited newspaper campaigns seeking to speed traffic on lower Market. This photo, of 1937 vintage, bore the following caption:

> "An illustration of how impossible it is to speed up streetcar traffic on Market Street under existing conditions! Down on lower Market, ferry-bound cars, in some instances, are switched from the inside to the outside track. This allows them to make the ferry loop in the same relative position at all times so passengers will not be confused. But look what it does to the other street cars! Note the car in the center switching to the outside track—while cars on TWO tracks behind it come to a full stop waiting for the switch to be completed. Everything has to wait!"

(LEFT) **EVEN IN OFFPEAK HOURS,** streetcar traffic on lower Market Street was intense, as shown in this 1936 photo. Taken at Market and Eddy Streets, the #31 Line car in the foreground is very effectively holding up outbound cars—while it, in turn, is delayed by a long procession of cars heading for the Ferry. In rush hour peaks, the situation greatly worsened, appallingly enough.

(BELOW) Third and Market in 1929. Note the monolithic streetcar loading zone visible at lower right.
BOTH: Charles Smallwood

(ABOVE) **OPERATION** could be difficult, if not hazardous, as witness this scene on Second Street between Harrison and Bryant Streets, in January, 1936. Construction of vehicle approaches to the Bay Bridge made this necessary. The car is an ex-Williamsport 725-class on the #28 Line. MSR shared Second Street with Southern Pacific (outer tracks) in this area.
Market Street Railway

(RIGHT) **DEMONSTRATORS** could also slow service. Here, Ninth, Polk & Larkin car 788 finds herself in the middle of one in front of the Main Library, on Larkin Street, 1930.
Randolph Brandt

BADGES IN THE SHAPE of the company's emblematic shield capped these 1927 era uniforms of Market Street Railway carmen.
Charles Smallwood

IMMEDIATELY TO THE NORTH of the Ferry loop was the terminal for the Sacramento-Clay cable line, a stone's-throw from the MSR #16 and Muni E line stub tracks. The loop track for the line at one point ran INSIDE part of a Market Street electric car line loop track. Note the conductor near the front of the car lifting the ''gypsy'' lever, a device used to bring a low cable up to sufficient height to be seized by the grip jaws.
Charles Smallwood

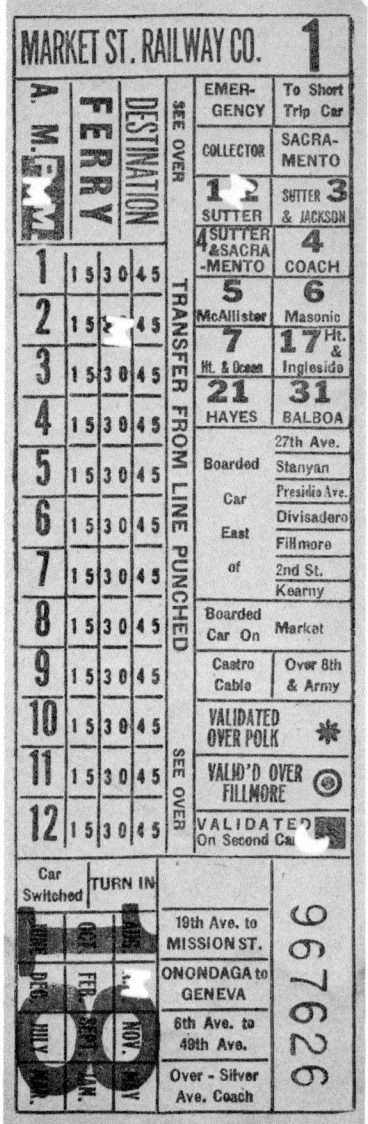
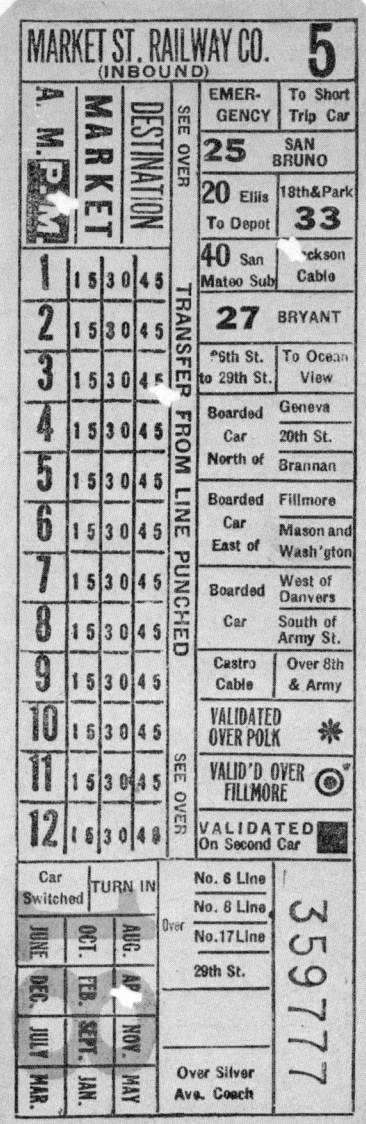

Transfer Sampler

SAMPLES of transfers used circa 1935. All used same back seen at left.

393

THESE TRANSFERS are very early in MSR's life. (ABOVE) One dating from 1923. (BELOW) Circa 1925.

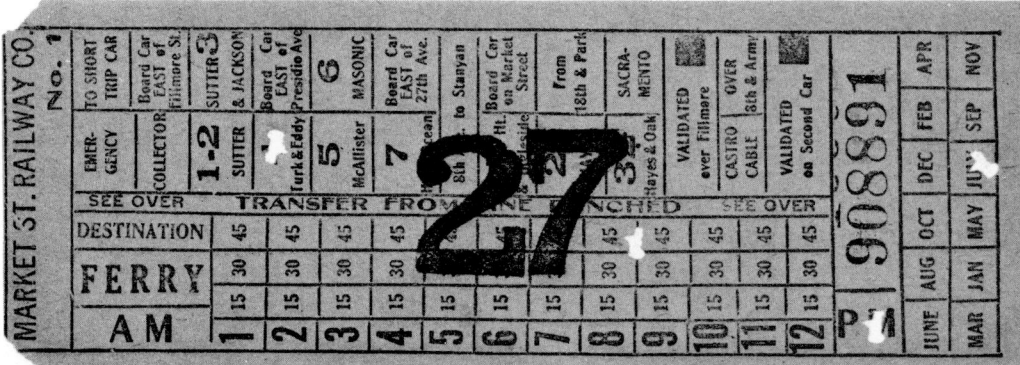

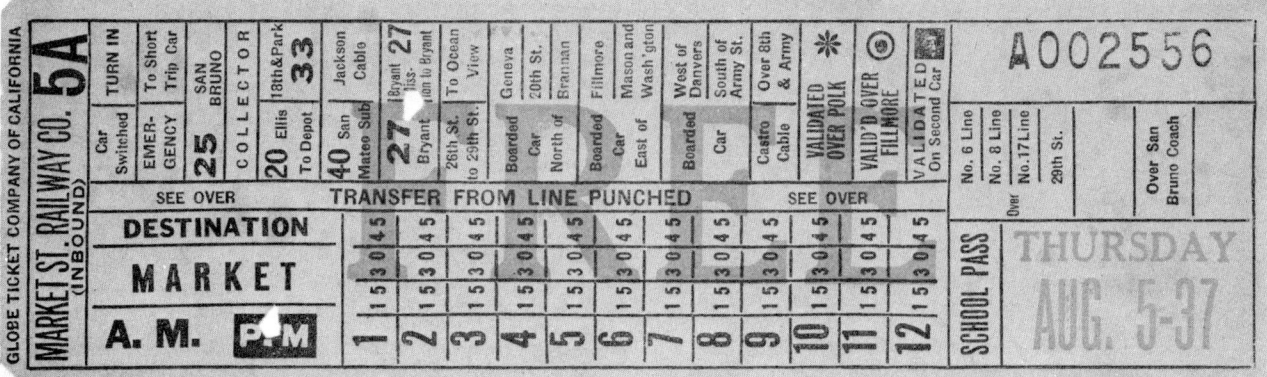

HERE ARE MSR transfers used in the 1937-38 days when the company was doing its best to increase revenues.

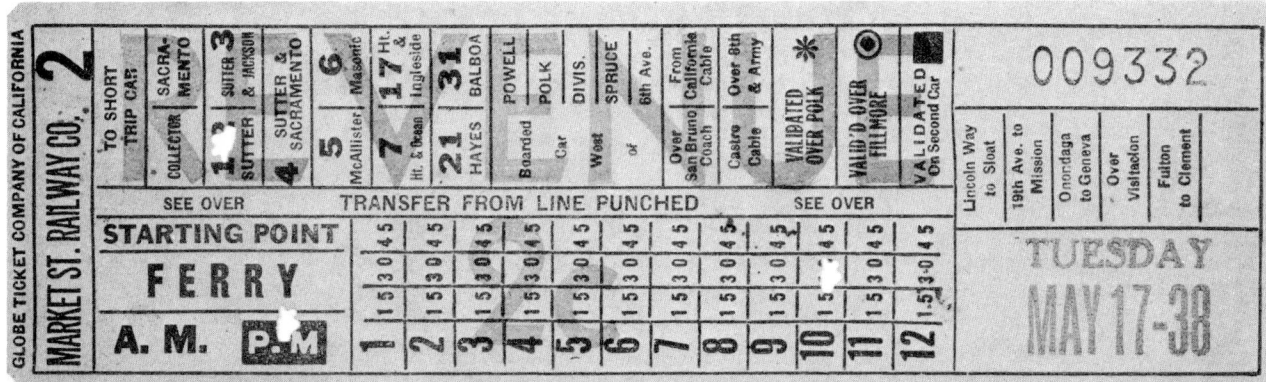

Tickets & Passes

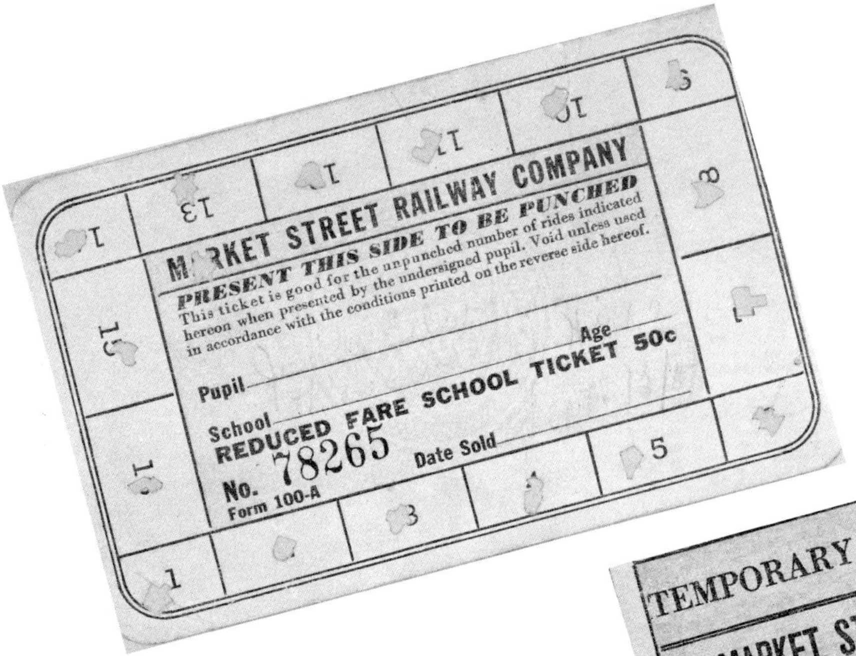

A SMILE at the crucial moment of collecting the fare was sure to please the gentler sex, and conductors with gallantry in their hearts were a big public relations asset to the company. C. 1928.　　**Charles Smallwood**

RELAYING MSR TRACK on Mission Street in the mid-1930s. This view looks south between 16th and 17th Streets. Note thermit rail joint welding setup in the foreground. Compressor car #0918 sits in the background. **Charles Smallwood**

MUNICIPAL RAILWAY BUILT the outside tracks on Market Street from Geary to Van Ness in 1918. In this scene a United Railroads #17 Line car carefully shoulders its way past workmen constructing the Muni tracks between Hyde and Leavenworth. The Municipal Railway's J and K lines began operation over the new rails on June 1, 1918. **Charles Smallwood**

Laying Track the MSR Way

THE MANY MILES OF TRACK on which cars of MSR rode swiftly and well represented much money, much hard work by the Engineering Department, and much dedicated and persevering research by the men who were devoting their life's work to this subject.

W.B. Farlow wrote an excellent series of articles on MSR's track in *The Inside Track*. As a matter of record, his first article appeared in Volume 1, Number 1, of MSR's monthly employees magazine; at the time the new magazine had no name. This may accent the importance attached by MSR administrative officers to the importance of the company's track construction and maintenance.

From the Farlow articles we have excerpted the material used in this chapter.

The year 1921 saw MSR's Engineering Department rebuild slightly more than six miles of track; 31,874 lineal feet of single track, to be exact. This work was not as simple as, on the face of it, it might seem. To carry out this work it was necessary to handle 17,590 cubic yards of earth for trench excavation; 16,893 cubic yards of rock for ballast and paving (all rock was quarried and crushed by the railway); then transporting and placing 15,937 redwood ties 6"x8"x8' long. This was followed by the laying of 63,748 lineal feet of steel rail weighing a total of 1,126 tons; each rail was 50 feet long. A total of 1,275 joint plates, each joint requiring 12 bolts (a total of 15,300 bolts) and each bolt had to be carefully tightened. To conduct the return negative current, each joint had four copper bonds—a total of 5,100 bonds to be pressed in place. A total of 63,748 rail spikes were necessary to fasten the rails to the ties. To keep the rails accurately in standard gauge, some 3,187 tie rods were emplaced at proper intervals. Over 25,500 sacks of cement were needed and 286,866 square feet of various kinds of paving were laid.

The above is for single track in city streets. More complex work was required at considerable greater expense when special work was renewed; switches, crossings and complex curves all meant more work and expense.

Market Street Railway in 1921 took over a system which had been constructed many years before. Much of the work of MSR's Engineering Department, therefore, was devoted to the reconstruction of track. Only one major track building project was to be carried through by MSR: the Balboa Extension in 1931.

The first step in rebuilding a stretch of MSR trackage was for the engineers to walk over the affected segment, noting carefully any and every condition which would affect their estimate of costs involved. A study of engineering records was next carried out to determine the type of construction of the existing track.

Where cable construction was involved, where a rebuilding would indicate electric traction, the removal of the old trackage would be a big job in itself; heavy yokes and massive concrete rope channels (and, in some cases, old sheave pits to be filled in) all escalated the cost.

With the estimate carefully worked out, it was then submitted to the MSR president. If he approved it, an authorization covering the necessary work was issued.

Once the authorization was received, engineers started the project rolling. Surveyors were sent out to run grades over the existing track and paving; rod readings were taken at 50-foot intervals except at street intersections where they were taken every 10 feet; readings were taken on each curb, gutter, two feet away from each outside rail and on each outside curb. This added up to eight readings at right angles to the track at every reading location.

With the field work complete, the notes of the surveyors were worked up and the elevation at each point was determined in relation to the city engineer's official grade.

This work was then plotted on a drawing which was submitted to the city engineer's office for approval. After approval and return, MSR's Engineering Department then made all necessary shop drawings for the project.

A temporary side track, built alongside the affected trackage, was then laid on top of the pavement for the use of work cars and other construction equipment, leaving one track free for passenger cars to be used by cars running in both directions between portable crossovers.

The first step in the physical removal of old track was to cut a groove in the paving two feet outside of the rail. This was done by a work car equipped with an adjustable cutting tool affixed to the underframe; the cutting tool could be swung up out of the way when it was not required. This cutting car moved down the street at about four miles per hour and caused considerable fireworks; the cutting point was burned off about every 500 feet. The paving was then plowed up by a work car pulling a plow very similar to those used back on the farm. The pavement was then loaded onto a gondola car by hand and was taken to the Market and Valencia Yard for possible further use.

An especially ingenious device known as an asphalt scoop was used wherever possible. This was mounted on small wheels and was pushed ahead of the work car; the scoop lifted a long ribbon of asphalt and automatically loaded it on the

CRANE #0130 is hard at work at Market and Valencia Yard in October, 1928.   S.F. Public Utilities Commission

NIGHT WORK on Market Street, near Eighth Street, in 1927, as crane #0130 removes a section of worn track. The crane's three-window front was changed to a single window in 1929.

Market Street Railway

k car, sometimes making a pile as high as the cab of the
 car without a single human hand touching the opera-

he location of the temporary crossovers was of great im-
ance, for the regular passenger cars had to be kept on
dule insofar as this was feasible. It was up to the Superin-
lent of Transportation to determine how far apart these
sshoppers" should be. They were installed on top of the
 and pavement and cars using them had to be operated at
emely slow speed as there was a lift of about six inches in-
ed to get the car onto the crossover and over to the other
 (or to remain on its own track if it was the other track
g reconstructed).

ny concrete in and about old track was broken up by a
0-pound drophammer mounted on a work car; this ap-
ed much like the familiar pile driver and after its passage,
old concrete was completely shattered.

t this point the crane car, operating from the side track,
 into the picture. It clamped onto a rail and lifted it
ly several feet up out of the trench; a number of old ties
ld be clinging to the length of rail and these were dis-
ged by the use of sledgehammers. The freed rail was
 dropped back into the trench for the time being. This

operation was repeated until all of the rails in the construction segment were free of ties. Those ties still embedded in the trench were cleared by running the plow along the edges of the trench.

Now came the process of salvaging whatever old material might be used again. Tie rods, for instance, were taken to Market and Valencia Yard and rehabilitated by cutting out all bad parts and welding what was left, making a suitable new tie rod. Joint plates were removed, being placed in stock at Market and Valencia. All usable old bolts were rethreaded and put back in stock. The old rails were loaded onto cars and taken to Market and Valencia where they were sorted and used further in maintenance or scrapped. Old ties were taken to Bryant Store Yard where they were sorted; the good ones were used in maintenance work, while the bad ones were cut into 32-inch lengths to be used as firewood at the Market and Valencia bitumen plant. The old copper bonds were scrapped for copper.

The old concrete that had been broken up by the drophammer and plowing was piled to one side of the trench and was later crushed by a portable crusher car running on the rebuilt track and discharged directly into the trench for ballast.

With the removal of the concrete from the open trench, the earth was removed by hand and loaded onto 22-cubic-yard work cars until the trench was nine feet wide and two feet deep. This earth was hauled to Kentucky Dump, where an unloader, similar to a large hoe, pushed the earth off the cars; Kentucky Dam, at 3rd and 23rd, was adjacent to Kentucky Car House and was at one time a deep hole. Constant dumping of earth over the years resulted in the final filling in of this property.

Ready for New Track

The new track trench, now complete, was ready for its new material. First came the ballast rock to a depth of eight inches; this rock was quarried and crushed at MSR's quarry at Daly City. Carried in motor gondolas, the ballast was discharged from the side as the car was moving along the temporary track, thus spreading it more or less evenly along the floor of the trench.

Next came the new 6"x8"x8' redwood ties which came from Bryant St. Store Yard aboard work cars; these were distributed in the trench on two-foot centers. The new rails then arrived from Geneva Ave. Yard; these were 106-lb. Lorain steel, each 60-foot length tipping the scales at 2,120 pounds. Rails were then spiked to ties with tie rods spaced every 10 feet, accurately holding the new rails in gauge. Temporary joint plates held the double line of new rails together.

More rock was then added and pneumatic tampers in skilled hands forced the new rock under the ties; this brought the new rails to exact grade and line. The temporary tie pla[tes] were then removed and four concealed copper bonds w[ere] pressed into place. Joint plates were then permanen[tly] installed and all bolts were thoroughly tightened.

The rock between the ties under the rail was dug out an[d] concrete stringer base was laid under the rails. This strin[ger] was mixed and placed direct by the concrete mixer fr[om] chutes. Then came a cushion for the header blocks, pla[ced] along each side of each rail; this was composed of one p[art] cement and four parts sand and was mixed and placed [by] hand. The basalt block headers were then laid along each s[ide] of each rail, flush with the top of each rail.

Next came the six-inch-thick concrete paving base co[m]posed of one part cement, three parts sand, seven parts ro[ck] mixed to the proper level for the bitumen top. This was [fol]lowed by grouting in the basalt block headers with a mixt[ure] of one part cement and two parts sand; this was mixed b[y] machine and poured between the blocks with a spout buck[et].

Finally came the bitumen (asphalt) paving. The concr[ete] base had to be swept thoroughly clean to permit a good b[ond] between the concrete and the bitumen. Header blocks w[ere] painted with hot liquid asphalt. The bitumen arrived fr[om] Market and Valencia Yard in special boxes each of which h[eld] about one cubic yard. The work car hauling these boxes ha[d a] collapsible crane for handling the boxes and placing the[m in] the proper location on the street; the car also returned [the] empty boxes to Market and Valencia for future use. [The] bitumen was smoothed with the proper tools and rolled w[ith] hot rollers.

THERMIT WELDING became standard policy in 1931, when the Sutter Street track underwent rebuilding as seen here. One mold has been lit off while the setup at the rail joint in the foreground awaits ignition. **Charles Smallwood**

(ABOVE) **RERAILING SUTTER STREET** from Van Ness to Market in 1930 required crane #0131 and dump #0930, seen near Hyde Street. Note both cars are on a temporary third track alongside the curb. A temporary crossover detours passenger streetcars around the construction.

(BELOW) **THREE WORK CARS** are visible in this Market Street scene circa 1930, as the inbound MSR (center) track is being rebuilt. A MSR Haight Street car operates on Muni's outer track.   **BOTH: Market Street Railway**

The final cleanup of the street ended the busy task. Old and new material of virtually every kind, from old cement sacks to 60-foot steel rails, had to be picked up and returned to their proper place in stock.

Several track rebuilding jobs were usually in progress at any given time back in the 1920s; the various gangs worked in follow-up manner. As one street was completed, another one started, making the work of the track crews never-ending.

Starting in 1931 with the Sutter St. rebuilding job, Market Street Railway went over to the use of thermit welds to create long stretches of jointless track. By the thermit welding process, superheated liquid steel at a temperature of approximately 5,000 degrees (twice that of ordinary molten steel) was joined to the preheated ends of the two rails being joined. The new steel's great heat melted those ends and amalgamated with them so as to form a single homogeneous mess—a true fusion weld. After the weld cooled, the excess metal above rail level was cut or filed off, and the final finish to an absolutely true running surface was made with a "Vixen" track file operated by two men.

The last and largest piece of new track construction by Market Street Railway was its Balboa Extension, running from Divisadero St. to 30th Ave. Performed in the very depths of the depression, the job was in answer to the approval by the voters of a new franchise to MSR; in the campaign MSR promised the Balboa Extension and its word was as good as its bond. This major job cost about $400,000 and kept a small army of men at work during the winter of 1931-32.

Opening for service on Sunday, May 15, 1932, the Balboa St. Extension involved new roadbed, new ties, new paving, new poles and wires—even new cars. It was thoroughly modern in every respect. The final bits of work at Turk and Divisadero streets saw all the various gangs bunching up to complete the finishing touches; a street literally covered with workmen was the result.

Market and Valencia Yard

When The Market Street Cable Railway was constructed in 1883, its power house was located on a big parcel of property at Market and Valencia streets, the location being, ideally, in the approximate center of the cable company's system of lines. After the great 1906 disaster and the subsequent conversion of cable lines to electric operation, the successor company, United Railroads of San Francisco, retained these spacious grounds and there established its paving plant as well as its special work track center.

Over the ensuing years, here was manufactured that black, tarry concoction known as "bitumen," used in paving around the track area (and two feet outside, as per city ordinance).

This bitumen, while still very hot, was loaded into large wooden boxes which were then covered with canvas tarpaulins to keep the heat from dissipating and hurriedly placed on small single truck open work cars (known as "bitumen cars") which were speedily dispatched to the proper location where paving work was in progress. The bitumen cars were fitted with a crane operated by hand, and these unloaded the bins of bitumen at the job. The car later returned and picked up the empty bins.

Market Street Railway Company in the 1920s began using motor dump trucks in hauling paving material from Market and Valencia Yard to the various jobs in progress, but the trucks did not replace the fleet of little bitumen cars; they

FIRST ON THE SCENE and last to leave any track job was this public relations-oriented "Improving San Francisco" warning sign. **Charles Smallwood**

were familiar sights well into the 1930s as they sped hither and yon over the company's lines with their smoking cargo.

The rail and special trackwork operations of MSR had been located at Market and Valencia Yard almost since the predecessor companies' very inception. Market and Valencia Yard continued to operate until well into the 1930s; by that time the property, on the fringe of the downtown district, became much too valuable to be used for such purposes.

A landmark for many years at this location was a portion of the great smokestack which once served the steam boilers of the old Market Street cable powerhouse. The top portion of the stack had tumbled to the ground during the great shake of 1906, but the stub lasted for many years and was used as the chimney of the paving plant. The pits of the paving plant were subsurface remnants of boiler and steam engine foundations of the old power plant.

Due to the spaciousness of the grounds, many large items such as poles were stored there; poles for the Turk and Balboa streets extensions were made at the yard in the early 1930s these poles were cast in concrete and utilized old cable line slot, rails running through the center of the pole for reinforcement. Although Municipal Railway made use of concrete poles on most of its system, those poles cast at Market and Valencia Yard were the only concrete poles ever used by MSR.

Market & Valencia Yard

THE COMPANY'S paving plant and its special trackwork manufacturing facility were located at Market & Valencia Yard, seen here as it looked in 1928. The great smokestack is a relic from pre-1906 earthquake days; it originally was part of the cable powerhouse, operated by steam power.

S.F. Public Utilities Commission

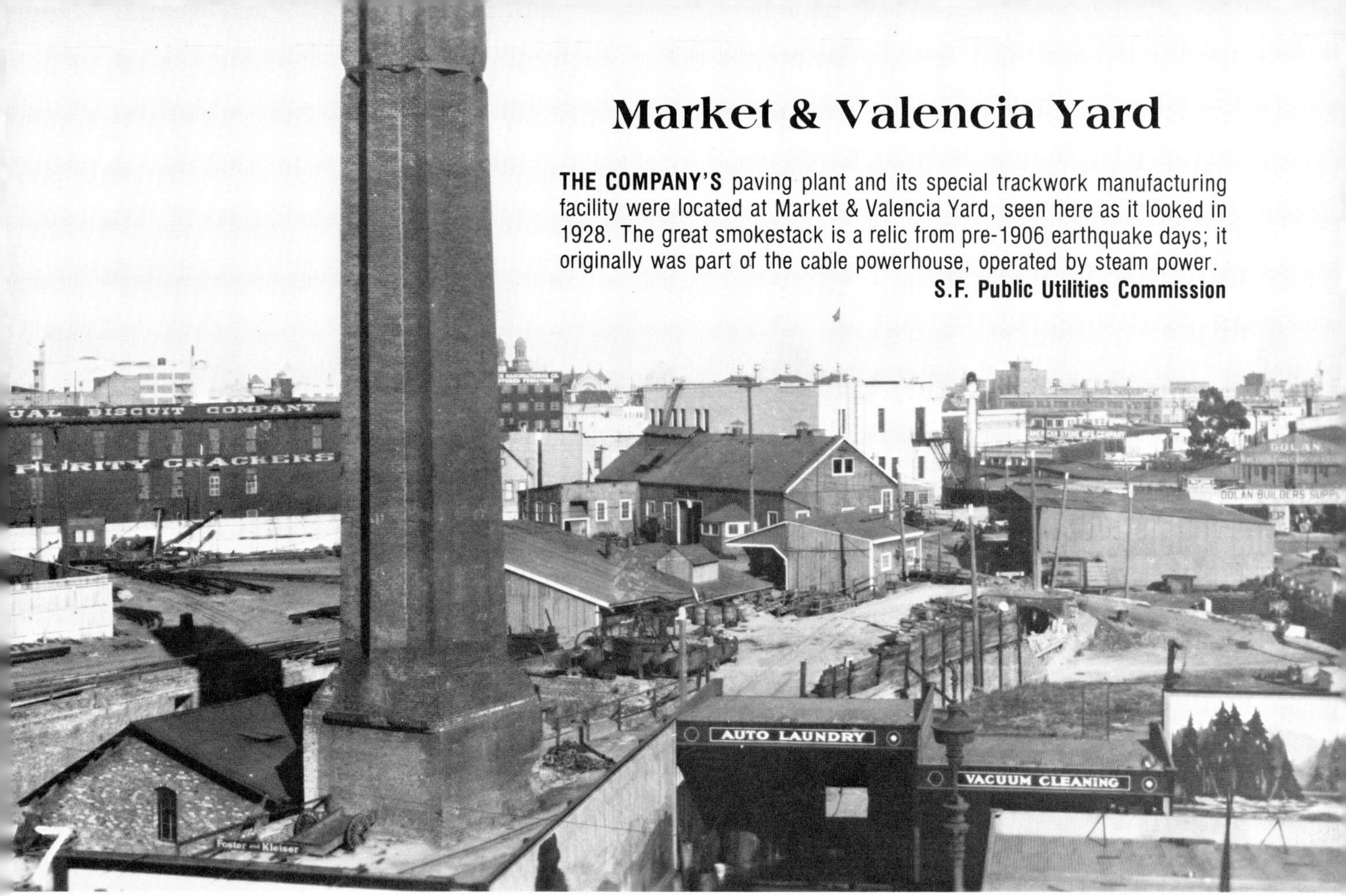

(BELOW) **THIS WAS THE PART** of Market & Valencia Yard which was devoted to manufacturing special trackwork.

S.F. Public Utilities Commission

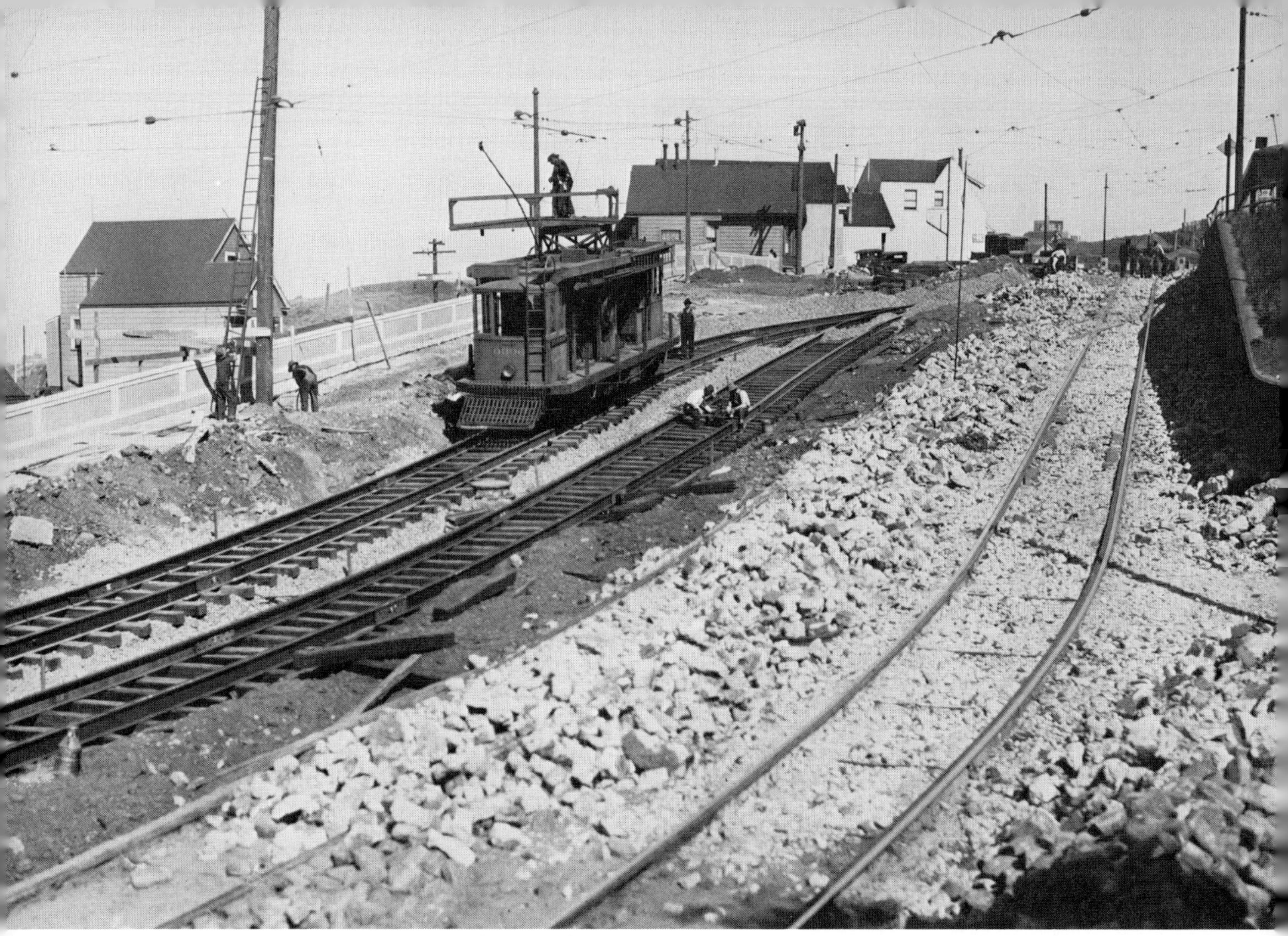

Upper Market Switchback

HARD AT WORK stringing wire over the relocated switchback on upper Market Street, at Clayton, in May of 1927, was line car #0306. Note this car's unusual three-window front.

(BELOW) **A SEDAN PAUSES** on the upper leg of the switchback as differential dump #0929 spreads ballast rock on the new track.
          BOTH: Charles Smallwood

HEAVY TRAFFIC during business hours made it advisable to perform much of MSR's special work renewals at night. Above, a 1925 scene shows the reconstruction of the diamond at Kearny and Sutter Streets. **Market Street Railway**

AN EARLY COMPRESSOR truck of MSR, mounted on a Ford Model-T chassis. **Market Street Railway**

ONLOOKERS ALMOST OUTNUMBERED the track crew removing the massive concrete and steel guideways on Stanyan Street from cable car days. **United Railroads**

Bryant Street Substation

BUILT IN 1893, the Bryant Street Substation furnished steam-generated direct current for the first electric cars of the old Market Street Railway. Its original equipment consisted of two 300-hp and two 600-hp engines, connected to six belt-driven 200 KW 550-volt generators. In 1896 a 1000-hp engine was added and three more 100-hp engines came in 1897. These four big engines were directly connected to eight generators with a rating of 400 KW each. This gave a total of 4400 KW (or about 5800 horsepower). Steam was furnished by 36 150-hp boilers. In 1911, six 1500-KW motor generator sets were installed, replacing the DC generators.

BOTH: S.F. Public Utilities Commission

The Power Picture

THE ELECTRICAL POWER distribution system of MSR was quite adequate for a large street railway system. Although much of the apparatus used for this purpose dated back to the original electrification of the old Market Street system in the mid-1890s, the energy supplied was both sufficient and reliable. Power failures during the Market Street Railway era were few and far between.

As was the case with many electric railways, Market Street Railway used 550-volt DC current.

The original power facilities used for generating electricity for the early trolley lines were actually steam-operated powerhouses. At one time there were five such steam-powered plants in San Francisco; they were as follows, listed in order of construction:

1. SAN FRANCISCO AND SAN MATEO ELECTRIC RAILWAY, located next to the original car barn of this pioneer road, on Sunnyside Ave. at Joost St. This opened in 1891 and was closed on December 21, 1900.

2. METROPOLITAN RAILWAY, also 1891 (a few months after the San Mateo road was established), and located adjacent to the company's car house on Carl St. This plant was not used after 1904.

3. MARKET STREET RAILWAY (original company); the pioneer plant of this system was located in the present brick building at Bryant and Division streets and was opened in 1893. The first drive between the steam engine and generators in this plant was by means of a manila hemp rope.

4. SUTRO RAILROAD. This rather small electric line which operated in the Richmond District had a small steam generating plant located in the northeast corner of the old Sutro Baths and Museum property at the Cliff House. This plant was the shortest-lived of all street railway power facilities in San Francisco, having been constructed in the latter part of 1896 and discontinued by 1902, when Sutro Railroad became part of United Railroads.

5. In the early part of this century UNITED RAILROADS, seeking to provide ample power to meet the increased demands of a greatly expanded electric railway system, con-

structed a large steam generating plant on the bay front at North Beach. This plant's output increased the company's power capacity so greatly that it was possible to abandon the small, obsolete plants of the pioneer San Mateo and Metropolitan roads; it did not, however, replace the Bryant and Division steam generating plant.

It is said the Bryant and Division plant was the first electric generating facility to reopen after the 1906 earthquake and fire; much of the downtown commercial power distribution then was direct current, so this large station was tied into those lines and thus supplied the only electric power in the stricken city for a time.

In later years, before the Market Street Railway days, the North Beach plant was sold by URR to Pacific Gas & Electric Company when the railway company established a firm policy of purchasing all its power.

Of all the properties and facilities of Market Street Railway Company that continued to exist and to function after the 1944 takeover by Municipal Railway, the substations were the most fortunate. At time of writing, all were either in daily use or are on standby status with the sole exception of the Millbrae substation, which was of no further use after the interurban line to San Mateo was abandoned in 1949.

Prior to the 1944 consolidation, much of Municipal Railway's power was purchased from MSR, especially for lines west of Twin Peaks and on lower Market Street; most of these lines are still running today. This situation, coupled with the fact that Municipal Railway replaced much of the streetcar service with trolley coaches, made necessary the retention of those power facilities which were in use.

LONG A LANDMARK in its busy neighborhood, Turk and Fillmore Substation was built to the colossal scale considered necessary in the era of its inception. Truly it was a cathedral of electricity. The exterior view was taken in 1921 as part of Market Street Railway's survey of its holdings. Inside was a mighty bank of motor-generator sets.
BOTH: S.F. Public Utilities Commission

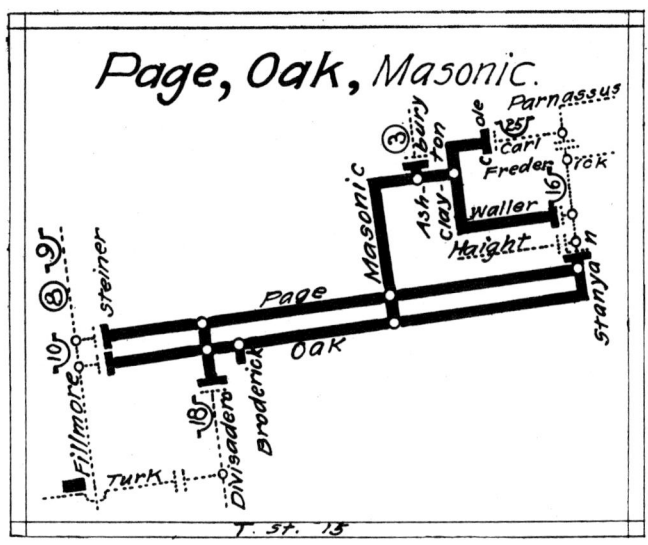

STARTING IN EARLY 1925, each substation feeder panel was equipped with a 4-in. by 5-in. map showing the sections of trolley lines fed by that feeder, with all branches and ends located by streets and corners.

The capacity of some substations had been increased, and that of others decreased, to conform to the company's load distribution. Downtown, Eighth Avenue and Geneva Substations had been increased by one machine each, while Turk Street and Bryant Street subs had each had one removed. This resulted in considerable shifting of feeder copper and made advisable the rearranging of sections fed by separate feeders.

These maps, like the sample shown above, enabled operators to memorize these changes, putting in front of them the information needed.

Substations

BRYANT STREET: Located at Bryant and Division streets, this substation was constructed by the original Market Street Railway Company in 1893 as a steam power plant. In 1911 the facility was downgraded to substation status. Equipment consisted of a halfdozen G.E. 1500 kw. motor-generator sets. The building still stands and today houses the Municipal Railway's Line Department.

When Bryant Station was completed in 1897, it was among the largest in the United States. A prominent engineer predicted that with its completion, the company would have sufficient power to supply its needs for all time to come. But by 1927 MSR's total capacity was about 48,000 hp—about eight times the old steam generating plant's top rating. The floor space of this station covered nearly a city block; in 1927 a station of similar rating could be contained in but five percent of that area. One 1927 boiler would equal all 36 of Bryant's, and AC current generators of up to 100,000 hp in that year would double the output of all fourteen generators in that old steam station. Time marches on!

TURK AND FILLMORE: Located on the southeast corner of Turk and Fillmore streets, this substation was built by the original Market Street Railway Company in 1896. Capacity of this station was increased until 1910, when it had risen to 9,000 kw., provided by six General Electric 1500 kw. motor-generator sets. About 1925 one of these 1500 kw. sets was removed and installed in the Millbrae Substation to upgrade power on the San Mateo interurban line.

Motor-generator sets in this substation, oddly enough, were not owned by MSR but by PG&E and/or its predecessors. This substation was still in use into the 1970s and supplying power to Municipal Railway trolley coach lines in the western part of the city. It was one of the last old-time street railway substations still in daily use in western America.

GENEVA AVENUE: This substation is located in the southerly portion of the present Geneva Ave. car barn building. It was constructed in 1901 for the *San Francisco & San Mateo Electric Railway* (the city's first trolley line) and became the property of United Railroads in 1902 when that company absorbed the interurban firm. Equipment in this plant is comprised of three General Electric motor-generator sets of 1500 kw. capacity each.

Like the motor-generator sets at Turk and Fillmore Substation, these three are also owned by Pacific Gas & Electric. The equipment in this facility is still intact today. In the 1950s this substation was relegated to standby status, replaced on the line by a rectifier station at West Portal and by an automatic station on Russia St. in the outer Mission district.

EIGHTH AVENUE: Located on the west side of Eighth Ave. between Geary Blvd. and Anza St., this substation was built in 1921 to serve the numerous car lines in the Richmond District. Its equipment consists of one General Electric 1500 kw., 60 cycle, 600 rpm, 2500 amp., 600 volt rotary converter. This machine was built in 1914 to help supply power for the heavy streetcar traffic generated by the 1915 Panama-Pacific International Exposition; and was stored in the old North Beach power station until 1921 when it was moved into the then-new Eighth Avenue building. A second machine in use at this plant is a General Electric 2000 kw., 600 volt, 3334 amp., 514 rpm rotary converter, built and installed in 1924. This station was used into the 1970s by Municipal Railway supplying energy to several trolley coach lines in the area.

BAY SHORE: This substation was established in 1913 to step up power on Third St., San Bruno Ave. and Visitacion Valley. It contained two Westinghouse 400 kw. rotary converters. For more than 15 years the Bay Shore sub served faithfully, but increasing demand for power made it mandatory to construct the new San Bruno automatic substation in 1927. The latter put out 1500 kw. yet was much smaller. Bay Shore's old rotaries were scrapped, with the crane car proving very efficient in removing them; each converter weighed more than 17 tons.

DOWNTOWN: Also built in 1921 was this substation, on Stevenson St. near Second St. in the downtown area. Somewhat unique in that it used Westinghouse manufactured equipment, Downtown originally was equipped with two 2000 kw. machines. One was a 2000 kw., synchronous type, 600 volt, 3333 amp., 450 rpm, six-phase, 50 cycle rotary converter; the other was a 3000 kw., synchronous type, 600 volt, 6000 amp., 400 rpm, six-phase, 60 cycle rotary converter.

In the latter part of 1923, a new 3000 kw. rotary was ordered from Westinghouse and installed here. With the two 2000 kw. machines and the new 3000 kw. machine, total capacity was raised to 7000 kw. Before 1944, one of the 2000 kw. machines was removed; its disposition is unknown.

This station was still in use by Municipal Railway to supply energy to streetcar and trolley coach lines in the downtown area.

MILLBRAE: Built in 1903 and located on the San Mateo interurban line, this was the only former Market Street Railway power facility not in existence in the 1970s. As built, Millbrae Substation was equipped with two General Electric 500 kw. motor-generator sets. The substation was extensively damaged in the 1906 quake, but was back in operation by 1907.

About 1925 a General Electric 1500 kw. motor-generator set was moved to this station from the Turk and Fillmore Substation. This set, as well as the two original sets, was owned by Pacific Gas & Electric.

Interurban car service on the San Mateo Line was discontinued on January 14, 1949, causing the closing of the Millbrae Substation. It was subsequently dismantled.

SAN BRUNO AVENUE: This substation was MSR's newest, and also enjoyed the distinction of being the company's only fully automatic sub. It was built in 1927 as part of the project of upgrading service in the district served by the Railroad Ave., San Bruno Ave. and Visitacion Valley lines; another major undertaking was the double tracking of the San Bruno Ave. line at this time from Wilde St. to the county line. This substation has been closed.

Located near the junction of Railroad Ave. and San Bruno Ave., this substation cost $55,000. It was built of reinforced concrete and much effort was devoted to making it an architectural asset; even the cables were buried under a front lawn.

Some 25 protective devices were provided to protect this sub's equipment. In case a trolley wire broke and fell onto the rail, a high-speed circuit breaker opened in a fiftieth of a second; five seconds after the wire was removed, the circuit reclosed. Any overheating, runaway, flashover, etc., automatically shut down the station pending arrival of repair crews.

The "automatic" feature of San Bruno Sub was that it started up when demands for power were severe, and shut down when the load demand dropped, thus saving the losses of running "empty."

Most of the energy used by MSR was brought in from hydro-electric plants in the mountains at 100,000 volts AC. It was delivered to Bay Shore substation as of 1925 where it was redistributed at 12,000 volts AC to the various MSR substations. The substations then converted it to 550 volts DC suitable for the cars. Steam generating plants were on standby to pick up the load in case of a failure of the hydro-electric power.

The 100,000 volts was a far cry from the 550 volts originally produced by the small steam plants in the city. Had hydroelectric power been available from nearby locations, it could have been transmitted in the form of 550-volt DC energy, but coming as it did from originating points hundreds of miles distant, it would have been impossible to have transmitted it at 550 volts, for by the time the current reached San Francisco the resistance from the conductors would have left little or no volts when it reached the place to be used.

Of course, high voltage transmission has its own unique set of problems. One of the most difficult is that of insulating conductors from "grounds" or the common short circuit. Expansion and contraction from heat and cold sometimes cracks the insulators so that moisture creeps in and causes trouble. Dust settles on insulators and then in comes the fog, particularly in the bay area; mud is thus formed, and mud is a good conductor. The current thus travels over the insulator, sets the crossarm on fire which often burns off the top of the pole and permits the wires to cross, setting off a short circuit so violent as to often shut down all the power stations.

Small boys with kites could accomplish the same result. MSR one day in 1925 had its entire system closed down as the result of a cat's crawling into the high tension bus of the Downtown substation, grounding one phase. On another occasion, the White Front cars ground helplessly to a halt when a rat started to crawl across from a 12,000 volt switch to an adjacent I-beam in a substation; the current grounded through the rat's body—but, small consolation, that particular rat did this only once.

MSR was always reminding its platform men to be on the watch for anything which might seem to endanger a trolley wire, such as burning crossarms and pole tops, a kite or other foreign substance lodged in the high-tension conductors, and by removing a broken trolley wire from the rail. Motormen were frequently reminded of a number of other "No-No's" such as feeding up too fast, running over sectional insulators with power on, slugging a car unnecessarily, etc.

GENEVA AVENUE SUBSTATION. Adjoining Geneva Car House, this substation provided power for the Outer Mission and Ingleside areas. Both buildings still stand and are changed but little from these 1936 photographs, although the substation has been downgraded to a standby status in the recent past.
S.F. Public Utilities Commission

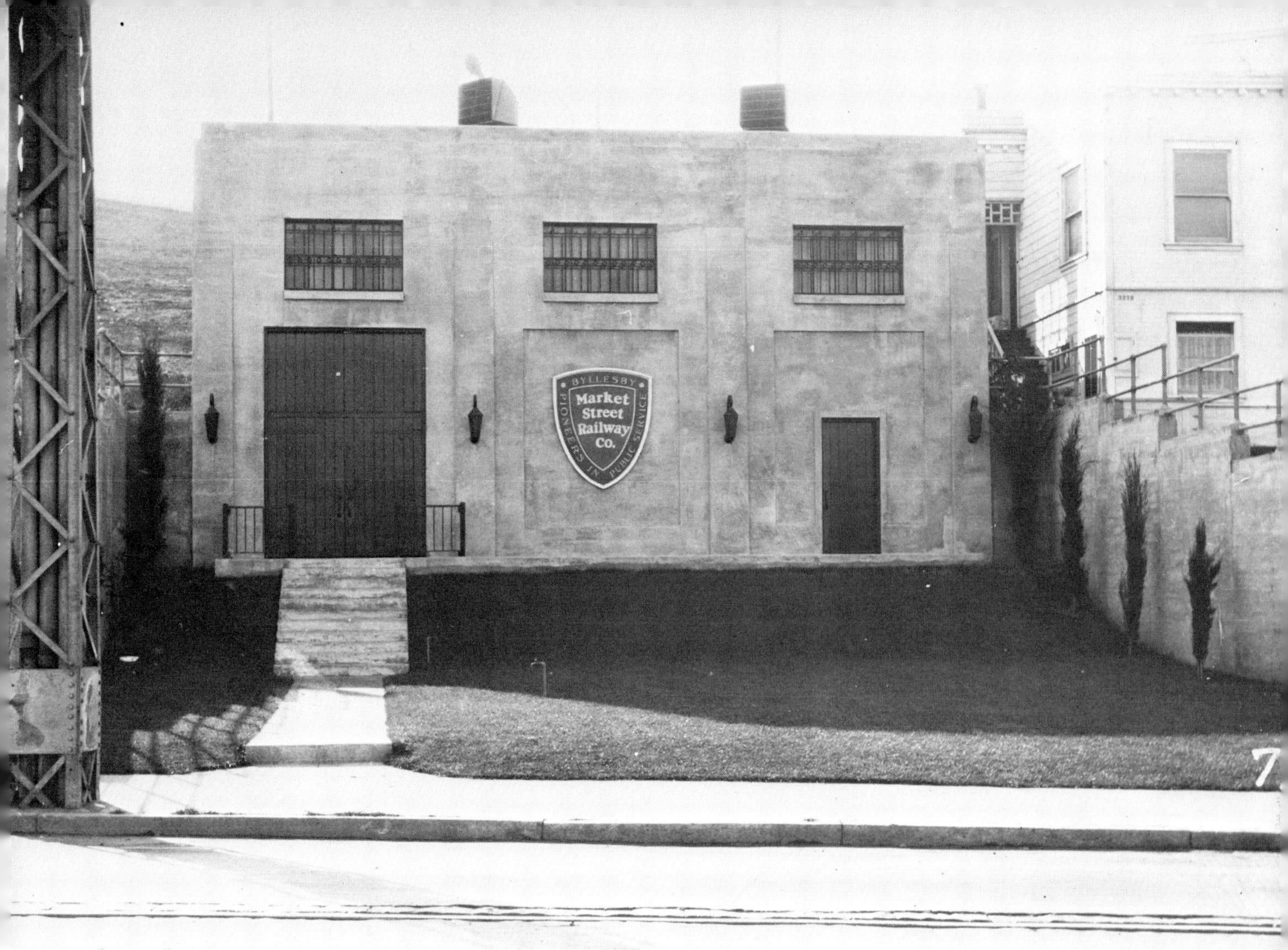

San Bruno Avenue Substation

COMPLETED IN November 1926, the San Bruno Avenue Substation greatly improved power conditions in the Bay Shore and Visitacion Valley districts, both of which were then growing rapidly. It contained a fully automatic 750-KW rotary converter and was located at San Bruno Avenue and Ordway Street.
S.F. Public Utilities Commission

FACING PAGE:

Millbrae Substation

ABOUT MIDWAY on the San Mateo Line was Millbrae Substation, housed in a rather large building for the amount of power it produced. Millbrae provided power for the interurban line from Holy Cross to San Mateo, and also powered the South San Francisco Line. These 1927 views show the structure shortly after it had been repainted green and white.
   BOTH: S.F. Public Utilities Commission

415

HARDLY AN ARCHITECTURAL BEAUTY, Downtown Substation was built in 1921 on Stevenson Street near 2nd Street. View was taken in 1921.
Market Street Railway

DOWNTOWN SUB-STATION, STEVENSON STREET.

FACING PAGE: UNDOUBTEDLY, the Eighth Avenue Substation was MSR's most attractive substation. Built of light color brick and trimmed with stone, Eighth Avenue was a credit to its Richmond neighborhood. This 1921 view shows ''United Railroads'' still emblazoned under the arch.
Market Street Railway

A GROUNDMAN tugs on the rope line while linemen prepare to place a feeder wire on the insulator of a freshly planted pole. By 1928, when this photo was taken for MSR's archives, motor trucks like this solid-tire model had supplemented rail line cars.
Market Street Railway

The Overhead

MARKET STREET RAILWAY'S Line Department spent only about one percent of the total operating costs of the system, but it occupied a most vital part in the operation of the transportation machine.

Cars might break down, but they could be towed to the car house and replacements sent out. Rails could be battered to pieces, yet carry the cars over. Generators might burn out and others put on a line to carry the load. But when an overhead trolley wire broke, the company's function came to a dead halt, and with it also the cash income of the company. There was no spare to fall back on, no taking the broken wire off to the shop for repairs, no inprovising; that wire must not come down and the constant purpose of the Line Department was to keep it up, rather than to rush out and pick it up.

Where the function of the Motive Power Department was to provide the current to the feeder wires, the Line Department's responsibility was to carry it through the feeders and into the trolley wire, then make sure it was properly picked up by the cars and converted into transportation for the passengers.

Heading the Line Department was the Chief Electrician; for many years this key post was occupied by S.L. Foster. Aiding him was an assistant chief electrician, three line foremen and a pole foreman. A total of about 40 men worked in this department.

Their responsibility was not alone to keep the overhead trolley wire functioning properly. In addition they were responsible for pole maintenance, block signals, electric track switches, the heavy underground feeder cables, overhead feeder cables, and they had to respond to all second fire alarms, day or night.

To the latter end, the two tower trucks were classified as auxiliary fire apparatus and were painted red and equipped with red lights and sirens. When they had to get somewhere in a hurry, they demanded and got priority in traffic.

IN MSR'S LATER YEARS, line car #0304 was sufficient to handle private rights-of-way, having been supplemented by tower trucks for lines on the streets.

Courtesy Mrs. C.D. Miller

One tower car was sufficient in later years, as its duties were primarily confined to track on private right-of-way which was not easily serviced by the auto tower trucks. That car, #0304, was extensively modernized in mid-1928, receiving relocated controllers, hand brakes, larger cab windows, plus a new lighting circuit and special headlights; topping off the transformation, the car got illuminated white ends, brass numbers and Byllesby shields.

When emergencies arose, and they invariably did at regular intervals, the Line Department was expected to react instantly. One memorable day—December 8, 1926—30 trolley poles on the San Mateo Line were blown down by a 50-mile gale; this catastrophe took place about noon. The Line Department had the line in operation by five o'clock that evening—quick work!

Inasmuch as Market Street Railway was by far the largest consumer of electric power in Northern California (its peak load at times reached 48,000 hp), men of its Line Department were carrying a heavy responsibility, indeed, for every turn of every car wheel was dependent on their performing quickly and efficiently.

But how could men of the Line Department protect their overhead against a crashing airplane? This actually was the problem at Leipsic Junction in December 1925, when a biplane, said to have been piloted by John Barleycorn, crashed, clipping off several trolley wire poles.

Night work on lines traversing downtown streets was mandatory after 1925, for traffic during daytime hours had grown to such proportions that it would have been unthinkable to cordon off a section of street to permit linemen to carry out their duties in safety. Such night maintenance work was carried out on Market St., lower Mission St., and Third and Kearny.

Preventive maintenance was the watchword of the Line Department. Conductors and motormen were urged to report immediately any dewirements apparently due to the overhead trolley wire. True, many things could cause a trolley to jump—too high speed on curves, weak trolley base springs, wet trolley rope, defective trolley wheel, improperly set trolley pole, etc.—but MSR's policy was to blame it on the overhead wire and an inspection was made as soon as possible. Repeated blows of wild trolley poles could do great injury to the overhead in a short time.

Among things the Line Department desired conductors and motormen to report were foreign wires lying across trolley wires, steam shovels and derricks being hauled under trolley wires, other dangerously high loads such as tanks and boilers on trucks, leaning trees and tree branches overgrowing the wires.

Much damage to poles was caused by automobiles running into them; if the pole was wood, it was cracked and if it was steel, it was bent. Carmen were asked to get the license numbers of such vehicles so their operators could be billed for damages.

One thing in particular was anathema to men of the Line Department: operating a streetcar on the front pole. Nothing could possibly do more damage to overhead trolley wire than a trolley pole protruding into it as a spear, ripping and tearing until the car could be stopped. Also, car motormen were cautioned against putting up two poles at once; where a dead section joined a live one, it was possible for the entire overhead current to pass through the car's wiring, causing burning of roof wiring and even setting the car roof ablaze.

(ABOVE) **MARKET STREET RAILWAY** linemen were proud of their trucks, like this shiny International extension ladder vehicle. That must have been quite a perch on which to stand after any length of time! All were painted red, signed ''Auxiliary Fire Apparatus,'' and equipped with sirens.
Charles Smallwood

(LEFT) **LIKE CROWS ON A TELEGRAPH LINE**, Market Street Railway linemen adorn a feeder span, while others pose atop horse-drawn tower wagons in an early company shot.
MSR ''Inside Track'' Magazine

Rough & Ready

ENGULFING A TOWER TRUCK, the doughty linemen and their foremen posed for the company magazine in 1922. One assumes the overhead wire system was on its best behavior during the conclave.
MSR ''Inside Track'' Magazine

THE VAST ELKTON SHOPS are shown in 1948, after Muni had taken over. The main shop building is at right, the paint shop is in center distance, and Geneva Car House is in the left distance. Ocean Avenue is in the foreground and San Jose Avenue is at left. On this spot now sits the new Muni shop complex.

Paul Ward

Elkton Shops

THE HEART of Market Street Railway's heavy repair and overhaul facilities was the sprawling Elkton Shops, located in the Outer Mission District. Elkton Shops property was bounded by Ocean Ave., San Jose Ave., Niagara St. and the old right-of-way of the Southern Pacific. The facility derived its name from a station on the old railway line that was located on the south side of Ocean Ave. and named "Elkton." This station was still in existence when the shops were constructed in 1907. The use of this name also served to differentiate the facility from the nearby Geneva Car House, immediately across the street.

Elkton Shops consisted of three main areas: the shop facility proper, the adjacent material and storage area, and the large paint shop. The latter was a building situated some distance apart from the main shops at the extreme southerly end of the property—this, doubtless, to minimize any possible fire danger.

The main shop building comprised the following departments necessary to maintain the large fleet of MSR rolling stock:

Motor overhaul and electric shop; machine shop; wood mill and car building plant; foundry; upholstery shop; wheel shop; truck overhaul shop; blacksmith shop; body overhaul shop; glass shop; special machine shop; and air brake shop.

Prior to 1935, every passenger car on the system went through Elkton Shops every two years for a thorough mechanical and body overhaul as well as a complete repainting. Cars suffering accident damage were repaired at the plant's carpenter shop; through the years a constant program for upgrading and modernizing older cars was instituted.

An important function of this well-equipped shop for many years was the turning out of a completely new car body every two weeks. These were the well-known "California Comfort Cars" which provided the bulk of the service on Market Street Railway's system for many years.

To give an idea of the extent of the activities of Elkton Shops, let us take the year 1929, one of the peak years in the shop's history and, happily, a year for which complete figures are available. In that year there were:

- 226 men permanently employed
- An annual payroll of $126,630
- 26 new car bodies constructed
- 316 cars overhauled and painted
- 297 cars receiving carpenter work
- 700 different items used on the system manufactured

The volume of brass castings turned out by the foundry and finished in the machine shop in 1929 were:

Finished brass fittings	202,917 lbs.
Trolley wire ears	17,066 lbs.
Journal brasses	3,295 lbs.
Axle liners	5,272 lbs.
Armature liners	2,713 lbs.
Trolley wheels	1,500 lbs.

The main shop building had 16 tracks leading into it from a ladder track on its west side. This building had a capacity of about 20 double-truck cars. The paint shop had two tracks which could accommodate 10 cars inside and two cars on the semi-open wash rack at the entrance. On the San Jose Ave. side of the paint shop was a spur track on which was located a large scale of sufficient capacity and size to weigh the largest electric cars as well as loaded freight cars which were received from the Southern Pacific through an interchange track located near Ocean Ave.

The yard area of the plant fronted on Ocean, San Jose and Geneva Avenues and was of ample size to enable much heavy and bulky material to be stored there, as well as providing considerable car storage area. Ever since the shop was established, obsolete car bodies were burned in the lower yard—this, of course, having been done in the days before public awareness of air pollution. Also located in the yard was a well-equipped first aid hospital with a staff of trained personnel.

MANY A STREETCAR was constructed in Elkton Shops over the years. Here, #941 takes shape, while at the right rear another 900 class car is virtually completed.
Market Street Railway

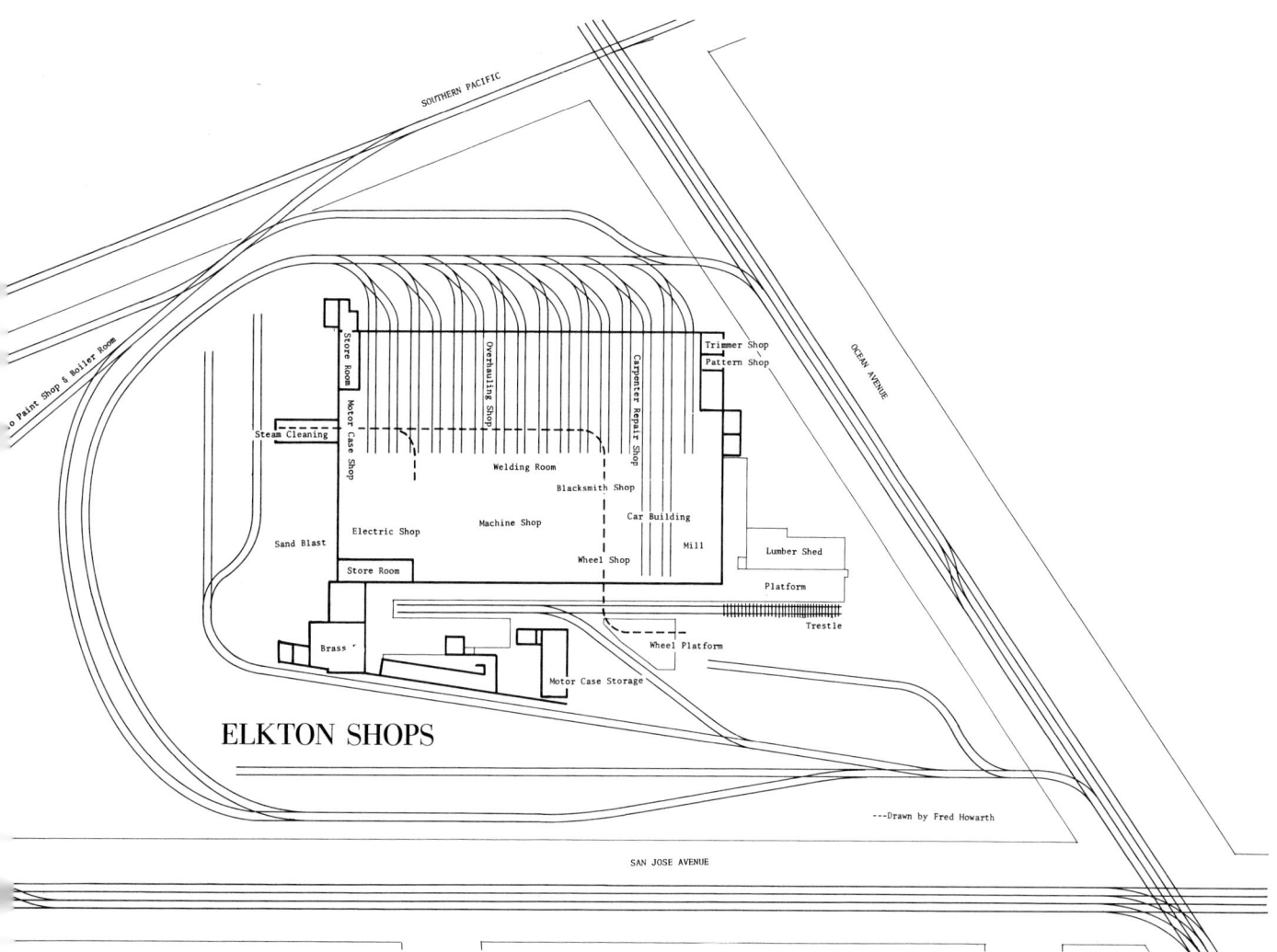

ELKTON SHOPS was a versatile facility, not only repairing but creating streetcars. It is interesting to contrast this map with the same area in the 1970s. On the left, where the Southern Pacific line ran, is the BART line from Daly City. BART's Balboa Park station sits about where the switch connects the MSR yard. On the rest of the site now sits Muni's new yard for its long-awaited LIGHT RAILWAY VEHICLES (a new word for streetcars).

Map by Fred Howarth

Car Maintenance and Repairing

In March 1928, Jesse M. Yount, Superintendent of Equipment of MSR, wrote a series of articles for the company publication, *The Inside Track*, on the subject of car maintenance and repairing. They afford us possibly the clearest and most exhaustive description of the company's procedures insofar as the car and well-being of its car fleet are concerned and are excerpted here in the following digest.

Market Street Railway [he wrote] owns 725 passenger cars, cable cars, and 67 miscellaneous cars. We have arbitrarily set our general overhauling period at 23 months, which approximates 70,000 car miles. No general repairs are made at any of the 13 car houses; car house employees simply look after running repairs and adjustments, such as brakes, controllers, etc. Changing wheels, armatures and fields for cars operating north of Market St. are made at Turk and Fillmore car house; some work of this nature for cars operating south of Market St. is done at 24th St. car house.

The general overhauling shops (Elkton) perform such work at Geneva car house. At Turk and Fillmore barn is installed a wet grinder for grinding flat wheels without removing them from the car; this machine takes care of the wheel grinding for the entire system.

Supplies from the shops to the various carbarns are delivered twice weekly; an old article must be given in place of a new or repaired article delivered by the supply car.

Let's follow the progress of a typical car coming to Elkton Shops for overhauling. The car enters from Ocean Ave., rolls down past the 16 tracks in back of the shop to the air reservoir tester, where its air reservoir is given a hydraulic test of 160 lbs. per square inch; this is done through a special connection without removing the reservoir from the car. The car is next run in on one of the 12 overhauling tracks and the body raised off the trucks. Trucks are then taken for sandblasting to remove dirt. The truck is next returned and run forward to a position over the overhauling stand, the monorail crane being above and between the trucks. Opposite each truck is a jib crane equipped with an 8″ air hoist. Motors are removed and taken to the motor overhaul department by monorail crane. Wheels are removed and go to the wheel shop. The truck frame is placed on wooden horses and the brake rigging is taken down and delivered to the blacksmith shop where it is placed in a furnace so that all oil and grease are burned off.

The foreman of the truck department now makes a thorough inspection of the truck and decides what can be repaired and what must be junked. While truck frames are on horses, they are tested for alignment and trued where necessary. Jour-

al boxes are next fitted to pedestals and guides are shimmed out where necessary. Brake rigging is replaced on trucks, wheels returned from the wheel shop and the truck is reassembled.

The motors are torn down; armatures are taken to the armature room for inspection and replacement of bearings. Fields are tested, connections inspected, fields painted and housing tested for undue wear. Where housings are worn beyond fixed limits, they are built up with electric welding and machined back to standard size. Motors are then reassembled and mounted on their trucks by air hoists attached to jib cranes. Motors are then tested on trucks, running them in both directions.

While the car body is on horses, the air compressor is removed and cleaned by steam; it then goes to the air compressor department where it is dismantled, all parts thoroughly inspected, valves ground, bearings fitted and reassembled.

Motorman's valves are removed and taken to the machine shop where they are reground and tested. Governors are removed, taken to the electric shop for inspection, repairs and adjusting. Air gauges are removed and taken to the test board and checked for accuracy. Circuit breakers and cutout switches are taken to the electric shop for repairs, adjusting and calibration. Controllers have power and reverse cylinders removed; the controller is thoroughly cleaned and repainted, segments and fingers adjusted and reassembled.

The car body is now placed on its trucks and run to the car building department where all body work is gone over and repaired. The car next goes to the paint shop for paint work. This consists of first priming all new work. The car is thoroughly cleaned inside and out, using acid cleaner for the outside. The body is puttied wherever necessary, then sanded. It next receives one coat of color varnish, then a coat of clear varnish, then lettering, striping, and the second coat of finishing varnish.

Windows are cleaned and the car is fitted up, ready for the road. Before the car leaves the shop it is thoroughly inspected by the inspector of equipment, who has charge of car house employees.

After this inspection, the car is returned to the car house from which it came. The average time a car is in the shop is 19 days, including Sundays.

(FACING PAGE, TOP) **IN 1912**, Elkton Shops displayed this typical busy, busy scene—a standard day in the extremely long service life of this facility. Work was carried on in this structure until the Muni Metro facility was built in 1977. **United Railroads**

(FACING PAGE, BOTTOM) **BOTH CABLE CARS** and electric cars were patients in Elkton's recuperative wards. This excellent 1938 view in the paint shop shows, at the right, three 800-class cars being repainted. At the left is Powell Street cable car #508 on flat car #04, the means by which these narrow-gauge cars were transported to and from Elkton. **Lorin Silliman**

AFFIXING THE BYLLESBY SHIELD to a 1550-class car, circa 1927; note the shiny new paint! This colorful shield —red, white and green—was a familiar emblem in San Francisco for many years. **Charles Smallwood**

The average number of cars in Elkton Shops for overhauling at any one time is 22. A grand total of 353 men are employed at Elkton Shops; these are distributed as follows, including foremen: machine shop, 38; brass foundry, 4; carpenter and car building, 25; wood mill, 3; electric repairs, 17; car wiring, 19; truck and motor overhauling, 32; blacksmith, 9; paint shop, 37; miscellaneous, 12; building repair, 8; outside wiremen, 2; plumbing, 1; special machine shop, 28; car house employees, 118.

Waste Not, Want Not

Human ingenuity being what it is, MSR shopmen came up with some interesting and, often, novel ideas to accomplish the desired result and effect it cheaply.

New car axles were five inches in diameter. As the motor fit became worn, axles were hammered and heat-treated for four-inch diameter. When the motor fit became undersize on four-inch diameter, the axle was then hammered and heat-treated for armature shafts and cable car axles. When these shafts and cable car axles wore out, they were cut up into door rollers!

HEADING INTO the overhauling and carpenter repair portions of Elkton Shops were 16 tracks off the lead trac The above two views indicate lots of activity. The left view was taken from across Ocean Avenue in August, 192 with the #12 Line tracks in the foreground. The right-hand photo, taken in October, 1928, looks toward Oce

Brake shoe wear in San Francisco was high due to steep grades. MSR used a brake shoe that was exceptionally hard, the ends being chilled. But there is a point in the wearing out of a brake shoe beyond which you cannot go or you will destroy the brake shoe head. There is always about 12 pounds of scrap on every shoe. MSR increased brake shoe mileage by increasing the weight of the new shoe from 30 to 40 pounds, the scrap in both cases being the same.

A big item of expense was car wheels. MSR used chilled iron wheels and the average mileage per wheel was regarded as being highly satisfactory. The chief objection to chilled iron wheels is chipped flanges, but MSR solved this problem to a great degree by having the rail grooves kept clean; even small steel balls from ball bearings could chip wheel flanges and many such balls were found in the grooves of girder rail.

Brake levers had all brake pin holes bushed so that when the holes became too large, the old bushings could be pressed out and new ones pressed in, thereby saving the levers and additional blacksmith work.

MSR Was a Landlord, Too

When Elkton Shops were built in 1907 the surrounding area was very lightly settled, the shop complex being built on land formerly devoted to truck farming. To house a limited number of shop and carbarn employees, Market Street Railway itself built about a dozen modest dwellings on its proper-

ty which were available to rent. These houses fronted on t west side of San Jose Ave. and on both sides of Geneva A where that street dead-ended in the shop area. Those on S Jose Ave. were four- and five-room cottages, while the gro on Geneva Ave. was rather large two-story flats. The dwe ings were well-built and reflected the rococo style of archit ture of the early 1900s.

Occupancy of the dwellings was restricted to employees the railway company. Interestingly, though rental rates housing in San Francisco increased several hundred perce from 1907 when the houses were constructed until 1944 (last year of MSR's existence), the company never raised rents; it continued to ask its tenants to the end for the sa amount of rent which was charged way back in 1907!

An interesting story was related to the author by a frie who worked for MSR. During the war year of 1942 he v desperately in need of a place to live for himself and his w Housing in San Francisco at that time was in extremely sh supply; when vacancies were found, rents were enormous. learned one of the company's San Jose Ave. houses would vacant the first of the following month and he immediat applied for it. To his great joy, he was accepted and he a his wife immediately moved in. As the first month of th occupancy drew to a close they started to wonder what rent on their newfound home would be; they had been thrilled at their good fortune in having found a place to that they had not thought to inquire as to the amount of r

.venue and has some interesting things to note: a 1500 class getting its open section enclosed, an Ingleside car (#1730) with a large headlight, and #0927, a center-cab shop switcher. **BOTH: S.F. Public Utilities Commission**

A TYPICAL COMPANY-OWNED dwelling on Geneva Avenue in the Elkton Shop complex. The low building at right is MSR's restaurant on San Jose Avenue. Note poles in storage. Geneva Avenue west of San Jose Avenue was MSR property when this photo was made in 1928.
S.F. Public Utilities Commission

they would be required to pay. They figured their rent would probably be $100 monthly, possibly more. On the day their rent was due, this man walked across the street to the Equipment office in Geneva Car House (the Superintendent of Equipment handled all of the company's rentals) to pay his rent; he was informed (to his great astonishment) that he owed the company a mere $20, his monthly rental rate! Whatever else, Market Street Railway was certainly the most reasonable landlord in all the city.

These houses passed into the hands of the city when Municipal Railway assumed control of MSR in 1944 and all of them were razed to make room for the present Ocean Ave. motor-coach division.

Other company ventures into the landlord's realm were a restaurant at the corner of Geneva and San Jose Avenues, a hot dog stand in the Sutro Terminal at the Cliff House, a small soft drink and candy store at Leipsic Junction, and a similar operation at Land's End along the Cliff Route.

In the mid-1930s the company established an auto parking lot on its large property at Market and Gough streets. A nominal parking charge was made, which also included two streetcar tokens which enabled the driver to ride to the downtown area and return. As this parking lot was on the fringe of downtown with its accompanying traffic congestion, many motorists took advantage of its convenience. It was short-lived (although successful) because of strong opposition from downtown garages. The company abandoned the project after a month or two and leased the lot to a used car dealer.

(BELOW) THE ELKTON PAINT SHOP, shown here in 1928, was a distance south of the main buildings. In this view, the venerable structure is surrounded by a cross-section of MSR's car fleet at that time. Visible are #1419, #227, #1535, and another 1400 class on the scrap track. **S.F. Public Utilities Commission**

Fender Problem

THE ECLIPSE FENDER, designed to scoop up the unwary pedestrian, more often yielded to errant autos. Car 1334's fender suffered some broken pieces and awaits repairs at Elkton Shops about 1924. It took a goodly crew of shopmen just to perform fender restoration. **Market Street Railway**

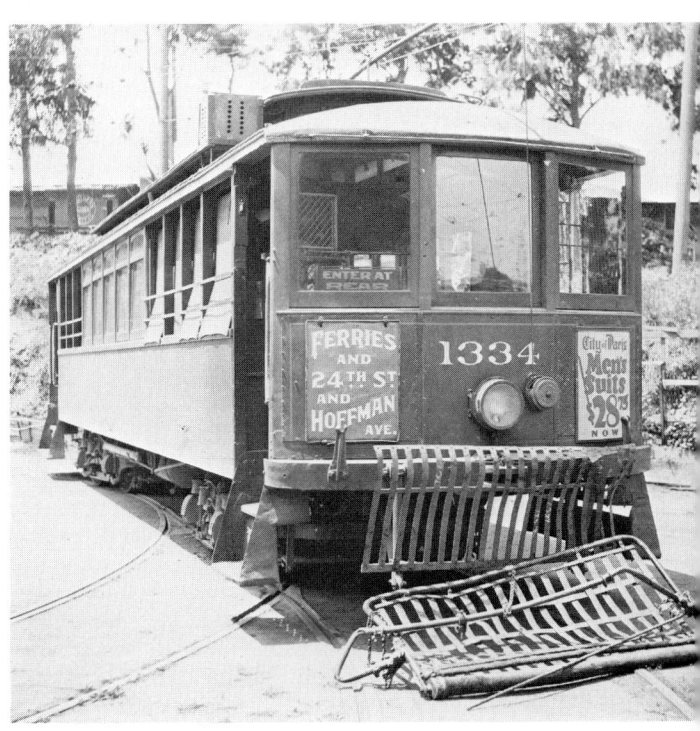

Inside Elkton

BRAND NEW streetcars were built to order at Elkton Shops. But that was just a portion of its activities. Here are some glimpses:

(RIGHT) **THE WOOD MILL** was neat and clean with plenty of light and air. A California Comfort Car takes shape (at left) in this 1927 photo. **United Railroads**

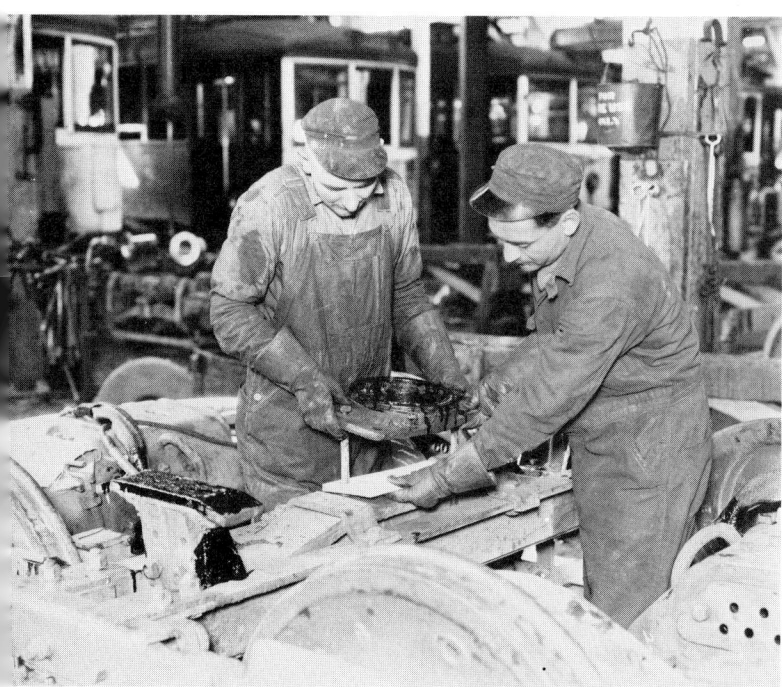

(LEFT) **FOLLOWING OVERHAUL** of this Brill 27-G truck, shopmen install a new truck center bearing. Dark, shiny surfaces have been lubricated to cut down friction on their bearing surfaces with the carbody. **United Railroads**

(RIGHT) **THE CLEANING DEPARTMENT** used a variety of methods. At left a monorail crane, with operator riding along with it, prepares to lower a motor case into the Oakite cleaning tank, while at right an air compressor is being steamed. **United Railroads**

Dissecting the Components

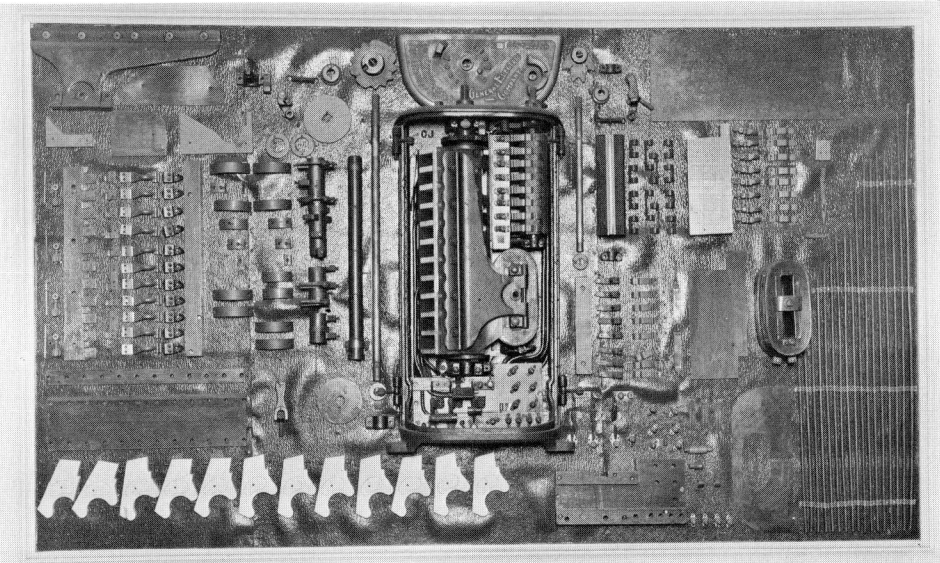

(LEFT) **THE SELF-SUFFICIENT** shops could manufacture all these parts for a General Electric K-12 controller. They were framed for permanent exhibition at Elkton.

(BELOW) **A POPULAR EXHIBIT** at Elkton back in the 1920s was this cutaway display of a General Electric No. 1000 streetcar motor.

Brass Foundry

ELKTON'S BRASS FOUNDRY was a never-ending wonder to those fortunate enough to visit it. Featured was a Detroit Electric Brass Furnace, modeled after the old arc lights. MSR made many new and replacement parts here, as shown in the photo at left.

ALL: Market Street Railway

COMBINE THE YEARS of experience of these skilled craftsmen with Elkton Shops' machinery and equipment, and you had the means to keep San Francisco's major street railway system in operation. (ABOVE, LEFT) **A MACHINIST** cuts a groove for an anti-noise lead insert in the motor gear of a truck. (ABOVE, RIGHT) **THIS GENTLEMAN** cuts out leather for repair of an upholstered seat. **BOTH: Market Street Railway**

ONE MORE LOOK at the ladder track at the west side of the shop complex. In this later (1940) view, car 212 is freshly painted in the late 1930s' modernized paint scheme while in the distance three cars await rehabilitation. **Charles Smallwood**

(ABOVE) **GENEVA CAR HOUSE, 1928.** Note the heavy timber braces in upper windows . . . a reminder of the 1906 earthquake damage—these remained for 50 years. At this writing, the structure still served its intended purpose pending completion of the new Muni Metro Center, catter-cornered on San Jose Avenue. **S.F. Public Utilities Commission** (BELOW) **THE CAR HOUSE LEADS** at Geneva as seen in 1921. **United Railroads**

Car Houses

MARKET STREET RAILWAY at its peak operated some 14 car houses, of which 11 were devoted to electric cars and three to cable equipment. Many of the barns used for electric cars were originally built to house cable cars; when they were transformed for electric use around the turn of the century, only the most necessary alterations were made to accommodate the new equipment.

To conserve supervisory expense, the 14 car houses were grouped into eight units. These barns, with their control groupings, were as follows:

1. Oak and Broderick
   Haight Street
   Lincoln Way Yard
2. Turk and Fillmore
3. Washington and Mason
   Pacific Avenue
4. McAllister
5. Kentucky (Third Street)
   24th and Utah
6. 28th and Valencia
   29th and Mission
   Castro Street
7. Sutro
8. Geneva Avenue

Little or no improvements were made on these buildings during the life of the company. One car house, located at 3rd and 23rd streets, was originally a horse car barn dating back to the 1870s.

Structurally, about half of the buildings were of brick and timber construction, the remainder were entirely constructed of wood. The condition of these structures ranged from fair to downright ramshackle; MSR did keep its car houses well painted, but coats of paint could not quite hide their decrepitude.

Fortunately the company and its predecessors never suffered that bane of many another traction property, a destructive and costly car house fire. Even in the great disaster of 1906 the only car house and power facilities lost were those devoted to cable operation.

We now examine these car houses individually, including histories, locations, descriptions and lines generally operating out of them.

GENEVA AVENUE: This brick building with frame interior is located on the southeast corner of San Jose and Geneva Avenues. It was constructed in 1901 by the *San Francisco & San Mateo Railway* as a replacement for that company's inadequate original barn, located on Sunnyside Ave. (now Monterey Blvd.). Before the SF&SM company could occupy its new quarters, the control of the road passed to the newly organized United Railroads.

Geneva housed MSR's first modest bus fleet, beginning with a half-dozen primitive buses in April of 1926.

This car house is still in use today, housing all remaining streetcar lines of Municipal Railway—and is the sole remaining car barn from which streetcars operate on the Pacific Coast. It is little modified today from what it was when first opened. Oddly, Geneva never received the garish green and white paint job that MSR applied to its other car houses in the mid-1920s.

Lines which operated from Geneva were:

- Route #10 — Glen Park-Guerrero St.
- Route #12 — Ingleside
- Route #18 — Mission
- Route #26 — Daly City via Guerrero St.
- Route #40 — San Mateo Interurban
- Route — South San Francisco local line
- Route — Visitacion Line

In 1939 the #14—Daly City line was operated from Geneva Division after the 28th and Valencia Barn closed. Still later, the #9—Valencia and the #11—Mission-24th streets lines w[ere] moved to Geneva when the 24th St. Barn was converted to [bus] use. At that time, more cars operated from Geneva than from a[ny] other car house in the history of the city's electric car era.

Geneva Car House passed to city ownership on September [?], 1944. Today it houses Muni's lines J, K, L, M and N, plus all [re]maining rail service equipment.

24TH AND UTAH: This car house is of brick walls and timber co[n]struction and is located on the square block bounded by 24[th], Utah, 23rd and San Bruno Ave. It survived into the 197[0s] although much altered, and was the main repair shop for Mun[ici]pal Railway's motor coach, automobile and truck fleet.

Built in 1903-04, this barn was considered the best laid-out [car] house on the MSR system during its electric car days; 13 of its tracks led directly to an outside ladder track on 24th St., so in c[ase] of fire its cars could have been removed rapidly from the str[uc]ture. It was also equipped to perform heavy truck and runni[ng] gear overhaul and provided such service for the 3rd St., 28th a[nd] Valencia and 29th St. Divisions, as well as for its own fleet of ca[rs].

Twenty-fourth and Utah Car House served the relatively uni[m]portant so-called "South of Market" lines; only two lines of a[ny] consequence—9th and Polk and Bryant-San Bruno—w[ere] housed here.

Over the years the equipment operating from this barn was t[he] most varied and interesting of any barn on the system; many f[ine] old series of cars were assigned to this division to run out their l[ast] year or two before being sent to the scrap line.

Lines which operated from 24th and Utah were:

- Route #19 — 9th, Polk and Larkin
- Route #25 — Bryant and San Bruno
- Route #27 — Bryant
- Route #34 — 6th and Sansome
- Route #35 — Howard Street
- Route #36 — Folsom Street
- Route — — 10th and Montgomery

FILLMORE CAR HOUSE, 1928, with its maze of overhead feeder cables from the substation across the street.

S.F. Public Utilities Commission

INTERIOR of Fillmore Car House, 1928, shows extensive use of wood. Car at rear is jacked up for a motor change.

S.F. Public Utilities Commission

In July, 1935, the #11—Mission and 24th streets line was moved to this barn when the 29th St. Barn closed. The #9—Valencia Line began operating from here in January 1939, when the 28th and Valencia Barn was abandoned.

TURK AND FILLMORE: Also of red brick and timber construction, this car house was located on the southwest corner of Turk and Fillmore streets. It extended along Turk St. west to Steiner St., and was built in 1896-97 by the original *Market Street Railway Company*. Like the 24th and Utah Barn, this barn was equipped to perform heavy truck overhaul (such as wheel changes and motor changes), as well as other major work.

Located here, too, was the only wheel grinder on the system; cars from all over the railway were at times seen at this barn for this grinding service.

Between 1907 and 1913, Turk and Fillmore Barn also did motor overhaul and wheel change work for the separately owned *Presidio & Ferries Railway*.

This barn performed truck overhaul, changing of wheels and motor replacements for the Sutro, Haight, McAllister and Oak and Broderick car houses. It also provided heavy wrecker service for all lines operating north of Market St.

Lines which operated from Turk and Fillmore were:

- Route #4 — Turk-Eddy
- Route #22 — Fillmore-16th Street
- Route   —— Fillmore Hill
- Route   —— Divisadero Extension
- Route #31 — Eddy-Balboa (after May 15, 1932)

Routes assigned to this car house remained fairly constant under MSR operation. After the 1944 merger, other routes from south of Market were housed here, including #25—Bryant-San Bruno, #19—Polk-Larkin, and #27—Bryant.

Turk and Fillmore Car House closed as an operating car barn on March 31, 1948. For a time thereafter it was used to shelter old streetcars and, later, some new trolley coaches. It was then sold and torn down.

SUTRO: This wood frame building was located on the block bounded by Clement, 32nd Ave., California St., and 33rd Ave. Its name was derived from the fact that it was constructed in the latter part of 1895 by *The Sutro Railroad Company*, and was opened in February 1896. The car house structure occupied about a third of the property, the remainder being used for open yard storage.

Lines operating from Sutro Division were:

- Route #1 — Sutter-California
- Route #2 — Sutter-Clement
- Route #3 — Sutter-Jackson
- Route #4 — Sutter-Sacramento (after June 16, 1935)

About 1940 the #4—Sutter-Sacramento Line was moved to the McAllister Division and Sutro acquired several out-of-service cars for storage.

It was acquired by Municipal Railway in 1944, and some Municipal lines operated from here—the only former MSR car house other than Geneva to have had this distinction.

It was finally closed as an operating division and abandoned on January 20, 1951.

Sutro

SUTRO VIEWS: The above view of the front of Sutro Car House dates from August, 1938, while the photo (below) of its yard was taken in 1928.
TOP: Ted Wurm; BOTTOM: S.F. Public Utilities Commission

24th & Utah

TWO ANGLES of the same view illustrate the front in 24th & Utah Car House. In the view below the office is seen at left.
TOP: S.F. Public Utilities Commission; **BOTTOM:** Charles Smallwood

HAIGHT STREET: Another wood frame structure of cable car ancestry, dating back to the 1880s, this car house was located on Haight St. near Stanyan St. The building housed cable cars until the disaster of 1906, after which it was remodeled to house electric cars of the electrified Haight St. cable system. In the 1890s it served as the office of *The Park & Ocean Railroad Company,* the steam line which ran on Lincoln Way to the beach from Stanyan St.

Haight Street Barn was equipped with a transfer table within its confines; only two tracks led into the barn from the street.

Routes operating from Haight Street Barn were:

- Route #7 — Haight-Ocean
- Route #17 — Haight-Ingleside
- Route #33 — 18th and Park

Aiding Haight Street Barn's pressing car storage problem greatly was MSR's "boneyard" at Lincoln Way and 14th Ave.; several runs of Haight's lines signed out of and terminated at the boneyard.

On October 6, 1935, San Francisco's first trolley coaches were housed at this barn; these were substituted for streetcars on the #33 Line.

Turned over to Municipal Railway in the 1944 consolidation, Haight Street Barn continued in service until December 7, 1946, when a trolley coach being switched within the barn accidentally struck one of the uprights supporting the barn roof; considerable damage resulted and forced the abandonment of this facility.

MCALLISTER: Like Haight Street Barn, McAllister also dated back to the 1880 cable car days and was converted similarly to electric car operation after the 1906 earthquake and fire. McAllister was also the only barn in the city to provide a right-of-way for an operating line—the #5-McAllister Line cut across its property from McAllister to Fulton streets between Central and Masonic Avenues.

Two outside yards provided car storage facilities, one large yard capable of caring for more than half the cars assigned to the division was not of the #5 Line's right-of-way, and a smaller yard just east of the car house.

Lines assigned to McAllister Division were:

- Route #5 — McAllister-Fulton
- Route #21 — Hayes

When the Third Street Barn was closed on April 7, 1941, remaining cars of the Third-Kearny Line were sent to McAllister; these operated out of this division on weekdays only and carried no route numbers.

McAllister Division became the property of San Francisco Municipal Railway in 1944 and continued as a car house until July 3, 1948, at which time it became an operating motor coach division; it continued in this capacity until its final closing on September 10, 1950.

HAIGHT & STANYAN BARN had just received its Byllesby paint scheme in this 1928 view.   Charles Smallwood

Haight Street

IN JUNE 1940 there was plenty of action at the Haight Barn. (ABOVE) Streetcars, autos, and a #33 trolley coach at right vie for the right-of-way. (BELOW) The barn was dominated by the 100s when this photo was taken in 1928.

TOP: Ted Wurm; BOTTOM: S.F. Public Utilities Commission

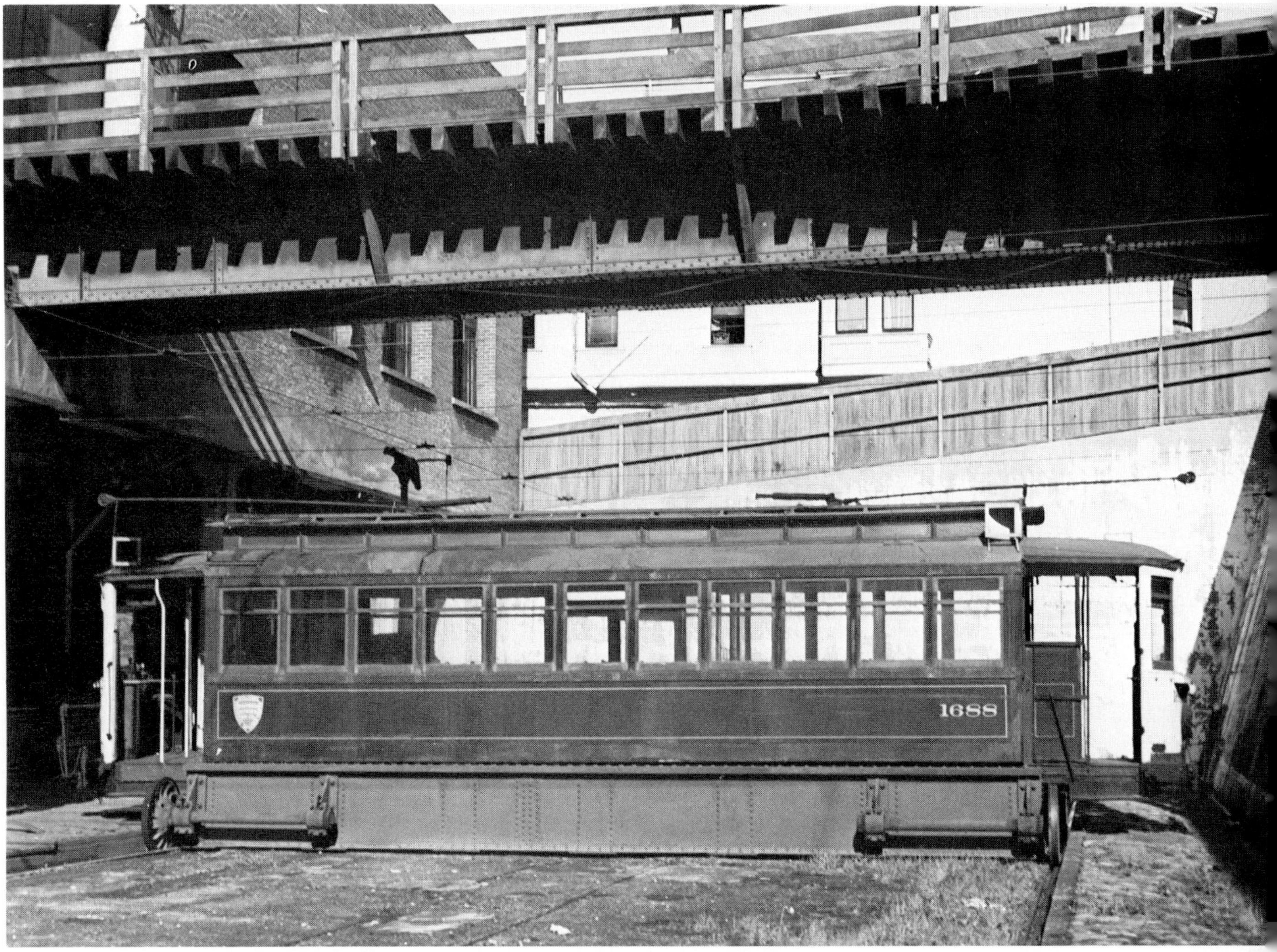

Transfer Tables

THE USE OF space-saving transfer tables to move streetcars sideways from track to track was a distinct need in densely populated San Francisco. (ABOVE) Car 1688 sits on the transfer table at the rear of 29th & Mission Car House in 1935. The trestle above led to the upper floor of the barn where the company's work equipment was housed. **Charles Smallwood** (BELOW) **THIS COMPACT** model ''shifter'' stands ready to receive a car inside the Haight St. Car House. **S.F. Public Utilities Commission**

29TH AND MISSION: This brick-walled, wooden-framed building, located on Mission St. near 29th St., was constructed in 1894 by the original *Market Street Railway Company* to house cars of its first electric railway operation on Mission Street.

This was a two-story building, with two lead tracks from Mission St. providing entrance to the first floor. A transfer table ran along the rear of the barn to distribute cars within the structure. Operating lines all ran from the ground floor; the top floor, reached by a natural grade up Virginia St. alongside the building, thence turning into Coleridge which ran in back of the barn, and so into the second floor from the rear. The upstairs floor provided maintenance and storage facilities for the company's large fleet of service equipment.

Lines assigned to 29th and Mission Barn were:

- Route #11 — Mission and 24th Street
- Route #23 — Fillmore and Valencia
- Route #24 — Mission and Richmond
- Route — — Bosworth Street

In the early days of the century, all of the special service cars (funeral cars, mail cars, party cars, observation cars, etc.) operated from this car barn.

On June 15, 1935, Lines #23 and #24 were discontinued and the #11 Line was moved to 24th and Utah Division. Twenty-ninth and Mission Car House was then closed as an operating car house and was used thereafter for storing surplus cars. It was sold in 1940 and was subsequently rebuilt into a bowling alley.

28TH AND VALENCIA: Located one block north of the 29th and Mission Car House, 28th and Valencia Car House was unique and of great importance to early-day operations of the company; it was built in the 1880s for the Market and Valencia cable lines, and in the mid-1890s was greatly expanded to include both cable and electric car storage and heavy maintenance. It became the main shops for the great Market Street cable system, as well as the main shop facility for the expanding fleet of electric cars. Many fine new electric cars were built here, and this shop also performed the conversion of the former *Omnibus* cable cars into electric cars between 1898 and 1900.

After the earthquake and fire of 1906 and the subsequent abandonment of cable operation, this barn was changed over entirely to electric operation. In 1907 the new Elkton Shops took over the heavy maintenance work, and 28th and Valencia became merely an operating division.

Lines assigned to 28th and Valencia Division were:

- Route #8 — Market Street
- Route #9 — Valencia Street
- Route #14 — Mission Street-Daly City

Twenty-eighth and Valencia Division ended its days as an operating division on January 14, 1939, in the interests of economy. Its lines were transferred to other divisions, the #8 Line going to Haight St. Division and the #9 and #14 Lines to Geneva Avenue Division. This barn was used for surplus car storage for a time and was finally razed to make way for a supermarket.

DATING BACK TO the 1880s, 28th & Valencia Car House was built to serve cable cars. It is seen in 1928 with fresh Market Street Railway paint.
Market Street Railway

Valencia Views

THE 28TH & VALENCIA Car House was entered on the bias. The top view was taken during a 1921 property survey. **Charles Smallwood** (BOTTOM) **THIS 1928** view shows the rear of the 28th & Valencia property, with car #1611 in the foreground. **S.F. Public Utilities Commission**

Lincoln Way Yard

LINCOLN WAY YARD was home base for certain runs of Lines 6, 7 and 17 back in 1930, when this photograph was taken. View looks southwest from Funston Avenue.

Market Street Railway

OAK AND BRODERICK: This barn was a brick and wood frame structure located on the northeast corner of Oak and Broderick streets. It was built in the late 1880s by *The Omnibus Cable Company* as a car house and cable power plant. It had been converted to electric operation by the late 1890s.

Oak and Broderick was a most difficult barn insofar as electric car operation was concerned; it had but one lead track in from the street, with a transfer table inside to distribute cars. There occurred occasions when a car would become derailed on the transfer table or the lead track in the rush hour period, in which case no cars could leave the barn. When such mischance occurred, a hurried plea to other divisions for loaners brought about some highly interesting temporary car assignments to the Oak and Broderick Barn's lines. Such perils hanging overhead doubtless caused the Operating Department's head officials to breathe a collective sigh of relief when the decision was made on August 15, 1938, to close Oak and Broderick Barn and transfer its lines to other, more relaxed, divisions.

Lines operating from Oak and Broderick were:

- Route #6—Haight and Masonic
- Route #20—Ellis and O'Farrell
- Route #32—Hayes and Oak
- Route — —Parkside Line (gone by 1928).

After closure of this car house as an operating division, it was used for a time as a storage facility for surplus cars. It was then sold for use as a warehouse; its new owners used it to store empty beer bottles, a function the old buildings was probably better able to perform than to serve as a streetcar operating center.

THIRD STREET: This rambling wooden structure had its genesis in the 1870 horse-car era, and was the oldest building used for any purpose by Market Street Railway Company. It was located on the south of Third Street between 23rd and 24th streets, and was originally known as the "Kentucky" barn—that part of Third St. having been known as Kentucky Street before the 1920s.

Inside Third Street Barn were the most spartan of repair and inspection facilities. Car storage was provided by a sprawling yard to the rear of and alongside the building. The latter had two entrances, located about a hundred feet apart and at the extreme ends of the barn, with the two tracks leading in from Third St. Distribution of cars within the barn was the task of a transfer table across the rear; the table was a somewhat flimsy affair as well as unreliable, and for many years the center tracks were used to store obsolete and surplus cars which seldom required moving. This, of course, resulted in leaving assigned cars to the elements outside, while the junk received loving protection inside.

Lines assigned to Third Street Division were:

- Route #15—Kearny-North Beach
- Route #16—Third Street
- Route #28—Ferries-Depot
- Route #29—Kearny-Broadway
- Route #30—8th and Army
- Route #41—2nd Street-Depot
- Route — —First and Fifth

On April 5, 1941, the main Third Street Division lines were changed to bus operation except the #15 Line between the Southern Pacific Depot and North Beach. It and the #41 Line were moved to other divisions and the Third Street Car House was closed after this date. The property was sold soon thereafter and the building torn down.

LINCOLN WAY YARD: Although not an operating division per se, this yard served as an adjunct to Haight Street Car House and some Haight runs operated from this yard. Lincoln Way Yard occupied the square block bounded by Lincoln Way, Funston (13th Ave.), Irving St. and 14th Ave. The property was purchased by United Railroads in 1905 and was intended to serve as the site of a major car house which would have consolidated the operations of no less than three existing divisions: Haight, Oak and Broderick, and the McAllister barns. Plans were drawn up and work began to the extent of transporting building materials to the site and installing an expensive ladder track when disaster struck the city on April 18, 1906. Work on the new car house was temporarily halted, or so it was then thought. Work was destined never to be resumed. The building material was carted away for use in making more urgently needed repairs to damaged URR property. Light, used rail was hastily spiked to the new ladder track to provide storage space for scores of Market Street cable cars whose lines and barns were being electrified.

In the months that followed the earthquake and fire of 1906, many new electric cars were arriving almost daily from eastern builders; eventually many of the original electric cars, made surplus by new equipment, came to Lincoln Way Yard to join the old cable cars. From then on until it was finally sold by the Municipal Railway in 1950, obsolete and surplus cars were stored there in greater or lesser numbers.

In 1906 this yard was in an area which largely consisted of sand dunes; eventually a substantial residential development sprang up around it. Known by all, both company employees and the general public, as "The Boneyard," Lincoln Way Yard was an unsightly plot of ground with its old cars in various stages of decrepitude. It generated no good will in the neighborhood, and unsuccessful attempts were made for years by residents of the area to have it removed.

In the mid-1930s, Market Street Railway revived the 1905 plan to construct a modern car house on this property and requested a building permit from the city for such a structure. As was to have been expected, the loud outcries of protest at the Planning Commission's hearing on the application were sufficiently loud and strong at City Hall to result in rejection.

So the infamous Lincoln Way Boneyard remained on the scene for another 15 years as the Sunset District's principal eyesore before it was finally removed. Its last task was to store long lines of former Market Street Railway cars made surplus after Municipal Railway converted their lines to bus and trolley coach operation after the 1944 consolidation.

WHEN THE McALLISTER BARN was built, it had the neighborhood pretty much to itself. It was 1890 when this photo was taken.
Charles Smallwood

McAllister

(ABOVE) **LOOKING TOWARD** McAllister Street from Fulton Street, the cameraman captures the McAllister Barn and yards as it appeared in 1937. **Ted Wurm** (BELOW) **ANOTHER VIEW** of the mass of wooden buildings at McAllister. **S.F. Public Utilities Commission.**

McALLISTER CLOSEUPS: (ABOVE) Facing Central Avenue, this portion of the McAllister complex was photographed in 1921 in its United Railroads livery. **Charles Smallwood** (BELOW) **THIS CLOSEUP** of the McAllister storage tracks shows how the #5 Line ran through the middle of the facility on the tracks running diagonally to the left. The ''San Francisco'' sign with arrow directs pilots to Crissy Field. **S.F. Public Utilities Commission**

Oak and Broderick

THE SINGLE TRACK entrance of Oak & Broderick Car House is behind the touring car at center right. **Charles Smallwood**

ACCESS TO STORAGE TRACKS inside Oak & Broderick Car House was via transfer table only (pit in foreground), fed by the single track from the street. **S.F. Public Utilities Commission**

3rd Street

THE FACADE of the wood-framed Third Street Car House is seen in 1925. **S.F. Public Utilities Commission** (BELOW) **THE MOTORMAN** of #877 lays over at the exit seen at far right in the top photo on this page. Route 22 cars en route to 23rd and 3rd Streets looped through the building. View circa 1940.

Charles Smallwood

BELOW) **29TH & MISSION:** This view looks down from the trestle over the transfer table pit into the rear of the building in 1937.
Charles Smallwood

(ABOVE) **THE STORAGE YARD** in the rear of Third Street Car House is seen in May, 1941.
Charles Smallwood

29th & Mission

(ABOVE) **THE BRICK FACE** of 29th & Mission Car House, as it looked in 1928. (BELOW) **THE INTERIOR** of this car house at that time reflected the transition period when 1300s were giving way to the new 800s. **BOTH: S.F. Public Utilities Commission**

Geneva

TWO MORE GENEVA SCENES: The [fr]ont of the Car House is seen at the [b]eginning of this chapter. (TOP) **THE [B]ARN TRACKS** are on different lev[el]s. View circa 1928. (BOTTOM) **THE [T]RESTLE TRACKS** over the pits, also [in] 1928. These views are virtually [u]nchanged 50 years later! **BOTH: [S].F. Public Utilities Commission**

CASTRO CABLES #6 and #4 pause in front of Castro Car House, at Castro & Jersey Streets, one of MSR's three cable barns, on the last day of operation, April 5, 1941. (BELOW) **A 1928 VIEW** of this same barn's interior, with transfer table pit in the foreground.
BOTH: Charles Smallwood

Cable Car Houses

WASHINGTON AND MASON: This is one parcel of Market Street Railway property that may be said to have made good. Today it is the operating center of San Francisco's world-famed cable car fleet. It is one of, if not the principal, tourist attractions in The City and is visited by hundreds of thousands annually.

This barn and power house has been beautifully refurbished, its new decor being strongly reminiscent of the fabled Gay Nineties era. A lavish balcony has been built over the massive cable propelling machinery for the accommodation of visitors, and work is progressing on the establishing within its confines of a transit museum. The property has been officially declared a National Landmark by the Federal Government, and a large bronze plaque in the visitors' gallery so attests.

Built in 1887 by *The Ferries & Cliff House Railway Company,* Washington and Mason Barn was originally three stories in height. The ground floor was given over to the cable machinery plant, while the two top floors provided storage for cars. In 1902, a small addition was added on the north side of the building facing Mason St.

The earthquake and fire of 1906 destroyed the building and its contents, but rebuilding got under way almost immediately. However, it emerged as a two-story structure.

The cable machinery was operated by steam power until 1911, when it was converted to electricity. The steam power plant was retained as an auxiliary until 1924, when it was removed.

During its ownership by Market Street Railway Company, cable lines operated from this division were:

- Powell-Mason
- Washington-Jackson
- Sacramento-Clay

On February 15, 1942, buses were substituted for the Sacramento-Clay cable car service. However, Powell St. service by cable continued until MSR passed into city hands in 1944.

WASHINGTON & MASON barn is the most famous of the cable facilities. It was rebuilt after destruction in the 1906 earthquake and fire, and today is still serving as an active facility . . . and also a popular museum. This view was taken in 1921.

Richard Schlaich

(ABOVE) **A TYPICAL SCENE** inside Washington & Mason car house, taken in October, 1941.

Ted Wurm

(BELOW) **CASTRO STREET CABLE'S** propulsion machinery was hard at work when this photo was taken back in 1928.

S.F. Public Utilities Commission

PACIFIC AVENUE barn as it appeared in 1929.   S.F. Public Utilities Commission

INSIDE THE CASTRO cable barn, October, 1938. From left to right are cars 4, 2, 6, 7, and 133.   Ted Wurm

CASTRO STREET: Built in the 1880s by *The Market Street Cable Railway* system for its Market and Castro line, this was the sole barn of many used by the Market Street cable system to remain a cable operating division after 1906. It served that portion of the old line not electrified: on Castro St. from 18th to 26th streets, this section being considered too steep to be negotiated by electric cars.

Castro Street Barn was located on the northeast corner of Castro and Jersey streets. It had ample car capacity, as but seven cars were operated from it after 1906. It boasted a most ingenious device in its depths: a transfer table which could also serve as a turntable.

On April 5, 1941, Castro St. cable service was replaced by bus operation. This building was sold soon thereafter and was eventually torn down to make way for a supermarket.

PACIFIC AVENUE: Like Castro Street, this building was both a car house and a cable power house. It was located on the north side of Pacific Ave. between Polk St. and Van Ness Ave. and was the smallest car house on the MSR system. It was built by United Railroads in 1908 to house the half-dozen cable trains (a dummy-grip car and its trailer) which were retained on the outer portion of the 9th-Polk-Larkin Line when that line, hitherto cable, was electrified in 1906. The remaining cable operation ran on Pacific Ave. from Polk St. to Broderick St.

The power plant to operate this tiny cable system was a General Electric No. 1000 streetcar motor!

On November 17, 1929, this archaic cable operation was abandoned and the barn torn down.

Carrying the Message

THIS EXACT SCALE MODEL of an MSR standard car was built by Elkton shopmen in 1927, and saw wide use as a display piece in shop windows and at various social functions.

Charles Smallwood

Putting MSR's Best Foot Forward

WHEN MARKET STREET RAILWAY Company took over the system of the United Railroads in 1921 it automatically inherited that company's unfortunate public image. Years of militant anti-labor exertions (including breaking two bloody strikes) and bribery (Mayor Schmitz and Abe Reuf, politician extraordinaire) had brought URR President Pat Calhoun to an eminence which today would be quite embarrassing to any corporation head.

From 1921 on, the objective of MSR public relations people was to mellow this negative image and in its place establish the company in the public's mind as one of progressive understanding and cooperation with any and all civic betterment movements.

How well did they succeed? All too well, if we are to judge by the surprised reaction of city officials who complained that MSR was spending altogether too much money on advertising —money which might better be spent on reducing fares.

But MSR's chief competitor was not the Municipal Railway; it admitted that a prospective streetcar passenger would catch the nearest car. No, MSR was out to get the man behind the wheel of his automobile. How it campaigned to influence him to leave his car at home and climb aboard a white front car is quite a tale.

Market Street Railway's aggressive public relations policy came full flower with the advent of President Kahn and the taking over of the railway by the Byllesby organization. The national advertising of the Byllesby group was quite up to the accepted par of the day, and when Market Street Railway's new management swung it into line, the results were startling to old-time San Franciscans.

Running down the long list of MSR public relations during the administration of President Kahn, one is impressed by the program's wide-reaching scope:

- NEWSPAPERS: Large advertisements were inserted, con[ve]ying to the readers of the city that a new day had dawned at [M]SR. In addition, full cooperation with reporters was a mat[te]r of policy; all questions as to service, accidents, special [ev]ents, etc., were fully answered, and quickly.

- BILLBOARDS: Kahn erected billboards wherever feasible [on] MSR property. Since many car houses occupied strategic [lo]cations on busy thoroughfares, this brought their message [ho]me to tens of thousands daily.

- EXHIBITS: Windows of downtown stores were used to [sh]ow MSR car models, photos, car equipment, and track [m]aps. These were rotated about the city and were viewed by [mo]re thousands daily. A feature of these exhibits was the [ni]ne-foot model of a Comfort Car, built at Elkton Shops in [19]27 and painted in the White Front colors; this model was [in] exact scale and was complete in every detail except elec[tri]cal equipment.

- STUNTS: Unusual uses of cars were always good for a [ne]wspaper story. Here were included a showing of a Harold [Ll]oyd talkie aboard a 100-Class car; a car encased in boxy [fra]mework supported exterior billboard signs; the private car [SA]N FRANCISCO wrapped up as a Christmas package and blar[ing] forth carols.

- THE SCHOOL CAR: The SAN FRANCISCO was "given" to the children of San Francisco and carried them over the system for years free of charge; a chief objective of these trips was Elkton Shops, where boys and girls were shown how Comfort Cars were constructed. Upon leaving, each child received a ruler with company advertising on both sides and each teacher was given a brass paperweight, cast in the Elkton brass foundry. Other trips were made to the beach, to downtown, and even to San Mateo. Many a San Franciscan grown old and gray recalls with fondness a trip aboard this famed car.

- ABANDONMENTS: Even this negative item was handled in a positive manner. When the Toonerville on Montgomery St. was abandoned in 1927, MSR turned the occasion into a publicity stunt which saw Mayor Rolph at the reins of an old horsecar; the farewell parade even included a cable car and two of the brand new California Comfort Cars. Invaluable columns of space resulted, along with a pleasing number of large photos.

- COMPANY PROPERTY: All car houses, shelters and stations received coats of green and white MSR paint. The advent of the Air Age was saluted when many car houses received large signs on their roofs identifying the city and with a large arrow pointing the way to the city airport.

Promoting the Riding Habit

(FACING PAGE, TOP) **THE ADVANTAGES** of leaving the family buggy in the garage were extolled by this billboard, at Fillmore and Turk Streets, in 1930.

(FACING PAGE, MIDDLE) **A WALL** of the 28th & Valencia Car House provided space for the MSR message, also in 1930.

(FACING PAGE, BOTTOM AND BELOW) **THIS 1930 SPREAD,** at Market & Gough Streets, sought to educate the public on the new features (including leather-upholstered seats) of its California Comfort Cars. **ALL: Market Street Railway**

Open House

NEWLY BUILT California Comfort Car, #937, held open house for six days in October 1929, at Fifth & Market Streets. An estimated 30,000 visitors inspected the new car during its display period.   **Market Street Railway**

- NEW CARS: The company's major car building program was accented by displaying the latest model cars at important locations, such as Fifth and Market. People were invited to board and inspect the new cars and were given brochures describing their advanced features.

- DASH SIGNS: Probably nothing had been as prosaic as a streetcar dash sign. Under MSR's new deal even these were brightened up. Cars heading for Playland displayed colorful signs on which the roller coaster was prominently displayed. Undoubtedly such imaginative use of the prominent space on the front of the cars resulted in additional rides being sold.

- SPECIAL MOVEMENTS: Baseball at Seals Stadium and football at Kezar Stadium generated big crowds for MSR cars. These movements were well publicized and the fact that the cars fortuitously were able to deposit their patrons right at the door was a big plus factor. Even Stanford Stadium got into the MSR act; connecting service to Southern Pacific peninsula trains to Palo Alto was publicized by big banners over the MSR cars at Second and Market which ran to the depot.

The Depression greatly curtailed the company's expenditures for public relations, but from 1926 through 1932 this important part of the merchandising picture was thoroughly exploited.

TERMINAL SIGNS at La Playa and Balboa reflect a downtown terminal change upon completion of the Oakland Bay Bridge in 1937. Signs in 1935 (left) and 1940 (right) demonstrate.   **BOTH: Charles Smallwood**

Flashy Dash Signs

PERHAPS NOT TYPICAL of the majority of dash signs, but nevertheless striking in eye appeal, was the novel design at right. Carried by cars on lines #5 and #7 serving the Playland amusement area in 1932, dash signs such as this could influence almost anyone to hop aboard and head for fun.

MORE PROSAIC but quite explicit were dash signs such as the one appearing below. Also prominent in this photo is MSR's virtual trademark: a small brass plate informing one and all of MSR's patent on its White Front area.

BOTH: Market Street Railway

COMPLETELY DISGUISED inside this traveling billboard is a 1550 class car, one of several fitted in the 1930s in an ill-fated attempt to boost company revenues. The boxy advertising shroud made the cars too wide to operate on the inner tracks on Market Street, and the plan was abandoned in a few weeks.
Market Street Railway

(BELOW) **A 100 CLASS CAR** models another publicity gimmick in the same period. A Harold Lloyd "talkie" was shown on board the car. **Market Street Railway**

PART OF CHILDHOOD in The City: As a souvenir of a trip on the school car "San Francisco" (see Electric Passenger Cars chapter), each student received a ruler, and each teacher received a brass paper weight cast in MSR's emblem. **Charles Smallwood**

September, 1930

WHY NO NEW LINES?

Much has been said about privately owned street railway lines in San Francisco failing to build new lines for some years past. To say they "**would not**" does not tell the story.

The whole truth is, they "*could not.*" And why?

Because the city charter for years has provided that new lines built by private capital must belong to the city twenty-five years after they are built, WITHOUT THE CITY PAYING A CENT FOR THEM.

Even those who lead you to think the companies **would not**; actually **could not** put their own money into such new street car lines. They **could not** because they **would not** get their money back in twenty-five years,—and probably **would not** even get interest on that money.

Extensions can be built privately if the charter is amended reasonably.

SAMUEL KAHN, President

Appendix

History: The Company's Narrative

THE MORE OFFICIAL narrative of the history of Market Street Railway Company was that appearing in the company's Annual Reports over the signature of President Samuel B. Kahn. The bulk of his reporting has been excerpted and covers the years 1930-1944. Three sources are thanked for making the Annual Reports available: Carl Blaubach of the California Public Utilities Commission, John D. Coll of the San Francisco Public Library's Special Collections Department, and the Stanford University Library.

1930

Gross earnings of MSR for the calendar year of 1930 were $9,196,340.40, a decrease of $393,853.38 (or 4.11%) from 1929. This decrease was due principally to the reduction in passenger revenues occasioned by the five-day work week for building mechanics and to other factors for which the national depression was to blame.

MSR executives made strenuous efforts to keep traffic, and their notable success resulted in a loss of revenue which was considerably under the average of the majority of traction companies—9%.

Because of the decline in passenger receipts, MSR made every effort to reduce operating expenses at no loss of its high quality of service to the public. Operating expenses, including taxes, declined a total of $221,732.09, some 2.75% better than 1929. This was effected partly through increasing the schedule speeds of cars plus such reductions in schedules as seemed to be indicated by the loss in passenger traffic. Despite the reduction in revenues, thorough maintenance of MSR property was continued during 1930 in spite of various economies effected; a total of $1,138,421.68 was spent for this purpose. Total operating costs, including taxes, amounted to $7,842,745.29.

TRACK AND ROADWAY: Work of this nature during the year consisted of rebuilding 0.187 miles (single) of electric track on Clayton and Turk Streets. Abandoned trackage removed totaled 1.343 miles (single) of unused track, mainly on 10th, Mission, Bosworth, and California Streets and 33rd Avenue.

ROLLING STOCK: The car fleet was maintained in good condition. Twenty-two new electric car bodies of the "California Comfort Car" type were built at Elkton Shops to replace a like number of obsolete bodies which were then scrapped and burned. In addition, seven electric cars were equipped with comfortable leather and rattan seats, making a total of 376 such cars in service on December 31, 1930. Twenty-three cars of the San Mateo suburban line were equipped with automatic field taps to increase their speeds; they also received quick-applying air brakes. Two hundred fifty-six electric cars and eight cable cars were thoroughly overhauled and repainted.

REAL ESTATE: Car houses and other structures were repainted and all necessary repairs made. A new pattern shop was built at Elkton Shops and other buildings there were remodeled and repainted.

SERVICE: Improved frequency of service, and increased car spee were inaugurated on many lines. Despite the faster speeds, t number of accidents was reduced due to intelligent observation orders issued to car men and others concerning care in car operatic

FRANCHISES: At a city election held on November 4, 1930, a proval was granted to MSR to surrender its remaining franchises the City and County of San Francisco and take in lieu thereof 25-year operating permit for all of its lines, whether operated un unexpired franchises or by sufferance under expired franchises. T proposition was adopted by a large majority and has since be ratified by the State Legislature. It thereby became a part of the c charter. During early February 1931 MSR surrendered its franchi and rights pursuant to the charter amendment and received 25-year operating permit for all of its lines. This 25-year operati permit clarified the franchise situation and enabled MSR to impr its property and make necessary extensions in the knowledge that property was inviolate for that period of time. This operating per was granted subject to the right of the city to acquire the property MSR upon payment of its fair share as determined by mutual agr ment or by the courts.

1931

Gross earnings for 1931 dropped $632,176.46—6.86%—co pared to those for 1930, chiefly due to the continued busin depression. MSR earned $8,589,034.30 for the year.

Revenue passenger traffic declined 6.51% during the ye although electric railways of the nation on a national average clined by 10.78% in passenger traffic. To offset this drop, ev effort was made by MSR chiefs to cut operating expenses with impairing service and maintenance. $1,010,178.49 was spent maintenance.

Total operating expenses, including taxes, were $7,339,662.60 decrease of $534,652.28—6.79% below 1930.

Fulfilling promises made to voters in the campaign to get 25-year operating permit, MSR applied for and received a permi construct a double-track electric railway west on Turk St. fr Divisadero across Arguello Blvd. to and along Balboa St. to 3 Ave.—a distance of 5.676 single track miles. Construction of this tension was started in November 1931 on Balboa St. from 6th A to 30th Ave., a distance of 2.860 single track miles; by the end of 1931 a total of 1.375 miles of single track and overhead had been laid. Work on the remainder was held up at year's end pending the start of grading work by the city on Turk Street.

Track reconstruction work completed in 1931 included a total of 3.108 equivalent single track miles, of which 1.631 miles were on Sutter St. and 1.477 miles were on Market St.

In cooperation with the city, temporary tracks were laid from 3rd and Berry streets through property of the Southern Pacific Company to and along 4th St. and back to 3rd St. This was in connection with the pending construction of a new bridge at 3rd and Channel streets.

Twenty new electric car bodies were built at Elkton Shops during the year, replacing a like number of obsolete bodies. The new cars were equipped with leather seats in the closed sections and rattan seats in open sections, and new line breakers were installed. On 20 additional electric cars the old style longitudinal rattan and wood seats were removed and replaced with cross seats of leather and rattan. Some 237 electric cars, five cable cars and six buses were thoroughly overhauled.

In November, 28 electric cars on Fillmore St. were temporarily equipped with "economy meters" as an experiment; their use indicates a 9.9% saving in power consumption on that line.

The exteriors of two car houses and one substation were painted; three car houses were whitewashed inside, and many waiting stations on the San Mateo Line were painted inside and out.

A special Wednesday 30¢ round-trip fare on the San Mateo Line has proved fairly successful.

1932

Earnings continued to plummet in 1932, as the Great Depression continued to hold the nation in a firm grip. MSR's gross earnings for 1932 were $7,822,181.55, a decrease of $766,852.75—8.52%. Revenue passenger traffic fell 8.96% in the year, compared with a drop for the entire street railway industry of the nation of 12%.

Operating expenses were cut to $6,955,997.22—a drop of 5.22% under 1931. MSR made every effort to maintain good service and continue maintenance of its properties; $1,002,967.90 was spent in 1932 for that purpose.

Among the outstanding economies effected in 1932 were: Skip stop operation on Balboa, California, Clement, Fulton, Geary and Lincoln Way, west of Arguello Blvd.; the abandonment of service on Divisadero St. between Sacramento and Jackson streets; and speeding up of car schedules to cut operating expenses yet give good service.

MSR realized $84,000 by selling to the city its property on which Kezar Stadium was later erected.

During 1932 the Balboa Extension accounted for 4.336 miles of single track and overhead trolley construction on Balboa and Turk streets; this new line went into service on May 15, 1932, as Line #31. It was 5.711 single track miles in length and quickly proved successful from a revenue standpoint and was greatly appreciated and commended by patrons and improvement clubs.

Three buses were purchased and two new bus lines were established in 1932. These were opened as follows: Southern Heights (2.65 route miles) on February 10, 1932; Sunset District (1.89 route miles) on February 12, 1932.

Cooperating with the city in the construction of Sunset Blvd. underpasses, MSR removed portions of its tracks on Sloat Blvd. and Lincoln Way, operating over detours, and relaid its tracks after completion of the underpasses. Abandoned track and overhead on Bosworth St. between Mission and Congo streets (0.68 miles) and unused special work at various locations were removed.

Twenty-one new electric car bodies were built at Elkton Shops during 1932; all got leather seats in the closed sections and rattan seats in the open sections and were replacements for an equal number of obsolete cars which were scrapped and burned. Some 224 electric cars and 11 cable cars were overhauled and repainted. Longitudinal rattan and wood seats were removed from 27 electric cars and replaced by lateral rattan seats.

Two electric cars were rebuilt into one-man cars and placed in operation on the South San Francisco Line.

The exteriors of these structures were painted during 1932: McAllister Barn, Haight Street Barn (front only), Clement Street Barn, and the roof and doors of the Bryant Street Substation and Storeroom.

1933

Although business continued to decline, MSR executives thought they detected a bottoming out. Gross earnings for 1933 were $7,422,816.20, a decrease of $399,365.35, or 5.10%, over 1932. The first ten months showed a continuing decline in electric railway travel over the same period of 1932, but passenger revenue for November and December showed a slight but encouraging increase of 2.56% over the same two months of 1932, indicating that a leveling-out process had definitely developed in the company's business. This increase was the first experienced in 45 months.

Operating expenses, including taxes, totaled $6,338,882.41, a reduction of $617,114.81, or 8.87% from those of the previous year, brought about by curtailing car miles and car hours operated. Notwithstanding such economies, MSR property was thoroughly maintained, the company spending some $946,824.98 for this purpose.

The company received $4,500 from the city for the sale of its Ocean Shore right-of-way, use of which was discontinued when the tracks and overhead were relocated in the center of Bay Shore Blvd. at the city's request in furtherance of the widening of that highway south of Army St.

The new Third Street Bridge was completed, tracks and overhead installed and streetcar service over the bridge resumed. The temporary detour tracks over property of the Southern Pacific were then removed.

The production of new car bodies at Elkton was cut to nine. In addition, one electric car body for one- or two-man operation was built, and modern safety equipment and leather and rattan seats installed in it. This new equipment replaced 13 obsolete bodies which were retired and cremated.

Some 203 electric cars, 18 cable cars and seven buses were overhauled, painted and revarnished. Longitudinal seats in 19 cars were replaced with rattan cross seats. Economy meters were installed in 18 cars, making a total of 122 cars so equipped.

The following structures were painted: Interior and exterior of two small stations at Broadway and Fillmore streets and Fillmore and Green streets; the front wall and cupola of the Eighth Avenue Substation; the roof of the office building at San Jose and Geneva Avenues; and the gymnasium and hallway at the same location.

To cut operating expenses, the company desired to operate one-man cars on some of its less profitable lines, and in 1933 requested the Board of Supervisors of the City and County of San Francisco to repeal an existing ordinance prohibiting one-man car operation. At the end of the year, no response had been forthcoming.

With a view to cooperating with the National Recovery Act (NRA) and to enable MSR to subscribe to the Code adopted thereunder for the street railway industry, MSR management advised the Public Utilities Commission of San Francisco of its willingness to apply to the California Railroad Commission for a six-cent fare, providing such increased fare, if allowed, were simultaneously adopted by the Municipal Railway. This proposal was declined by the city.

A company union was formed (reflecting NRA) to be known as "Market Street Railway Employes Cooperation Association"; about 90% of the company's employees became members, and on August 24, 1933, MSR entered into an agreement with this union for the period ending December 31, 1934, regulating the working hours and wages, and establishing a plan to hear, consider and act upon the grievances of employees.

Through the Employes Cooperative Association, MSR management submitted to its employees for approval an agreement under which there would be distributed to employees (except officers and department heads) 55% of the annual net profits of the company for a period of three years starting January 1, 1934, and guaranteeing that such annual compensation for the year 1934 would be a sum at least equal to an increase of 2¢ per hour over and above the present hourly wage of each platform man and a proportionate amount for every other employee. On January 16, 1934, approximately 67% of the membership voted to accept this agreement. Distribution of profits would be made in quarterly installments.

1934

Operating revenues for 1934 were $7,288,300.37, a decrease of $134,515.83, or 1.81% compared with 1933.

The uptrend in business expected due to the increased passenger revenue for November and December of 1933 continued through the first five months of 1934, but the remainder of 1934 showed a decrease over the same months in 1933, particularly July, due to the fact that on July 15th, anticipating the general strike which took place in San Francisco from July 16th to 19th, MSR employees went on a strike which continued to and including July 28, 1934.

Operating expenses were $6,375,444.46, an increase of $36,562.05, due mainly to a wage increase of 2¢ per hour guaranteed to employees by an agreement in effect January 1, 1934. Every effort was made to cut expenses by reducing car miles and car hours operated without materially affecting service to the public. The maintenance of properties was continued throughout the year, $970,474.83 being spent for this purpose.

Track removed amounted to 0.495 miles of single track, this being done on Divisadero St. from Sacramento to Jackson streets and on First St. from Brannan to Townsend streets, where service had been abandoned.

To facilitate sewer construction work being done by the city on Harrison, Bryant, Brannan, 16th and other streets, 2.796 miles of single track and overhead wires were temporarily removed, of which 0.547 single track miles had been restored by the end of 1934.

Sixteen obsolete electric cars were cremated; 205 electric cars, 10 cable cars and five buses were overhauled, touched up and revarnished. Wooden seats in nine cars were removed and replaced with rattan seats.

The fronts of the Turk and Fillmore car house and substation were painted.

Cooperating with the California Highway Commission and the city and county of San Francisco to the end that Harrison St. west of Fifth St. might be utilized as an avenue of approach to the westerly terminus of the San Francisco Bay Bridge, now under construction, MSR agreed to remove its streetcar tracks on Harrison St. west of Third St. and along the route of its #33 Line, except such portions thereof as were used by other lines, in return for a permit to operate trolley buses along and upon a route substantially the same as that operated by the #33 Line.

On May 1, 1934, MSR entered into an agreement with Division 1004, Amalgamated Association of Street and Electric Railway Employees of America, covering working hours and wages, similar in all intents and purposes to the agreement executed in 1933 with the Market Street Railway Employees Cooperative Association. This agreement was signed by the company and by officers of Division 1004 and was approved by the officer representing the International Association. In spite of this, the agreement was later repudiated by the International Association and MSR employees went on strike, which not only adversely affected the company's earnings but seriously inconvenienced its patrons. After extended discussions, MSR management agreed with International Association officials to submit the matter of wages to arbitration.

On December 14, 1934, the Board of Arbitration rendered its award which increased wages by about 12 to 25%, effective February 1, 1935. In making this award the Board of Arbitration exceeded the powers granted under the agreement, and recognized the inability of the company to pay such an increase of wages out of its present revenues, but suggested that the union and the company cooperate to the end that an increase in revenue be obtained with either a fare increase or by other means.

The company, desiring to avoid further wage controversy, took steps to meet the increased costs imposed upon it by the Board of Arbitration, requesting the city of San Francisco to rescind an ordinance forbidding the operation of one-man cars. The city denied this request and, upon advice of counsel, the company appealed to the Federal Courts in the belief that the ordinance is unconstitutional. A temporary restraining order was obtained and MSR management was hoping for a permanent injunction. At the end of the year the company was operating six one-man cars and was adding others as quickly as cars could be converted to one-man operation.

1935

The year 1935 brought a 0.69% upswing in operating revenues; $7,338,740.97 was received, an increase over 1934 of $50,440.60.

Operating expenses were $6,247,243.01, a decrease of 2.01%, realized by a reduction in service and car hours operated which became necessary and unavoidable to offset the increased wage scale effective February 1, 1935. Further economies were secured by one-man car and trolley coach operation.

A total of $837,452.73 was spent in maintaining property.

Some 5.40 single track miles of track was rebuilt in the year, principally on Mission St. from the county line to Colma and on Sloat Blvd. between 38th and 42nd Avenues.

Cooperating with municipal authorities and the State Highway Commission in the construction of sewers and Bay Bridge approaches, approximately 9.103 single track miles of track were abandoned, of which 3.62 miles of single track and overhead lines were removed on Bryant St. from Sterling to 2nd streets, Sterling St. from Bryant St. to Harrison St., Harrison St. from 1st to 2nd streets and 3rd to 10th streets, 5th St. from Bryant to Harrison streets, 6th St. from Brannan to Bryant streets, and 8th St. from Bryant to Brannan streets. In addition, 1.58 miles of single track were covered over and overhead construction removed on 18th St. from Guerrero to Church streets, on Ashbury St. from Frederick to Clayton streets, and on Harrison St. from 10th to 14th streets. The remaining 3.903 were pending removal at year's end.

Sixty-one obsolete electric cars were cremated. Forty-one electric cars, seven cable cars and six buses were thoroughly overhauled. Eighty-two electric cars, seven cable cars and one bus were repainted. Rattan cross seats were installed in six electric cars and eighteen cars received new motors.

On March 14, 1935, one-man cars were placed in operation, the first line so equipped being #36 on Folsom St. As rapidly thereafter as equipment became available, additional one-man cars were operated on other lines in the following order: Line 35—Howard St.; Line 27—Bryant St.; Line 20—Ellis and O'Farrell streets; Line 25—San Bruno Avenue; Line 39—Visitacion Valley.

To furnish equipment for these lines, 12 used one-man cars were purchased and 47 two-man cars converted for one-man operation; at the end of the year MSR owned 61 one-man cars.

In November 1935, the Master in Chancery, to whom the hearing of evidence in the one-man car case was referred by the Federal Court, submitted his report to the Court; he found in favor of the company on all points and recommended that the city be permanently enjoined from enforcing its ordinance requiring operation of streetcars by two men. Subsequently the Federal Court rendered its decision in the one-man car case in favor of MSR, perpetually enjoining the city of San Francisco from enforcing the ordinance requiring two men on all streetcars.

Approximately 10.169 round-trip miles of double overhead trolley lines were constructed for trolley coach operation, and on October 6, 1935, eight new trolley coaches began operating over practically the same route as the abandoned #33 rail line. They proved popular with patrons from the start, and the new line's receipts were practically double those of the former car line. An additional trolley coach was ordered to help meet the increase in riders.

1936

The depression was lifting its heavy hand from the nation's economy and MSR's operating revenues reflected the fact by increasing 2.52% to $7,523,415.34—an upsurge of $184,674.37. This improvement was principally due to better business conditions and more employment in the territory served. In fact, MSR's business would have been even better but for the West Coast maritime strike, called in the latter part of October.

Operating expenses, maintenance and taxes amounted to $6,242,016.62, a decrease of $5,226.39, or 0.08%. These savings were principally attributable to increased operation of one-man cars.

Twenty-nine one-man cars were purchased during the year and additional MSR cars were rebuilt for one-man operation; the company owned 174 one-man cars at the end of the year.

The Bay Bridge opened for auto traffic on November 12, 1936—too late in the year to affect 1936 revenues. In its desire to cooperate with the city in eliminating areas of congestion, MSR relocated some 700 trolley poles at various points, transferred certain feeder lines, discontinued other lines and removed their poles, wires and track from street on which service had previously been abandoned.

The United States District Court's verdict upholding MSR's position in the one-man car case and perpetually enjoining the city from enforcing its two-man crew ordinance was appealed by the city to the United States Circuit Court of Appeals, and there the matter rested as 1936 ended.

1937

Total gross revenues were $7,192,721.83, a decrease of $330,693.51 or 4.40% as compared with 1936.

Operating expenses were $5,991,530.14, up 0.96% to $56,700.05.

Sixty-eight percent of the decrease in net operating revenue was attributable to decreased passenger revenues caused partly by strikes, including a waterfront strike which completely suspended shipping from October 30, 1936, to February 5, 1937, and a three-month strike of all Class A hotel employees. Taxes went up some 12%, also adding to the poor showing.

On March 23, 1937, MSR entered into an agreement with Division 1004 of the Amalgamated Association of Street Electric Railway and Motor Coach Employees of America covering wages, hours and working conditions of all employees except office forces and a few monthly employees in the operating department. The agreement, effective March 14, 1937, continued through March 31, 1939. For the first year of the agreement, wages of car men went up 5¢ per hour; shopmen and linemen received 7.5¢ more per hour; trackmen 2.5¢ more hourly with a minimum of 50¢ per hour. On and after March 14, 1938, the wages of all employees covered by said agreement were increased 2.5¢ per hour.

To raise money to meet these increased payrolls and taxes, MSR applied to the State Railroad Commission for a fare increase from 5¢ cash with free transfers to 7¢ cash or four tokens for 25¢, 16 rides for 50¢ for schoolchildren and 25¢ for Sunday and holiday passes with free transfers to remain. The Railroad Commission denied the plea and of its own motion ordered that the 5¢ cash fare with half fare and free transfers for schoolchildren be retained, but that transfers issued with full fares be sold for 2¢ each. This plan went into effect on July 6, 1937. The sale of transfers reached expectations but normal 5¢ fare riding fell off to such an extent that no financial advantage was realized.

Operating expenses were cut by reducing headways during off peak hours and in certain other ways without impairing efficient operation and good service.

Maintenance expenditures for 1937 continued at a relatively high level: $957,871.13. The policy of replacing old bolted rail joints with thermit welded joints was continued. Old track and special work was rebuilt at various locations, and abandoned track, principally on Geneva Ave. and Taylor St., aggregating 3.041 miles of single track, was removed.

Rolling stock received necessary repairs, overhauling and painting. Nineteen electric cars received longitudinal leather seats, replacing cross seats, in their open sections, thus increasing passenger capacity. Twenty revenue and six non-revenue cars, retired as obsolete, were cremated.

Two 23-passenger Twin Coach buses were purchased, as were nine motorcycles with sidecars, the latter for use of inspectors and track oilers.

The Visitacion Valley right-of-way, extending on Geneva Ave. from Mission St. to the San Mateo county line, owned by *The Gough Street Railroad Company,* and leased to MSR, was sold during 1937 to the city and county of San Francisco for street purposes. The city thereupon asked MSR to discontinue operation of the street railway over this right-of-way and remove its tracks. This was done, and a permit to operate buses in lieu of streetcars over the same route, tying in with the existing Crocker-Amazon and Excelsior bus lines was secured.

Also sold in 1937 was the easterly half of MSR's sand block located at 21st Ave. and Ortega St. Going too was the old cable power house property on Pacific Ave. west of Polk St.

On May 27, 1937, the Golden Gate Bridge opened to pedestrian traffic and to vehicular traffic the following day. The week of Fiesta celebrating the event added to the company's passenger receipts.

A new city ordinance prohibiting automobile parking on Market St. and in other downtown areas during morning and evening rush hours went into effect on August 16, 1937. This bettered streetcar service greatly.

Accidents were reduced by 21% in 1937 over 1936, and MSR attributed this to a large extent to one-man cars.

1938

Gross revenues for 1938 fell to $6,482,370—a decrease of $710,350 from the 1937 total. Kahn attributed the downswing to "unemployment and depressed business conditions, changes in fare structures hereinafter referred to, and fewer revenue car hours..."

Operating expenses fell to $5,594,584—a 6.63% decrease amounting to $396,945. This was due to the many economies effected during the year.

The necessary amount of maintenance work was done during the year, $880,324 being spent. Tracks and special work were rebuilt at various locations. Nine obsolete cars were cremated. Rattan seats replaced wood seats in open sections of eight electric cars, while 10 cars received leather seats in their open sections. When necessary, cars, buses and trolley coaches were overhauled and repainted. Three worn-out gas buses were scrapped and replaced by two new Twin Coaches and one used Fageol bus.

Effective March 14, 1938, wages of all carmen, shopmen, linemen and trackmen went up 2.5¢ per hour, in accordance with the company's agreement with Amalgamated Association of Street Electric Railway and Motor Coach Employees of America, Division 1004.

Economy measures included the closing of the Oak and Broderick car house on August 15, 1938; cars formerly operating therefrom were reassigned to Haight and McAllister car houses. The 28th and Valencia car house was closed on January 15, 1939, and its cars reassigned to 24th and Utah, Geneva and Haight car houses. The number of car hours operated in off peak periods was reduced.

Revenue derived from selling transfers at 2¢ each, authorized by the Railroad Commission in 1937, proved inadequate and application was made on March 19, 1938, for an increase in fares in San Francisco to seven cents, with free transfers; schoolchildren 16 rides for 50 cents, Sunday and holiday passes 25 cents, and interurban fares seven cents where five cents was being charged. On May 9, 1938, the Railroad Commission approved this fare schedule, but authorized the use of tokens and directed that they be sold at the rate of four for 25 cents. This fare structure went into effect on May 29, 1938.

469

What happened next? Quoting President Kahn: "The defection of our regular patrons to other and competing lines which maintained the five-cent fare and increased service in anticipation of the change, was much greater than expected and occurred principally on Market St. where the Municipal Railway also operates, and on other lines closely paralleled by Municipal Railway lines or California Street Cable Railway lines."

To meet such decrease in revenue, the company applied to the Board of Supervisors for permission to abandon its unprofitable Castro St. cable and Guerrero St. electric lines, but the Board refused.

On October 8, 1938, the company again asked the Railroad Commission to set a straight seven-cent fare in San Francisco and South San Francisco, eliminating tokens. At the hearing before the Commission, the Manager of Public Utilities of the city of San Francisco testified that the Municipal Railway had no jitney competition (the city refused to permit jitney buses to operate on streets having Municipal Railway lines) and that if it desired to abandon or curtail service on unprofitable lines it did so without reference to any regulatory body whatsoever, a privilege definitely not enjoyed by Market Street Railway Company.

On November 23, 1938, the Railroad Commission issued a most interesting order: it directed MSR to ask the appropriate boards or officers of the city and county of San Francisco for permission to abandon operation, in whole or in part, of 11 unprofitable street railway lines, and for such relief as might be necessary to eliminate jitney competition. Should such relief not be given before January 1, 1939, the Commission's order continued, the fare structure requested by MSR would automatically go into effect.

Accordingly, MSR on November 28, 1938, filed with the Board of Supervisors of San Francisco an application for repeal of certain city ordinances permitting and regulating jitneys; on November 30, 1938, MSR applied to this same Board of Supervisors for authority to abandon, either wholly or partly, the operation of the 11 lines. On December 12, 1938, the Board of Supervisors refused to permit the abandonments or to repeal the jitney ordinances and on January 1, 1939, the straight seven-cent fare automatically went into effect. For the convenience of the public, MSR sold tokens at the rate of five for 35¢.

The company also lost its last hope for one-man car operation in 1938. MSR's suit against the city and county of San Francisco to enjoin the enforcement of the ordinance prohibiting the operation of one-man cars, which was decided by the United States District Court in favor of MSR in 1935, was appealed by the city to the Circuit Court of Appeals; that court on July 7, 1938, reversed the District Court's decision. MSR thereupon appealed this decision to the U.S. Supreme Court, but the latter court on January 3, 1939, declined to review the decision of the Court of Appeals. An application for a rehearing of the case before the Supreme Court was also denied.

Another proposal to buy MSR and combine it with Municipal Railway was defeated at the polls at a special election held on September 27, 1938. President Kahn had agreed to recommend to his stockholders that MSR be sold to the city for $12,500,000. In submitting this proposal to the Board of Supervisors for their action with respect to a bond issue, the Public Utilities Commission added to the $12,500,000 price tag a sum of $11,980,000 for rehabilitating the combined properties in the event of sale. The voters refused to go for the $24,480,000 bond issue, defeating the proposal by an 88,837 to 49,511 score.

Subsequently, and on its own initiative, the Board of Supervisors placed upon the ballot at the general election held on November 8, 1938, proposals for the purchase of MSR's properties for $5,000,000, and for the purchase of 750 gasoline buses to replace streetcars in San Francisco. In President Kahn's words, "These were merely policy measures and involved no bond issues. Both proposals were badly defeated, as they deserved to be, for there was no basis for supposing that the Company's properties could be purchased for $5,000,000."

A big event influencing 1938 was the continued construction of the Bay Bridge railway and its terminal in San Francisco. The construction of the terminal loop was exclusively a Municipal Railway operation, with MSR participating in the role of tenant. The bridge railway service opened on January 15, 1939.

During the year three wholly owned subsidiaries were liquidated. The corporate charter of The Sutter Street Railway Company expired and was not renewed. *The South San Francisco Railroad & Power Company* and *The Gough (Street) Railroad Company* dissolved and wound up their affairs, effective December 30, 1938; all properties owned by the companies, consisting of franchises, track and rights-of-way, were conveyed to MSR.

The unfortunate financial condition of MSR was emphasized during the year. The company was unable to meet the sinking fund installments due in July and October 1938, or any of the interest on bonds held in the sinking fund. The trustee gave notice to bondholders of the non-payment, but they made no request for action by the trustee (Wells Fargo Bank & Union Trust Company) in regard thereto. Interest on bonds outstanding in the hands of the public was paid.

Two brighter items occurred in the year. The Railroad Commission on December 28, 1938, ordered a revision of charges for electric energy purchased by MSR which resulted in a reduction in the company's power bills of approximately four percent.

And accidents were reduced 20% during 1938, due in large part, according to Kahn, to the work of the Accident Prevention Department, created in 1937.

1939

The total gross revenues for 1939, $6,436,315.72, were down slightly from those of 1938 ($6,474,502.29), the decrease amounting to $38,186.16.

Passenger revenues decreased $48,737.54—0.75% from 1938. This drop was blamed on unemployment, labor strikes, and loss of patronage due to a fare increase to seven cents cash fare in 1938. However, it was felt that the drop would have been even greater had it not been for added business generated by the Golden Gate International Exposition, from which MSR benefited somewhat.

Operating expenses' downward trend was credited to consolidation of car houses, reduction in rate paid for electrical energy and other economies.

The MSR subsidiary, *South San Francisco Railroad & Power Company,* was dissolved in 1938.

Some $710,883.87 was spent on maintenance in 1939, but this was only for necessary maintenance work on properties and equipment. A total of 2,596 bolted rail joints were replaced by thermit welded joints, while certain special work was renewed and some track raised to grade.

Elkton Shops overhauled and repainted 84 electric cars, eight cable cars, five buses and trucks. Other cars and buses were touched up, white fronts repainted where necessary. Obsolete rolling stock consisting of 22 electric cars and three buses were disposed of, the former being burned and the latter sold.

The cable machinery department maintained the plant and road machinery in the best possible condition, and installed approximately 22.5 miles of new cable to replace worn-out cable.

Twelve 25-passenger, 14 27-passenger, and 20 36-passenger motor coaches were purchased, some of which were in operation by the end of the year. These supplemented streetcar service, principally on the 9th-Larkin-Polk Line. The remainder were put in service on several lines on January 28, 1940.

The interior of the 24th and Utah car house was remodeled to serve as a central garage for all motor coach equipment. Streetcars formerly housed here were moved to other car houses.

A new streamlined green, white and yellow color scheme was adopted for MSR's rolling stock, and during 1939 34 electric cars and 46 motor coaches were so painted. The remainder of the company's rolling stock would be repainted in the new scheme as soon as convenient. MSR asserted that the new color scheme received much favorable comment from the public.

The new seven-cent cash fare with free transfers went into effect January 1, 1939, replacing the sale of four tokens for 25¢. The price of school tickets (16 for 50¢) remained unchanged. Tokens continued to be sold as a convenience, but at a straight seven-cent rate.

Operation of the South San Francisco streetcar line, from Leipsic Jct. on the San Mateo suburban line to South San Francisco in San Mateo County, which had been operated at a loss for several years, was permanently discontinued on January 1, 1939. About 3.5 miles of single track was abandoned by this move.

Complying with the San Francisco ordinance which required two-man crews on all streetcars (declared constitutional by the U.S. Supreme Court in 1938), all MSR cars were changed over to two-man operation between February 12 and 26, 1939.

The Golden Gate International Exposition opened on Treasure Island February 18, 1939 and closed October 29, 1939, with a total attendance of 10,496,203. It attracted large numbers of tourists to the city and undoubtedly increased MSR's passenger revenues. The company, however, was unable to reap the most possible benefit from this tourist influx due to the fact that its lines on Market St. leading to the Exposition ferries were operating in direct competition with those of Municipal Railway which charged a five-cent fare.

A new contract, dated June 9, 1939, was entered into with the Amalgamated covering wages, hours and working conditions from June 1, 1939 to May 31, 1941. This provided for modification in spread of work of regular platform employees, immediate increase of 2.5¢ per hour for Miscellaneous Department employees, and increase in wages for all employees covered by 2.5¢ hourly effective September 1, 1940. Annual vacations with pay were allowed all employees covered, the length of such vacations being graded according to length of service but not to exceed six days. Wages of motor coach operators were voluntarily increased 2.5¢ hourly effective September 16, 1939.

At the request of the city, operation of cars on Howard Street was discontinued because the franchise had expired and this service had not been included in MSR's Operating Permit. About 6.7 miles of track was cut.

An initiative ordinance designed to restrict the operation of jitney buses to outlying residential districts of the city was submitted to the voters on November 7, 1939 but was defeated. Thus MSR continued to suffer competition from these transit parasites, principally on Mission St.

A strike of shipping clerks employed on the waterfront from November 10, 1939 to January 3, 1940 tied up all shipping, resulting in diversion of ships and passengers to other Pacific Coast ports. This had an adverse effect on MSR revenues.

Coming due on April 1, 1940 was MSR's bond issue (First Mortgage 7% Bonds, of which $4,689,000 was outstanding at the close of 1939) and President Kahn reported MSR financially unable to retire the issue on the maturity date. Rather than take action under the National Bankruptcy Act, he proposed to bondholders that they consent to the extension of the maturity dates of the bonds from April 1, 1940 to April 1, 1945, with a reduction in the interest rate from 7% to 5% per annum during the life of such extension. This plan would become effective when the owners of 95% of the outstanding bonds consented and deposited their bonds in accordance therewith. At the end of the business day of February 29, 1940, some 85% of the bonds had been deposited.

1940

Total gross revenues for the year, $6,068,623.67, represented a drop of $367,692.46 from the 1939 total—5.52%. This decrease was due largely to decreased use of cars by visitors to the Golden Gate International Exposition; in 1939 high bridge tolls and parking fees on the island induced many to ride cars and ferries. The short 1940 run of the Fair (only 128 days vs. 1939's 254) with lowered toll charges and parking fees caused many to take their autos to the Treasure Island fantasyland.

Operating expenses dropped to $5,065,438.70, or 3.94%, due to substitution, wherever practicable, of motor coach for streetcar operation, reductions in cost of power, and lowered payments for injuries and damages.

The net result of operation for the year (after interest and appropriation for retirement reserve) showed a loss of $265,810.13.

Track, roadbed, plant and equipment were properly and adequately maintained by the various departments during the year at an expense of $714,351.02.

The track department rebuilt 0.97 miles of single track on outer Mission Street between 2nd and Army streets, removed previously abandoned tracks aggregating 4.71 single track miles at sundry locations, principally Visitacion Valley, Post and Ninth streets, and installed 1,592 thermit welded track joints. A new cable car turntable was installed at Bay and Taylor streets.

One hundred fifty-one electric cars, two cable cars, nine trolley coaches, 25 motor coaches, 10 auto trucks, sundry waiting stations, structures and miscellaneous equipment were overhauled and repainted as needed. Fifty-three obsolete electric car bodies were cremated, their trucks, electrical and other usable equipment being salvaged and the metal sold as scrap. One old motor coach was retired and sold.

Cost of electrical energy purchased during 1940 decreased $102,487.89 (13.55%), but this reduction was largely offset by increased use of gasoline and diesel fuel for motor coaches.

The Plan for Extension of Maturity of MSR's First Mortgage Bonds for the period of five years from April 1, 1940, and reduction of interest rate thereon from 7% to 5% per year was declared effective on March 30, 1940—more than 95% of the owners of said bonds outstanding on that date having approved the plan and deposited their bonds thereunder.

The alterations at 24th and Utah barn to make it the motor coach operating center were completed in the year and a total of 150 motor coaches could be cared for there.

The city and county of San Francisco requested MSR to remove its tracks on Third St. and the southerly portion of San Bruno Ave. from Channel St. to the county line, and replace streetcar operation on this stretch with motor coaches. Streetcar operation on Third St. between Market St. and the Southern Pacific Depot at Townsend St. was to continue as before.

Permission was received from the city to operate motor coaches from 26th St. via Castro, Divisadero, Jackson, Fillmore, Broadway, Steiner, Filbert and Fillmore streets to Marina Blvd. When the necessary motor coach equipment for this new crosstown line was received, it would be substituted for the present cable car service on Castro St. between 18th and 26th streets and cable-electric car service on Fillmore St. from Broadway to Marina Blvd.

Motor coaches added during the year were three 27-passenger, seven 32-passenger, two 36-passenger gasoline units, and 11 36-passenger diesel coaches. In addition, 39 36-passenger gas buses were ordered for the operation of the Third St. and Castro St. lines. Delivery of this new equipment could be delayed by war defense orders.

A charter coach service was started in 1940, offering clubs, fraternities, lodges, schools and private parties exclusive motor coach facilities for picnics and excursions anywhere in or out of the city at reasonable rates. This new service resulted in 79 charters during the six months of its operation.

The Mayor of San Francisco strongly urged the purchase of the properties of MSR by the city for unification and consolidation with its municipally operated street railway.

1941

Total gross revenues were $6,062,673.99, up over 1940 by $5,949.68 (0.14%). While small, this increase indicated a reversal in the trend of patronage. Revenues in the first eight months were below corresponding months of 1940, but beginning with September, revenues increased over the same 1940 months sufficiently to more than offset the losses recorded earlier in the year. This upward trend was attributable to increased employment and activity incident to the program of national defense.

Operating expenses decreased $129,109.91 (2.55%) to $4,936,328.79. This was due to reductions in maintenance of track and overhead and wages of platform men as a result of substitution, wherever practicable, of motor coaches for streetcars.

Net result of operation for the year was a loss of $114,810.00, an improvement of $151,000.13 over 1940.

The track department rebuilt 0.021 miles of single track on Townsend St. between 3rd and 4th streets and removed abandoned tracks, consisting of 6.145 single track miles, in various locations, principally on Third St., Castro St. and Leavenworth St., the Third Street Car House and Yard, and 29th and Mission Streets Car House. Some 1,133 thermit welded joints were installed.

Elkton Shops overhauled and repainted a total of 135 electric cars, 11 cable cars, three trucks, seven motorcycles, various waiting stations, structures and miscellaneous equipment. One hundred forty-nine obsolete car bodies were cremated, their trucks, electric and other usable equipment being saved and sold as scrap.

Twenty-one miles of new cable were installed.

Maintenance cost $665,911.25 during 1941.

The cost of electric energy consumed during the year decreased $68,973.36, or 10.54%, but this was more than offset by an increased use of gasoline and diesel fuel, resulting in a net increase in cost of power of $4,761.03 and an increase of $9,202.34 in lubricants.

The company received a permit from the city to operate motor coaches instead of electric cars on Third St. from the county line to North Beach and the ferries. Thirty 37-seat coaches for this line and nine 36-passenger coaches for the Castro St. line were purchased and placed in operation during the year. Later in the year a permit was secured to substitute motor coaches for cable cars on the Sacramento St. line to enable the company to give better service and simultaneously reduce its operating expenses by more than $100.00 daily. Six coaches required for this change were received and placed in service during February 1942, thereby increasing MSR's fleet to 121 motor coaches.

There were four sets of tracks in Market Street, with MSR cars using the two inside tracks and Muni cars the two outside. Cars of each railway turned into streets intersecting Market St. as they proceed in a westerly direction, resulting in greatly reduced traffic in the outer end of this artery. Municipal Railway proposed the removal of the two outside tracks and the reconstruction of the two inside tracks at its own expense on outer Market St. west of Valencia St. for joint use. MSR agreed. The rebuilt tracks were to belong to Municipal Railway, but MSR reserved the right to operate over these tracks during the life of its franchise. Power costs and maintenance were prorated on the basis of the number of cars operated by each railway.

The purchase of the operative properties of MSR by the city did not receive the consideration anticipated as the public was obliged to focus its attention on the acquisition of facilities of Pacific Gas & Electric Company for the distribution of power in San Francisco.

1942

Market Street Railway Company enjoyed a remarkable upsurge in total gross revenues for the year 1942, the increase to $7,574,541 being a 25% improvement over the $6,062,674 of 1941—$1,511,867 more, in fact. The increase was attributable to war conditions: greater military and civilian population, rationing of rubber and, subsequently, also of gasoline (the latter taking place in December 1942). The month of December showed an unbelievable 44% increase in revenues over December 1941.

In his 1942 statement to stockholders, Kahn observed the situation well: "The magnitude of war activities, particularly the construction of naval and cargo vessels, caused an influx of labor which relied largely on your company's facilities for transportation. Notwithstanding the company's shortage of manpower and the difficulty of obtaining essential materials for maintenance, in common with other street railways throughout the country, it has handled the greater loads with credit to itself and the community which it serves. The company has additional streetcars which may be used for any reasonably greater loads to which it may be subjected, provided the manpower shortage is alleviated. Such shortage could be rectified promptly if San Francisco permitted the operation of one-man cars, which are widely used throughout the country, but the city has not suspended the ordinance prohibiting the use of such cars, even as a war emergency for the duration, notwithstanding the U.S. Office of Defense Transportation's request for such action."

Operating expenses increased 13% due to (1) wage increases; (2) large payments for overtime; (3) 110,000 more car hours operated than in the previous year; (4) increase in gasoline and lubricants required for the operation of buses; and (5) increase in cost of claims and actions for injuries and damages.

The company had a net income, after interest and appropriation for retirement reserve, of $754,478—an increase of $869,288 over 1941 and the greatest for more than a decade.

The shortage of manpower was particularly acute in 1942. During the year 1,046 employees left the company's service, 148 joining the armed forces, but the majority entering shipyards and other war production units, due to the higher pay. During the same period, the company employed 1,103 men and women; in July the labor shortage became so acute that MSR was obliged to employ women to fill positions wherever practicable—becoming one of the first railways in the nation to do so. At the close of the year MSR had 138 women on its payrolls, 101 working as conductorettes, 15 as motorwomen, six as bus operators and 16 in the garage as helpers. Women meeting the public were garbed in a smart uniform and performed their duties satisfactorily and were well received by the public.

The Maintenance of Way Department rebuilt 0.56 miles of track, principally on Mission St. between 5th and 7th streets. It removed 7.397 miles of abandoned single track, principally on 3rd, Castro and Chenery streets.

Rolling stock received all necessary maintenance to keep it in first-class operating condition. One hundred thirty-one electric cars were overhauled and repainted. Buildings were properly equipped for air raids. Part of the city was designated a dim-out area by military authorities and cars and buses operating within that area were equipped with dim-out lights.

All cable machinery and cables were kept in first class operating condition. Approximately 14 miles of new cable were installed to replace worn-out cable.

On July 1, wages of employees were increased: electric car motormen and conductors received 8¢ more per hour, trolley coach and bus operators got 5¢ more, engineering department people 5¢, and all others, 8¢. To get new employees, MSR was obliged to begin paying platform labor during the breaking-in period.

Changes in service included the conversion of the Sacramento-Clay cable line to motor coach operation. Morning and evening coach service on Army St. was started to transport workers to shipyards. To obtain buses for war workers, streetcars were substituted for buses on the San Bruno Ave. (#25) and Folsom (#36) lines during the daytime, since these tracks had not been removed.

Ten new motor coaches were added during the year but seven more, on order, were cancelled as a war measure.

To meet any possible war emergency, MSR organized its employees into a utilities operation group to care for the company's property should a bombing attack occur and to have experienced personnel ready to restore service in such event. A group of 267 employees was organized and assigned duties in case of blackouts or actual air raids. Properties were equipped with sand buckets, long-handled shovels, and other fire-fighting equipment. All sprinkler systems, fire hoses and other protective devices were carefully maintained and all lights were shielded. A direct telephone line was installed between the city hall and MSR headquarters switchboard at 58 Sutter St., and another direct line connected the chief of police with 58 Sutter. In all MSR buildings the gas shut-off valves and the master electric switches had special markings affixed.

Emergency vehicles were dispersed between Turk and Fillmore, Haight and Geneva car houses; they had formerly all been stationed at Turk and Webster garage. At 24th Street Garage provision was made to store 20 to 30 bus units outside in the streets to eliminate danger of loss in the event of that facility's being bombed.

Another proposal to purchase MSR's operative properties was submitted to the electorate at the general election held on November 3, 1942. The price to have been paid was $7,950,000. This had its inception in July 1940 when a representative of one of the New York firms which underwrote MSR's outstanding bond issue convinced the company he could interest the city in the purchase of MSR's operative properties. At that time, and for years past, MSR's finances were at low ebb. Revenues had been declining steadily and expenses, especially labor, were rising. The onerous competition presented by the Municipal Railway continued unabated, and bankruptcy, with all its attendant evils, seemed inevitable. Bearing all these in mind, MSR was willing at the time that a sale be negotiated which, if consummated, would permit it to discharge its debts, provide for claims and damages, pay its expenses for the remainder of its corporate existence, and leave a balance for distribution upon liquidation. In view of these circumstances MSR authorized the New York firm of Ladenburg, Thalmann & Company to negotiate for the sale of its operative properties. Had the voters approved the purchase, Kahn would then have recommended to his stockholders for whatever action they might have deemed appropriate.

But again the voters turned down the purchase. It was close—100,904 against, and 94,243 for. A simple majority of the votes would have been sufficient for passage. Shortly after the election the mayor announced that he would endeavor to have the proposed purchase submitted again to the citizens of San Francisco at a special election to be held in the spring of 1943.

1943

Gross revenues surged upward again, this time by almost a million. Nineteen forty-three's $8,549,296 was $974,754 more than 1942's $7,574,541—an up of almost 13%. Operating expenses, including taxes, went up to $6,933,249—an increase of $928,622. Net income fell to $589,557 from $754,478.

War conditions were responsible for the growth in riding, of course. Greater military and civilian population and further rationing of rubber and gasoline gave MSR a remarkable number of new riders.

The manpower shortage continued. MSR owned many idle cars which slept out the war because no operators were to be found. Nor did the city relax its stand against the use of one-man cars; had these been permitted, MSR would not have had to report, as it did in 1943, that 145,507 fewer car hours were operated in 1943 than in 1942. MSR did all it could to repeal the anti-one-man-car ordinance; with the approval of many civic and military bodies the company was instrumental in placing on the ballot at the general election held on November 2, 1943, a proposal to repeal the one-man ordinance; it was roundly defeated, 143,608 to 33,683, despite the built-in assurance that it would be valid only for the duration of the manpower shortage.

Nineteen forty-three marked the emergence of Hunters Point as a major passenger generating point. Construction there of major dry docks and a submarine base brought such a demand for additional service that the Navy Department leased MSR 19 45-seat diesel motor coaches to supplement its own equipment. MSR was commended by the Navy for the excellent service rendered this vital area.

The upswing in operating expenses was attributed to the following factors: increased cost of maintaining cars and buses due to overloading, large overtime payments, increased claims and damages as a result of additional accidents due to large labor turnover.

Some 1744 employees left MSR employment during 1943, most of them entering shipyards and other war production units due to higher wages offered; 1692 men and women became MSR employees during the same period. To obtain men and women, the company used every means possible: ads in all newspapers, radio announcements, personal solicitation, posters in all cars and buses. As an inducement, wages of platform employees while breaking in were increased from 37.5¢ to 73¢ per hour and money was advanced them for several days until they collected their first checks. Women workers, in general, proved to be capable but turnover was very high because of heavy loading of cars, night work and inclement weather.

Track rebuilt included 0.74 miles, principally on Mission St. Track removed totaled 1.42 miles of single track in various locations, including Third St. A total of 212 electric cars was overhauled and repainted and 16 miles of new cable were installed.

As a result of the closeness of the November 3, 1942 election at which the voters turned down the purchase of MSR by the city by 100,904 to 94,243, the identical proposition (to purchase MSR for $7,950,000) was resubmitted at a special election held on April 20, 1943. This time it wasn't even close: it was rejected by 87,399 to 53,441. It placed MSR in the unique position of having had its properties rejected twice in six months! However, a new mayor was elected in November 1943, and he announced repeatedly that his first undertaking would be directed towards better transportation which could only be accomplished by merging MSR with Municipal Railway.

Also working for a unified street railway system was the United States Office of Defense Transportation. It attempted to obtain an equalization of fares (MSR's seven cents vs. Muni's five cents), universal transfers and interchange of facilities to improve transportation within the city. ODT decided to hold the issuance of directives in abeyance in order to give the city ample opportunity to solve its local problem without the interference of the Federal Government.

But a much more serious development occurred when the Railroad Commission, acting on its own volition, ordered (in April 1943) an investigation inquiring into the reasonableness of rates, adequacy of operations, service and facilities of MSR. Hearings were held before the Commission in May, July and September 1943. On November 30, 1943, the Commission rendered its decision reducing MSR's basic fare from seven cents to six cents, effective December 20, 1943. MSR petitioned for a rehearing which was denied, but the effective date of the order was extended to February 11, 1944 (subsequently to February 29, 1944). MSR in the meantime appealed to the California Supreme Court for a stay suspending the effect of the decision to permit the continuance of the seven-cent fare until the matter was determined.

In effect, the Railroad Commission had told MSR publicly that the service it was providing the public was not worth seven cents.

1944

On March 8, 1944 the California Supreme Court issued an order staying and suspending the order of the Railroad Commission during the pendency of the review but required MSR to offer to each of its cash and token patrons a coupon good for one-cent refund in the event the Supreme Court were to sustain the Railroad Commission; it further required that any unclaimed funds would go to the State. The company was required to file an approved bond in the amount of $100,000 at once with an additional $100,000 on the first day of each month while the case was under consideration. These monies represented, in round numbers, the excess passenger revenues collected by MSR when charging a seven-cent fare as compared with a six-cent fare from March 1, 1944. The Court order covering the refund coupons (good for one cent each in the event the Railroad Commission's decision were ultimately sustained) was unique in the history of the electric railway industry in California.

On July 1, 1944, the California Supreme Court upheld the Railroad Commission's Order, and MSR at once appealed the case to the United States Supreme Court. The $100,000 monthly impound had grown to $700,000 when there occurred the final drama, the sale of MSR.

At a Special Election held on May 16, 1944, voters approved the purchase of MSR's operative properties for a total purchase price of $7,500,000. The successful campaign was a tribute to new Mayor Roger Lapham who, true to his promises, worked earnestly to formulate another plan to acquire MSR's properties for consolidation with Municipal Railway. Lapham discussed this issue in every section of the city and by carrying his message directly to the people was successful in convincing a substantial majority of the electorate that such acquisition and consolidation was fundamental to the solution of the transportation problem which had seemingly always faced the city.

Prior to the election MSR management held numerous conferences with the mayor and other city officials, finally agreeing to recommend the sale of the operative properties of Market Street Railway Company to its stockholders for the sum of $7,500,000.

The Board of Directors of MSR on July 27, 1944, authorized the sale of the company's operative properties to the City and County of San Francisco for the above sum and a special meeting of stockholders on August 3, 1944, approved and consented to the sale; shares voted in favor of the sale were 232,533 (72.9%) while those in opposition were but 4,867 (1.5%).

On September 14, 1944, a contract authorized by the new Section 119.1 of the Charter of the City and County of San Francisco, now voted into law and approved by the California State Legislature, was entered into between the City and County of San Francisco and Market Street Railway Company, the chief provisions of which were:

(1) Purchase price was $7,500,000—$2,000,000 being paid immediately from surplus funds of Municipal Railway.

(2) The balance of $5,500,000 to be paid from 57% of the gross revenues of the consolidated system after deduction therefrom of operating expenses, repairs, maintenance and provisions for reconstruction and replacements.

(3) Unpaid balance to bear interest at four percent.

(4) A uniform fare of seven cents to be charged on the unified system until purchase price paid in full.

(5) City and County of San Francisco to have the right to pay any part of the balance of the purchase price and interest thereon at any time from any funds of Municipal Railway appropriated by the Board of Supervisors for that purpose.

(6) Upon delivery of the necessary instruments of conveyance, all rights, privileges and obligations under the operating permit of MSR be terminated, canceled.

(7) MSR to have access at all reasonable times to the operating financial records of the City and County of San Francisco applicable to the operation of its unified street railway system and would be furnished quarter-yearly statements in respect thereto.

(8) The City and County would not make any extensions, radical changes or alterations to the operative properties acquired from MSR, or abandon any substantial portion thereof, except only to the extent that such extensions or abandonments were required by reason of the unification of the operation of said operative properties with those of Municipal Railway.

(9) The City and County to, until the purchase price be paid in full, operate the operative properties of MSR and maintain same in good running order and otherwise utilize said properties in an efficient and economical manner in accordance with the established operating and business standards and practices of the street railway industry.

On September 29, 1944 at 5:00 A.M. (Pacific War Time) Market Street Railway Company delivered its operative properties to the City and County of San Francisco and received the initial payment of $2,000,000. Thus ended private operation of a street railway system in the city that had its inception back in 1857.

Thereafter, MSR was a skeleton. Its officers, attorneys, auditor, claim agents and their clerks and stenographers remained on the payroll. The operating personnel automatically became municipal employees.

Since the city could not take title to the operative properties of MSR unless they were delivered free and clear, MSR was obliged to borrow from a bank the sum of $2,000,000 which, with the city's payment of $2,000,000 together with its cash on hand, enabled MSR to redeem its outstanding bonds in the principal amount of $3,580,500 and interest thereon, to retire a bank loan of $255,750, to pay its pro rata of taxes on properties transferred to the city, and to provide a balance for working cash.

Thus only final dissolution awaited MSR, but the company would not be in a position to satisfy all of its obligations and inaugurate a program leading to the final settlement of its affairs until it:

(1) Received the balance of the purchase price of its operative properties ($5,500,000 plus interest).

(2) Sold its remaining real estate, appraised independently at $437,755 and its office equipment.

(3) Paid off its indebtedness to the bank.

(4) Disposed of 418 actions for damages pending as of December 31, 1944, asking for $6,338,674.

(5) Disposed of claims for compensation and benefits arising from compensable injuries or the death of former employees in accordance with the Workmen's Compensation laws of California.

These all came to pass and Market Street Railway Company was eventually dissolved.

Operation of MSR's street railway system ceased on September 29, 1944, when its operative properties were transferred to the City and County of San Francisco. Thus the financial records cover only nine months of 1944:

Gross revenues were $6,531,028, while total operating expenses were $5,582,562. Net income before appropriation for fare refund reserve amounted to $202,991; it became a loss of $502,804 when the reserve for refund of fare reduction from seven cents to six cents of $705,795 was applied.

President Kahn's final remarks to his stockholders as operating head of MSR's street railway system reflected his bitterness over the one-cent refund order:

"The results of operation for the first nine months prove in no uncertain terms that the Railroad Commission of California was not justified in reducing the fare charged by your company in San Francisco from seven cents to six cents effective February 29, 1944. Even with a seven-cent fare an adequate return was not earned, largely due to increased labor costs, and such return, when deducting therefrom an amount representing one cent for each revenue passenger, resulted in a deficit of over $500,000 for the nine months' period ended September 30, 1944."

The final act, as chronicled in *Moody's Transportation Manual, 1956* was indeed a terse obituary: "On January 12, 1955, a final liquidation dividend of 75¢ per share was paid to Prior Preference stockholders. . . . Any of these funds remained unclaimed after three years will be distributed among stockholders previously paid. The First Preferred Stock, the Second Preferred and Common had been declared worthless as of December 19, 1950."

Market Street Railway was dissolved as of January 9, 1959.

Selected Car Plans

These eight car plans, from the collection of author Charles Smallwood, represent a sampling of many different types in terms of age and design. Some of these illustrations are from original tracings and others are from blueprints. In the latter instance other tones not a part of the drawing (but a characteristic of the process) will be seen.

Modified for one-man service (900 s

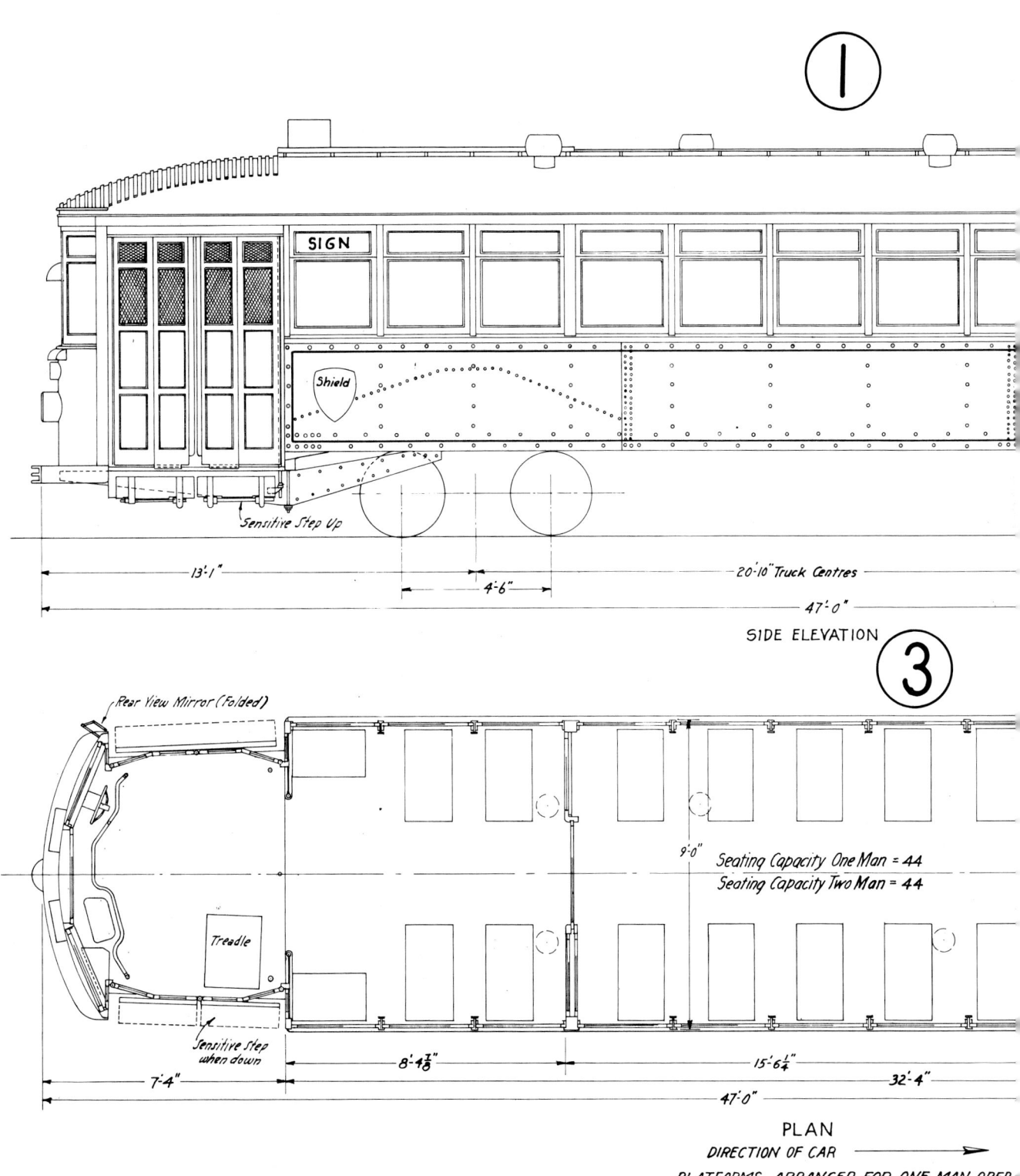

ries). See page 181.

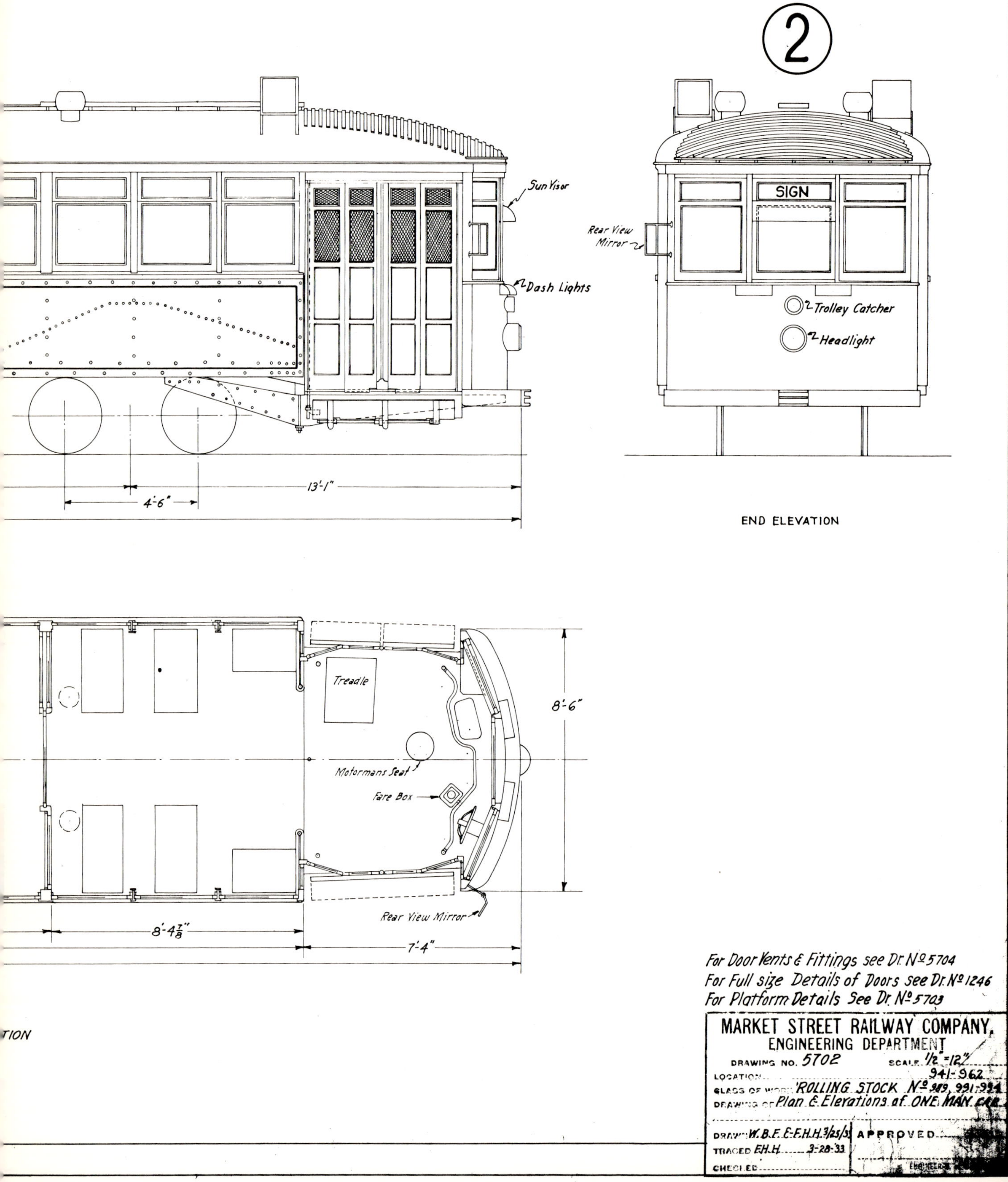

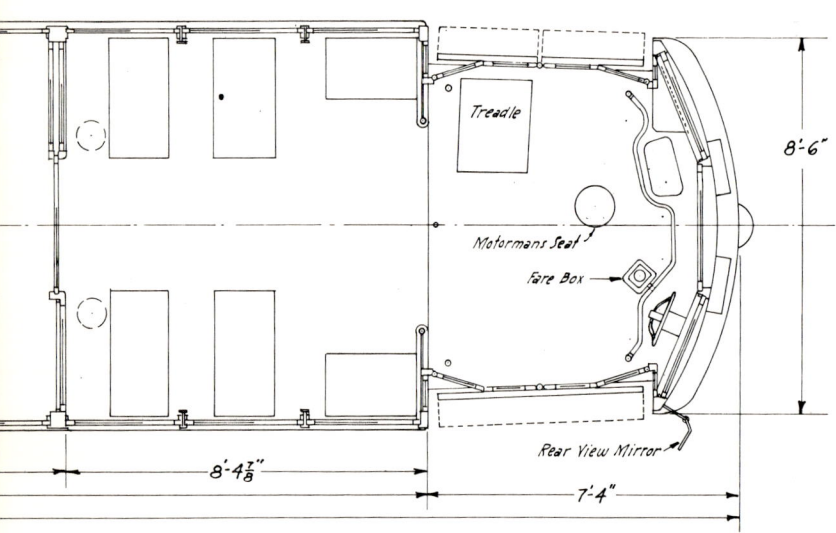

END ELEVATION

For Door Vents & Fittings see Dr. No 5704
For Full size Details of Doors see Dr. No 1246
For Platform Details See Dr. No 5703

MARKET STREET RAILWAY COMPANY,
ENGINEERING DEPARTMENT
DRAWING NO. 5702   SCALE ½"=12"
LOCATION: 941-962
CLASS OF WORK: ROLLING STOCK No 989, 991-994
DRAWING OF: Plan & Elevations of ONE MAN CAR
DRAWN W.B.F. & F.H.H. 3/25/33   APPROVED
TRACED E.H.H. 3-28-33
CHECKED

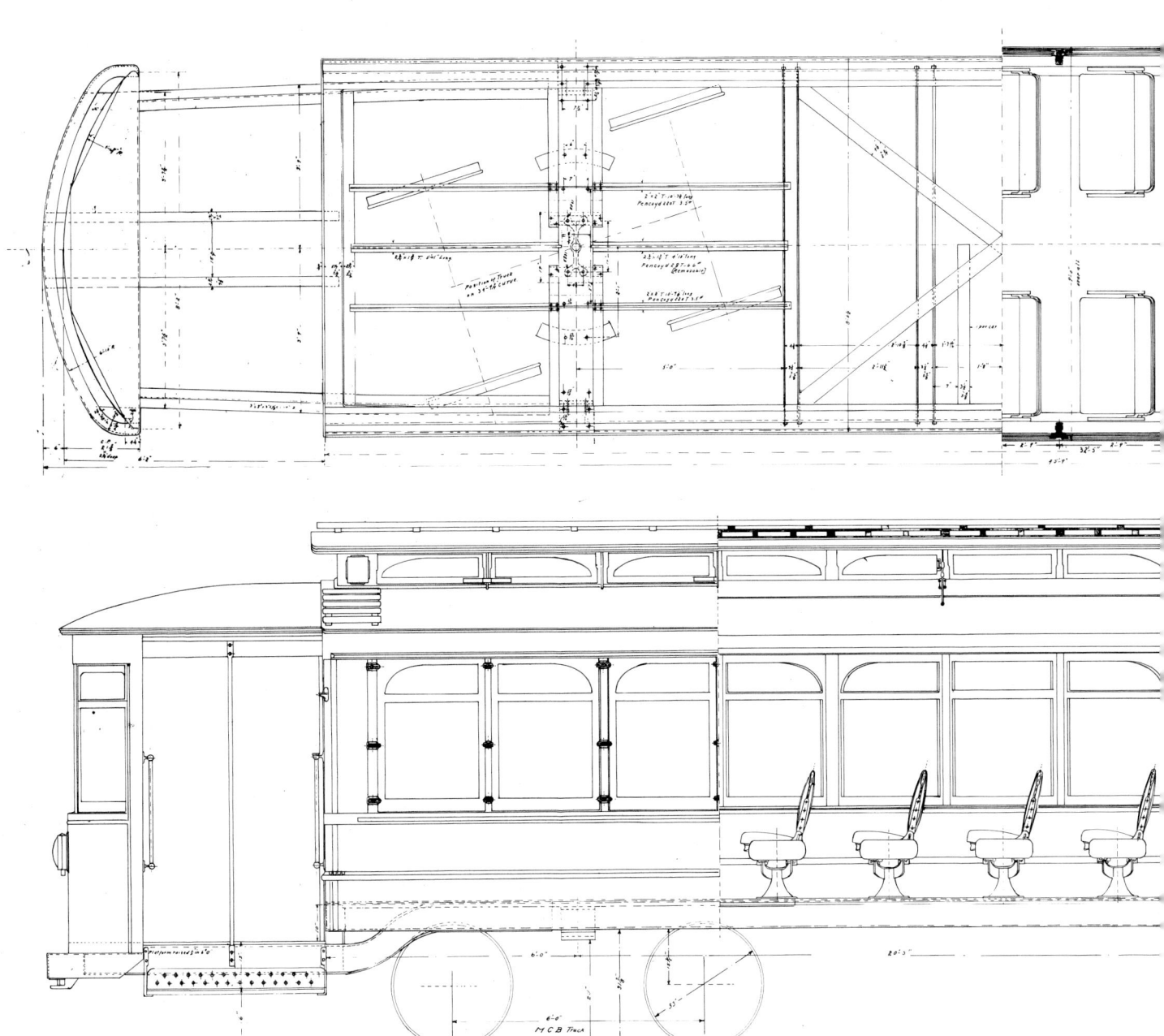

The "C

Cars 1500-1549, originally built for th[e
cisco to help the system rebuild after

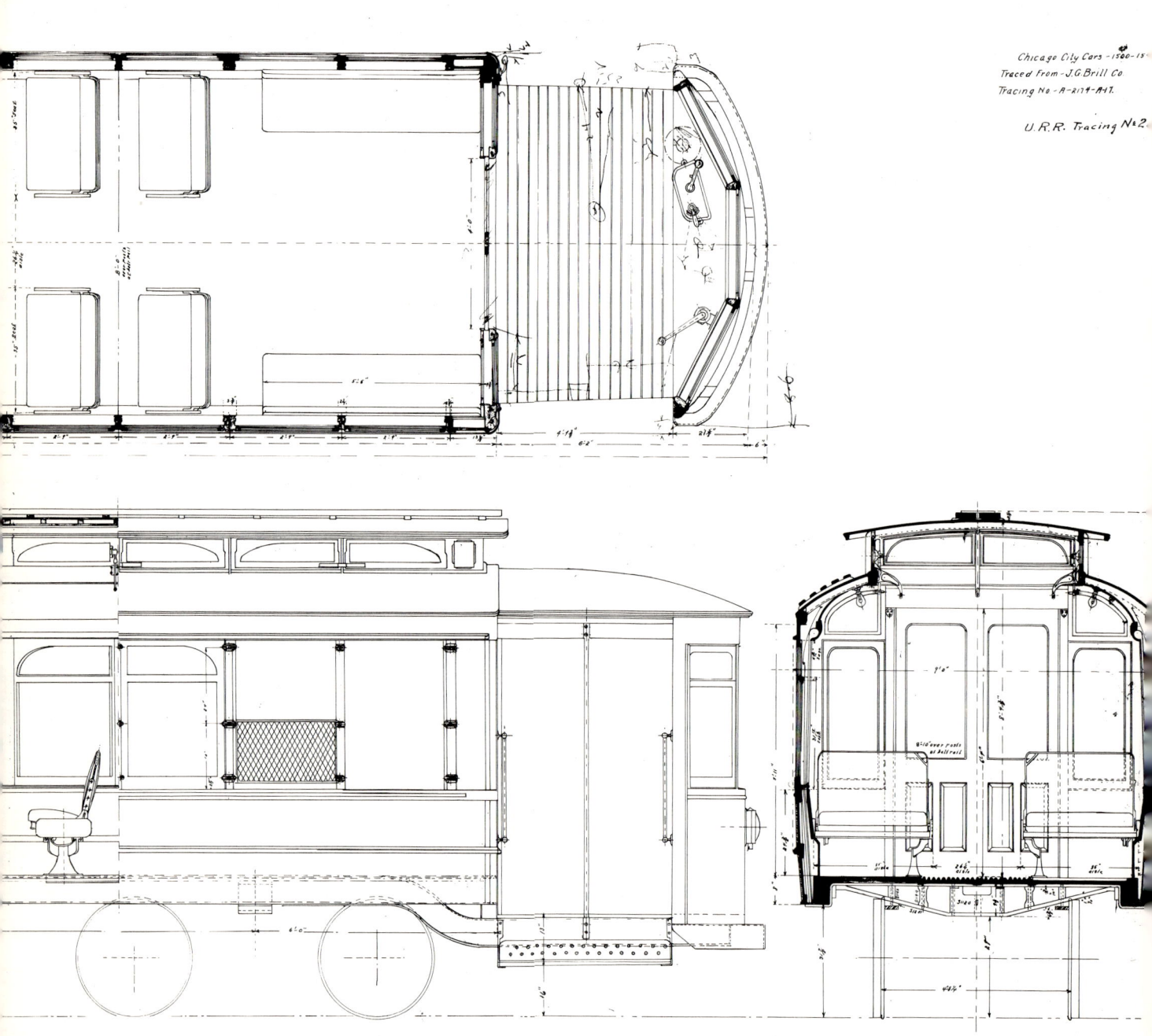

"Chicagos"

Chicago City Railway but diverted to San Fran-
the 1906 earthquake and fire. See page 269.

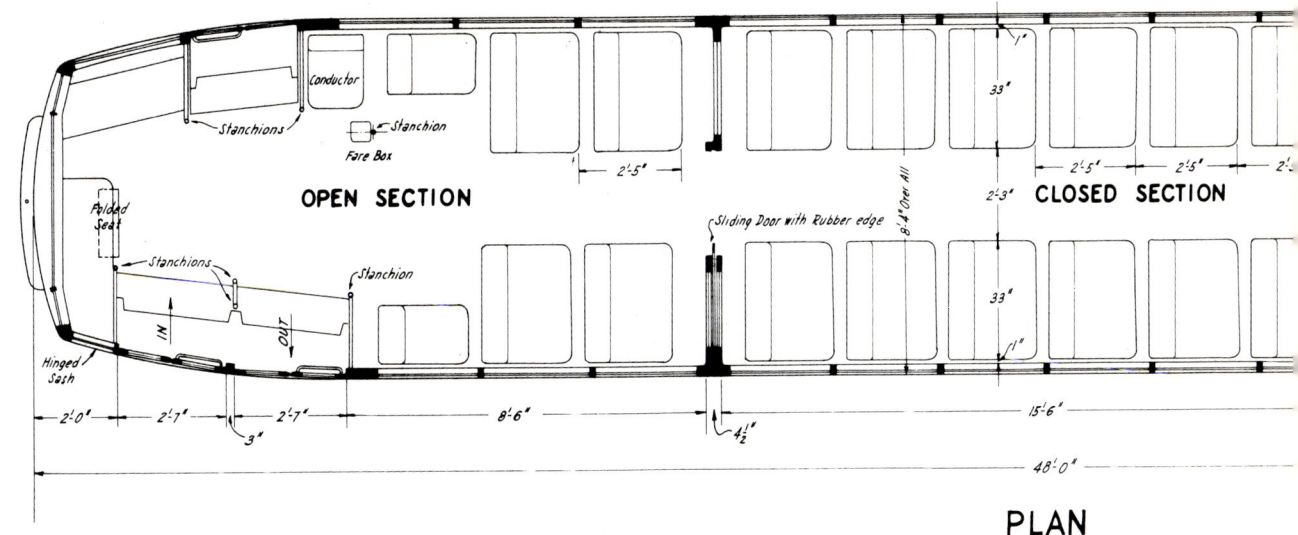

PLAN
SEATING CAPACITY 49

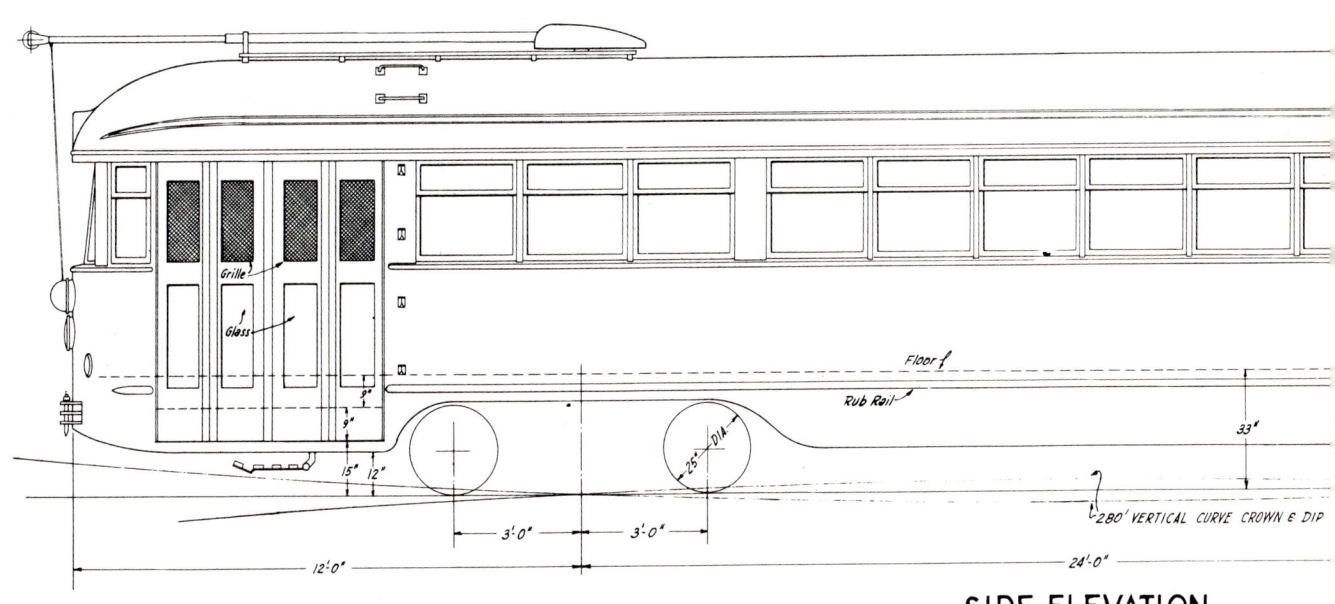

SIDE ELEVATION

SPECIFICATIONS

TYPE OF TRUCK	97-ER-1.
WHEEL DIAMETER	25 INCHES.
MOTORS	FOUR G.E. CO. TYPE G.E. 1198.
CONTROL	G.E. CO. FLOATING TYPE.
TRACK BRAKE SHOES	G.E. CO. TYPE ES-109 E.
OPERATION OF CONTROL & BRAKES	FOOT.
BRAKES	DYNAMIC, MAGNETIC & AIR.
AUXILIARIES	BATTERY OPERATED 32 VOLTS.
DIMENSIONS — OVERALL LENGTH	48'-0".
" WIDTH	8'-4".
" HEIGHT	10'-2".
SEATING CAPACITY	49
BODY FRAMING	STRUCTURAL STEEL, PRESSED STEEL & ALUMINUM.
FLOOR	PLYWOOD.
SASH	ALUMINUM, TOP SASH TO LOWER.
DOORS	STEEL WITH GLASS & SCREENED PANELS, AIR OPERATED.
SEATS IN CLOSED SECTION	THROW OVER TYPE, TAN COLOR LEATHER.
SEATS IN OPEN SECTION	THROW OVER TYPE, STERLING FIBRE.
STANCHIONS	ANODIC COATED ALUMINUM.
FLOOR COVERING	PABCO.
INTERIOR FINISH	SHEET AND EXTRUDED ALUMINUM.
DESTINATION SIGN	HUNTER ILLUMINATED.
VENTILATION	FORCED DRAFT (NO HEATERS).
LIGHTING & SIGNALS	LOW VOLTAGE (32).
PAINTING EXTERIOR	MARKET ST. RY. CO. NEW STREAMLINE.
PAINTING INTERIOR	WHITE CEILING, TAN COLOR FROM WINDOW SILLS TO ADVERTISING RACK, PLUM COLOR FROM FLOOR TO WINDOW SILL.

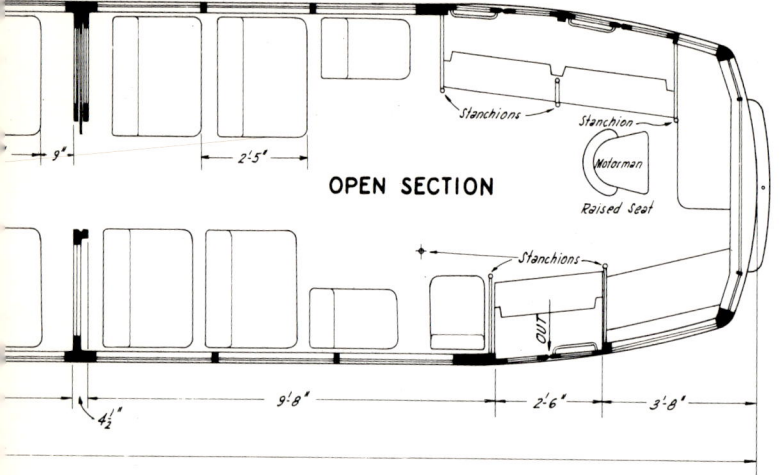

Here is a car type you won't find in the book because it never got beyond the drawing board. This is Market Street Railway's proposed "California Type" PCC streamliner, a double-end vehicle designed for two-man operation. Note the grilles on door windows instead of glass and the three sections. In another version, both end sections were shown *without* window glass. The drawing dates from 1939, but diesel buses and poor finances made the plan academic.

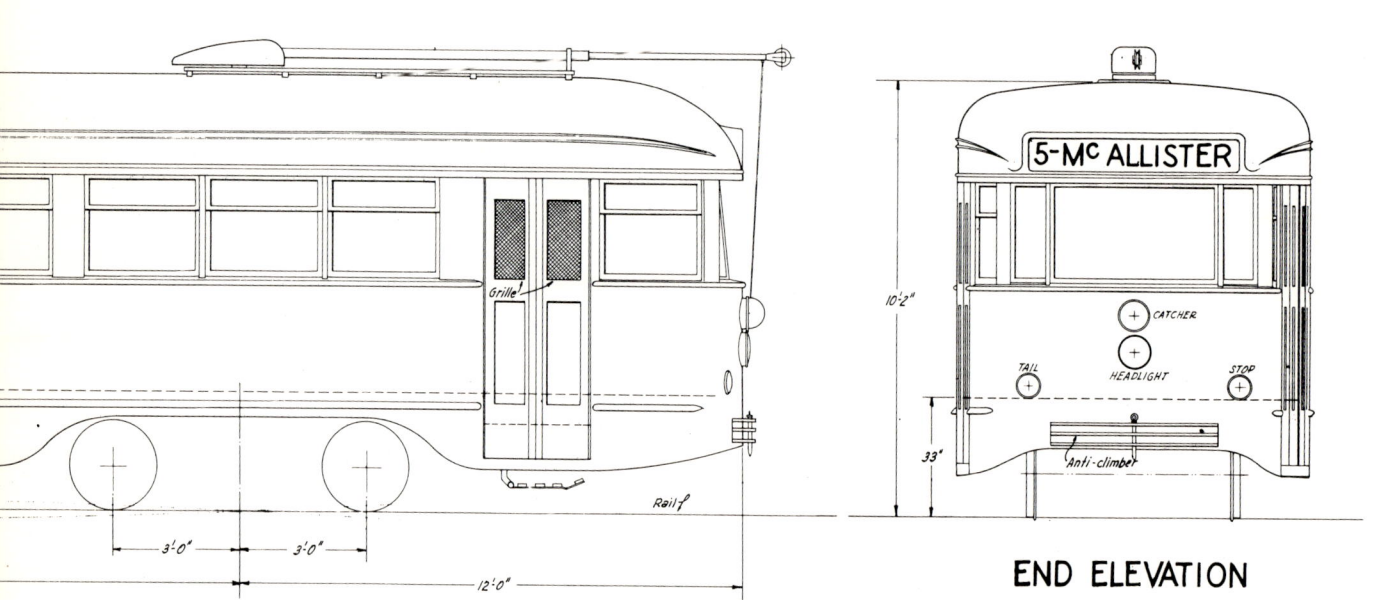

A Market Street PCC?